Teaching: Professionalization, Development and Leadership

David Johnson • Rupert Maclean
Editors

Teaching: Professionalization, Development and Leadership

Festschrift for Professor Eric Hoyle

 Springer

Editors
David Johnson
University of Oxford
United Kingdom

Rupert Maclean
UNESCO-UNEVOC
International Centre for Education
Bonn, Germany

ISBN 978-1-4020-8185-9   e-ISBN 978-1-4020-8186-6

Library of Congress Control Number: 2008921704

Printed on acid-free paper

9 8 7 6 5 4 3 2 1

springer.com

This volume comprises original contributions to the field of teacher professionalization, development and leadership written by leading international scholars in the field. Each contributor has in some way been professionally associated with Eric Hoyle during the past four decades and has influenced, or been influenced by, his work.

We dedicate this Festschrift to Professor Hoyle in celebration of his continuing contribution to this vitally important field in education.

David Johnson and Rupert Maclean

Emeritus Professor Eric Hoyle

Contents

Reflections

Contributors

Ibrahim Ahmad Bajunid
UNESCO-Regional Centre for Educational Planning, Sharjah,
United Arab Emirates

Ray Bolam
School of Social Sciences, Cardiff University, United Kingdom

Patricia Broadfoot
University of Gloucestershire, United Kingdom

Harold Entwistle
Department of Education, Concordia University, Montreal, Canada

John Furlong
Department of Education, University of Oxford, United Kingdom

Ron Glatter
Institute of Education, The Open University, United Kingdom

David H. Hargreaves
Wolfson College, University of Cambridge, United Kingdom

Eric Hoyle
Graduate School of Education, University of Bristol, United Kingdom

Peter D. John
Thames Valley University, London/Reading/ Slough, United Kingdom

David Johnson
Department of Education, University of Oxford, United Kingdom

Rupert Maclean
UNESCO-UNEVOC International Centre for Education, Bonn, Germany

Thangavelu Marimuthu
Cyberlynx International College, Kuala Lumpur, Malaysia

Agnes McMahon
Graduate School of Education, University of Bristol, United Kingdom

Paul Morris
Institute of Education, University of London, United Kingdom

Marion Myhill
Faculty of Education, University of Tasmania, Launceston, Australia

Marilyn Osborn
Graduate School of Education, University of Bristol, United Kingdom

Anthony Sweeting
History Department, University of Hong Kong, China

William Taylor
Centre for Higher Education Policy and Management, University of Southampton, United Kingdom

Mike Wallace
Cardiff Business School, Cardiff University, United Kingdom

John Williamson
Faculty of Education, University of Tasmania, Launceston, Australia

Foreword

Harry Judge

It is doubly fortunate that a foreword is not an introduction. Since it is mercifully brief, it should not be expected to mention respectfully each of the distinguished contributions which constitute "the word" before which it modestly stands as herald. For the same reason it cannot be expected to constrain within one overarching framework contributions which are essentially varied in subject matter and method. The brief of a foreword-writer might indeed be compared to that of a musician commissioned to write an overture to an opera which he had not written. To write such a piece for a volume devoted to Eric Hoyle is nevertheless a privilege as well as a pleasure. Partly, of course, because this volume celebrates a long and distinguished career devoted to the application of intelligence and (less assertively) theory to the improvement of practice. And partly because this abbreviated overture is privileged by being placed before a set of virtuoso performances throughout which consistent and coherent themes do insistently resonate.

Those themes are the very same that distinguish Eric Hoyle's own work. Running through them, of course, is a preoccupation with the development of teaching as a profession (and an exploration of what exactly that means), and a focus upon a deeper understanding of schools as organisations. They have been audible since his first major contribution to the literature in 1969. But it is the modesty of his presentations, even more than the persuasiveness of his argument, that gives his work its permanent value. If he had, like too many others, fallen into the prophetic trap of proposing monistic theories to encompass all that is known and not yet known about teachers and organisations, he would soon have been forgotten as his disillusioned disciples wandered off into the desert in search of yet another guru. This volume now proves decisively that they have not. His steady devotion to the utility of 'theories of the middle range' has ensured that his insights have abiding value not only across societies and cultures, but equally across time. Those insights remain pragmatic without ever degenerating into the technicist, and underpinning all his work is a commitment to the improvement of practice.

The key facts of his biography illustrate such simple truths. Born in the North of England, where neither pretentiousness nor nonsense is appreciated, and educated in the kind of school for which his later work has most relevance, he taught for a decent number of years in secondary schools. Have many sociologists become heads of English departments in such places? That experience, I allow myself to believe, helped to root his work in the rich but messy world inhabited by teachers. He then followed what was for a while the royal road for teacher educators and educational researchers, with a spell in a College of Education before joining the more refined world of the University and then being translated to Bristol, where (happily for so many) he remained, and indeed remains. As the following pages exemplify more than once, that path was kept open in part by the particular circumstances of the day. Men and women like him were needed to produce—through the Universities in which they taught—the college lecturers (in the fundamental disciplines of education) who would in turn elevate the quality of the preparation given to all teachers. Many recent developments, by no means all of them regrettable, do now raise in an acute form such questions as: "How is this endangered heritage to be preserved? How are the Universities to develop the distinctive role proper to them in the education and professional development of teachers?".

For a number of years in the early 1980s Eric Hoyle edited, in partnership with others, *The World Yearbook of Education*. The first of the sequence bearing his name was launched under the banner "Professional Development of Teachers". Even Eric is not infallible, for he asked me to contribute a piece entitled "Teaching and professionalization: an essay in ambiguity" which worried away at the tensions between the academic and the practical overtones of that slippery word. Professor Hoyle enjoys irony, and his keen eye will certainly alight upon the title of the Introduction on which the opera house curtain now rises.

14 April 2008

Introduction

Chapter 1
Hoyle: Ambiguity, Serendipity, and Playfulness

David Johnson and Rupert Maclean

> *Silence fell in the great hall of the palace at Anuradhapura.*
> *The oldest of the three princes of Serendip was about to relate*
> *a story for his father, the king, and members of the royal court.*
>
> *The monarch ... had once sent his sons forth to travel in the*
> *great world that they might grow in virtue and wisdom. By*
> *happy chance and not a little sagacity, they met with fortunate*
> *adventures, heard marvellous tales, and gained extraordinary*
> *friends.*
>
> *(Hodges, 1966, p. 3)*

It would be unusual to come across a piece of writing on the subject of the teaching profession in which there is no reference to the work of Eric Hoyle. Since the publication of his very first book on this topic, '*The Role of the Teacher*' in 1964, there is no doubt that his writing and lectures over the last forty years has deepened the understanding of all who work and teach in the field of teacher education. But Hoyle would be the first to recognise that we, all of us, are today where we are in our thinking about the teaching profession as a result of *intersubjectivity*; that is through our interaction with each other, in writing or other forms of communication, we mediate the viewpoint of the other. This book is testament to this fact, and therefore, it is by happy chance and not with a little sagacity that Hoyle met with fortunate adventures, heard marvellous tales, and gained extraordinary friends and colleagues, many of whom are contributors to this volume.

There is little doubt that his teaching, examining and research of teachers, and the teaching profession, in countries both more and less developed, has given him a broad outlook and a sympathy for the status of the profession everywhere. But, for those who know his work, this can hardly be described as travellers' tales, nor as simple chance discoveries or blind leaps of faith. Serendipity as we use it here is therefore better understood as sagacity, the ability to link together apparently innocuous facts in order to come to a valuable conclusion. And in a distinctive way, Hoyle, the influences of Merton clear in his work, prefers logically interconnected conceptions which are limited and modest in scope, rather than all-embracing and grandiose. This is what Merton refers to as *theories of the middle range*, or theories that are intermediate to the minor, everyday working hypotheses, and the all-inclusive

D. Johnson, R. Maclean (eds.), *Teaching: Professionalization,*
Development and Leadership,
© Springer Science + Business Media B.V. 2008

speculations of the 'master conceptual scheme'. It is precisely this degree of inci-
siveness, far sightedness and the ability to discern between fashionable policy and
the reality at the coalface that has come to define Hoyle's writing.

Hoyle's work is best described as trying to make sense of the autonomy-control
binary that dictates the nature of teaching, management and professionalization
today. Hoyle in this volume reflects on this:

'... forty years of engagement with the idea of teaching as a profession suggests
that there is an endemic dilemma entailed in the relationship between two modes
of organizing teachers' work: the bureaucratic (managerial) and the professional.
At the heart of this is the balance between autonomy and control.'

Hoyle's interest in the nature of management arises from his interest in the
nature of organisations. But his work is best defined by his focus on a theory
for understanding organisations rather than management theory, or a so-call
theory for action. For Hoyle, it is more useful to answer the question how leaders or managers can best support and develop teachers as professionals, hence
the notion of 'temperate' leadership (Hoyle and Wallace, 2005), as opposed to
putting into practice much of the prevailing rhetoric of 'transformational' or
'my way' leadership. His reference point on this is the organisational theorist
James March (1999). March adopts an interdisciplinary approach to the study
of organisations which draws on sociology, politics, economics and various
meta-theories, such as decision-theory, game theory, and choice theory. Like
March, Hoyle insists on seeking to understand how organisations actually function. But, as we have said before, it is not the grand theories of organisation that
interest him. Hoyle prefers a conceptual playfulness in making sense of the
complexity of organisations. Little wonder then, his affinity for the counter-
intuitive perspectives of March, such as, organisations 'running backwards', or
the notion of managerialism as a 'solution in search of a problem' (March and
Olsen, 1976). Hoyle and Wallace (2005) show how some of the metaphors
generated by March to capture the complexity of organisations, such as the
'garbage can' theory, or the description of universities as 'organized anarchies'
(March and Olsen, 1976), are at once simple and profound. But the lowly metaphor has the power to be insightfully playful (as are those used by March) or to
become dangerous, almost fundamentalist gospel; sadly, such metaphors as the
'learning organisation' or the 'transformational school', examples of the latter. For Hoyle, perhaps the central challenge for professionals is to read the
metaphor more as a playful heuristic that unlocks our capacity to understand and
appreciate the nature of organisations, rather than as a rubric for doing
management.

But most of all, Hoyle is fascinated by ambiguity and dilemma (see Hoyle
this volume). Building on the work of March (March and Olsen, 1976) and
Weick (1976), Hoyle and Wallace argue that 'because of the incommensurable
values and demands which are endemic to all organisations, a variety of inevitable dilemmas and ambiguities are generated, which no amount of rationality,
efficiency or control will eliminate'. Rather, these ambiguities may have effects
opposite to those intended by policy-makers and legislators. Sometimes, pro-

fessionals, recognising that certain policy imperatives are unworkable, actually rescue its larger aspirations through a 'principled infidelity' – a conscious decision not to implement policies in the way that they are intended. The message from Hoyle and Wallace is that 'successful' practitioners are those who are aware of ambiguities, ironies and dilemmas, generated by the nature of organisations. Teachers would do well to collaborate in their local contexts, and in a neo-Vygotskian way, co-construct meaning relative to their own local contexts and shape and mould policy imperatives and ideas accordingly, rather than to adopt a 'big idea' from elsewhere. They thus argue for a more localised approach to 'making things marginally better for those students who are in a particular school at a particular time'. To achieve this, they argue, 'teachers must be given the space to manage the inherent ambiguities and ironies of the contexts in which they work'.

But alluring as ambiguity is as a concept, the suggestion that it constrains the options that professionals have to achieving a 'radical transformation' of the status quo is not universally shared. Bottery (2007) for example, accuses Hoyle of conservatism and argues that a 'fixation' on the local is unhelpful in sensitising students and their communities to the national and the global.

Stinging criticism for what we have come to recognise as the Zeitgeist of Hoyle? We asked Hoyle about this and found his reply interesting:

> *I'm surprised to find that my value position in terms of education has become increasingly conservative in the sense of taking the view that education remains essentially a conservative institution in that it transmits culture and that there is a relatively unchanging, deep structure of schooling that teachers get on with everyday. 'Choice', covert and not so covert, selection, league tables, city academies and so on, have an impact, of course, and greatly exercise parents (and grandparents) who are preoccupied with these matters but underneath it all the old verities of education persist and the professionalization of teachers should be concerned with helping them to improve teaching rather than engage with these epiphenomenal issues'.*

Personal communication, 2007

Of course Hoyle is right in pointing out that education remains for all intents and purposes a conservative institution and parents, where it concerns their own children, organise around local issues. This of course does not preclude teachers, parents or indeed their children from organising more globally too, and in many different ways; some content with a twinning arrangement with a school in The Gambia, while others might seek to be more active in contributing to global change, for example through doing Development work. And while Bottery is right about the need for a more national and global movement to combat the ever pervasive culture of compliance that schools, universities and other public sector institutions are engulfed in, perhaps we need to recognise that whilst in organisations are embedded a set of incommensurable values, people within organisations, and within each person, there is likely to reside a full spectrum of value positions. So while it is true that ambiguity plagues organisations, many of us live with ambiguity in terms of our own ideals. Our working lives, our political lives, and our social lives shape in very different ways, our identities and ontological stances. So yes, we do need a global movement to turn the tide of narrow instrumentalism that dictates the way in which schools and other social institutions are managed, but is the site of teaching the best place around which to organise such a movement? Perhaps not, first because it is unrealistic; second because, in typical liberal fashion, the argument assumes that teachers or other professionals do not occupy other public and political spaces, or that they should be in the vanguard of the proposed revolutionary transformation; and third, because there is a fundamental flaw in a political position that assumes that educational transformation is in itself a sufficient condition to transform the culture of control and accountability, so deeply embedded in all sectors of public, social and political life.

Hoyle recognises what he calls, his own 'lived ambiguity' even though this is not always clear in his writing. But how could it be? Like all good writing, where the arguments are cogent, the style proficient, and the stance uncompromising, it rarely permits us more than a glimpse into the inevitable philosophical struggles that he, like all of us, has to endure in his 'search for meaning' (Frankl, 1963).

Frankl discusses three broad approaches to finding meaning: through experiencing something, by doing (an existentialist idea of finding meaning by becoming involved in a project or occupation), and by adopting an attitudinal or value position.

Hoyle touches on all three aspects and talks of living with ambiguity in relation to his value position in relation to knowledge, his own teaching and research, and his epistemological stance. In respect of the first, Hoyle unwittingly touches on an issue that has split the academic community and is likely to determine the organisation of institutions of Higher Education for many years to come. In a recent paper, Johnson (forthcoming) argues that the higher education sector in the Britain has found itself swept into a maelstrom of competing ideas and philosophies about the changing role of the modern university, some wanting to hold on to the core values of the nature of knowledge and the search for truth. Others, many of whom had been systematically under-funded and under-resourced, seek to occupy a strategic position within a growing 'market' of higher education where courses and programmes are sold to meet commercial and industrial demands. And then there are those who feel that these two 'missions' are not incompatible and that such bifurcation is the only way forward.

Hoyle might argue that these value positions are incommensurable, and drawing on Berlin (1969) he would suggest that this does not preclude one 'from arguing the case for one over another' (Hoyle and Wallace, 2005). But what we have here is probably more than a problem of incompatible values. Perhaps a few years ago, the positions were in flux and might have been construed as a problem to be resolved. Now, it seems, the positions have hardened and the organisation of higher education is more a dilemma than an ambiguity. According to Johnson (forthcoming) the different value positions can be chartered along a 'looking in-looking out continuum' which reflects an interesting but irreducible tension between those with strongly held views about the nature of knowledge, its scientific and disciplinary foundations, and the core mission of the university. In the former view, in brief, universities are above all concerned with the search for truth. Applications are secondary; this is essentially an inward looking, philosophical view of knowledge; the alternative view is that the production of knowledge is a condition of productivity, innovation and creativity and that its production is not confined to the academy alone. Rather, the sphere of activity is widened beyond the university to include a more diverse set of researchers and practitioners; this constitutes an outward looking, more economically driven view.

Clearly we cannot simply replace a disciplinary form of enquiry that emphasises fundamental epistemological principles, and that forms the basis for understanding the discipline, with one that is solely needs driven. But, at the same time, we should not close off the opportunity for academics to contribute to societal need. After all, academics are, or should be, concerned and active citizens too. The flip side of the coin suggests that research more orientated to application and development should not eschew the fundamental principles upon which research in any one tradition is built. This tension appears to be at the heart of the dilemma between control and autonomy referred to by Hoyle.

In relation to theory, we have highlighted above Hoyle's preference for the theories of the middle range which inevitably, entail the development of taxonomies and typologies, and the summarising of concepts. Hoyle has always been happy to typologise and label and it is fascinating that since boyhood, he has been a great admirer of Linnaeus who was born just over 300 years ago this year.

Yet Hoyle admits that typologies greatly oversimplify the complexity of the world, and argues that they must be complimented by a more rounded view of the social world - hence the importance of good novels and ethnographies. Typologies and concepts provide a good starting point for exploration because they are heuristic. It is for this reason that Hoyle as a teacher has always encouraged students to be sensitive to the meanings of the words that constitute our working concepts and to 'play' with meanings, principally because that for much of the time our concepts function as metaphors (Lakoff and Johnson, 1980).

Hoyle also feels particularly sensitive of his lived ambiguity in respect of his teaching and writing, both which have focussed on improving our understanding of organisations (i.e., organisation theory rather than prescriptive management theory). He says:

> 'I try to teach students to understand organisations but their jobs often involve the management of change. I sometimes wonder if, in improving understanding, I am undermining their capacity to manage by emphasizing ambiguity, paradox, contingency, complexity, unintended consequences and so forth thereby inducing analysis paralysis. But I console myself with the thought that (a) others will teach them management and (b) effective management is dependent on understanding. In any case, my teaching and my writing can hardly be said to be 'value free', but at least I hope that I'm up-front about where I stand'.

Personal communication, 2007

Analysis paralysis? Surely not! Indeed, it is his ability to play with concepts that we would argue is a defining characteristic of Hoyle the teacher. Much of his teaching shows the ease with which he is able to interrogate complex concepts, sometimes weighing one against the other in a curious contrapuntal form, while at the same time extending both, analogous to an operatic Fugue. This is also evident in his writing. Little wonder then that some of the commentators on his work refer to 'levels of literary complexity that few books published in the field can match' (Brundrett, 2007:434 reviewing (Hoyle and Wallace, 2005). We cannot say for certain that this is the case, but there is no doubt that not many teachings have been able to achieve a serious analysis of complex forms of human behaviour in organizational settings, with quite the same playfulness as that managed by Hoyle.

It is appropriate therefore, to end this piece on the following note:

'His life ... entailed more than authorship. He was a wonderful teacher, with a vivid speaking style, clear and witty, and a terrific memory for facts. His lectures often packed the hall, his private tutoring earned him extra money, and he made botany both empirical and fun by leading big festive field trips into the countryside on summer Saturdays, complete with picnic lunches, banners and kettledrums, and a bugle sounding whenever someone found a rare plant. He had the instincts of an impresario. But he was also quietly effective in mentoring the most talented and serious of his students, of whom more than a dozen went off on adventuresome natural history explorations around the world, faithfully sending data and specimens back to the old man. With his typically sublime absence of modesty, he called those travellers the apostles'.

Of course we speak here of Linneus but it hardly goes unnoticed that Hoyle shares many of his characteristics. We cannot vouch for Hoyle's knowledge of Flora and Fauna, nor his leading his students into the countryside with banners and kettle drums; But more typical of him, for one who has tutored the perceptions of so many, and perhaps unlike Linneus, is his modesty.

References

Berlin, I. (1969) *Four essays on liberty*. Oxford: Oxford University Press

Bottery, M. (2007) Book Review Symposium: Educational Leadership: Ambiguity, Professionals and Managerialism (Hoyle, E. and Wallace, M. (2005)). *Educational Management Administration and Leadership*, 35, 3, 429–439

Brundrett, M. (2007) Book Review Symposium: Educational Leadership: Ambiguity, Professionals and Managerialism (Hoyle, E. and Wallace, M (2005)). *Educational Management Administration and Leadership*, 35, 3, 429–439

Frankl, V. E. (1963) (I. Lasch, Trans.) *Man's search for meaning: an introduction to logotherapy*. New York: Washington Square Press

Hodges, E. J. (1966) *Serendipity tales*. New York: Atheneum.

Hoyle, E. (1969) *The role of the teacher*. London: Routledge Kegan Paul

Hoyle, E. and Wallace, M. (2005) Educational Leadership: Ambiguity, professionals and Managerialism. London: Sage

Johnson, D. (forthcoming) Globalisation, knowledge and innovation: a sting in the tail for the British entrepreneurial university? In D. Johnson, R. Maclean and A. Hollender (Eds.) *Globalisation, vocationalisation and mass higher education*. Dordrecht: Springer

Lakoff, G. and Johnson, M. (1980) *Metaphors we live by*. Chicago: University of Chicago Press

March, J. and Olsen, P. (1976) *Ambiguity and choice in organisations*. Bergen: Universitetsforlaget

Merton, R. (1957) Social theory and social structure. (2nd edn) New York: Free Press

Weick, K. (1976) Educational organisations as loosely-coupled systems. *Administrative Science Quarterly*, 21, 1–19

Part I
The Professionalization of Teaching

Chapter 2
The Predicament of the Teaching Profession and the Revival of Professional Authority: A Parsonian Perspective

Peter D. John

This paper entails a reflection on the recent and current predicament of the teaching profession. In so doing it argues for a normative interpretation of teacher professionalism based on a re-evaluation of the work of the sociologist Talcott Parsons. Such a conception grounds teacher professionalism in the expert authority of the practitioner which, according to Parsons, means aligning the interests of clients with those of society at large. It also means a renewed emphasis on the fiduciary relationship between client and professional and the implications such a conception has for the authority, knowledge and autonomy of the teaching profession under new managerial conditions.

To achieve this, the paper is split into three sections: the first outlines the current predicament of the teaching profession with an emphasis on the constraining and mediating effect of the 'new managerialism'. The second presents a brief explication of the work of Talcott Parsons and the ways in which expert authority forms the foundation for the fiduciary relationship between clients, communities and professionals. Building on the work of Parsons, the final section will offer a way forward for the teaching profession focusing on the continued importance of trust, the centrality of knowledge and the re-establishment of autonomy and responsibility.

The Professional Predicament

The classical literature on the professions used a variety of trait models to define and describe the professions. The characteristics that emerged from author to author usually focused on key dimensions summarised in Table 2.1. This checklist method helped to evaluate occupations based on their conformity or deviance from the standard taxonomy. The approach, however, came under increasing scrutiny in later decades as scholars rightly questioned whether the ability or inability to conform to the traits was influenced by forces outside the functional value of the knowledge the profession controlled. Also, some derided the approach because it gave ontological priority to occupational groups rather than to particular practices; still others felt that it described professions in purely denotative terms whereas the everyday use of the word has a decidedly normative cast (Latham, 2000).

D. Johnson, R. Maclean (eds.), *Teaching: Professionalization, Development and Leadership,*
© Springer Science + Business Media B.V. 2008

Table 2.1 Typical characteristics of a profession

- Knowledge based on empirical techniques and theoretical complexity
- Mastery of that knowledge base requiring lengthy periods of education and training that are usually university based
- Specialised training designed to both equip and socialise into the culture and symbols of the profession
- Tasks that are inherently valuable to society and relevant to key social and human values
- Members are motivated by a desire to prioritise the client's welfare
- Members exhibit a long term commitment to the profession and to continuous up-grading of their knowledge and skills
- Performance of tasks are characterised by a high degree of autonomy
- The profession is guided by a well developed code of ethics that guides practice and defines the profession's values

Despite the criticisms, the trait approach has proved remarkably resilient and is proving useful in providing us with a set of places to look for changes in professional life. In short, trait explanations may not explain the development of the professions very well or the process of change within or across them but trait theories do point us toward a set of well established institutional markers whose disappearance may be indicative of deeper change than the initial reaction may have signalled.

The current predicament of the teaching profession draws attention to some of these institutional markers. In particular, they highlight a number of ambiguous and contradictory conclusions that have been driven by the assertion that professionalism under 'new managerial conditions' has led to teachers' work being re-defined. These conditions, it is argued, are part of a wider accountability movement that has, according to Woods et al. (1997), resulted in a sometimes inconsistent effect best characterised by the tension between constraint and opportunity (Hoyle and Wallace, 2005). Put simply, for some teachers the reforms of the last decade have opened up new avenues of opportunity leading to a new extended or expanded professionalism. For others, however, the changes have led to a gradual loss of control, creativity and independence leading to a more restricted or distended professionalism.

Both interpretations draw on studies of teachers' work carried out mostly in the 1990s and early 2000 at the height of the reform movement. Broadly, the majority of these investigations highlight increased workloads, a growing loss of autonomy, increasing control over the curriculum and assessment, and a compliance culture driven by harsher inspection regimes combined with the imposition of nationalised professional standards. These changes were shaped by a combination of 'new right' and 'New Labour' policies that reflected a drive to improve standards through market oriented definitions. This approach has seen education re-cast as a product to be produced and consumed while *pari passu* directed by the economic norms of effectiveness and efficiency where measurable output combined with greater choice and personalisation. This process was driven in part by the urge to 'informatize' teachers through the explosion in policy documents and curriculum directives. It was also guided by what Brown (1990) calls 'the parentocracy' which sought to place parent power in the ascendancy (Troman, 2000). This idea of greater parental interest and involvement is not in itself problematic, rather it is the shift in the nature of the engagement and the underlying assumptions upon which it is based. These tend toward greater consumer control leading to fears of client capture imposing new and multiple demands on schools and teachers (Troman and Woods, 2001).

Much of the writing in this constrained conception has focused on the negative effects that 'New Labour' policy discourse has had on teachers' workplace and professionalism. Here the language of performance, accountability, standards is used interchangeably with the discourse of life-long learning, personalisation and partnership – all leading to a new expanded professionalism. At the core of this expanded approach has been a shift from a meso (school level) to a micro bureaucracy (teacher level) where rather than checking and monitoring pupils' performance, teachers are now required to audit progress and carry out skills audits. And instead of keeping records they now have to regularly assess, record, report, measure and account for individual pupil performance. National and local targets drive this process where the responsibility for learning (or the lack of it) lies with the teacher not the learner. This has led, in some cases, to a distended professionalism where teachers are over-stretched in terms of their workload where their traditional pedagogic activities are curtailed in favour of compliance and over personalisation. Smylie (1999), Hargreaves (2000) and Woods (2002) have shown that teachers have responded by trying to strive for perfection by meeting all the new expectations but with less and less success.

A great deal of the literature on the policy effects has characteristically painted teachers as powerless victims operating under a state of siege. Ball (2003), for instance, uses evidence to illustrate the continuing demoralisation where the technocratic intrusion drives 'performativity into the day to day practices of teachers' and forces them 'to play the game' in terms of school inspections, for instance. Further studies (Helsby, 1999; Osborn et al., 2000; Woods, 2002) have highlighted the de-motivation, stress and insecurity that have emerged in the wake of reforms leading to widespread dissatisfaction, illness and resignation.

Many scholars have further highlighted the intensification of teachers' work as playing a major role in this process. Driven by 'less down time' (Apple and Jungck, 1996); a chronic and persistent sense of work overload (Hargreaves, 1997); professional isolation and increasing diversification of role, teachers experience de-professionalization. Many of the characteristics of intensification also creep into the home life of teachers with further unintended consequences. However, studies also show that the way in which intensification is experienced is highly personal and differentiated. Troman (1997) for instance, talks of the 'ambiguities of intensification' where teachers use their own subjective educational theories (Klechtermans, 2005) to adapt to change thereby creating elements of re-professionalization. This often manifests itself in further professional development, the adoption of new roles, and an acceptance that change can bring opportunities. Many teachers in fact adapt wholesale to the changes and align themselves with the new settlement thus carving out new careers. Often termed the 'new entrepreneurs', these professionals become the 'trail blazers' of reform, driving change across institutions.

Some researchers (Helsby, 1999; Woods, 2002; Barlett, 2002) have further argued that the effects of policy changes have not always had a constraining impact because schools and teachers mediate their effect. Helsby (1999), for instance, shows that teachers are not always reactive subjects but have degrees of freedom in deciding how to interpret and cope with imposed change. Furthermore, studies show that the complex and diffuse nature of schools and classrooms acts as a natural filter for such policy demands as do teachers' personal theories and perspectives (Troman and Woods, 2001). This straining out process – both individual and collective – has led to various reforms being moulded to suit personal and local needs and many examples exist of the ways in which teachers have used the reform movement to their own (and their students') professional advantage.

In essence, teachers seem able and willing to accommodate and integrate changes which are seen as having a positive effect on pupils' learning (Osborn et al., 2000) while rejecting others. This rapprochement is often derived from the interpersonal rather than legalistic relationship teachers have with their students. It is also part of a greater sense of collegiality that has emerged from the need to approach problems of implementation collectively where responsibility for new curricula and pedagogy has to be negotiated. Teachers thus work in the interstitials creating and mediating change in the best interests of their students. And as Troman and Woods (2001) show the culture of collaboration that emerges within a school can mediate and alleviate the paralysing effect of some external demands. Schools, it seems, can play a crucial role by further mediating the impact of change by helping to determine the space for interpretation and negotiation (Acker, 1999; Helsby, 1999; Troman, 1997; Troman and Woods, 2001; Huberman, 1993).

Furthermore, teachers are often accepting of reforms when they perceive the changes to be in the best interest of pupils and when they are congruent with their values and personal theories. In this sense they are able to discriminate amongst and between policies, creatively shaping them where appropriate and discarding where necessary. As Troman (1996) concluded 'Even in the face of the most stringent control of school work human agency creatively shapes the teachers' responses.' In addition, this agency operates beyond the workplace and appears to influence changing conceptions of professionalism and the ways in which autonomy, responsibility and knowledge are understood (Day, 2006).

In summary, teachers react to, interpret and interact with change and re-structuring in a differentiated, complex and sometimes contradictory way. Of central importance is the dynamic relationship between individual and context (Ballet et al., 2005) where both compliance and adaptation operate with equal measure driven by a continuing sense of agency and pragmatism. In terms of the latter, both Moore (2000) and Hoyle and Wallace (2005) have argued for a more subtle interpretation of teacher pragmatism and its effect on professional engagement with reform. As Moore (2004) points out this involves teachers in continually positioning themselves in relation to each other, their organisations and the national policy structures. It also implies making accommodations with the perceived tension between external function and internal purpose. As Britzman (1991) suggests, no teaching identity is ever singular or without contradiction and that teachers' conceptions are rarely, if ever, neatly packaged or consistent (Billig, 1988). This means that teachers must be willing to trade off some of their autonomy, cede certain levels of curriculum control, and introduce change into their practice for continued classroom and pedagogical autonomy. This 'principled pragmatism' (Moore, 2004) is preferred to 'contingent pragmatism', which appears to be more opportunistic and less durable.

This brief analysis raises a number of important questions in terms of the teaching profession and its future orientation. If teachers' professionalism is to be developed then it must be grounded in some conception of their expert authority because it is this that makes the whole idea of professionalism necessary. Furthermore, it is only through this professionalism that sufficient trust can be re-established in the minds of their clients (students, parents, carers, etc.). In order to throw light on this predicament and to indicate a possible future direction, I propose to re-introduce some elements of Parsons' original conception of a profession. This gives ontological primacy not to groups and structures but to the important work carried out by the professionals themselves – not just in organisational but also in normative terms.

A Parsonian Perspective

At the outset Parsons (1952) drew attention to and built on Weber's ideas on legitimate authority. Weber outlined three broad categories including: legal authority, traditional authority and charismatic authority. Parsons, however, believed that Weber had missed a fourth crucial variety: expert authority and in so doing explicitly linked this with the work of professionals. In later essays Parsons (1975) developed his ideas believing that professionals were essentially double agents or go-betweens whose job it was to mediate between clients and society. Professionals, he claimed, also used their authority to curtail their clients' deviance and to help align their clients' interests and actions with broader social norms. In Parsons' view, professionals are therefore continuously 'invoking their authority to negotiate and re-negotiate the normative boundaries between individuals and society'.

Parsons (1939) went on to explain that for this negotiated approach to be successful, professionals had to maintain a certain outlook – put simply they must not be overly motivated by a desire for power and wealth; a position that could be balanced only by a stronger desire for status and reputation. In this sense professional authority is exercised for the social good in a way that balances the individual needs with that of the community and it is by 'speaking forth' through the public articulation of values and norms that the profession maintains its trust and public esteem (Parsons, 1954). Crucial to this trust and respect are the standards of professional competence and ethicality that must be open and transparent to the public at large. The core element of Parsonian

professionalism is that a profession is an occupational group that uses its legitimate expert authority to mediate between the individual and society (Parsons,
1975; Latham, 2000).

This model of professionalism was critiqued (persuasively) in the 1970s and
1980s by a range of scholars (Becker et al., 1961; Larson, 1972; Freidson, 1975;
Abbot, 1984) who argued that Parsons ignored the exploitative actions of professional monopolists who were power and status hungry often at the expense of the
quality and the client. However, even if Parsons' analysis has conceptual and
empirical weaknesses there is still much to recommend it as a normative description of what the teaching profession ought to look like, in particular, the ways in
which the authority, expertise, and trust of teachers might be rekindled in the light
of the erosion that has taken place in wake of two decades of reform.

At the core of the Parsonian idea is that the authority of professionals is grounded
in their knowledge and expertise. However, in order to develop a normative conception of teacher professionalism that might restore what Freidson (2001) terms 'the
soul of professionalism' a more detailed understanding of professional authority is
required. Put simply, a professional's authority allows him or her to secure actions
or beliefs without coercion and without undue persuasion. But what if anything
makes teachers' exercise of their authority normatively legitimate? Why should students, parents, carers and others accept the bare statements and actions of the teacher
as a reason for belief or for action? Put simply why should they trust the teacher?

We can perhaps find an answer of sorts in the etymology of the word authority.
Authority comes to us from two different Latin roots: *auctoritas* and *auctor*.
The former is a legal term usually referred to as 'a surety in a transaction, the testimony
of a witness, or the means of verification of some fact – usually a document.' It
then emerged to mean the respect, dignity or weight attached to the person or the
document involved (Freidman, 1990). The latter – *auctor* – is derived from the
verb *augere* 'to augment, increase, enrich and tell about', similar to author – usually
defined as either one who 'brings about the existence of something' (as in the
author of his action) or to one who 'promotes the increase or prosperity of…or
by his efforts gives greater permanence or continuance to it.' (Freidman, 1990)
Auctor then can usually be understood to refer to a founder or author, to whom a
line of action can be traced back as the source; or to one who augments or
enriches such an act; or one who bears witness to or gives an account of such a
foundation (Latham, 2000).

Taking the two derivations together, an authority can be seen as 'an intermediary
between the thing he is an authority on and the persons who accept him as an
authority on that thing' (Freidman, 1990). The authority has, for reasons of superior
wisdom, experience or knowledge, privileged access to some body of knowledge;
and the subjects of that authority recognise that privileged access and agree to
accept the judgement of the authority and trust it with regard to a proper interpretation of that wisdom, experience and knowledge. To put it in Parsonian terms, those
with professional authority are intermediaries who have direct access to a body of
knowledge and expertise while the subject has access to such resources which at
best can only be vicarious.

The Revival of Professional Authority

My aim is now to show that Parsonian professionalism with its claims to exclusive cognitive authority, its emphasis on responsibility and autonomy and its commitment to the authority of practice is the only credible way of countering the excessive managerialism, consumerism and standardisation that Freidson (2001) claims are the main threats to the quality of professional practice.

Such comments point to the need for teachers – as professionals – to develop the capacity to determine their professional responsibility not only towards each student but also a capacity to be knowledgeable about the characteristics of their profession and the nature and specificity of their expertise. They also need to understand and be able to explain the goals and the values of their practice and the basis of their professional knowledge. This means being prepared to evaluate their practice, to question the evidence upon which their practice is based, and to see themselves as agents of change who are confident and able to defend their work and the quality of their practice. This ability to respond to and to question change and to put forward an explicit rationale for their practice will be crucial to the ability to maintain a strong professional profile and the trust of the public at large.

In order to restore the 'soul of professionalism' (Freidson, 2001) the constraining influences that have limited teachers as professionals need to be challenged. Of crucial importance is the centrality of the social contract which Wear et al. (2004) define as 'the norms of the relationships in which professionals engage in the care of their clients.' This recognises the centrality (though not exclusively) of the relationship between the client and the professional while being cognisant of the shifting societal norms that influences those relationships. The key to this relationship, as Parsons pointed out, is trust. However, the public trust held by teachers has not been sufficiently celebrated – or investigated (Frowe, 2001). In particular, we often call attention to the character of the teacher-pupil relationship but seldom recall that virtually every professional encounter has implications for the 'community' that supports and cares for the pupil. Furthermore, the actions and pronouncements of teachers also frame the social relations of their pupils with their families, peers and carers. The teacher's authority is thus, *ipso facto*, also an authority over the pupil's 'community' and trust must be maintained over both.

So how is trust to be re-established? I argue that this can only happen through the 'acts of profession' but what are these acts exactly? The 'pro-fession' of professionals is fundamentally a speaking forth in public; it is a public commitment to socially accepted standards of both ethics and of competence (Latham, 2000). These commitments, as Pellegrino and Thomasma (1981) reminds us, are always re-affirmed in the relationships between professionals and their communities and are the procrustean bed from which the fiduciary relationship is built. This relationship has both primary and secondary characteristics (Frowe, 2005). The former are entered into voluntarily where both truster and trustee agree to act in an agreed way; while the latter involves a range of tacit agreements that guide behaviour. Logically, according to Frowe (2005) primary trust precedes secondary trust although often both categories become blurred. In many ways this categorisation aligns with Becker's (1996) distinctions between cognitive and non-cognitive trust where the cognitive involves gathering information about the relative trustworthiness of a particular person, persons or institution whereas non-cognitive consists of a series of attitudes and disposition to the formulation of trust (Frowe, 2005).

Trust is an essential feature of the professional–client relationship and much of it emanates from the quality of the knowledge and the capabilities possessed by the practitioner. This allows professionals to use their judgement or discretionary powers in the furtherance of the clients' and their communities' interests (Frowe, 2005). Knowledge is crucial to this relationship because as Oakshott (1989) points out 'judgement is essential for knowledge to work' and that it is 'the acquisition of judgement that is the real substance of our inheritance'. The current attempts by governments to reduce professional judgement through the 'informatizing' of teachers fails to appreciate the complexities of the judgements need to practice as a teacher. It is also predicated on the idea that teachers must internalise imposed elements of prescriptive knowledge and exhibit this in a series of competent behaviours audited by set national standards. This inevitably limits the need for cognitive or primary trust because it is externally imposed – leaving the only room for manoeuvre in the tacit field of relationships. As Offe (1999, 52: 53) points out trust begins with knowledge and then only develops when we stop calculating, enforcing and monitoring.

However, the relationship between teachers' knowledge and practice has been and continues to be problematic. Jackson (1968) as long ago as 1968 highlighted some of the issues. He claimed (somewhat over-simplistically) that teachers, because their language was conceptually simple, seemed uninterested in the causal or underlying theoretical patterns that informed their practice. They preferred, he claimed, intuition to analysis and opinion to evidence. In the years since those pronouncements, researchers have gradually built a picture of teachers' knowledge that is rich in its complexity and universal in it application (Clandinin and Connelly, 1995; Huberman, 1993) Nevertheless, the role of knowledge – in all its forms – remains in tension with the professional aspects of teachers' roles. I propose a number of sources or categories of knowledge that might help ameliorate those tensions and provide the platform for a re-establishment of the authority and expertise that Parsons felt was so vital to professionalism.

First, however, it is important to define the territory – here teachers' professional knowledge is defined as the knowledge comprising all the profession-related insights that are potentially relevant to the act of teaching. These insights can pertain to the formal theories often derived from empirical research of various types and often informed by various discipline based theories (knowledge for practice) as well as codified craft knowledge that has emerged from research into the beliefs, values, practices and experiences of teachers (knowledge of practice). Much of this practical knowledge remains tacit, being both embedded and embodied in practice (knowledge in practice). We follow Fenstermacher (1986) in claiming that the main function of the first two is to improve the practical arguments or warrants that engage teachers when thinking about their practice – both *in situ* and *post factum.*

It is important to realise that this knowledge, however configured, is not only cognitive but normative and patterned into a shared set of values, beliefs, and ways of reasoning. The third, however, comes from within teachers' own personal and practical experience. According to Eraut (2002) it is constructed from 'an implicit aggregation of a series of episodes' often snatched from busy crowded environments and usually drawn form atypical behaviour patterns. This is inevitable, claims Eraut (2002) because teachers work in 'busy kitchens' where the action is hot and their knowledge inevitably becomes 'experienced based, tacit and ready for instant use as opportunities arise (Huberman, 1983).'

For these differentiated forms of knowledge to cohere into what Parsons would term professional knowledge and cognitive authority, a number of key processes and features need to be more apparent. First, this knowledge needs to be connected to the processes of teaching and learning that occur in the classroom and that the motivation to use it emanates from specific 'problems of practice'. Second, this knowledge needs to be storable and sharable as well as represented through exemplar. Making the more abstract or empirical elements more usable will involve concretising these exemplars so they can be understood and adapted to the specifics of practice. Third, new technologies need to be harnessed since they provide a useful storage and exchange medium both for individual teachers and institutions. Of central importance, however, is that this knowledge is accurate, verifiable and continually put to the test (Hiebert et al., 2002) as well as being open to communication thus rendering it genuinely public and open not only to teachers but to other consumers and users of education including parents.

However, if teachers are to recover their classroom responsibility and the essentials of their autonomy, they will also have to show a willingness to engage with 'knowledge for' practice described above. Usually defined as evidence, this type of knowledge has always been a significant defining trait of all professions. It may be research based evidence within subject pedagogy or it may be generic; it might be linked to how children learn or it may be based in policy or governance studies; it might be highly generalised built from large scale studies of literature reviews or it may be findings drawn from qualitative studies of various kinds. Of central importance, however, is that teachers have to think how the connections can be made to practice. This is complex and requires much investment of time and effort; it also means encouraging the educational research community to become more attuned to the needs and demands of practitioners as well as communicating their findings and ideas in ways that matches teachers' discourse (Bartels, 2003; John, 2004). New technology has a role to play in developing the enabled professional by providing the platform which might facilitate such an engagement.

Confronting teachers' practical knowledge with formal theory might also be the answer to the often rehearsed criticism of the conservative nature of teachers' practice and its tendency to reflect the well established routines and traditions. It might also bring about the situation described by Thiessen (2000) where practically relevant propositional knowledge and propositionally interpreted practical knowledge interconnect to inform practice. As Eraut (1994) suggests, such a blending requires critical review and control and understanding of one's knowledge base. In this sense 'knowing about' the profession is considered to be as important as 'knowing in' the profession so that the rationales for thinking, acting and relating within the profession become explicit. This heightened sense of professional awareness might also confront the narrow 'fitness for purpose' knowledge agenda that underpins the current attempts to constrain and re-model the teaching workforce.

The impact of professional knowledge on teachers' professional authority and trust therefore relies on them engaging in a number of continuous knowledge engagement processes. These include:

- Continually expanding and refining their knowledge base – both subject specific and generic
- Translating their practice and knowing into articulable knowledge
- Learning in action and testing their knowledge through reasoning and the use of practical arguments
- Developing a deep understanding of the procedural knowledge and processes underlying their thinking
- Constantly challenging and developing various interpersonal and professional skills
- Continually up-dating their knowledge and professional competence
- Assessing the utility and relevance and adequacy of their knowledge with the aim of improving
- Testing that knowledge in a variety of contexts

The enactment of these processes relies heavily on *reflection and self-awareness*. The Parsonian perspective is once again significant here in that it rehabilitates the idea of uncertainty in professional practice and stresses the need for teachers to theorise the contemporary complexities of practice through reflective pedagogy. Such intellectual activity will, in the final analysis, be guided by sets of individual and collective values; these frameworks will also be the filter through which practice is expressed. Furthermore, if professional goals are to held sovereign amidst competing claims for practice, the act of reflection – where individuals reflect on both the essential characteristics of professional practice over a period of time and on the underpinning assumptions of professional knowledge it presupposes – becomes of primary concern as a tool to maintain the autonomy of practice. A commitment to 'interpretive reflection' or what might be termed 'meta-cognition' is therefore central. Meta-cognition – here defined as the ability to become conscious of both how and why one is learning a particular thing in particular ways and thereby helping to gain control over the process – offers the opportunity for teachers to abstract themselves from the daily detail of practice and consciously take a strategic overview of their professional thinking, behaviour and decision making in the contexts in which such activities occur. This ability to recognise and regulate one's practice and the thoughts underpinning it (sometimes termed reflexivity) is an essential skill for retaining and maintaining autonomy; one that should feature explicitly in all accounts of teachers' practice.

This emphasis on the autonomous, problem solving, and regulatory aspects of reflection is in marked contrast to the functional reflection that is a feature of constrained professionalism. Here the cycle of reflection is too often seen as 'a micro quality assurance mechanism' where chunks of learning are evaluated against set objectives or targets. In this sense teachers rarely move beyond concrete reflection of the perceived effectiveness of the lesson or series of lessons.

If the idea of a knowledge driven profession defined by levels of autonomy and reflectivity is to emerge then a new *language of practice* needs to develop along-side; one that integrates the concepts, ideas, knowledge and skill that emerge from both the practical and the formal domains. Architects and medical practitioners, for instance, have developed a 'way of thinking' that enables the profession to take ownership of their practical problems (Yinger, 1987). Teachers and educational researchers likewise need to develop a professional language in order to share their understandings. This would mean recognising that teaching is a social practice and that language enters this practice as a means of articulating and formulating rules, principles and standards that inform it (Frowe, 2001). In this sense language makes practice possible in a procedural and cognitive sense. The primary role of this language would be to facilitate communication amongst practitioners who would also articulate their goals, principles, rules and routines. This means that in education, language has a more essential role to play than in a more formal discipline such as physics or geology where beliefs and values often stand in some contingent relationship to practice, rather, as in education, being actually constitutive of it (Frowe, 2001). The emergence of such a language of practice needs to be mindful of these issues because as Fielding (2001) points out, the language of performativity does not simply refer to a pre-existing reality – it actively engages with and shapes the actions themselves.

Conclusion

It has been argued in this chapter that teachers as professionals have faced a number of challenges over the last two decades; challenges that do not easily fit into ready-made terms such as proletarianisation, de-professionalization, de-skilling or re-professionalization. Rather there are a myriad of forces which act to both afford and constrain professional practice. Of significance, however, is the trend towards neo-institutionalism (Deakin, 1998) in schools where new enabling or entrepreneurial structures are supposed to encourage self-activity, accountability and new forms of collaboration and teamwork which often achieve the opposite. These have been reinforced by new funding arrangements, including the greater use if semi-autonomous agencies and revised contractualism. These explicit attempts to incorporate new forms of coercive power into schools and classrooms rely on key actors – senior managers and practitioners – realising the considerable personal and career gains that can accrue from being a part of the change process.

It is my contention, that to counter-balance these forces (which I have argued are at the core of the current predicament of the teaching profession) we need to re-visit some of the verities of 'classic' professionalism as evinced by Talcott Parsons.

His insights support a view of professionalism as the mobilisation of collective action to achieve agreed social goals; action that ties professional authority to consensus. The authoritative professional argued for in this chapter is therefore dependent upon a number of principles. For these to be realised it is crucial that:

- There should be a core knowledge base agreed by the profession and enacted through the GTC.
- This knowledge base must be underpinned by a set of values and principles and both need to be integrated into all continuing professional development programmes.
- All education and training be informed research findings.
- Management decisions be informed by professional needs and that there be an increasing isomorphism between the two.
- Ownership of the education and training (ITE and CPD) must lie with the profession and it should manifest itself in life-long career credentials and continuous professional learning.
- This commitment to continuing professional learning should be an individual, institutional and national obligation and resources need to be committed to this aim.
- Teaching comes to terms with differentiated tasks and a differentiated work force and that is underpinned by complementarity not substitution.
- All teachers (and teaching assistants) see themselves as part of a profession underpinned by an exacting but nationally agreed set of standards and that self-regulation be maintained within the remit of the GTC.
- There is collaboration to achieve appropriate status and career structure for all in the profession, and the infrastructure to ensure that all who acquire that status deserve it by having the pre-requisite knowledge and by demonstrating the necessary skill.

References

Abbot, A. (1984) *The System of Professions: An Essay on the Division of Expert Labour* (Chicago, IL: University of Chicago Press)

Acker, S. (1999) *The Realities of Teachers' Work: Never a Dull Moment* (London: Cassell)

Apple, M. W. and Jungck, S. (1996) You don't have to be a teacher to teach this unit: teaching, technology and control in the classroom. In A. Hargreaves (Ed) *Understanding Teacher Development* (London: Casell)

Ball, S. J. (2003) The teacher's soul and the terrors of performativity. *Journal of Education Policy*, 18(2), 215–228

Ballet, K., Klechtermans, G., and Loughran, J. (2005) Beyond intensification towards a scholarship of practice: analysing change in teachers' work and lives. *Teachers and Teachers: Theory and Practice*, 12(2), 209–229

Barlett, L. (2002) Teachers work in times of reform: professionalisation or intensification. Paper presented at the annual meeting of the American Educational Research Association, New Orleans, April 7–12

Bartels, N. (2003) How teachers and researchers read academic articles. *Teaching and Teacher Education*, 19, 737–753

Becker, H., Geer, B., Hughes, E., and Strauss, A. (1961) *The Boys in White: Student Culture in Medical School* (Chicago, IL: University of Chicago Press)

Becker, L. (1996) Trust as a non-cognitive security about motives. *Ethos*, 107, 433–461

Billig, M. (1988) Social representation, objectification and anchoring: a rhetorical analysis. *Social Behaviour*, 3, 1–16

Britzman, D. (1991) De-centering discourses in teacher education: or, the unleashing of unpopular things. *Journal of Education*, 173, 75

Brown, P. (1990) The 'third wave': education and the ideology of parentocracy. *British Journal of Sociology of Education*, 11(1), 65–85

Clandinin, D. J. and Connelly, F. M. (1995) *Teachers' Professional Knowledge Landscapes* (New York: Teachers College Press)

Day, C. (2006) Teachers in the twenty-first century. *Teachers and Teaching: Theory and Practice*, 12(2), 98–114

Deakin, S. (1998) Collective learning as a contribution to reflexive governance. Application to EU Social and Bio-diversity Protection Policy Unit

Eraut, M. (1994) *Professional Knowledge and Professional Competence* (London: Falmer)

Eraut, M. (2002) Menus for choosy diners. *Teachers and Teaching: Theory and Practice*, 8(3/4), 371–379

Fenstermacher, G. D. (1986) The philosophy of research: three aspects. In M. C. Wittrock (Ed) *Handbook of Research on Teaching*, 3rd edn, pp. 37–49 (New York: Macmillan)

Fielding, M. (2001) *Taking Education Really Seriously: Four Years Hard Labour* (London: Routledge/Falmer)

Freidman, R. B. (1990) On the concept of authority in political philosophy. In J. Raz (Ed) *Authority*, pp. 56–91 (New York: New York University Press)

Freidson, E. (1975) *The Profession of Medicine* (New York: Dodd-Mead)

Freidson, E. (2001) *Professionalism: The Third Logic* (Cambridge, UK: Polity)

Frowe, I. (2001) Language and educational practice. *Cambridge Journal of Education*, 31(1), 89–101

Frowe, I. (2005) Professional trust. *British Journal of Education Studies*, 53(1), 34–53

Hargreaves, A. (1997) Re-thinking educational change. In A. Hargreaves (Ed) *Re-thinking Educational Change with Heart and Minds* (Alexandria, VA: ASCD)

Hargreaves, A. (2000) The four ages of professionalism and professional learning. *Teachers and Teaching: Theory and Practice*, 6(2), 151–177

Helsby, G. (1999) *Changing Teachers' Work* (Buckinghamshire, England: Open University Press)

Hiebert, J., Gallimore, R., and Stigler, J. W. (2002) A knowledge base for the teaching profession: what would one look like and how might we get one? *Educational Researcher*, 35(8), 1–14

Hoyle, E. and Wallace, M. (2005) *Educational Leadership: Ambiguity, Professionals and Managerialism* (London: Paul Chapman)

Huberman, M. (1983) Recipes for busy kitchens: a situational analysis of routine knowledge use in schools. *Knowledge: Creation, Diffusion and Utilisation*, 4(4), 478–510

Huberman, M. (1993) Professional careers and professional development: some interaction. In R. T. Guskey and M. Huberman (Eds) *Professional Development in Education: New Paradigms and Practice*, pp. 193–224 (New York: Teachers College Press)

Jackson, P. (1968) *Life in Classrooms* (London: Holt, Rinehart & Winston)

John, P. (2004) Contentions, conceptions and connections: how teachers read and understand different genres of academic research. In R. Sutherland, G. Claxton, and A. Pollard (Eds) *Learning Where World Views Meet*, pp. 231–244 (London: Trentham Books)

Klechtermans, G. (2005) Teachers' emotion in educational reforms: self-understanding, vulnerable commitment and micro-political literacy. *Teaching and Teacher Education*, 21, 995–1006

Larson, M. S. (1972) *The Rise of Professionalism* (Berkeley, CA: University of California Press)

Latham, S. (2000) Medical professionalism: a Parsonian view. *Mount Sinai Journal of Medicine*, 9(6), 303–309

Moore, A. (2000) *Teaching and Learning: Pedagogy, Curriculum and Culture* (London: Routledge/Falmer)

Moore, A. (2004) *The Good Teacher: Dominant Discourses in Teaching and Teacher Education* (London: Routledge/Falmer)

Oakshott, M. (1989) Teaching and learning. In T. Fuller (Ed) *The Voice of Liberal Learning* (Yale, CT: Yale University Press)

Offe, C. (1999) How can we trust our fellow citizens? In M. Warren (Ed) *Democracy and Trust* (Cambridge: Cambridge University Press)

Osborn, M., McNess, E., Broadfoot, P. with Pollard, A. and Triggs, P. (2000) *What Teachers Do: Changing Policy and Practice in Primary Education* (London: Continuum).

Parsons, T. (1952) A sociologist looks at the legal profession. In Parsons, T. (Ed) *Essays in Sociological Theory* (New York: Free Press)

Parsons, T. (1954) The professions and social structure (1939). In Parsons, T. (Ed) *Essays in Sociological Theory*, pp. 34–49 (New York: Free Press)

Parsons, T. (1975) Professions. In D. L. Sills (Ed) *International Encyclopedia of Social Sciences*, vol. 12 (New york: Macmillan)

Pellegrino, E. and Thomasma, D. (1981) A philosophical reconstruction of medical morality. In E. Pellegrino and D. Thomasma (Eds) *A Philosophical Basis of Medical Practice* (Oxford: Oxford University Press).

Smylie, G. (1999) Teacher stress in a time of reform. In R. Vendenberghe, M. R. Vanderburgh, and M. Huberman (Eds) *Understanding and Preventing Teacher Burnout* (Cambridge: Cambridge University Press)

Thiessen, D. (2000) A skilful start to a teaching career. *International Journal of Educational Research*, 33, 515–537

Troman, G. (1996) The rise of new professionals: Re-structuring primary teachers work and professionalism. *British Journal of Sociology of Education*, 17(4), 475–487

Troman, G. (1997) The effects of re-structuring on primary teachers' work: a sociological analysis. Unpublished Ph.D. theses, Open University, UK

Troman, G. (2000) Teacher stress in the low trust society. *British Journal of Sociology of Education*, 21, 331–353

Troman, G. and Woods (2001) *Primary Teachers' Stress* (London: Routledge/Falmer)

Wear, G., Delese, S., Kuczewski, M., and Mark, G. (2004) The professionalism movement: can we pause? *American Journal of Bioethics*, 4(2), 1–10

Woods, P., Jeffery, B, Troman, G., and Boyle, M. (1997) *Reconstructing Teachers: Responding to Change in the Primary School* (Buckinghamshire, England: Oxford University Press)

Woods (2002) The reconstruction of primary teachers' identities. *British Journal of Sociology of Education*, 23(1), 89–106

Yinger, R. (1987) Learning the language of practice. *Curriculum Inquiry*, 17(3), 293–318

Chapter 3
Under 'Constant Bombardment': Work Intensification and the Teachers' Role

John Williamson and Marion Myhill

Introduction

There has been a growing interest in the work of teachers in recent years, particularly in their increasing workloads and in the changing nature of their work. While the significance of teaching and the importance of teachers continue to be strongly affirmed, there are growing concerns being expressed at the extent to which recent changes are impacting on the teaching profession. In particular, concerns have been expressed about the intensification of teachers' work and the negative impact that this may have on teachers, their work lives and their work-life balance – and also by extension on the quality of teachers' work and on their students' learning experiences.

This intensification which is central to the changes in teachers' work may well reflect more general workplace trends, from which the education sector is not immune or protected. Trends such as increasing work demands and constraints on workers, the pervasiveness of a business management-oriented framework with a focus on 'marketization' and managerialization' have all been cited as impacting on teachers – as well as the special demands of being required to educate children for the future in a fast-changing and globalised world (Helsby, 1999).

However, there are certain aspects which are central to teachers' experiences. The intensification of teachers' work appears most commonly to have resulted from a documented trend towards considerably longer working hours than in the past, an ever-expanding teaching role, and most noticeably, a significant increase in non-teaching and largely administrative duties (Gardner and Williamson, 2004).

With longer working hours and constantly expanding teaching and non-teaching roles and duties, concerns have been expressed that these changes are undoubtedly producing negative effects on teachers. Supportive evidence is provided by consistent reports of increased teacher stress and the growing number of research studies that have investigated teachers' work lives. Such studies have documented that teachers are now considered to be working longer than reasonable hours (Gardner and Williamson, 2006a), to be engaged in a greater number of non-teaching duties (Gardner and Williamson, 2005), to be complying with more accountability demands (Hoyle, 1995) and to be experiencing higher levels of

D. Johnson, R. Maclean (eds.), *Teaching: Professionalization, Development and Leadership,*
© Springer Science + Business Media B.V. 2008

stress. What is of particular concern is that all of these pressures are likely not only to have a negative impact on teachers personally, but also to affect their teaching performance.

Intensification of teachers' work lives therefore is a current issue of concern which is being examined, not only to assess its nature and extent, but also to determine its impact on teachers and their capacity to fulfil positively their role as teacher.

In this chapter, we shall review current trends in the intensification of teachers' work, focussing on the nature, sources and impact of intensification. These three issues will be examined from a general perspective and then from the perspective of a particular group of working teachers who participated in a recent case study of teachers in the Australian state of Tasmania.

Intensification of Teachers' Work

Intensification in the teaching context has been described as the "increasing pressure to do more in less time, to be responsive to a greater range of demands from external sources, to meet a greater range of targets, to be driven by deadlines" (Galton and MacBeath, 2002: 13). This has been coupled with a corresponding loss of a 'sense of control' over one's own 'planning, decision-making, classroom management and relationships' (Galton and MacBeath, 2002: 13).

The first key element of the intensification raised here by Galton and MacBeath (2002) is the identification of increasing pressure on teachers which has resulted from being required 'to do more in less time'. The second element is that this pressure is identified as arising largely from external sources. This has led to a sense that these pressures are largely out of the control of teachers themselves; and that this is turn has led to a feeling of a general erosion of teacher professionalism (e.g., teacher planning, decision-making and classroom management judgements).

The third element is an expansion in the range, variety and nature of the 'more' that teachers are being asked to do. Doing 'more in less time' now encompasses not just an increase in work hours, or in general busyness or in just getting more of the same work done in a shorter time. It also involves an expanded teacher role, more-non teaching duties and activities, more deadlines, targets and responsibilities – and as a result, greater in and out-of-school work hours and increased reported stress.

The related major issue, also raised by Galton and MacBeath (2002), is teachers' loss of a 'sense of control'. This issue had been reported earlier by Hoyle and John (1995) and Churchill and Williamson (1999); and it is evident in comparative national research, such as the international series of studies described by Poppleton and Williamson (2004). This perception of a loss of control is both a separate area of concern and also one that impacts interactively with the work intensification issue and to create a much larger and more pervasive concern.

We shall examine both of these major areas – teachers' work intensification and a loss of a sense of control – both separately and then in relation to the Tasmanian case study findings.

What Is the Nature of the Intensification?

Considerable data have now been gathered which document the nature of the intensification of teachers' work.

International trends have shown changes in teachers' work which have resulted in increased teacher hours, class sizes and tasks (UNESCO, 1998). In addition to the international research studies monitoring these trends, various national studies have also focussed on those issues that reflect national, rather than international, research and policy priorities and interests. In the USA, for example, teacher pay has been a major focus (Moulthrop et al., 2005; Stronge et al., 2006) while the focus has been on teacher workloads in both the UK (Galton and MacBeath, 2002; Helsby, 1999), and also in Australia (Gardner and Williamson, 2005, 2006a, b).

The general consensus is that there is a current trend for teachers in many countries to be working much longer hours than previously. Teachers are spending more time at work, as well as more time at home working on teacher-related activities. The related concerns that have been expressed are that this trend has led to high levels of stress and a negative work-life balance for the teacher and ultimately a loss of teaching quality, which is turn creates a negative outcome for students and their learning.

Several comprehensive studies of teacher workloads have been undertaken in Australia over the last decade. Williamson and colleagues have conducted a number of studies of teacher workloads (Churchill et al., 1997; Gardner and Williamson, 2004, 2005, 2006a, b), as well as studies of the workloads of principals and other school employees (Gardner and Williamson, 2004). In many cases, these studies have been conducted with the support and involvement of teacher education unions (e.g., Gardner and Williamson, 2004).

What Are the Sources of Intensification?

The sources of the intensification can be linked to a range of factors: an increased political interest in and focus on education, a tendency toward constant change in education systems, financial constraints, increased pressures from society and the community, and an increased complexity in teachers' roles. Related issues have been teacher pay and the nexus between workload, performance and pay.

The source factors can be identified as having their origin in pressures both external and internal to teachers. External pressures arise from system-level policies and changes, which operate at a number of levels (school, state, national or international)

and are beyond the classroom teacher's ability to influence. However, they have the capacity to have a strong impact on the teacher's work and work-life.

A number of external sources of intensification and pressures on teachers have been identified:

- A trend towards international educational outcomes comparisons, such as cross-national 'league tables' of student performance by country (e.g., PISA)
- A politicisation of education at various levels of national government (e.g., state and federal governments in Australia); also leading to a proliferation of some-times competing policies and practices
- A trend towards centralised systems of state school education (e.g., the move from the local LEA/council to a centralised system based in Whitehall, in the UK)

These centralised systems tend to lead to approaches which create extra pressures for teachers. These new pressures arise from several sources:

- 'One size fits all' systems: these are based on economic rationalist principles and are characterised by aggregated student results, an outcomes-focussed approach, attempts to identify 'best teachers' (for the purposes of differentiated salaries), and the ranking of schools (regardless of background factors).
- An assessment-driven approach.
- Limited recognition of schooling context variation: few allowances are made for meeting the needs of all children within a wide range of local conditions.
- Tensions between teachers and bureaucrats: teachers focus on children and their learning needs, while bureaucrats focus on testing/outcomes and resources.

Internally driven pressures arise largely from teachers' professionalism and their commitment to students and their needs:

- Teachers focus on 'their children' and have a commitment to meeting their students' learning needs; this commitment may also extend to a broader concern with their students' personal lives and long term futures.
- Teachers focus on the reality and immediacy of the classroom and its demands and practices, rather than on what they perceive as abstract (economic, political and ideological) policies.

What Is the Impact of Intensification?

The impact of intensification can be seen at the levels of: the school system, the individual school and on the individual teacher. One of the broad consequences of intensification, as reported by one teacher, is that 'we [teachers] are changed out'. This comment contains both a negative view of change more generally and the fact that the constant competition between time for quality teaching and for coping more generally with the workload may impact on personal health and well-being. Teachers see the rise in societal and employer expectations as leading to much more 'out-of-school' work being done and this is not just anticipated individual preparation and marking but also for more time to be spent in meetings and joint planning.

An important system-level outcome is that innovations are implemented in a 'spotty' fashion. Many teachers report that in the face of the constant rise in expectations they have become more selective about what innovations they implement in their class. As a consequence they proactively consider initiatives through the lens of 'what is worthwhile for my students?', and disregard those other initiatives they deem not applicable. In this situation policy-makers cannot be sure that policies are being implemented at the system level and this has significant consequence for policies such as inclusion.

A consequence which is becoming more evident is the trend for many teachers to refuse to apply for more senior positions within the school and, at the same time, for the number of fractional appointments also to increase. This trend is a concern as the very competent and committed teachers that schools would wish to see in leadership positions are not being considered as the 'costs' to the individual and the teacher's family are deemed to high.

The View from the Coal-Face: A Case Study of Tasmanian Teachers' Worklives

What Are Working Teachers' Experiences of Intensification?

In 2003–2004 an education union-commissioned study of teachers' workloads was undertaken state-wide in Tasmania.

Tasmania is one of the smaller states and territories in Australia, but the main education issues that are evident in the wider Australian context are also evident in Tasmania. The smaller scale also allows for a comprehensive research sample to be gained and a more epidemiological approach to be taken in the conduct of the study. While it is the case that the six states and two territories in Australia operate as separate jurisdictions and education systems and they also differ considerably in terms of size and scale, they are quite similar in terms of the broad challenges that they face and the general approaches that they take. This allows for some confidence in generalising issues and challenges across the systems – while still recognising the unique challenges for state systems with large indigenous populations (e.g., Northern Territory) and with multi-ethnic schools (e.g., Victoria and New South Wales). In addition, the states and territories have also all been similarly influenced in recent years by the increasingly pro-active educational policies of the Australian federal government (e.g., national literacy and numeracy benchmark testing).

The Tasmanian study arose from the recognition that there was 'increasing concern about education workers' workloads' (Gardner and Williamson, 2004: 1). The key purposes of the study were to identify the factors that determine the workloads of teachers, principals and other education workers (e.g., laboratory technicians and teacher's aides), and to suggest ways of distributing resources to ensure their most effective and innovative use – in order to promote student learning. The significance of the study was increased by the support of the Australian Education Union (AEU) and the contents of the ensuing report being taken up in political debate at the state parliament level.

Using a multi-method approach employing questionnaire, diary entries, and interviews (both focus and individual) and a quasi-grounded approach to the analysis, several major themes emerged from the data: length of working hours, intensification of work, impact of recent changes, satisfaction with role-related decision-making involvement and the identification of aspects of the workplace that hindered or assisted the work.

As background, it should be stated that approximately 95% of the teaching-force in Tasmania are members of the Australian Education Union (AEU). The study used a stratified sampling technique to ensure a minimum of 10% of each of the main groups (primary teachers, secondary teachers) and a higher percentage for selected groups with comparatively small membership numbers than the teacher groups (guidance officers, social workers) (Gardner and Williamson, 2004).

The Nature of Intensification: Teachers' Working Hours

From the 'snapshot' data of hours worked based on diary entries, the findings indicated that close to half of the surveyed teachers reported working hours that placed them in the Australian Bureau of Statistics' (ABS) 'very long working hours' category. This is based on a definition of at least 50 hours of work per week. However, many teachers worked much longer hours that this: more than half (54%) of the secondary teachers worked more than 50 hours a week, with some working more than 60 hours (8%). The great majority of primary and senior secondary teachers worked between 40 and 60 hours (89% of primary teachers; 79% of senior secondary teachers). So it seemed that long working hours had become something of a norm.

Working 50–60 hour weeks necessitated considerable work at home as well as at work. Respondents also reported an increased amount of time devoted to work during the week – and at the weekend.

At work, teachers reported an increased workload, not just in teaching, but also in administrative and other non-teaching tasks. Ironically perhaps, given the efficiency claims for on-line communication, teachers perceived that the introduction of computers for staff, and particularly email communication, were perceived to have added very considerably to the their workload:

> We have to do all our own letters and worksheets. I still [at the time of interview] have a couple of hundred emails to read. An increasing number of people are complaining about email. It's an extra job on top of preparation and marking. I feel as though I'm not spending enough time on what I should be doing. It doesn't have defined end-points … I'm trying to do my best for the kids … trying to be professional. *(Senior secondary teacher, female, >21 years experience, individual interview)*

> (Gardner and Williamson, 2005: 6)

What is concerning about this teacher's comments is that she is clearly struggling under the weight of increased non-teaching tasks, which not only takes up more time than she is willing, or capable, of giving. It has also have impacted on her to the extent that she now feels she has a job that has 'no defined end-points' and that she is only capable of 'trying to be professional'. Overall this comment suggests a feeling of being overwhelmed by ('drowning in') the current non-teaching demands of the job.

What is of further concern is that this teacher is not a new and inexperienced graduate, but a very experienced teacher. If she is not able to survive, let alone thrive, in the current system, then what teacher can? This situation is clearly of more general concern for all teachers and schools, not just for this particular teacher; and considerable future systemic problems are indicated.

A second issue that arises from this teacher's comment is that her non-teaching workload creates for her a high level of concern about her capacity to do what she sees as her 'core business', which is teaching students and being a professional teacher.

Tensions Between Teacher Collaboration and Isolation

Another recent change in the role of the professional teacher has been the systemic trend toward demanding teachers to be involved in collaborative planning and teamwork. While collaborative planning and teamwork may well be an admirable ideal – and well justified by the pedagogical literature – this approach requires, by definition, more time devoted to planning and organisation than does individual teacher planning (Gardner and Williamson, 2006a).

This time commitment again has a cumulative effect; and the time commitment to working out of hours comes at a cost. One teacher gave a very clear account of the impact of the workload on her private as well as her work life, the steps she took to create a better work-life balance – but also the serious toll that this took in terms of the negative impact on her career aspirations:

> When I started teaching I did hours of preparation and marking night after night, year after year. After seven or eight years I decided I could *not* continue working day *and* night. I no longer existed as a social person. My family life was greatly diminished. So I decided not to take work home [as a rule], Work (the place) is for work (the activity). Home is home! I had to change the way I teach; I gave up aspirations of promotion… I believe that my teaching has been improved (by the changes I made). I have more energy, better health, I'm more child-centred and I'm a more interesting person. However, at times I regret that I haven't been able to work in senior positions. I feel I could contribute lots, but the workload requires lots of work in 'home' time. *(Primary teacher, female, 21+ years experience, questionnaire; emphasis in original)*
>
> (Gardner and Williamson, 2006a: 3–4)

Perhaps this time issue is at the basis of the finding that female teachers are five times more dissatisfied than male teachers about working 'out of hours'. As one female

teacher commented, "I have three jobs. I am a mother, a wife and a teacher...."
(Gardner and Williamson, 2004).

 It may also be the reason why some teachers had chosen to work part time in order to thrive:

> Teaching has become more pressured due in part to changes in teaching emphasis and in part to behavioural issues (across the school). I prefer to put in long hours at school ... and find .8 perfect. My work is challenging ... rewarding, but exhausting. Stress leave and illness ... evidence of this. Many envy my .8 but cannot afford to do so themselves. *(Primary teacher, female, 16–20 years' experience, questionnaire)*

(Gardner and Williamson, 2006a: 4)

 Or just survive:

> I go home at 5pm and then work for another two hours at night. I decided to go part-time because of a 'lack of a life' and I questioned my capacity to do a fulltime load. *(Primary teacher, female, focus group)*

(Gardner and Williamson, 2006a: 4)

What is of concern here is the concept that fulltime work as a teacher is not condu-cive to a healthy, balanced life; the work of a teacher has become so demanding and that the only way to survive, let alone thrive, is to work part time. Is this going to be the pattern of the teaching work force of the future? While at one level this may be a viable and potentially positive option, there are also inherent problems related to the provision of quality teaching. If part time work were to become the majority pattern of work rather than the minority, then what would schools be like? School organisation would be considerably more complex, and potentially less cohesive, coherent and connected. And then what impact would this have on students and their learning, particularly at the primary level?

A related finding was that many of the respondents reported working very long days at work (10–12 hours), but only taking – or only being able to take – minimal breaks. It was rare for respondents, for example, to report having taken the half hour uninterrupted breaks during the day which was an industrial requirement:

> Yesterday I worked from 7.30am until 7.10pm with a recess break of 15 minutes, a lunch break of 25 minutes, 10 minutes coffee break and 30 minutes for tea. I had 7 periods of contact time, including an evacuation for [a safety threatening incident] and professional learning ... we are expected to be "on call" for professional learning whenever manage-ment see fit during Monday to Thursday. *(Secondary teacher, female, >21 years' experience, questionnaire)*

(Gardner and Williamson, 2005: 6)

It is interesting to note the teacher's reference not just to the longer working day, which is likely to have spanned both the workplace and the home, but also to the large amount of class contact, the brief break periods, and the perceived lack of control by the teacher over her working day.

This perceived lack of control is exemplified by her reference to the unforeseen time spent on an unplanned event (e.g., a safety evacuation) and by being "on call" for professional development as arranged by the school's senior management team. The unplanned activities during a teacher's day, while doubtless necessary, are likely to impact both on the teacher's day in terms of extended time, but also in terms of her personal control over that time (e.g., the lack of certainty expressed about when professional development would occur) and the suggestion that her working day is somewhat at the whim of management. This lack of control seems to be both an indicator of work intensification, and also of the wider changes in teachers' work and professional autonomy.

It is also interesting to note that the teacher's use of the term 'management' suggests a perceived separation of the classroom teacher from the school or system hierarchy, which further indicates the current influence and extent of managerialism in schools. This trend had earlier been reported in the UK and has been cited as a factor that had changed significantly the nature of teachers' work (Helsby, 1999).

The Nature of the Intensification: Teachers' Perceptions of Change

In addition to teachers' concerns about work intensification was the related issue – and reality – of change, particularly changes over the last 5 years (Gardner and Williamson, 2005).

Change and the change process were reported as one of the most important and influential aspects of the intensification of work; and one which both separately and in combination with work intensification created considerable additional stress.

Teachers were not only engaged in on-going teaching activities, which were inherently challenging, but also had to adapt to large-scale whole-of system changes, which brought additional pressures.

This combination led to teachers expressing concerns about the pace of change, and the new complexity and contradictions inherent in their role. Teachers reported a wide range of issues that could be grouped broadly as related to one of three main change factors: _time/pace, task demands and complexity, and change process._

The particular issues identified by the teachers in the study were:

Change factors	Issues identified by teachers
Time/pace	• More time needed to implement change while dealing with the exigencies of day-to-day work in schools
	• Being required to teach more curriculum, or a broader curriculum, in less time
	• Increasing demands on time of non-teaching duties
	• Typically having to discuss essential work matters 'on the run'
Task demands and complexity	• Feelings of having to juggle too many demands and expectations
	• Feelings of being close to losing control of the 'juggling act'
	• Having rising case loads but a corresponding fall in staff numbers

(continued)

Change factors	Issues identified by teachers
Change process	• Having to perform more, irrelevant or conflicting responsibilities • Being unable to sleep at night because of thinking about the day's activities and planned actions for the next day • The amount of change • The incoherence of change

(from Gardner and Williamson, 2005:9)

Change for teachers is not an ephemera or an abstraction. Those teachers with 5 or more years experience in the education system clearly perceived that considerable change/s had occurred and they were also well able to list a range of factors that supported their perceptions. What was of particular note was that more than 50% of the teachers (and principals) were in 'strong agreement' that these changes were 'significant' in the way that they had affected their work.

Four key areas of workplace changes were identified as having had an impact on teachers and their work. These were curriculum and pedagogy, student needs (and inclusion), accountability and control, and reduced resources.

Curriculum and Pedagogy

Teachers reported that changes in curriculum and pedagogy were having a significant impact on their work. While this has been reported in other settings (Poppleton and Williamson, 2004), the situation in Tasmania was exacerbated by the fact that the data were being collected at a time when the Tasmanian government school system was undergoing a period of major curriculum change. A new state wide curriculum was in the process of being introduced and implemented. This new curriculum was considered to be significantly changed from the previous curriculum and it was also accompanied by major shifts in the underpinning pedagogy and in the teaching and planning practices that teachers were now being ask to employ.

This context may explain why one teacher felt herself to be in a situation akin to being under fire in a battle zone:

> There is constant bombardment with pedagogy and [new curriculum] documents. ...
> *(Primary teacher, female, focus group)*
>
> (Gardner and Williamson, 2005: 10)

Teachers experienced a range of responses to both the changes and the manner of their implementation – from frustration and irritation to a loss of confidence and low staff morale. In addition, a perceived lack of (system) support and a perception that their previous teaching experience was either undervalued or irrelevant in the new 'change environment' added further to these negative responses.

The same teacher, for example, reported that the introduction of the changes 'implied what you were doing before is not right' and gave rise to the feeling of frustration that arose from a perception of wasted time and energy:

I've had experience of putting in time on learning new things.... and then we haven't used it. *(Primary teacher, female, focus group)*

(Gardner and Williamson, 2005: 11)

Time was also clearly a major factor in explaining why the implementation of the new curriculum was not always well received. Teachers argued that change requires time to implement and negative responses occur when teachers feel that insufficient time has been allocated to their needs. This was also reflected in the perception that the change was incoherent; and that there was a lack of recognition of the reality of teachers' lives by those charged with implementing the new curriculum, which led to frustration. So the 'standard' pressures of increased time and task commitments were augmented by the 'new' pressures – and stresses – of the change requirements:

A big frustration at the moment is trying to come to terms with the [new curriculum], while at the same time teaching, marking, preparing lessons, running extra curricular activities, etc. Things seem to be in a mess.... *(Secondary teacher, female, > 20 years' experience)*

(Gardner and Williamson, 2005: 11)

Student Needs and Inclusion

There is an increasing emphasis on teachers' recognising and meeting a wide range of student needs both inside and outside the classroom. This is seen as an inevitable consequence of social change and, while debated at times, the responsibility of teachers. In addition, Tasmanian government schools operate on an inclusion policy which means that teachers are likely to have a wider range of students in the classroom, including those with special needs (e.g., autism, Down syndrome), than previously.

In the Tasmanian study, teachers were in general agreement with the state systems' 'inclusion policy' – in principle. However, there was considerable disquiet and anxiety with its implementation, largely because of a perceived lack of support and resources:

Good to have inclusion, but [it] needs proper funding. Your planning and preparation times are doubled plus the students take up the teacher's time in the classroom ... There may not be enough room in the classroom for special equipment. You have to do PD out of school time to learn, for example, how to lift a child. There's a lot to learn about special needs ... when you're on your own, it's lonely. Unless you practise some things regularly, you need to be shown again. *(Primary teacher, focus group interview)*

(Gardner and Williamson, 2005: 11)

It was also noticeable that the implementation of the inclusion policy added further time directly to teacher's work in school and indirectly to their work time through the need to undertake (voluntary) professional development outside their school work time. There was also a reference to a lack of adequate resources which added to the teacher's work time (e.g., through extra preparation), but it was also likely to be an additional source of further stress.

The aspect of resource shortfall problems was supported by one of the principals in the study:

> The discrepancy between the hours we are funded for this student [i.e., one with special needs] and the time he needs support means that we have to take resources from the general resource package. This will affect the general program for other students. *(Principal, <5 years' experience, questionnaire)*
>
> (Gardner and Williamson, 2005: 11)

The specific inclusion policy clearly added considerable time to a Tasmanian teacher's workload; and this is likely to be found widely elsewhere, as it is a general policy in many national education systems to include students with 'special needs' in regular classrooms. However, what also adds to teachers' time is an increased assumption that teachers are the most suitable people (rather than parents or health professionals) to meet a much broader and more general set of student needs (e.g., social and emotional, as well as academic and learning) that all students might experience, than previously would have been seen as an integral part of a teacher's work. This added teacher responsibility for implementing the student inclusion policy, combined with an assumed and comprehensive responsibility for meeting student needs (and a perception that there are many more students now who are 'needy'), would have to add significantly to *all* teachers' workloads.

With special needs students, teachers reported feeling both under-prepared and inadequately equipped, as well as not in control. One teacher's description not only of her current situation, but more particularly of her expressed feelings and concerns about what might happen *the following year*, highlight the high level of anxiety and stress associated with this policy; and what is even more concerning is that this was a teacher of more than 20 years of teaching experience:

> While I am out on duty in [playground] I see around me at least twelve [grade identified] children with disabilities. As there are going to be only two grade [grade identified] classes next year I foresee several of them in my class. I can imagine just what next year will be like and I have only had experience with children with [named condition]. I am not looking forward to feeling totally inadequate and not in control. It is quite depressing actually. Shouldn't staff be educated before they are confronted with these problems? *(Primary teacher, female, >21 years' experience, questionnaire)*
>
> (Gardner and Williamson, 2005: 13)

One professional support service staff member summarised this situation and reflected on the stress factors for teachers:

> Inclusion means more pressure.... central support for kids no longer [available] ... so less support for teachers working with at-risk students and students with disabilities. This is stressful for teachers. *(Support service staff, focus group interview)*
>
> (Gardner and Williamson, 2005: 12)

Accountability and Control

A significant source of stress comes from work situations where staff perceive themselves to have little or no control (Hoyle, 1995; Poppleton and Williamson, 2004). In this study teachers (and principals) expressed concern and frustration that they were being held accountable for outcomes that were largely outside their control:

> Teaching well is an incredibly complicated process ... integrating and orchestrating multiples of factors, many of which teachers have little ability to control or prevent. *(Secondary teacher, male, >21 years experience, questionnaire)*
>
> (Gardner and Williamson, 2005: 13)

Teachers also expressed concerns that they were accountable for 'everything' and certainly for larger issues than they could personally control:

> Kids have changed ... kids today think that everything is our responsibility; ... to make the subject interesting, to get them to do their work, to behave. Parents and hierarchy too put these things on to teachers. Kids have to take some responsibility ... if they don't do their work, surely some of the responsibility lies with them? *(Secondary teacher, female, >21 years experience, individual interview)*
>
> (Gardner and Williamson, 2005: 13)

Principals too expressed concern that they were now accountable to a range of agencies, both state and federal. For both teachers and principals the issue was not so much the increase in accountability, but that this was not accompanied by (appropriate) support. In fact their concerns were linked to greater accountability in situations of reduced resources.

One principal's comment typified his colleagues' views on accountability and resourcing:

> If we were truly self-managing then decision-making would be much quicker and easier. Interference at Department level outside school does not take into account individual differences. This includes decisions to do with resourcing – money and personnel. I would prefer to be left to run my school rather than continually answering to someone else. Accountability for federal funding is also a huge problem ... paperwork is endless. *(Principal, male, >21 years' experience, questionnaire)*
>
> (Gardner and Williamson, 2005: 13)

Reduced Resources

Concerns were expressed by teachers (and principals and teacher assistants) about resourcing levels for all school activities and particular mention was made of the limited resources available for professional learning for teachers (and TA's). This concern most likely arose from the pressures of increased curriculum and other changes, for which teachers felt they needed greater professional learning time and support.

Principals had a particular concern that their expertise should be recognised with a closer nexus to be made between schools and resources. Many of them saw this in terms of a scenario where policies had been predicated on a 'one size fits all' model and where the geographically and professionally distant head office of senior bureaucrats who had developed the policy failed to venture out into the schools to see first hand the impact of their policies.

Several of the principals also commented that they were spending significant amounts of time writing bids for competitive funds for what they considered to be part of the school's core activities. For example, they described how contested funds were available for some aspects of the implementation of the inclusion policy but in their view these resources should have been provided as a matter of course.

The effects of government political decisions and funding priorities could be felt in the teachers' physical work environment – school buildings, classrooms and teachers' office space. The appropriateness of the fact that teachers' office space is often very cramped and routinely shared with other teachers was challenged. As one highly experienced primary school teacher asked:

> "[H]ow many managers of 25–30 people wouldn't have their own office?" *(Primary teacher, female, >21 years experience, individual interview)*

(Gardner and Williamson, 2005: 14)

Another teacher spoke about the effects of diminishing resources on his and his colleagues' core work with students – and the conflicting pressures they felt between maintaining teaching quality and meeting budgetary expectations:

> Given a budget, our team plays around with and we may have to cut classroom resources. I am concerned about … the tightening of budget strings. … there are pressures from above about the quality of work and classrooms and teachers, yet strategies we're able to use are opposing quality at the 'coal face'. *(TAFE teacher, male, >10 years experience, individual interview)*

(Gardner and Williamson, 2005: 14)

Involvement in Decision-Making

There is evidence to suggest that teachers are more likely to be able to adapt to rapid changes if they are involved meaningfully in the school's decision-making processes (Poppleton and Williamson, 2004). The Tasmanian study focussed on teachers' satisfaction with their involvement in role-related decision-making. While many teachers were happy with the decision-making related to their roles (with the exception of teacher assistants and TAFE teacher respondents), there were particular areas of concern and complaint.

'Symbolic' decision-making: Many teachers felt that their involvement in decision-making was more 'symbolic' than real; that there was the appearance of consultation, but not the substance:

> There appear to be structures enabling teachers to participate, but many decisions are imposed from above, i.e., by the hierarchy. *(Secondary teacher, female, >21 years experience, questionnaire)*

(Gardner and Williamson, 2005: 15)

Interestingly this view was also shared by principals, who might have been expected to be more involved in decision-making than teachers:

> Over my years as principal, I have generally found that principals are not listened to. Consulted in appearances, yes, but listened to, no. *(Principal, male, >21 years experienced, questionnaire)*

(Gardner and Williamson, 2005: 15)

Opportunities to participate in decision-making: The lack of involvement in decision-making seemed in part to be the result of a lack of serious planning for comprehensive staff involvement:

The timing of communication can restrict opportunities to have input to the central level, for example [when material is distributed for comment at] the end of term or the school year. *(Support service, focus group interview)*

(Gardner and Williamson, 2005: 16)

And the teacher's employment status may be a barrier. There were some teachers, such as those on temporary contracts, who felt themselves outside the decision-making process (and perhaps the system as a whole), no matter how experienced they were:

As a temporary teacher, I am disposable. *(Secondary teacher, male, 4–10 years' experience, questionnaire)*

(Gardner and Williamson, 2005: 16)

In many schools and in many classrooms with included students there are teacher support staff or aides. In Tasmania these allied educators are seen as very important to promoting student learning. However, they are only paid for the time they work during the school year (i.e., exclusive of school holidays) and they are often employed on annual contracts with no ongoing tenure. In the context of wishing to have better communication with all members of the teaching and support staff within the school, a teacher assistant reported:

TAs are not involved in planning meetings, they should be. Teachers are reluctant to ask TAs to give extra time for meetings given the current working conditions of TAs. There needs to be meetings … staff meetings … we *are staff.* Ultimately we're all here for the children. *(Teacher assistant, female focus group interview, interviewee's emphasis)*

(Gardner and Williamson, 2005)

Similarly, a library technician reported:

I am not included in staff meetings and briefings, therefore I'm often not aware of things that are going on in the school, changes in policies, etc. unless someone remembers to inform me…I feel the lack of consultation with me about my role … denigrates my qualifications and … experience and service at the school. *(Library technician, female, 4–10 year's experience, questionnaire)*

(Gardner and Williamson, 2005)

The Workplace as a Supportive Environment for Teachers

The respondents were asked to identify those aspects of the workplace that both assisted and hindered the work of teachers and allied educators (Gardner and Williamson, 2004). Those factors that were perceived to provide a supportive setting were: support from colleagues, support from senior staff/principal, a supportive environment and proactive programs. However, for those at the head of a school, the principal, this support was often lacking, as one relatively new principal described:

It can be very lonely, when things are not going well; you question your own ability. …that can be very stressful. *(Principal, <5 years' experience, questionnaire)*

There were also a number of factors that were identified as hindering the work of staff. These were given as: school processes and programs; time issues; inclusion policy; and student needs.

Conclusion

The nature of Tasmanian teachers' work lives has been shown to be similar to those elsewhere (Galton and MacBeath, 2002; Helsby, 1999). Likewise the impact of this work intensification has had similar outcomes on teachers' reported ability to perform their roles and duties.

Teachers have reported, for example, not just the pressure of intensification, but also the impact that it had on their perceptions of their capacity to perform their roles, or even to maintain good health given the level of stress it induced:

> We are expected to do *more* in seemingly less time. Children have become more demanding ... the Department has become more demanding ... parents are more demanding ... senior staff are more demanding. ... I personally know five teachers who have been on prolonged stress leave over the past five years ... one of our staff is currently on stress leave. *(Primary teacher, female, 16–20 years' experience, questionnaire, emphasis in original)*
>
> (Gardner and Williamson, 2005: 7)

The respondents reported – largely in negative terms – four broad issues that they identified as the key features of intensification:

- That they were forced to do their planning and decision-making 'on the run' as the school day was full
- That the changes were generally imposed from outside the school with little or no consultation
- That they had limited opportunity for quality work time on those matters they saw as 'core', i.e., teaching and student pastoral care, rather than administrative tasks or accountability reports
- That they were working to unrealistic change implementation timetables

These issues were reflected in the comments of one senior secondary school teacher who summarised the complexity of the current teacher's role. However, what also seems to add to the issue for this teacher is the lack of community recognition of teacher's work which may have potentially negative consequences for the future of the profession:

> The role of the teacher has changed considerably to the extent that we are social worker, surrogate parent, administrator and lastly, an educator, yet our status in the community ... or salary ... does not acknowledge any of this ... If we don't address it soon, there will be too few people going into the teaching profession and I'm saying this as someone under the age of 30. *(Senior secondary teacher, female, 4–10 years' experience, questionnaire)*
>
> (Gardner and Williamson, 2005: 8)

Teacher Responses to Intensification

Teacher responses to the current work intensification suggest that they are 'surviving but not thriving' under the pressure. While these Tasmanian teachers may have been under particular intensification pressure due to the implementation of a new state-wide curriculum, the evidence from elsewhere suggests that this situation is more standard than particular. Worldwide, teachers in industrialised countries are experiencing increased time/pace and complexity factor pressures in their work. Much of this is due to general workplace change, but the teacher's workplace is particularly affected by these changes – and exacerbated by the particular commitment that teachers feel toward the professional and vocational aspects of their job and their commitment to students (Churchill et al., 1997; Helsby, 1999).

The outcomes of the intensification can be seen in two clear teacher strategies for coping with multiple and complex changes:

- *Teacher resistance and selective change implementation* – with the sheer number of changes and policies, teachers find that they cannot implement all of them (*policy change fatigue*), so they 'cherry pick' the policies they want to implement on the basis of those they consider to be of the most benefit to the children in their class or school.
- *Teacher 'inertia' or 'cynicism'* – experienced teachers tend to recognise externally generated change (or fad) cycles and, if they are not convinced of the merits of the change or if they are not concerned with personal promotion in the new era, they tend to follow one of three options: they continue their usual practice, they may incorporate or accommodate some aspects of the new 'fad' into their current repertoires, or, they re-name their activities to reflect the current ideology (e.g., Tasmania's 'Essential Learnings' curriculum).

It is interesting to note that expert and novice teachers appear to respond differently to change and that change affects the two groups of teachers differentially. The teaching-force is Tasmania is an aging one; the average age of Tasmanian teachers is now 48 years. There are important implications for the profession in the fact that so many teachers are now leaving before they serve 5 years; one consequence is that it will mean a 'churning' of beginning teachers with few progressing their skills and knowledge to the levels of competent or expert (Berliner, 2002). It may be argued that if there is this hollowing out of experienced teachers consequently the teaching force will not offer the same quality of teaching of earlier years.

The data from the Tasmanian study show that increased workload both leads and contributes to:

- Extreme busyness: no time for reflection, and professional issues such as consideration of teaching, matching teaching to students, and so on.
- Increased tension between 'teamwork' and 'whole school' policies versus individual decision-making.
- A broadening of considerations of what constitutes teacher expertise: this is typically in terms of generalist versus specialist teachers (where the 'system view' is that "a teacher is a teacher" which gives administrative ease to staffing schools), rather than an expertise-based view (Berliner, 2002). This consideration, in turn, leads to downplaying of specialist curriculum knowledge/expertise and an increase in multi-skilling, which results, at least in the short term, in increased employability but more limited personal/professional empowerment.

- Shifts in perceived accountability: the data suggest a cleavage between commitment and accountability to the profession versus accountability to external 'masters' and, likewise, a view of accountability that is hierarchical and external or one based on individual professional decision-making.
- System- or school-level determined professional development activities rather than personal needs based; the resultant tendency is to encourage staff to engage in school/system change-related PD, rather than personal professional development.
- A shift from more autonomous schools to a more centralised and bureaucratic model. Schools consequently are more like government departments where there is limited capacity for the individual teacher to choose curriculum, or assessment approaches that best suit her students rather what is mandated by state or federal curricula (or school), assessment requirements, and national testing, finally
- Increased levels of teacher and allied educator stress: with too many policies implemented at the one time especially as they involve curriculum, testing and assessment procedures and concomitantly the implementation of the inclusion policy.

Where To from Here?

The data from the Tasmanian study of teachers' workloads are consistent with those from other countries (Galton and MacBeath, 2002; Helsby, 1999; Poppleton and Williamson, 2004). These different countries all report intensification in teachers' work lives and, therefore, it is not a matter that will disappear simply be being ignored and swept under the carpet at the school- or the system-level.

Teachers have reported that there are number of practical ways to assist them to deal with this increased workload, such as them being involved in decision-making that relates to the adoption and implementation of major policies for new curricula or new strategies to include children with a spectrum of behavioural and psychological needs in regular classrooms. This shift to involve teachers more meaningfully in school decision-making will require a substantial mind change from many school leaders and employers.

At the system-level there needs to be more thought given to the number and size of the innovations that are introduced to the schools. In Tasmania, for example, in the 5 year period 1995–2000 it has been calculated that 80 major policies were announced and schools were expected to implement all of them. This amount of change would suggest it is clearly beyond the scope of any organisation to achieve implementation fully and successfully. Rather than creating situations where teachers will inevitably fail to implement all policies as decreed by the policy makers it would make more sense to have fewer but more meaningful innovations.

More teachers report a down-sizing in their employment either through not applying for senior administrative positions within the school or with a move to a fractional level appointment. If the schools are to continue to offer quality teaching to all students major policy changes need to be made to the support provided to teachers in terms of their on-going professional development and learning and the amount of work they are routinely expected to engage in out of school time.

Employers of teachers will need to move quickly in two important areas. First, to assist those teachers who are not coping with the present changed work context and conditions, and second, to provide appropriate mentoring and support for those beginning teachers who have not yet served 5 years in the classroom.

References

Berliner, D.C. (2002) Teacher expertise. In B. Moon and A. Shelton Mayes (Eds.). *Teaching and learning in the secondary school.* London: Routledge/Open University.

Churchill, R. and Williamson, J.C. (1999) Traditional attitudes and contemporary experiences: Teachers and educational change. Asia-Pacific Journal of Teacher Education & Development, 2(2), 43–51.

Churchill, R., Williamson, J. and Grady, N. (1997) Educational change and new realities of teachers' work lives. *Asia-Pacific Journal of Teacher Education*, 25(3), 141–158.

Galton, M. and MacBeath, J. (2002) *A life in teaching? The impact of change on primary teachers' working lives.* A report commissioned by the National Union of Teachers (NUT). Cambridge: University of Cambridge Faculty of Education.

Gardner, C. and Williamson, J. (2004) *Workloads of government school teachers and allied educators in Tasmania.* Report commissioned by the Australian Education Union Tasmanian Branch.

Gardner, C. and Williamson, J. (2005) *Teaching is not the job it used to be.* Paper presented at the 2005 AERA Annual Meeting, Montreal, Canada.

Gardner, C. and Williamson, J. (2006a) *My home has become another workplace.* Paper presented at the 2006 AERA Annual Meeting, San Francisco, CA.

Gardner, C. and Williamson, J. (2006b) *Having a life outside teaching: The nature and amount of teachers' out-of-hours work.* Proceedings of the 2006 Australian Teachers' Education Association Conference, pp. 157–171.

Helsby, G. (1999) *Changing teachers' work: The 'reform' of secondary schooling.* Buckingham, UK: Open University Press.

Hoyle, E. (1995) Changing conceptions of a profession. In H. Busher and R. Saran (Eds.). *Managing teachers as professionals in schools.* London: Kogan Page.

Hoyle, E. and John, P. (1995) *Professional knowledge and professional practice.* London: Cassell.

Moulthrop, D., Calegari, N.C. and Eggers, D. (2005) *Teachers have it easy: The big sacrifices and small salaries of America's teachers.* New York: New Press.

Poppleton, P. and Williamson, J. (Eds.) (2004) *New realities of secondary teachers' work lives.* Oxford: Symposium Books.

Stronge, J.H., Gareis, C.R. and Little, C.A. (2006) *Teacher pay and teacher quality: Attracting, developing and retaining the best teachers.* Thousand Oaks, CA: Corwin Press.

UNESCO (1998) *World Education Report 1998: Teachers and teaching in a changing world.* Paris, France: UNESCO Publishing.

Chapter 4
Teacher Professionalization in Hong Kong: Historical Perspectives

Anthony Sweeting

Introduction

Professionalization, like localization, refers mainly to a process, a process, which, by implication, is incomplete. Eric Hoyle emphasized this aspect of its meaning over thirty years ago, deeming it worthy of reinforcement on several subsequent occasions (e.g., Hoyle, 1974, 1975, 1980, 1982, 1995, 2001; Hoyle and John, 1995). More specifically, he defined professionalization as "the process whereby an occupation increasingly meets the criteria attributed to a profession" (Hoyle, 1982: 161). The incompleteness of the process suggests that its history is of importance. And, even on the occasions when professionalization is considered complete, more as product than process, it is commonly viewed retrospectively, thus highlighting again the significance of historical perspectives.

Over the past decade, the decline, if not the demise, of the history of education has received several notices of regret (McCulloch, 1997; Aldrich, 1997; Robinson, 2001). Robinson, herself, makes a convincing case in favour of "finding" for historians of education "our professional niche", enlisting such unlikely bedfellows in this regard as Simon (1981), Fullan (1993), and Woodhead (1998). Although Aldrich, McCulloch, Robinson, and others are perfectly correct in emphasizing the mere lip-service that is paid to historical perspectives in many policy documents issued by national governments, they might have also acknowledged the attempts made by several scholars in various countries to rectify this situation. In the field of teacher professionalization, for example, Hoyle, with and without co-authors, has not been alone in making such efforts. His work was slightly preceded, then succeeded and complemented by such publications as Eddy, 1969; Gosden, 1972; Ozga and Lawn, 1981; Herbst, 1989; Kam and Wong, 1991; Engvall, 1997; Hargreaves, 2000; Hall and Schulz, 2003; Sachs, 2000, 2003; Hypolito, 2004; and Furlong, 2005. A major goal of the present chapter is to extend and supplement this research by applying it to the situation in Hong Kong.

The selection of Hong Kong depends partly on convenience, partly because of the multiplicity of influences on the development of its education and its teachers – Chinese, British, Asia-Pacific, and possibly cosmopolitan or World Systems-amenable.

D. Johnson, R. Maclean (eds.), *Teaching: Professionalization,*
Development and Leadership,
© Springer Science + Business Media B.V. 2008

And, particularly in terms of Hong Kong's most recent developments, mere lip-service to historical perspectives would serve only to exaggerate an already notice-ably tendency – the emergence of a 'tabula rasa syndrome', by which the 1997 change in sovereignty is deemed to have wiped the slate of earlier educational developments clean (Sweeting, 2007: 105). Because another chapter in this Festschrift also tackles Hong Kong issues, focusing mainly upon the last few dec-ades (Morris, 2008: pp. 119–138), the present author will pay special attention to more remote periods, convinced of their relevance to an understanding of teacher professionalization.

The concept of profession is, unsurprisingly, regarded as "contested" (Hoyle and John, 1995: 1; Furlong et al., 2000: 4; Hargreaves, 2000: 152). It is a descriptive or normative term that applies variously – perhaps indiscriminately – to a broad range of occupations. Nowadays, it is commonly used about (and by) medical doctors, lawyers, architects, engineers, and the clergy; sometimes as an aspiration by teachers or as form of mollification about them. It is also, however, a term that is applied to sportsmen, artists, musicians, journalists, mercenaries and prostitutes. The breadth of usage is such that, although the usual antonym of professional is ama-teur, other possibilities include gentlemen, dilettantes, neophytes, line-workers, volunteers, laity, and lovers. Adjectives used in association with professionals include "skillful", "hard-working", "thorough", "earnest", "true", "complete", "devoted", and "seasoned", but also, if more rarely, "ruthless", "selfish", "hard-nosed", "rule-bound", and "narrow-minded". Advocates of professionalization clearly support the positive epithets and disregard the negative.

The initiative for professionalization may derive from different sources. There is commonly a passive sense of "the professionalization of teachers", in which the process depend ultimately on agencies or forces external to teachers. It is some-thing that happens *to* members of a particular occupation, characteristically involv-ing the control of that occupation, rather than something done *by* them. It is this sense that Roger Soder emphasized when he made a preliminary analysis of the professionalization of medical doctors, focusing on a combination of economic and social factors (Soder, 1990: 62–63). Song and Wei (2005) used the same interpreta-tion in their distinction between the concept of teachers' professional development and that of their passive professionalization. One can infer, however, that medical doctors, as well as members of other occupations, have made various active contri-butions to their own professionalization. Endogenous, together with exogenous, factors will have played some part in the process(es). Moreover, bearing in mind historical contingencies, one should query the idea that a wide range of occupations achieved professional or quasi-professional status and improved their own knowl-edge and skills in essentially the same ways.

As far as several occupational groups are concerned, several factors complicated and often delayed the professionalization process. These include (not necessarily in order of importance) social class, gender, race, and fragmentation (Apple, 1986; Grosvenor, 1999). Most noticeably in past centuries, differences in working conditions, expectations, and rewards reflected social class, gender, and ethnic origin, together with the particular segment of the occupation to which the individual belonged (e.g., in the case of teachers, whether they worked in kindergartens, primary schools, secondary schools, or tertiary institutions). With teaching, more than with most of the other occupations, there was a distinct possibility that forms of professionalization would prove to have non-education-specific effects and, for example, encourage individuals to treat professional preparation as a stepping stone to other, more lucrative or prestigious employment. Alternatively, even if particular individuals remained involved in education, their "promotion" prospects, at least in some societies and for some periods, were typically away from the classroom and from the actual activities of teaching, towards administration, academic research, or even politics.

The two poles ("liberal" and "technical"), to which, according to Borrowman (1956), re-stated by Urban (1991: 59), most characteristic endeavours in the field of teacher preparation gravitate, may help to de-mystify the paradox between apparently increasing teacher professionalization and the commonly observed "teacher de-skilling" (Apple, 1979, 1986; Ozga, 1988; Ginsburg, 1988; Ginsburg and Lindsay, 1995). In general, it is clear that many trends in teacher preparation practices during the past four decades – such as microteaching, competency/ performance-based teacher education, "teacher-proof" curriculum packages, externally-imposed "standards" for teachers, together with standardized curricula – have gravitated towards the technical pole. These developments may well be, as Bates (1986) suggested, in line with the evolution of industrial capitalism, in which control is based on "bureaucratic systems of rule specification, incentives and task evaluation". Within such systems, the teacher's task is likely to be perceived as helping deliver student achievements, which are measurable as a production function. Governments, especially those that reveal convictions that merit a "New Rightist" label (which, in England, include "New Labour" and, in Hong Kong, the post-colonial government), may conceptualize the "professional" teacher as someone who is technically competent, rule-compliant, and highly flexible in bending to the wishes of the educational planners. In this situation, technical discourse replaces ethical questions and, although teachers may not see themselves as having been proletarianized, their actual roles and working conditions have come to resemble more closely those of line-workers. On the whole, the more that teachers consider the process of their professionalization as something external to themselves, determined by, say, government policy, the more likely it is that their own de-skilling does not represent a genuine paradox with professionalization.

Especially with regard to the possibly passive nature of at least some aspects of teacher professionalization, it is interesting to note that the most common metaphors used about the process are "the struggle for …", and "the path (or march")) towards professionalism. Perhaps an historical observer of teacher professionalization in Hong Kong could maintain a more stable balance is he/she were to think in terms of the "Long March towards …" and "the survival of a series of Encirclement Campaigns".

The Chinese Background

The traditional Chinese respect for teachers is closely related to their reverence of scholars. Indeed, it was taken (almost literally) as read, that scholarship was the goal of education, which was essentially text-based, male-specific (at least in its formal manifestations), and hortatory in style.

There is certainly authority to be cited from the classical Confucian canon to confirm not only the importance of teaching and teachers, but also the social dimensions of their role. For example, in the *Analects*, "the Master said, If a man keeps cherishing his old knowledge, so as constantly to be acquiring new, he may be a teacher of others' (II, XI). Mencius declared teachers to be of higher importance than ministers of state (*Works*, IV, II, XXXI) and urged them not to lower their standards simply in order to 'cause learners to consider them attainable' (*Ibid*., VII, XLI). The establishment of the central bureaucracy controlling education in China is usually associated the name of the Emperor Han Wudi and especially with the setting up of the Imperial University in 124BC, with a professorial chair for each of the classical books. At the provincial level, an earlier initiative by Wen Weng, Governor of Sichuan, created a department of education, administered by scholars he had trained himself. This has been considered the beginning of government education in China (Needham, 1954: 106). At a more quotidian level, the first book that countless Chinese children read (and/or had read to them) made it clear that

Men at their birth are naturally good. Their natures are the same; their habits become widely different. If foolishly there is no teaching, their nature will deteriorate. The right way in teaching to attach the utmost importance to thoroughness (*Sanzijing* ['Three Character Classic': 1).

From the earliest days of formal schooling (normally seven years of age), children also learned to memorize the dictum that 'The Emperor values bold heroes and would have you learn writing. Other occupations are lowly in rank; study alone is high' (*Youxue shi* [Verse for Young Learners], 1, cited in Sweeting, 1990: 95). High valuation of study, thorough ways of teaching, and the encouragement of writing would appear to indicate correspondingly high social status and at least an incipient sense of professionalism inhering in persons recognized as teachers. This, however, oversimplifies the situation.

In the various regions of Imperial, Republican, and Communist China, a range of educational institutions provided opportunities for different types of teachers, with different status, but often with little or no sense of (or occasion for) collegiality. In the case of the humblest institutions, such as the single-class, single-teacher *sishu* (or private elementary school), the teachers were customarily disappointed candidates at the provincial civil service examinations. Formal, face-giving respect, therefore, may have sometimes been a substitute for good working conditions and satisfactory remuneration. The nature of the tasks fulfilled by *sishu*-teachers ensured that they were isolated adults commissioned to be *in loco parentis* and expected to wield a martinet's powers of discipline over their custodial charges, but with little or no room to take curricular initiatives. Unsurprisingly, they were frequently encouraged to assume other non-pedagogic roles, such as palm reading, the interpretation of spirit-writing, and *feng-shui* consultancies. At more elevated institutions, such as the famous academies, teachers received a level of respect bordering on veneration. Again, however, they tended to be individuals lionized more because of their personal qualities of scholarship, refinement, and personal talents (especially as calligraphers and artists), than because of their pedagogic skills. And again, they had little chance to amend the curriculum. Instead, most of their energies were devoted to the interpretation of text and to exhortation. This remained largely true throughout Chinese history, although, of course, the particular texts and (sometimes) the styles of hortatory transmission changed. More fundamental change in the direction of *professional* cohesion, concern about control of entry into and exit from the profession, the analysis and questioning of professional ethics, the assumption of professional standards, and claims to participate in decision-making over curricular and other policy-related matters occurred only very slowly in China, including Hong Kong.

A complicating factor in the case of Hong Kong, of course, was the incursion of other cultural values. These included colonial British and, briefly, colonial Japanese attitudes towards individual teachers and towards teachers as a work force. On the whole, such historical forces did little positively to encourage the professionalization of Hong Kong teachers other than by providing initially rudimentary mechanisms to prepare teachers for their tasks. They had more impact as symbols of centralized (and alien) power against which teachers could protest, argue, organize, and begin to adopt some of the characteristics of a discrete group.

In terms of organization, one can detect efforts in Hong Kong mainly during the second half of the twentieth century to enhance both solidarity and a sense of professionalism among teachers "from above" and from somewhere near the grassroots. The top-down approach, although compatible with much in Chinese cultural tradition and certainly availing itself of exhortation techniques, was almost as futile as trying to force people to take initiatives. Ultimately more fruitful bottom-up efforts tended to achieve clarity of purpose by adopting the attributes of one or other of a set of historical analogies (e.g., interest groups, pressure groups, friendly societies, trade unions, and closed shops). In order to reach firmer conclusions about the significance of the historical trends, however, and, in doing so, to see *whom* the teachers in Hong Kong have been and from *where*, in literal and metaphorical terms, they have been coming, one needs to take a more comprehensive view of the various developmental phases. The remainder of the chapter attempts to do this.

Gestures Towards Professionalization in Pre-colonial Hong Kong

In what became the known as the Hong Kong region, as elsewhere in China, teachers even in the most elementary of *sishu* were accorded respect (Luk, 1984), sometimes in ways very important to the local life-style, by gifts of the most succulent chicken and other treats. There were, however, times when the outward show of respect provided scant consolation for failed ambition, poor working conditions, and modest remuneration. As was to happen on many later occasions, appeals to the "higher valuations" (Myrdal, 1944) of a teacher's sense of vocation diverted attention from basic 'rice-bowl' considerations. Vocationalism was an uneasy precursor of professionalization, serving at times as a substitute and even as an obstacle to be overcome.

Further up the educational ladder, the "Hong Kong" region could also boast of a college that gained quite a widespread reputation from the late eleventh/early twelfth century. A member of the scholar-gentry, Deng Fuxie, having recently retired from government service, moved his family to the Kamtin district in what is now the New Territories. There, he not only founded Liying College and provided it with a library of many thousands of scrolls, but also occasionally lectured in the college himself and paid for full-time teachers to be employed, taking an interest in their training. In this sense, Deng was following the model earlier set by Wen Weng. There is plenty of evidence to show that colleges and study halls continued to exist in the region through the Sung, Yuan, Ming, and Qing dynasties, though inevitably their fortunes fluctuated and there was even a temporary halt to their activities during the Qing-inspired evacuation of coastal villages during the 1660s. Their teaching staff comprised scholars who had experienced Imperial Civil Service Examination successes, up to and including the *chujen* degree, and who might have originated from the locality, neighbouring districts, or further afield in China (Lo, 1963; Sung, 1974; Hayes, 1983; Ng, 1984; Faure, 1986). At the humbler level of the *sishu*, the family-centred *jiashu*, and the charitable *yixue*, teachers were less highly qualified and usually, but not invariably, from the locality, itself. One might conclude that, on the whole, professionalism as it is understood nowadays, especially in contradistinction to amateurism, was not a feature of education in the Hong Kong region before the arrival of the British, although some of the prerequisites for its development, including concern over standards, already existed.

Gestures Towards Professionalization in Early Colonial Hong Kong

The arrival of the British and their occupation of Hong Kong from the early 1840s made little difference in the short term to teacher professionalization. The early missionary schools were actually run by the missionaries themselves (and, often, by their wives). Some of these were charismatic, but few were professional teachers. One of the few for whom this status could be claimed was Samuel Brown, the American headmaster of the first western-style school to be established in Hong Kong. His training and earlier experience teaching the deaf and dumb in New York was considered suitable preparation for his stint in Asia by the president of his alma mater, Yale College (Chinese Repository, pp. 568–569). Chinese teachers quickly took up the opportunity of a growing population in the new colony of Hong Kong to set up their own schools, but, at the outset at least, they were not essentially different in terms of professionalism or professionalization from teachers elsewhere in China.

Grounds for differences became firmer in 1848 when the Hong Kong Government set up a small Committee of Superintendence to ensure that its recently approved 'modest' support for three Chinese village schools was money well spent. The new committee was empowered to satisfy itself about the standards of teaching and learning in the Government-supported schools. Eventually, it drew up rules for the conduct of these schools (Lobscheid, 1859; Sweeting, 1990: 27) and made proposals about their curriculum (Committee for Superintending Chinese Schools, 1851; Sweeting, 1990: 180), as well as about half-yearly examinations, the use of prizes as incentives to study, and the supply of 'reliable' teachers for the future via a new pupil-teacher scheme (Committee for Superintending Chinese Schools, 1853; Sweeting, 1990: 147). This top-down approach did little to enhance the professionalism of local teachers, but it does serve as an early example of a move towards what has been earlier described as "passive teacher professionalization" and is explicable in the context of an insecure colonial government at a time of deteriorating Sino-British relations.

The urge towards parsimony combined with an instinct to control what seemed unfamiliar and a possible threat to motivate further moves in the direction of the closer supervision of local teachers. Initially, supervision of teachers had been vested in the part-time and amateur Committee of Superintendence, comprising a few missionaries and one or two government officials. In 1857, at the height of the Second Anglo-Chinese ("Arrow") War, the responsibility was handed over to the first full-time Inspector of Schools, a German missionary, Wilhelm Lobscheid. Although more sustained inspection might have increased possibilities for the professionalization of the local teaching force, in fact, both Lobscheid and his successor as Inspector, Frederick Stewart, expressed themselves forcefully about the unpromising nature of local teachers and were more involved in criticism than they were in training. Lobscheid, for example, reported that "they are so lazy and useless that the corruption of teachers has become proverbial" (Lobscheid, 1859: 14); Stewart, that "A Chinese Schoolmaster is truly an object of pity. He is simply a drudge" (Stewart, 1865: 280).

Thus, cultural distance between government and governed emphasized the need to monitor what was happening in classrooms where, of course, teachers could act as powerful forces on the minds of the younger generation. It is in this context that one can view Stewart's abandonment of Bible reading at the Government Central School mainly on the grounds that Chinese teachers tended to make comparisons between classical Chinese texts and the Bible, to the detriment of the latter – itself, a possible indication of the growing independence and, perhaps, incipient professionalism of some local teachers (Sweeting, 1990: 220). And it is a similar context that surrounds the 1883 report by the government's Surveyor-General of "classrooms arranged as requested by Mr. Wright [the second headmaster of the Central School] in such a manner that each large classroom opens into two smaller classrooms with glass doors to enable one European teacher to supervise two Chinese assistant teachers" (cited in Sweeting, 1990: 36).

Moves Towards Professionalization in Colonial Hong Kong

Driven by perceptions of a shortage of competent and reliable teachers, the government, as mentioned briefly above, approved the introduction of pupil-teacher schemes of "professional" preparation, similar to those in contemporary Britain, initially at the Anglican St. Paul's College as early as 1853 and eventually at its own showpiece establishment, the Central School, from 1865. As Stewart, then also headmaster of the Government Central School, reported, however, the latter faced major implementation problems. This was because many of the youths selected as pupil-teachers left the school for more lucrative employment (mainly as translators and interpreters) as soon as they felt that their fluency in English warranted the change (Stewart, 1866: 279–280). The pupil-teacher scheme at the Central School continued, as evidenced by examinations in "Pupil Teachers' Theory" set for the school's senior class (Sweeting, 1990: 37). It was, however, probably more significant in Hong Kong's social history as a stepping-stone for young Chinese and Eurasian men who had aspirations to serve as middle-men – in the context of commerce, administration, and diplomacy – between colonizers and colonized.

In the early 1880s, the new Inspector of Schools and former German missionary, Ernst Eitel, was largely responsible for launching a different experiment in teacher-preparation and incipient professionalization. It illustrated the progressive nature of some educational thought in Hong Kong, but its abandonment after only two years also indicated that these specific signs of embryonic professionalization had been aborted. This was the Wanchai Normal School, established in 1881 through Eitel's enthusiastic advocacy, the support of the maverick governor, Sir John Pope Hennessy, and the work of its headmaster, A.J. May. It was, however, deemed 'unnecessary' by the Education Commission (1880–1882), which considered that, "when the Central School had been put on a proper footing, the Headmaster would be able to make all the necessary arrangements for the training of the limited number of teachers required" (Sweeting, 1990: 212). And the British Colonial Office had only reluctantly permitted the scheme to continue, pending a full report on the vacancies expected for teachers, the total cost, and the nature of any "bond" demanded of students in return for their grants (Sweeting, 1995: 338). The actual demise of the Wanchai Normal School was precipitated by May's insistence that the students agreed to a bond to teach for five years, on their completion of the course, at a modest salary rate. The immediate result was that four of the ten students left for the medical college at Tientsin, three joined commercial firms, one became a government interpreter, and only two of the original intake eventually became teachers (Sweeting, 1995: 339).

For the next couple of decades, the rather elderly, but cheap, type of apprenticeship scheme again became the only institutionalized source for the preparation and possible professionalization of local teachers. This was reinforced by Hong Kong's adaptation of a "Payment by Results" approach, as exemplified by the Grant-in-Aid Codes (initiated in 1871, with significant revisions in 1879 and 1903).

The opening of evening "extension classes" for in-service teachers at the new Technical Institute in 1907 was justified on grounds of value for money. In the atmosphere of the early years of the century, when Chinese nationalism was spreading and strengthening, it is likely that political considerations played a part in securing the support of the Hong Kong Government. The fact that the new classes were held in Queen's College, as the Government Central School had been renamed, and that instructors for the extension classes comprised teachers from this school probably also facilitated support. The establishment of the "Department for the Training of Teachers" in the Arts Faculty of the fledgling University of Hong Kong was clearly related to early forms of manpower planning, especially to the employment of school leavers from Queen's College as masters in Government and Grant-in-Aid schools. However, the political ramifications of "serving China" (as well as Hong Kong and territories in Southeast Asia) through supplying graduate teachers who might be pro-British also contributed to its motivation (Sweeting, 2002: 68–69). In the cases of both the in-service courses at the Technical Institute and the pre-service courses run concurrently with other undergraduate studies at the University of Hong Kong, much of the professionalization that was achieved was initiated by sources external to the teachers, themselves. It merits description, therefore, like many of the students, themselves, as "passive". On the other hand, student-teachers took some extra-curricular initiatives. For example, in the University, they supported their "Education Society" (formed in 1919), which eventually established a "Free Night School", opening in 1931 for the benefit of impoverished children (Sweeting, 2002: 83–84).

Catering for the teaching force needed to man (or, more likely, woman) the increasing number of vernacular primary and secondary schools in the interwar period, two small Vernacular Normal Schools (for Men and Women) opened in 1921. These derived mainly from the initiatives of voluntary societies organized by Chinese residents of Hong Kong, particularly the Tung Wah Hospital Committee, the Confucian Society, and the District Watch Committee. They received the blessing of the government, but very little financial support (Sweeting, 1995: 339). Much the same can be said of the Government Tai Po Vernacular Normal School, although, as its name implies, the financial support of this institution, catering for schools and teachers in the newly stabilized New Territories was more generous.

One problem that persisted in the case of both pre-school and in-school teacher education related to the political reliability of the teachers. This was particularly true as the May Fourth Movement (1919) in China influenced nationalism, feminism, anti-colonial and, especially, anti-British sentiments and actions, eventually culminating in the 1925–1926 General Strike and Boycott of British Goods, the proselytizing of the Guomingdang's New Life Movement, and the activities of its Overseas Chinese Education Committee (Sweeting, 1990: 351–353). Partly as a result of these political pressures, partly as the outcome of recognition that the existing forms of teacher preparation and professionalization were, at best, rudimentary, by the late 1930s the climate of opinion, even the opinion of some government officials, became more favourable to change. The consequence of this, as reinforced by the hyper-critical Burney Report on Education (1935), was the formation of a committee under Justice R.E. Lindsell and its report (1939). This report recommended that the University of Hong Kong should introduce a more rigorous and "consecutive"/postgraduate teacher education programme and that the various normal schools should be replaced by a fully-fledged teacher training college. The Government Teacher Training College (soon to be renamed, after the current

Governor, Northcote Training College and, from the 1960s, Northcote College of Education) opened in 1939 (Sweeting, 1990: 357–359).

At about the same time, the first signs of teacher unionization appeared, with the Hong Kong Teachers' Association established in 1934. This body was, however, more accurately comparable with a Friendly Society, being largely preoccupied with such matters as Widows' and Orphans' benefits and very much under the influence of the government's Education Department (Sweeting, 1990: 355, 361). Other signs of professionalization of a more active form include the formation of subject associations to enhance developments in a number of curriculum areas. In practice, however, the overwhelming concern of most members for the details of various public examinations tended to make the subject associations very susceptible to influence and direction from examination (i.e., largely government-paid or appointed) officials.

Teacher Preparation and Status During the Japanese Occupation

Both the Northcote College and the University of Hong Kong closed down for the duration of the Japanese Occupation of Hong Kong. Despite several promises, the Japanese authorities made no provision for university level education throughout the three years and eight months of the Occupation. They considered the questions concerning school teaching important enough, however, to merit special crash-courses for teachers – mainly in an attempt to ensure some facility in the Japanese language and a degree of anti-colonial political correctness – before they permitted some schools to reopen in May 1942. Similar concern about the influence of teachers persuaded them to arrange further short courses and to insist that one of the principal functions of the *Toa Gakuin* (East Asia Academy), which they opened in the grounds of a girls' secondary school in 1943 as a pale substitute for the University, was to offer "normal school education", focusing on the training of elementary school teachers (Sweeting, 2002: 91–92). As conditionsx deteriorated towards the end of the Occupation, the Japanese reinforced their acknowledgement of the importance of teachers by paying them in rice, rather than in drastically devalued Military Yen. This, together with discussions held at the end of 1943 between Japanese officials and Chinese heads of the new District Bureaux about the possibilities of introducing compulsory education, might, of course, have encouraged their sense of distinctiveness and professional status.

Limitations to Teacher Professionalization During Postwar Reconstruction

There is plenty of evidence to suggest that Hong Kong Government officials formally acknowledged the importance of teacher professionalism and, by implication, their professionalization during the first couple of decades following the end of the Japanese Occupation (Sweeting, 1993: 142–149). Teachers, themselves, however, as well as later policy analysts, could find grounds for believing that this acknowledgement represented little more than lip service. For example, the first postwar Director of Education, T.R. Rowell, who had earlier been principal of the Northcote Training College, ostensibly called for cooperation between the College and the Department of Education (the more modern name for the Department for the Training of Teachers) at the University of Hong Kong. It seems likely, however, that, in actuality, he was proposing that the training college should take over at least some of the Department's responsibilities and was quite happy to try to delay the latter's reopening (Ibid., p. 144). Moreover, the government's reliance on very brief, emergency or "crash" training courses and its readiness to use the services of completely untrained teachers also suggests that the main factors influencing policy and practice about teacher preparation were financial constraints and supply considerations (Ibid., pp. 50, 70). In years that witnessed enormous pressures on school places caused by demographic factors, it is hardly surprising that government commitment to teacher professionalization was limited and did not reflect an urgent priority. The results included an ever increasing number of untrained teachers, particularly but not only in Hong Kong's private schools, problems concerning teacher morale, and a conspicuous lack of teacher participation in education policy making, particularly as it related to the school curriculum and their own training. Even so, some progress was made, both in terms of new institutions or courses and in terms of the nature and aspirations of teachers, themselves.

Progress Towards Teacher Professionalization During the Second Half of the Twentieth Century

Basic considerations related to teacher supply in a time of rapid school expansion influenced the creation of new teacher training institutions and courses. New institutions included the Rural Training College (1946–1954), replacing the Government Tai Po Normal School, Grantham Training College (1951), Sir Robert Black Training College (1961), the School of Education at the newly established Chinese University of Hong Kong (1966), and the Technical Teachers' College (1974). Potentially of even greater importance was the establishment of what might seem to be the significantly named "Professional Teacher Training Board" in June 1952, officially to coordinate the various efforts in the field. As a purely advisory body without any executive powers, however, this soon became recognized as a mere "talking shop" and fell into desuetude. New courses included the already mentioned emergency measures. The new In-service Courses of Training for Teachers (ICTT), offered from 1953 by the government-run Training Colleges for unqualified non-graduate teachers during the time of very rapid growth in student numbers (Lai, 2002), University in-service courses for unqualified graduate teachers, starting at the University of Hong Kong in 1956, and technical teachers' training courses, starting in 1970 and organized by the Morrison Hill Technical Institute with help from the Colleges of Education offered sustained training (Sweeting, 2004: 169, 260). Accompanying these various top-down initiatives and several examples of rhetoric espousing teacher professionalization, officials typically remained quite dismissive of teacher quality, especially in Hong Kong's private schools (Sweeting, 1993: 156–157).

Perhaps understandably, at much the same time a relatively new trend towards teacher activism developed, at least amongst some of the teaching force, including private school teachers who resented their exploitation by profit-making school operators. The 1960s and 1970s witnessed a growth in subject associations, education-related pressure groups, and a more interventionist trade union, the Professional Teachers' Association (PTU), which soon became the predominant representative of teachers' interests.

As far as specific events are concerned, one should note the contributions made by teachers and principals of the "Patriotic" (i.e., China-oriented schools) to Hong Kong's 1967 "Disturbances" (Sweeting, 2004: 254–255, 324–325), as well as the Certificated Masters' dispute of 1971–73. The latter galvanized an alliance of "educational groups" and facilitated the formation of the PTU in 1973 (Sweeting, 2004: 68–70, 247, 263–264). Growing in confidence, the PTU played a major part, supporting a group of dissident teachers and pupils at a government-assisted secondary school, in the 1977–1978 "Precious Blood Golden Jubilee School Affair", which was eventually resolved at the cost of face-loss by the government Education Department (Sweeting and Morris, 1993: 209–211). In the latter case, however, although the government made overt efforts to improve its channels of communication with teachers (and parents), it also established a special, monitoring committee on pressure groups and did little to counteract a backlash against progressive teaching methods and curricular proposals in schools controlled by conservative principals (Sweeting, 2004: pp. 326–327). Thus, it might be concluded that the struggles of the teachers, either as individuals or in groups, to make significant progress on their "Long March" towards professionalization continued to be hampered by "Encirclement Campaigns" organized by the Hong Kong Government and its allies. On the other hand, teachers' support for activist unions is not necessarily compatible with self-motivated professionalization. And, in the case of Hong Kong, despite the PTU's title and its rhetoric espousing the professionalism of teachers, the new trade union soon gave the impression of being more concerned with political and economic issues than it was with ethics, the enhancement of teaching skills and pedagogical knowledge, service to clients, or collegiality.

In the early 1980s, a visiting panel of educationalists and administrators, appointed to create an overview of educational developments in Hong Kong, issued its report, which recommended, *inter alia*, the establishment of a "Teaching Service" to promote enhanced professionalism within the workforce and to remove disparities in qualifications and conditions of employment within the teaching force (Llewellyn, 1982: 96–101). Unsurprisingly, especially in view of the growing strength and political clout of the PTU, this was one of the panel's recommendations that the government balked at implementing. In its place, the new "Education Commission", itself a watered-down version of another proposal by the visiting panel, approved one rather general and another specific innovation. The former involved the "fostering of a sense of professionalism by encouraging teachers, principals, school managements and sponsors to cooperate, through the coordination of the (government's) Education Department, in the "writing of a 'code of practice' for the teaching profession". The latter adopted a less radical suggestion of the Panel to set up "regional teachers' centres" (Education Commission, 1984: 65). As it happened, a "Code for the Education Profession in Hong Kong" was eventually produced (as a revised edition in October 1990). It was, however, generalized, platitudinous, and difficult to "police", being the outcome of hard bargaining among pressure groups, educationalists, and administrators and, ultimately of inevitable compromises (Sweeting, 2004: 379). The first teachers' centre was opened in June 1989 and, together with others set up in subsequent years, it probably played a small, practical part in teacher professionalization, by providing some resources, less isolation, and more exhortation. However, the remark by Leung Siu-tong, who alternated as Chairman and Vice-chairman of the Hong Kong Teachers' Centre for several years, that the Centre (and the Code) represented "games" played by the government are particularly significant (Interview with Leung Siu-tong, cited in Sweeting, 2004: 517). Leung and others regarded both the Teachers' Centre and the Code as ploys to divert attention away from the Teaching Service idea. Similarly, officials' support in 1992 for the Education Commission's proposal to set up a "Council on Professional Conduct in Education" (Education Commission, 1992: 93) is open to different interpretations. One is that the government was sincere in its focus on teachers' conduct (or more frequently, misconduct). Another is that it was an attempt to distract teachers and their unions from campaigns to establish a "General Teaching Council", comparable in functions, powers, and status with the General Medical Council (see, for example, Cheng, 1993; Lee, 1993; Sze, 1993). In the meantime, relatively new social and political developments had interesting, but by no means simple, effects.

By the late 1980s, a new type of demographic factor began to affect opportunities for at least some aspects of teacher professionalization. Political considerations, especially as provoked by the Sino-British Agreement on the Future of Hong Kong (1984) shaped this new factor. Towards the end of 1987, for example, there was sustained public discussion, largely anxious, about the educational connotations of the journalistically emphasized "brain drain". This phenomenon was beginning to affect Hong Kong as growing numbers of the well educated sought to obtain foreign passports or immigration permits as a form of insurance against a worst-case scenario regarding the forthcoming resumption of sovereignty over Hong Kong by China. The outflow of well-qualified, often relatively young people from Hong Kong, including increasing numbers of teachers and newly qualified graduates, soon had a marked impact both on Hong Kong's schools and on the recruitment of teachers in institutions of teacher education. In the latter case, motivation to undertake full-time study in particular was drastically reduced by the fact that opportunities for employment as teachers without professional qualifications were increasing as a by-product of the brain drain. Furthermore, for an aspiring emigrant, professional teaching qualifications were not valued since they tended not to improve an individual's attractiveness to the potential host country – typically, Canada, the United States, Australia, New Zealand, and the UK) which already possessed enough teachers (Sweeting, 2004: 366, 485). Eventually, once they had secured their passports or "green cards", many of the successful emigrants (or "astronauts", as they were called, locally) returned to Hong Kong. Back home, they helped to ease problems regarding the supply of professional teachers, but they and their families tended to exacerbate different problems, mainly concerning pressures on the learning and teaching of the English language.

Another politically oriented development, of some titular significance for teacher professionalization, was the establishment of a special ("functional") constituency for teachers in the indirect Legislative Council elections of 1991. Functional constituencies represented one of the tentative steps towards electoral democracy, taken in the last years of the Hong Kong colonial government. Their establishment, especially for the teaching, legal, and medical professions, enabled large numbers of Hong Kong residents to be represented in the Legislative Council on the basis of their occupation. The functional constituency for teachers almost certainly enhanced their status in that it accorded formal recognition of this by the government. For this reason, it might be regarded as a key step in the Long March towards professionalization. Inevitably, it led, however, to the capture of the Legislative Council seat, in 1991 and in every subsequent election, by PTU leaders. This, together with the creation of the other functional constituencies and, eventually, the direct election of some other members to the Legislative Council, contributed to the politicization of education policy making. It also contributed to the amount of "busy work" that the Government Secretariat had to undertake. The main reason for such a development was to enable spokespersons for the Education and Manpower Branch and the Education Department to be seen to be responding to formal questions posed by individual Legislative Council Members or its Education Sub-committee (Ibid., pp. 374, 379). In practical terms, therefore, the functional constituency of teachers did not invariably serve the cause of teacher professionalization. Much the same is true of a whole miscellany of "education reforms" in which Hong Kong became embroiled towards the end of the twentieth century and in the early twenty-first century.

Education Reforms and Teacher Professionalization

As was true, contemporaneously, of several other societies, the education reform movement comprised mainly top-down initiatives. Typical of the Hong Kong Government, some of the early "reforms" were confined to quantitative expansion. These included the "blister programme" at the University of Hong Kong and the Chinese University of Hong Kong, which commenced in September 1984 and was completed in June 1987, to be succeeded by a "second blister", which lasted from 1987 to 1990. As early as 1982, government officials had reached the conclusion that the situation with regard to the supply of qualified graduate teachers was so critical that it should provide special earmarked grants to the two Schools of Education in the two universities. The basic purpose of these was so that the Schools of Education (later renamed Faculties) could deal with the backlog of untrained graduate teachers in secondary schools via appointing additional staff on short-term contract terms. Together, the two programmes did facilitate a radical reduction in the proportion of untrained teachers in secondary schools. However, the intense nature of the training and the temporary nature of the appointments also caused disruption organizationally and, for some staff, in personal terms (Ibid., pp. 283, 388).

The establishment of a new Institute of Language in Education (ILE) in 1982 to train or re-train non-graduate teachers of Chinese and English in specialist language skills at least partially represented another instance of expansion. In addition, in 1992 the government approved the opening of a Faculty of Education at the Open Learning Institute (later, the Open University of Hong Kong) which began its first course, a B.Ed. for Primary School teachers in 1994 and both a Department of Educational Studies, which started its part-time Postgraduate Diploma in Education (PGDE) in 1993, and a School of Continuing Education, which ran a B.Ed., at the Baptist College (later, the Baptist University) in 1994. In 1992, the Education Commission Report No. 5 (ECR5) recommended that the Colleges of Education and the ILE should be combined into a new Institute of Education, with its own governing body and eventually its own custom-designed campus. The new Institute would be empowered to offer some courses at degree level, but suggestions in favour of a fully-fledged Teacher Training (or "Normal") University or alternatively, an institution comparable with the earlier Area Training Organizations in the UK (i.e., with universities as leading members) were rejected (Education Commission, 1992: 59–60). These and other government initiatives, when implemented, led to some improvements, both in quantitative and in qualitative terms. However, it is more than likely that the government's main motivation related to teacher supply and control, rather than teacher professionalization, and that the various initiatives were significant as typical instances of "bureaucratic incrementalism" (Sweeting, 2004: 24–25, 371). This encouraged territoriality disputes, together with a typical government strategy to divide and rule. Other innovations stimulated by ECR5 included the government appointing in 1993 a Committee on Home-School Cooperation and an Advisory Committee on Teacher Education and Qualifications. In the former case, although several chairpersons and members were well-intentioned, the committee was under-resourced and focused more on general exhortations than on practical coordination; in the latter, business tended to concentrate on credentials, rather than on teacher education quality. In both cases, the new committees resembled distractions and possibly "encirclement campaigns".

Despite official rhetoric concerning its contribution to the enhancement of teachers' status, Hong Kong's new Institute of Education had a shaky start. The mass media conveyed critical comments about the first President's lack of qualifications and experience related to school-based teaching (although similar ignorance was also typical of all Education Commission chairpersons, most Secretaries of Education and Manpower, and several other senior education policy makers). As importantly, large numbers of College of Education lecturers resented their loss of privileges and security consequential on the fact that transfer to the Institute would mean that they would no longer be government employees. Eventually, about half of the 400 lecturers initially seconded to the Institute decided to reject a permanent transfer, preferring to return to government service (Ibid., 428–429). Moreover, although new staff soon solved the most obvious problems, the resignation or non-renewal of the contracts of its three most senior staff followed a visit and enquiry into the Institute by Sir William Taylor and the non-validation of its PGDE course. The Presidential tenures of Professors Ruth Hayhoe (1997–2002) and Paul Morris (from 2002) certainly helped to rehabilitate the Institute. Hayhoe consolidated the institute and Morris was especially successful in upgrading both its teaching and research profiles (largely via the clearing away of residual "dead wood" and the appointment of new, internationally reputable academics as fulltime staff or visitors). Unfortunately, however, Professor Arthur Li Kwok-cheung, initially as Vice-chancellor of CUHK and, allegedly, later as Secretary of Education and Manpower, pressed the Institute to merge with (and be submerged by) the CUHK's Faculty of Education. Morris resisted these efforts and his own advocacy of university status for the Institute, a prospect that Li rejected on the grounds that the Institute was a monothematic body, the Institute led to unpleasant consequences. The Institute's Council, the members of which were predominantly nominees of the Education and Manpower Bureau, refused to renew Morris's own contract and almost all of the internationally renowned academics announced that they planned to leave the Institute (*South China Morning Post*, 30 January 2007). Thus, although the Hong Kong Institute of Education undoubtedly contributed to the professionalization of large numbers of local teachers, continuing problems have tended to distract attention from these contributions.

Similarly, the Council on Professional Conduct in Education, although it provided some teachers and academics with some experience and despite the official rhetoric about its purposes and importance, was under-funded and under-deployed. On his resignation from the body, its chairman, Professor Cheng Kai-ming, described it as "useless" (Sweeting, 2004: 534). As already noted, it almost certainly represented a stratagem by the government to deflect attention from the campaign to secure the creation of a General Teaching Council (GTC) supported by, amongst others, Cheng Kai-ming as well as the PTU. Although the GTC was clearly promised "within two years" by Mr. Tung Chee-hwa in his Policy Address of October 1997 (cited in Sweeting, 2004: 601), to date it has not materialized – presumably because of official anxieties that it would be dominated by the PTU.

Quite recently launched exercises that ostensibly facilitated teacher professionalism and professionalization included the "Accelerated Schools Project", an alliance formed in 1998 between the CUHK and HKIEd, which amongst other objectives, aimed to enhance training of staff at certain secondary schools, and its contemporary "Unified Professional Development Programme" at the University of Hong Kong, with similar aspirations. The Hong Kong Government's Quality Education Fund (QEF) funded both of these, the former more generously than the latter, but a member of its advisory committee alleged that the main motive was to be seen to "share the spoils" between the two principal stakeholders in graduate teacher education. Despite QEF pressure to ensure positive evaluation, especially of the Accelerated Schools Project, the results of the evaluation exercise and of the projects themselves were mixed.

Mixed feelings and a sense of a less than constructive impact on teacher professionalization also apply to the various schemes whereby native-speakers of English, usually from abroad, were deployed to teach the English language in Hong Kong's schools. These began as a part of the "Language Enhancement" measures during the 1980s. The first scheme was run by the British Council and termed the "Expatriate English Teachers Scheme". Some local teachers expressed dissatisfaction with a system that offered foreign teachers, unfamiliar with the culture and problems of local pupils significantly better terms of employment and the PTU, which had criticized the scheme from its outset, supported the local teachers. Despite this, a renamed "Native English Teachers" (NETs) scheme was implemented in the 1990s. It was extended even after the resumption of sovereignty over Hong Kong by China in 1997 and in following years. Although some individual NETs probably contributed to the more efficient and idiomatic learning of English by local pupils, others expressed criticisms, if not contempt, of the local teachers and certainly did not contribute to their professionalization (Sweeting, 2004: 18–19, 584, 622). Indeed, it is likely that, in any educational "balance of payments" that can be envisaged, greater benefits accrued to the NETs than to local teachers.

Largely because of pressures from commercial enterprises, which influenced the government about alleged failings in English by Hong Kong's students, local English language teachers began to face and be upset by "benchmark tests" (recommended by ECR6 (1995) and implemented with apparently increasing rigor after the 1997 change in sovereignty. These, together with other "Managerialist" techniques in Hong Kong, as elsewhere tended to hold back teacher professionalization.

Moreover, the whole package of education reforms, bundled together by the Education Commission from 1999 to 2001 (including, as it did, top-down proposals about pedagogy, curricula, assessment, parent-teacher relations, and, especially, the "mechanics" of schooling) also did little to advance teacher professionalization, other than as a focus for opposition. Most teachers were and are dissatisfied with the reforms, as the PTU and a series of surveys has made clear (Lee, 2001; Sweeting, 2004: 627–628). Because of the non-cooperation of many teachers, the reform movement has remained, in practice, scantily implemented. Even so, it has clearly placed new pressures or threats of pressures on the teachers' already heavy workload and added to their stress. Several teachers have committed suicide during the past few years and alarming statistics about depression and anxiety disorders have emerged from various surveys (Lo, 2004). According to recent polls, about a third of the teaching force were seriously considering leaving the "profession" (Law, 2006; Tong, 2005).

According to some observers, Hong Kong needs further reform at both policy and school levels for genuine professional autonomy to be actualized (Lai and Lo, 2002).

On the other hand, during the summer of 2006, teachers massively subscribed to professional development courses run by the various local universities. For example, over 2,500 teachers registered for the "update" courses at the City University on "embracing change", designed to assist their adaptation to reforms, particularly the new 3 + 3 + 4 structure of secondary and tertiary education to be introduced in 2009 (Clem, 2006). Since most courses were either commissioned or at least approved by the government's Education and Manpower Bureau, these reactions suggest that its stick and carrot approach is having some impact on teacher professionalization. Moreover, Elizabeth Cheung's research into the career patterns of local teachers provides convincing evidence about grass-roots level developments in professionalism and professionalization (Cheung, 2000).

Conclusions

This very last point, which shows that at least some teachers are making efforts to professionalize themselves, creates the firmest grounds for optimism about the prospects for teacher professionalization in Hong Kong. The whole long history of gestures or even actual efforts on its behalf have ranged from developments in the basic economic and pragmatic domains, through the enhancement of teachers' social and institutional coherence, all the way to a self-motivated and/or client-oriented concern for quality and professional ethics. There are now signs are that individuals who resemble what Judyth Sachs calls "the activist professional" are emerging in Hong Kong (Sachs, 2003: 181) and that some of them are beginning to operate together in what Wenger terms "communities of practice" (Wenger, 1998).

As many of the details outlined above have shown, the nature of teacher professionalization in Hong Kong comprised both a (very) Long March *and* a series of Encirclement Campaigns. In Hong Kong, as elsewhere, professionalization and unionization may have been uneasy bed-fellows, but they have been bedfellows. Likewise, professionalization, especially in the late twentieth and early twenty-first centuries has benefited significantly from newer, classroom skills and reflection oriented, teacher education programmes. However, the academicization of teacher educators, with the higher priority many of them now place on research and publications, has not invariably improved the quality of the training that teachers receive.

It may also be of some significance that the actual usage of the term "professional" and its derivatives has increased markedly over the past decades – with the high-sounding, but soon moribund, Professional Teacher Training Board (1952), the Professional Teachers' Union (from 1973), the Professional Code for Educational Workers (1990), and the non-statutory Council on Professional Conduct in Education (1994) serving as illuminating examples. It is more than possible, however, that this form of terminological inflation, like other forms, leads inevitably to devaluation. In Hong Kong, as Whitty appears to espouse for the United Kingdom (Whitty, 2006), it is the concept of professionalization, itself, that is being devalued.

References

Aldrich, Richard (1997). *The End of History and the Beginning of Education*. London: Institute of Education, University of London.

Apple, Michael (1979). *Ideology and the Curriculum*. London: Routledge

Apple, Michael (1986). *Teachers and Texts: A Political Economy of Class and Gender Relations in Education*. New York: Routledge & Kegan Paul.

Bates, Richard J. (1986). 'Instructional Leadership and Educational Control: A Cultural Perspective'. Paper presented at the Annual Meeting of the American Research Association.

Borrowman, Merle L. (1956). *The Liberal and the Technical in Teacher Education: A Historical Survey of American Thought*. New York: Columbia University, Teachers' College Bureau of Publications.

Cheng, Kai-ming (1993). 'A Matter of Professional Legitimacy: ECR5 Recommendations and Confusions'. In Amy B.M. Tsui and Ivor Johnson (eds.). *Teacher Education and Development*. Education Papers 18, Hong Kong: University of Hong Kong Faculty of Education, pp. 148–165.

Cheung, Elizabeth Lai-man (2000). 'Hong Kong Secondary School Teachers' Understanding of Their Careers'. Ph.D. dissertation. Hong Kong: The University of Hong Kong.

Chinese Repository (1841–1851). Missionary Journal. Guanzhou: Chinese Repository.

Clem, Will (2006). 'Teachers Swamp Free Professional Development Courses'. *South China Morning Post*, 24 June 2006.

Committee for Superintending Chinese Schools (1851). *Report*. Hong Kong: Government Printer.

Eddy, Elizabeth M. (1969). *Becoming a Teacher: The Passage to Professional Status*. New York: Teachers College Press.

Education Commission (1984). Education Commission Report No. 1. Hong Kong: Government Printer.

Education Commission (1992). Education Commission Report No. 5. Hong Kong: Government Printer.

Engvall, Robert P. (1997). *The Professionalization of Teaching: Is It Truly Much Ado About Nothing?* Lanham, MD: University Press of America.

Faure, David (1986). *The Structure of Chinese Rural Society: Lineage and Village in the Eastern New Territories, Hong Kong*. Hong Kong: Oxford University Press.

Fullan, Michael G. (1993). *Changing Forces: Probing the Depths of Education Reforms*. London: Falmer.

Furlong, John et al. (2000). Teacher Education in transition: Re-forming professionalism. Buckingham: Open University Press.

Furlong, John (2005). 'New Labour and Teacher Education: The End of an Era'. *Oxford Review of Education*, 31, 1, 119–134.

Ginsburg, Mark B. (1988). *Contradictions in Teacher Education and Society: A Critical Analysis*. London: Falmer.

Ginsburg, Mark B. and Lindsay, Beverly (1995). *The Political Dimension in Teacher Education: Comparative Perspectives on Policy Formation, Socialization, and Society*. London: Falmer.

Gosden, Philip (1972). *The Evolution of a Profession: A Study of the Contribution of Teachers' Associations to the Development of Schoolteaching as a Professional Occupation*. Oxford: Blackwell.

Grosvenor, Ian (1999). '"There's no place like Home": Education and the Making of National Identity'. *History of Education*, 23, 3, 235–250.

Hall, Christine and Schulz, Renate (2003). 'Tensions in Teaching and Teacher Education: Professionalism and Professionalization in England and Canada'. *Compare*, 33, 3, 369–383.

Hargreaves, Andy (2000). 'Four Ages of Professionalism and Professional Learning'. *Teachers and Teaching: History and Practice*, 6, 2, 151–182.

Hayes, James (1983). *The Rural Economies of Hong Kong: Studies and Themes*. Hong Kong: Oxford University Press.

Herbst, Jurgen (1989). *And Sadly Teach: Teacher Education and Professionalization in American Culture*. Madison, WI: University of Wisconsin Press.

Hoyle, Eric (1974). 'Professionality, Professionalism and Control in Teaching'. *London Review of Education*, 3, 2, 13–19.

Hoyle, Eric (1975). 'Professionality, Professionalism and Control in Teaching'. In V. Voughton et al. (eds.). *Management in Education: The Management of Organizations and Individuals*. London: Ward Lock in association with the Open University Press.

Hoyle, Eric (1980). 'Professionalization and Deprofessionalization in Education'. In Eric Hoyle and Jacquetta Megary (eds.). *Professional Development of Teachers*. World Yearbook of Education. London/New York: Kogan Page/Nicols Publishing, pp. 42–54.

Hoyle, Eric (1982). 'The Professionalization of Teachers: A Paradox'. *British Journal of Educational Studies*, XXX, 2, 161–171.

Hoyle, Eric (1995). 'Changing Concepts of a Profession'. In Hugh Busher and Rene Saran (eds.). *The Management of Professionals in Schools*. London: Longman.

Hoyle, Eric (2001). 'Teaching: Prestige, Status, and Esteem'. *Educational Management and Administration*, 29, 2, 139–152.

Hoyle, Eric and John, Peter D. (1995). *Professional Knowledge and Professional Practice*. London: Cassell.

Hypolito, Álvaro Moreira (2004). 'Teachers' Work and Professionalization: The Promised Land or Dream Denied?' *Journal for Critical Education Policy Studies*, 2, 2, www.jceps.com/print. php?articleID = 33.

Kam, H.W. and Wong, R.Y.L. (1991). *Improving the Quality of the Teaching Profession: An International Perspective*. Singapore: International Council on Education for Teaching.

Lai, Kwok-chan (2002). 'Lessons Learnt on the Long Road Towards an All-Trained Profession – Fifty Years of In-Service Training for Non-graduate Teachers in Hong Kong'. Paper presented at the symposium "Learning from the Past, Informing the Future: Education Then, Now, and Tomorrow", Hong Kong, Baptist University, 13–14 May.

Lai, Man-hong and Lo, Leslie N.K. (2002). 'Decentralization and Teacher Autonomy: Reflections on the Education Reform Experiences of Hong Kong and Taiwan'. *Bulletin of Educational Research*, 48, 4, 53–74 (in Chinese).

Law, Niki (2006). 'Third of Teachers Think of Quitting, Poll Shows'. *South China Morning Post*, 10 September.

Lee, Wing-on (1993). 'Developing Teacher Professionalism – But What Kind of Professionalism?'. In Amy B.M. Tsui and Ivor Johnson (eds.). *Teacher Education and Development*. Education Papers 18, Hong Kong: University of Hong Kong Faculty of Education, pp. 118–133.

Lee, Wing-sze (2001). 'Teachers Dissatisfied with Education Reforms'. *South China Morning Post*, 18 May.

Llewellyn, John et al. (1982). *A Perspective on Education in Hong Kong*. Hong Kong: Government Printer.

Lo, Hsiang-lin (1963). *Hong Kong and Its External Communications Before 1842: The History of Hong Kong Prior to the British Arrival*. Hong Kong: Institute of Chinese Culture.

Lo, Alex (2004). 'Depressing Numbers', South China Morning Post, 3 July, City Section, C2.

Lobscheid, Wilhelm (1859). *A Few Notices on the Extent of Chinese Education and the Government Schools of Hong Kong, with Remarks in the History and Religious Notions of the Inhabitants of the Island*. Hong Kong: Printed at the *China Mail* Office.

Luk, Bernard Hung-kay (1984). 'Lu Tzu-Chün and Ch'en Jung-Kun: Two Exemplary Figures in the 'Ssu-Shu' Education of Pre-War Urban Hong Kong'. In David Faure, James Hayes, and Alan Birch (eds.). *From Village to City: Studies in the Traditional Roots of Hong Kong Society*. Hong Kong: Centre of Asian Studies, University of Hong Kong.

McCulloch, Gary (1997). 'Privatizing the Past: History of Education Policy in the 1990s'. *British Journal of Educational Studies*, 45, 1, 69–82.

Morris, P. (2008). Teacher Professionalism and Teacher Education in Hong Kong (Chapter 8, this Volume).

Myrdal, Gunnar (1944). *An American Dilemma: The Negro Problem and Modern Democracy*. New York: Harper.

Needham, Joseph (1954). *Science and Civilization in China*, Volume 1. Cambridge, Cambridge University Press.

Ng, Lun Ngai-ha (1984). Village Education in the New Territories Region Under the Ch'ing'. In David Faure, James Hayes, and Alan Birch (eds.). *From Village to City: Studies in the Traditional Roots of Hong Kong Society*. Hong Kong: Centre of Asian Studies, University of Hong Kong.

Ozga, Jennifer (1988). *Schoolwork: Approaches to the Labour Processes of Teaching*. Milton Keynes, UK: Open University Press.

Ozga, Jennifer and Lawn, Martin (1981). *Teachers, Professionalism, and Class: A Study of Organized Teachers*. London: Falmer.

Robinson, Wendy (2001). 'Finding our Professional Niche: Reinventing Ourselves as Twenty-first Century Historians of Education. In David Crook and Richard Aldrich (eds.). *History of Education for the Twenty-First Century*. London: Institute of Education, University of London.

Sachs, Judyth (2000). 'The Activist Profession'. *International Journal of Educational Change*, 1, 1, 77–95.

Sachs, Judyth (2003). 'Teacher Professional Standards: Controlling or Developing Teaching?' *Teachers and Teaching: Theory and Practice*, 9, 2, 175–186.

Simon, Brian (1981). 'Why No Pedagogy in England?'. In Brian Simon and William Taylor (eds.). *Education in the Eighties: The Central Issues*. London: Batsford, pp. 124–145.

Soder, Roger (1990). 'The Rhetoric of Teacher Professionalization'. In John Goodlad, Roger Soder, and Kenneth A. Sirotnik (eds.). *The Moral Dimensions of Teaching*. San Francisco, CA: Jossey-Bass, pp. 35–86.

Song Guangwen and Wei Shuhua (2005). 'On Teachers' Professional Development'. *Educational Research*, 26, 7, 71–74 (in Chinese).

Stewart, Frederick (1865). *Report on Education*. Hong Kong: Government Printer.

Stewart, Frederick (1866). *Report on Education*. Hong Kong: Government Printer.

Sung, Hok P'ang (1974). 'Legends and Stories of the New Territories: Kam Tin'. Reprinted from *The Hong Kong Naturalist*, 6–8, 1935–1938 in the *Journal of the Hong Kong Branch of the Royal Asiatic Society* 13 (1973), 110–132 and 14 (1974), 160–185.

Sweeting, Anthony (1990). *Education in Hong Kong, Pre-1841 to 1941: Fact and Opinion*. Hong Kong: Hong Kong University Press.

Sweeting, Anthony (1993). *A Phoenix Transformed: The Reconstruction of Education in Post-war Hong Kong*. Hong Kong: Oxford University Press.

Sweeting, Anthony (1995). 'An Introduction to the History of Teacher Education in Hong Kong: In-service, Pre-service, and Lip-Service'. In ITEC'95. *Teacher Education in the Asian Region*. Hong Kong: Department of Curriculum Studies, University of Hong Kong, pp. 332–341.

Sweeting, Anthony (2002). 'Training Teachers: Processes, Products, and Purposes'. In Chan Lau Kit-ching and Peter Cunich (eds.). *An Impossible Dream: Hong Kong University from Foundation to Re-establishment, 1910–1950*. Oxford: Oxford University Press, pp. 65–97.

Sweeting, Anthony (2004). *Education in Hong Kong, 1941 to 2001: Visions and Revisions*. Hong Kong: Hong Kong University Press.

Sweeting, Anthony (2007). 'Education in Hong Kong: Histories, Mysteries and Myths'. *History of Education*, 36, 1, 89–108.

Sweeting, Anthony and Morris, Paul (1993). 'Educational Reform in Post-war Hong Kong: Planning and Crisis Intervention'. *International Journal of Educational Development*, 13, 3, 201–216.

Sze, Wai-ting (1993). 'The Cat, Pigeons, Hawks, and Headless Chicks: ECR5 and Aspects of Teacher Professionalism'. In Amy B.M. Tsui and Ivor Johnson (eds.). *Teacher Education and Development*. Education Papers 18, Hong Kong: University of Hong Kong Faculty of Education, pp. 134–147.

Tong, Nora (2005). 'Teachers Would Rather Quit or Die'. *South China Morning Post*, 3 December.

Urban, Wayne (1991). 'Historical Studies of Teacher Education'. In W. Robert Houston (ed.). *Handbook of Research on Teacher Education*. New York: Macmillan, pp. 212–233.

Wenger, Etienne (1998). *Communities of Practice, Learning, Meaning and Identity*. Cambridge: Cambridge University Press.

Whitty, Geoff (2006). 'Towards a New Teacher Professionalism'. Paper presented at the twentieth anniversary event of the Institute of Education Old Students' Association, City University, Hong Kong, 17 June.

Woodhead, Chris (1998). 'Academia Gone to Seed'. *New Statesman and Society*, 20 March, 51–52.

Chapter 5
Teacher Professional Identity Under Conditions of Constraint

Marilyn Osborn

When we as researchers write about the impact of recent educational reform on teacher's work and sense of professional identity we often seem to infer that the constraints which operate on teacher professional autonomy are relatively new. However, the struggle for control over teachers and teacher's work is a long-term rather than a new phenomenon (Reynolds, 2005). Teachers have long worked under conditions of constraint and 'have always been under structural controls' (Reynolds and Smaller, 1997: 15) although there is a long history of teachers managing to mediate, accommodate and resist state incursions into teaching and learning.

From at least the 1930s onwards many researchers and writers have argued that the affective and emotional dimensions of teaching are central, yet, in practice, teachers have often been besieged by external directives or controls which mitigate against these aspects of education. Waller (1932), for example, argued that human relationships were vital in schools, arguing, 'let no one be deceived, the important things that happen in schools result from the interaction of personalities, a theme which was echoed in D.H. Lawrence's portrayal of Ursula's first experiences of teaching in 'The Rainbow'. Yet both the fictional Ursula and the real teachers in Waller's study often fought a real battle against implacable school authorities to keep these values alive. In the 1960s and 1970s the teachers studied by Lortie (1975) and Jackson (1968) accepted the legitimacy of the prescribed curriculum but saw their role as more than just implementing this. They were 'moral agents' as well, emphasising the social and personal development of children and the close connection between this and successful learning. For these teachers and those studied in the 1980s by Nias (1989), the main rewards in teaching came from the affective dimension of classroom events, from children responding well and from being influenced by their teaching.

It is clear that these values have long been deeply held by teachers, particularly those working in primary education. Yet at a time when school systems are being restructured to meet ever-increasing demands for accountability, for greater rationality and for technical competencies in teaching, these sources of professional satisfaction are under threat as never before (Hoyle and John, 1995).

In England, for example, with the introduction of the National Curriculum, national assessment, the literacy and numeracy hours, a system of performance

D. Johnson, R. Maclean (eds.), *Teaching: Professionalization, Development and Leadership,*
© Springer Science + Business Media B.V. 2008

management, school inspection by OFSTED and the introduction more generally, of the values of the marketplace into education, it has become apparent that teachers are required to have an increasing range of more technical, cognitive and managerial skills which may come into conflict with more personal and moral dimensions of professional responsibility.

The current range of professional responsibilities delineated by the School Teachers' Pay and Conditions of Employment Act are extensive. A classroom teacher's professional duties are deemed to include planning and preparing courses and lessons, personalising teaching according to the needs of individual children, marking work and assessing, recording and reporting on the development, progress and attainment of pupils.

In addition they are responsible for a whole range of other activities, including the personal and social needs of pupils, advice and guidance on matters which include further education and future careers, keeping records and writing reports on the personal and social needs of pupils; communicating and consulting with the parents of the pupils, communicating and co-operating with persons or bodies outside the school; and participating in meetings. They are responsible for taking part in a scheme of performance management, and in some cases carrying out the performance management of other teachers, including responsibility for continuous professional development and in many cases, a range of other management and administrative tasks.

The list of duties and requirements above cannot possibly represent the turbulent changes that have taken place in the last 18 years to the working life of the classroom teacher in England. This article aims to identify some of the principal changes which have taken place in English primary teachers' attitudes to their work and in their practice as a result of recent policy changes and to consider the significance of these changes for the teachers themselves, their pupils, their schools and for the education system and society as a whole. It draws principally upon the PACE (Primary, Assessment, Curriculum and Experience) study (Osborn et al., 2000; Pollard et al., 2000), but also draws upon a programme of comparative research on teachers in England, France and Denmark (Osborn et al., 2003) and on the work of researchers on teaching elsewhere. In framing some of the dimensions of these studies the work of Eric Hoyle has made a significant contribution.

Comparative studies of teachers in England and France, carried out by myself and Patricia Broadfoot with French colleagues before and after major educational reforms, drew upon Hoyle's conceptions of 'restricted' and 'extended' professionality (Hoyle, 1974) to characterise the professional identities of primary teachers in England and France (Broadfoot, Osborn 1993; see also chapter 14 in this volume). To summarise briefly, our research suggested that French teachers had a narrower, more 'restricted' and more classroom-focused conception of their role, which centred on what they saw as their responsibility for children's academic progress. English teachers, in contrast, saw themselves as having a more wide-ranging, diffuse and 'extended' set of responsibilities relating to work outside as well as inside the classroom, including extra-curricular and sometimes even community activities, all aspects of school relationships, accountability to parents, colleagues and the head-teacher. At each extreme, a French teacher's perception of her role centred on 'meeting one's contractual responsibility', whilst a typical English teacher characterized her role as 'striving after perfection'. As Eric Hoyle's theoretical framework had predicted, for some English teachers this meant a certain amount of conflict and confusion about their role and a sense that they were setting themselves, and being set, goals they could not hope to fulfil (Broadfoot and Osborn, 1993).

This French/English research suggested that before the Education Reform Act (1988), although English teachers were becoming increasingly constrained on all sides, they nevertheless believed in their autonomy (in contrast with French teachers who believed they had very little autonomy), and saw it as central to their 'extended' role that they would be able to decide for themselves both what they would teach and how they would change it.

A later, much larger scale national research project, the PACE (Primary Asssessment, Curriculum and Experience) study carried out with a team of colleagues, studied 150 teachers and headteachers in 48 schools in eight English local education authorities over the course of eight years following major educational reforms. The study focused in more depth on the perspectives and practices of nine teachers in nine case study schools for each year of the study (54 classrooms and teachers being reported over the whole study). All teachers were interviewed and in addition the 54 studied in more depth were observed extensively in their classrooms throughout the study.

The study explored the changes that might have taken place in primary teachers' perceptions and definitions of their work and professional responsibilities as well as in their professional practice. It also examined the way in which national policies for teachers had been mediated by teachers' perspectives, cultures and behaviour and, in particular, their perceptions of their professional responsibility. In the sections which follow I examine the context for change, and the impact of this on teacher's sense of professional identity and on their working lives.

The Context for Change

Educationalists in other countries are frequently amazed that there was no tradition of a national curriculum in England and Wales until the 1988 Education Reform Act was implemented. Historically England has been almost unique in having no national curriculum and teachers, particularly at primary and lower secondary level, had enjoyed considerable freedom in respect of both *what* was taught and *how* it was taught since they were constrained neither by a formal curriculum nor by the requirements of a formal examination system. All this changed dramatically when the 1988 Education Reform Act, a policy initiative almost unprecedented in its ambition and scope was introduced with the aim of raising teacher expectations about pupil achievement. The introduction of the National Curriculum was complemented by provision for a standard and comprehensive assessment system with children undergoing national assessments at the ages of 7, 11, 14 and 16. These reforms and the multiple changes which followed them in the next 18 years represented a profound shift in the way in which primary teachers' work and role were defined by government policy directives. The changes included the introduction of new forms of management into schools, new requirements for the teaching of literacy, numeracy and for assessment, new forms of evaluation of teachers' work, and the increased infiltration of the market place into education.

When the New Labour government came into power in May 1997, the White Paper Excellence in Schools (DfEE, 1997) was published and it was evident that the pace of new education policy making was to continue. However, there was a reappraisal of focus and priorities, and this resulted in a new concern for social inclusion and an ever-increasing emphasis on the basics of literacy and numeracy. In 1999 plans for a revised National Curriculum were published. This Curriculum 2000 was the result of much more extensive consultation with teachers than previous versions. However, it was not as "slimmed down" as previously anticipated, and still gave relatively little scope to teachers to exercise their professional judgement.

New Labour also increased pedagogic prescription through establishing a compulsory framework for literacy and numeracy hours in primary schools, introducing a more demanding process of inspection of schools by OFSTED (Office for Standards in Education) and the "naming and shaming" of failiing schools. These developments were further reinforced by the gradual development of target-setting systems for schools and local education authorities and the linking of teacher's classroom performance and continuing professional development to salary enhancement through "performance management". Taken as a whole, these various policy initiatives have ensured that primary school teaching has become increasingly framed by requirements and pressures that are external to the school itself. Paradoxically, in terms of finance, primary schools have been given increased autonomy to manage their own budgets. Unlike most other European countries, schools are also free to recruit their own teachers and non-teaching staff although the staff remain the employees of the Local Education Authority.

In the rest of the article I discuss the significance of these multiple initiatives for teachers' work and professional identity looking particularly at the challenges that were posed to their sense of professionalism, their work and their values. I also examine the teachers' strategic responses and their classroom practice.

Challenges to Teachers' Professional Identity

Evidence from the PACE research (Osborn et al., 2000) showed that teachers felt overwhelmed by the 'avalanche' of policy initiatives of the late 1980s and 1990s. Their responses suggested that they were increasingly besieged by critics and demands for accountability from outsiders, especially parents, whilst losing little of their deeply held sense of moral accountability to pupils. Many teachers experienced high levels of increasing stress as the growing proliferation of external requirements left them less and less space for personal professional discretion.

As one teacher put it:

> There's so much pressure now from paperwork and record-keeping and from attending
> meetings after school. I have no time to myself. I live, eat, drink and sleep school. We are
> expected to give an awful lot more of ourselves than other professions yet we are not given
> any credit.

For many, the effects of this increase in pressure and constraint were exacerbated by their belief that what they were being asked to do was not educationally desirable or in the best interest of their pupils. The increasingly high profile and externally controlled national assessments provided one of the most widespread causes of such conflict. However for some teachers, particularly those working with pupils from difficult social and economic backgrounds, the National Curriculum itself caused stress and frustration since teachers felt it could not meet such children's particular needs.

One Year 6 teacher said:

> Well I don't know the children any more. ...You feel that you are under this obligation to
> get work done and as a consequence... This notion that we've got a certain amount to get
> through is just pressurizing – for the teacher and for the children. It's difficult to include
> the education of the whole child because of it.

Significant changes also characterised teachers' professional identity and values (Acker, 1999; Campbell, 1996; Troman, 1996; Webb and Vulliamy, 1996; Woods et al., 1997). In the PACE research we reported the growing sense of resignation and instrumentalism of many as they found themselves constrained in terms of curriculum content and teaching methods. In the media, teachers were subjected to a barrage of criticism and to what Ball (1994) has referred to as a "discourse of derision". For many teachers this shift from professional autonomy to contractual responsibility as the basis for accountability was associated with increased stress, value conflict and reduced job satisfaction.

As one Year 6 teacher put it:

> I would like to leave tomorrow if I could, I used to love teaching. I can genuinely say I used
> to love teaching and now I don't feel that I'm actually communicating with the children in
> the way I was when I went into teaching in the first place.

They began to feel bound by the demand for 'delivery of performance' beyond all other considerations. Further, they felt that the more "affective" side of teaching – the sense of vocation and investment of self – was being undermined by pressure to become 'expert technicians' in transmitting predefined knowledge and skills to their pupils (Hargreaves, 1994; Jeffrey, 1996; Nias, 1989). The policy emphasis of successive governments on education as a 'commodity' to be delivered and measured was at odds with many teachers' views of education as being fundamentally concerned with personal development.

Another Year 6 teacher said:

> My workload has increased enormously and the paperwork. I spend an hour after day on
> paperwork, another hour on marking and planning.... My enjoyment is not so great.
> I am tired all the time. I feel I'm doing a bit of everything, not doing anything properly.

However this teacher, like many others stayed in teaching because of the satisfaction she derived from working with children.

> I still get satisfaction out of working with the children. I wouldn't go for a job out of the classroom.

Ironically, as Hoyle has argued, it is this relationship with their clientele, children, that is in part a contributor to the relatively low status of teachers (2001). While teachers are seen as mainly mediators between the child and adult world they will derive their status from the low status of children. It is arguable then that reforms which require teachers to work more closely with others, in particular, with other adult professionals have the potential to raise teachers' occupational prestige and professional status (Hoyle, 2001).

Teachers' Strategic Responses

It is this work with other professionals which has been a positive outcome of reform for a considerable number of teachers. For them, the worst effects of the changes described above were mediated by a growth in collaboration and collegiality. This had often been a strength within primary schools, in particular (Nias et al., 1989), and in the circumstances of the early 1990s teachers increasingly felt the need to work together to cope with the new challenges and its effects. Thus curriculum planning, whole-school co-ordination, preparation for inspection and external communication, as well as teaching itself, were increasingly likely to be characterised by teachers pooling their different knowledge and skills in complementary ways. At their best, these developments were highly creative and empowering, resulting in some or all teachers in the school feeling a new sense of professional achievement.

This collaboration might be seen as a central element of what Eric Hoyle has called the 'new professionalism' (Hoyle, 1986) a term which was taken up by other researchers to describe 'new professional' teachers who often accommodated to the reforms but also sometimes contested or resisted them (Troman, 1996; Woods et al., 1997).

These creative responses to change were more widely documented in the PACE study. We suggested that while teachers adopted a range of strategies in response to change, which ranged from 'incorporation' to 'resistance' to 'retreatism' (Osborn et al., 2000: 67), some of these teachers could be seen as 'creative mediators'. They were able to take active control of the changes and put them into practice in a creative, albeit selective, way (Osborn et al., 1996, 2000). The changes were filtered through their values so that they took on board those aspects which more closely accorded with their own beliefs and values as teachers and worked with them creatively.

As one teacher of a Year 5 and 6 class put it:

> You have to accept that you never know it all, be open to new things and go on learning. You need to be prepared to take risks and have confidence to do what you see is necessary in your class It's that skill to have the power of your own conviction, to create the right environment and know where you want to go....What I got at the end of the year was phenomenal in terms of children's response, but I had to take risks, not just stick to papers and worksheets, and be prepared to follow the needs of the children at certain times.

Other research, such as Woods (1995) and Woods and Jeffrey (1996), has documented the skill and creativity of teachers in protecting their values, imagination and engagement with pupils *despite* the National Curriculum and other requirements. Common to all these accounts of creative teaching is the ability to make choices, to be adaptable and flexible, to see alternatives, although working within constraints, and to have the confidence and motivation to put values into practice. These teachers were able to resist pressures to become technicians carrying out the dictates of others and to avoid the trap of 'over-conscientiousness' (Campbell et al., 1993).

Examples of such developments have also been documented by other related studies such as Richards (1998), who refers to the 'confident domestication' of the National Curriculum in small rural primary schools, with a pragmatic adaptation of policy directives to their own particular classrooms. Assessment understanding and expertise have grown (Gipps et al., 1995; Torrance and Pryor, 1998). Nixon et al. (1997) also refer to the emergence of a 'new professional' whose values and practices represent a creative incorporation of new requirements into core professional values. Hargreaves (1994) links this to organisational development.

However, in some cases teachers' experience of an often more autocratic school management produced 'contrived collegiality' (Hargreaves, 1991) and a contractual, rather than a professional, engagement. This was particularly the case when collaboration was managerially imposed in a 'top-down' way and was centred on producing documentation and paper-work rather than collaboration more directly related to teaching. These teachers were 'collaborating under constraint' (Woods et al., 1997) and often felt that the enforced requirement to attend constant meetings and take part in 'managed collaborative cultures' (Webb and Vulliamy, 1996, 2006) was threatening their strong sense of moral, personal and professional responsibility to the children in their class. Other studies, such as that of Menter et al. (1996), have talked of teachers' 'fragmented identity', torn between a model of a responsible and accountable professional and private experiences of bitterness, anxiety and overload. A number of researchers have related the erosion of primary school teachers' commitment to their repositioning and commodification within a more managerial labour process (Ozga, 2000).

Overall we found that where the individual teacher, or the school as a whole, lacked the confidence to engage in the 'creative mediation' of external policy directives, or where individual or personal circumstances made this difficult, the picture was likely to be one of conflict, stress and disillusion. Thus, whilst some teachers were able to generate a creative response to the new, very challenging educational environment, others, often for reasons to do with personal biographies or the challenges posed by particular pupil intakes, were depressed and disheartened by it. These tended to be older, more experienced teachers who objected to new requirements on principle, or found it difficult to revise their professional values and educational practices. However, a key variable in the capacity to cope with change was found to be confidence, both in terms of each individual teacher's professional skills and knowledge and more generally as a person. Some just could not cope, for instance, with greater subject knowledge requirements. Others, skilful, knowledgeable, committed and confident, simply became tired of the struggle or were unwilling to compromise. Many experienced teachers and headteachers took early retirement or left the profession under sickness schemes. Whilst the reconfiguration of the profession has continued through new training, appraisal and pay structures, our evidence showed that younger or more recently trained teachers accommodated to the new structures and requirements and began to take them for granted as 'the way things are'. This trend appears to have continued. Recent research on teachers and professional status has shown an increasing acceptance and accommodation by teachers to many central government directives (Hargreaves et al., 2007).

Although teachers in England have traditionally believed more strongly in their professional autonomy than teachers in many other countries (Broadfoot et al., 1993), the research evidence suggests that 'creative mediation' is a feature of teaching as a profession which transcends national and cross-cultural differences. Darmanin (1990) and Hargreaves (1994) provide evidence of this in Malta and Canada, respectively. In France, for example, following imposed reform teachers talked of the need to 'internalize the changes, to be selective', and of the importance of 'taking the best from the reforms, but using their own judgement in the end' (Osborn, 1996). This is not restricted to the Western world. Angeline Barrett (2005) has shown how teachers working in the low-income context of sub-Saharan Africa construct their professional identity in relation to their working context. In particular the teachers in Barrett's study saw their social identity and professional responsibilities as being co-constructed and shared with parents, the local community and education administration. Like teachers in many high income countries, they tended to mediate and adapt the implementation of new policies and educational ideas according to their educational values and their particular contemporary situation and circumstances.

Classroom Practice

Returning to the PACE study, over the eight years of reform it documented, the powerful combination of National Curriculum directives and public rhetoric on the one hand, and national assessment and OFSTED inspection requirements on the other (Jeffrey and Woods, 1996), left little room for individual teachers or schools to redefine what was to be learned, when and to what standard. Discretion concerning time, space and control over the content of learning was increasingly denied to both teachers and pupils. Indeed, the progressive reduction of both teacher and learner autonomy is arguably the most pervasive and significant result of the policy agenda of multiple reforms of the late 1980s and 1990s.

The findings of the PACE research documented a clear shift away from teacher commitment to 'constructivist' models of learning, towards new understandings framed by a perception of teaching and learning in terms of the delivery and incorporation of an established body of knowledge. Whilst important continuities with the past should be acknowledged (Alexander, 1997, 2004), the evidence suggests that there were also significant changes in classroom practice.

The PACE study found a situation in which the curriculum was increasingly strongly 'classified', in Bernstein's sense of an explicit division between subjects

(Bernstein, 1996). Classrooms were also increasingly strongly 'framed', in that teachers' discretion over how to teach was progressively diminishing and this structuring was being relayed on to pupils. Finally, assessment was becoming increasingly categoric, regular and high-stakes as requirements for accountability and performance measures became more prominent and explicit.

The potential effects of the trend towards whole-class teaching, teacher instruction, subject timetabling and ability grouping were thus reinforced by an assessment system which increasingly commodified achievement, shifting the educational balance in favour of cognition rather than an affective dimension, and emphasised product rather than process. The result is an increasingly pressured classroom life, permeated by an instrumental focus on pupil performance (Osborn et al., 2000;Pollard et al., 2000).

It would be wrong to assume, however, that the picture of change has simply been one of teachers accommodating to the requirements placed upon them. Policy initiatives are not translated wholesale into school and classroom practice, but rather are subject to a series of mediations which are the product of successive interpretations and reinterpretations of them by actors at various levels of the system (Ball, 1994). Osborn et al. (2000) also highlights the way in which teachers had become 'policy-makers in practice' striving in particular to protect their pupils from what they perceived to be the worst effects of recent policy changes. They also document a range of changes and strategies at school level.

In seeking to understand teachers' different responses to recent policy initiatives and the significance of these differences, the issue of professional motivation is crucial. The PACE research documented the gradual movement from a covenant-based professionalism, linked to *intrinsic* satisfaction, to a contractual, performance-based motivation, driven by the demands of external accountability and assessment. We hypothesised that this is likely to lead to a decline in teachers' sense of moral, self-imposed accountability and commitment. Although largely indefinable, such facets of professionalism are nevertheless fundamentally important and have a significant effect on the quality of the classroom experience of *pupils* (Pollard et al., 2000).

The diagram which follows summarises this discussion of the significance of these policy initiatives set in motion in the England of the late 1980s and 1990s for the nature and quality of teachers' professional motivation and practice. The diagram characterises this shift from a 'professional covenant' model of teaching based on personal and individual accountability and responsibility which sees teachers as facilitators of individual learning to one which is based on 'performance' which emphasises defined outcomes and prescribed bodies of knowledge.

Thus recent years have witnessed increasing central specification of the range of competencies to be achieved in Initial Teacher Training and hence, of the 'inputs' to the education system. They have witnessed too, the growing powers of OFSTED (Office for Standards in Education) and the imposition of a comprehensive inspection system based on a framework that defines what constitutes 'quality' in educational 'processes'. Last but not least, teachers are subject to the control of externally imposed definitions of 'outputs' through the publication of league tables of pupil results. Moreover, as has already been suggested, the system of 'performance management' now in place in schools, with radical reforms to teachers' pay and career structure, are also based on the assumption that it is both possible and desirable to judge an individual teacher's performance in relation to explicit criteria. Thus teachers, like pupils, are increasingly being required to respond to a 'performance'-oriented system of education based on external measures of quality. Both teachers' working lives and pupils' learning experiences are increasingly the subject of formal, 'categorical' assessments.

Table 1 displays some of these issues in contrastive ways for analytic purposes, although of course the situation is more complex than this device allows.

Table 1 Contrasting 'professional covenant' and 'performance' models of teaching (Adapted from Osborn et al., 2000)

	'Professional covenant model'	'Contractual performance' model'
Management style	'Invisible management' with relative professional autonomy	'Visible management' with relative professional regulation
Organisational form	Professional, with flat management structure. Control through self-regulation, socialisation and internalisation of norms	Mechanistic, with hierarchical structure and bureaucracy. Standardisation for control and co-ordination
Management style	Collegiate, with emphasis on proficiency, dialogue and consensus. Informality in relationships	Managerial, with emphasis on efficiency and target setting for results. Greater formality in relationships
Teacher roles	Teachers as facilitators, with affective dimensions seen as intrinsic to the teaching role	Teachers as instructors and evaluators, with emphasis on cognitive and managerial skills
Teacher professionalism	Professional covenant based on trust, and commitment to education as a form of personal development. Confidence and sense of fulfilment and spontaneity in teaching	Professionalism as the fulfilment of a contract to deliver education, which is seen as a commodity for individuals and a national necessity for economic growth. Less confidence, fulfilment and spontaneity in teaching
Teacher accountability	Personal and 'moral' accountability	External and contractual accountability, backed by inspection
Whole school co-ordination	Relative autonomy and informal teacher collaboration	Formal school planning with 'managed' collegiality
Economic costs	Expensive, because of sophisticated teacher education and time-consuming school practices	Cheaper, because of more explicit teacher training and systematised school practices

Although this diagram is based on the PACE data, recent studies of teachers have also found teachers talking of a lack of trust in teachers, and a feeling of being'undervalued' by government. Teachers' comments in a 2007 study of teacher status frequently referred to 'targets, testing, SATs or OFSTED' as being associated with the low status of teachers. One teacher commented:

> The continuous reform since the 80s has undermined teachers and the status of the profession. The constant pressure to 'do better' has made both teachers and the public perceive teaching as a failing profession.
>
> (Hargreaves et al., 2007: 114).

Thus teachers, especially in England, have become subject to a growing 'performance' model of practice, which seeks to govern not only the inputs and processes but also the outputs of education (McNess et al., 2003). These pressures operate to a greater or lesser extent in other European countries and are likely to become more intense (Elliott, 1996; Levin, 1998). Elliott (1996: 16) argues that this new emphasis on 'performativity' as a policy device is not simply, or even mainly, about raising standards, but rather plays a central role in: *changing the rules which shape educational thought and practice... part of a language game which serves the interests of power and legitimates those interests in terms of the performativity criterion.* There is already evidence that this 'policy epidemic' will continue to spread to other national systems with issues of effectiveness and performance becoming more prominent (Van zanten, 2000; Klette, 2002; Rasmussen, 2000).

However the teachers in the various studies I have reported above were not simply the passive victims of imposed educational reform. They had the potential to actively, and creatively, mediate policy change and in some cases to adapt, change or subvert it. As we have seen, there is evidence of teachers seizing the potential for a margin of manoeuvre between centralized policy change and its implementation to become "creative mediators" of policy change (Osborn et al., 2000), developing professionally as a result. Recent research has also suggested that teachers attitudes to government reform have softened compared to earlier cohorts as new school systems have became 'bedded down' (Hargreaves et al., 2007). There are signs that teachers perceive their status as higher than in recent years, even though centralised control is perceived to have increased. These teachers still see as central elements of their professional identity not only the traditional aspects associated with classroom teaching but also an 'extended' dimension (Hoyle, 2001) going beyond the classroom to 'external collaborations and partnerships, CPD and research' (Hargreaves: 94).

Both these and other studies suggest that teachers' response to imposed policy change is multi-faceted and complex. They indicate the extent to which differences in teacher values and expectations of their work are reinforced by policy and practice and "embedded" in particular policy contexts (McLaughlin and Talbert, 1993). Thus externally imposed requirements are mediated by the perceptions, understandings, motivation and capacity of both individual and groups of teachers in different contexts to produce particular practices and actions. Although the danger is great that in the long-term the prevailing 'performance culture' may shape individual teachers' views of themselves and silence alternative voices concerning other goals for education it is still the case that policy change is unlikely to be achieved by the imposition of centrally derived directives alone and that genuine reform needs to engage and challenge teachers' own values so that they become part of the reform process.

Conclusion

This chapter has documented the effect of increasing managerialism on the work of the teacher in England and demonstrates the pressures which have shifted the teachers' role from relatively autonomous semi-professional towards that of skilled worker with technical expertise or 'new professional', depending on whose perception is foremost. It is unquestionable however, that the recent reforms in England have required teachers to respond to a "performance"-orientated system of education based on external measures of quality.

Thus teachers' working lives are increasingly subject to formal "categorical" assessments. As I have shown here, it is appropriate to recognise that these tensions are not confined to one country although they find their more extreme expression in the English case. This body of research also shows how much of what it means to be a teacher or a pupil is socially and culturally constructed and how teacher identity becomes defined and re-defined in different settings.

Recent government directives in England raise the question again of how far we are moving to a common notion of the 'European teacher', and perhaps, by extension the 'European pupil'. Teachers' work in England, as defined by government policy, has already changed dramatically as a result of the school workforce agreement (2003) and recent government directives on CPD and performance management (2007) and looks set to change still further, bringing teachers' work closer to the French model, which is similar to those in Belgium, Italy, Spain and Portugal. By contrast, in Denmark and in other Scandinavian countries (and to a lesser extent in the Netherlands) teachers still have a wide range of duties and are encouraged to take a "holistic" approach. Sometimes, as in Denmark, they remain as class teachers of the same group of children for some years and know them and their families well.

Our research suggests that, in spite of pressures to Europeanisation and globalisation, and increasingly common educational policies and pressures towards a 'performance' culture for teachers and pupils, there are distinctive cultural and historical traditions which will lead to policies being interpreted and mediated differently by teachers. We need to understand the importance and complexity of teachers' response in any policy change. As Hargreaves et al. (2007) suggest, more could be done by government 'treating teachers as professionals, respecting their expertise, consulting with them on policy formation, reducing the external control to which teachers feel they are subject and, in particular, by making it clear to teachers that they are trusted professionals' (Hargreaves et al., 2007: 98). We need to think more carefully about the characteristics of a 'learning individual', whether teacher or pupil, who is ready, willing and able to go on learning throughout life, and whether current policy changes look likely to achieve this. Significantly we have to decide what we want our teachers to be and what kind of learners we want to develop, and to work with schools to achieve this. These are issues to which Eric Hoyle's research has contributed an unusual depth and breadth of insight and understanding and for which other educational researchers owe him a great deal.

References

Acker, S. (1999) *The Realities of Teachers' Work: Never a Dull Moment.* London: Cassell.

Alexander, R. (1997) *Policy and Practice in Primary Education.* London: Routledge.

Alexander, R. (2004) Still no pedagogy? Principle, pragmatism and compliance in primary education. *Cambridge Journal of Education,* 34(1), 7–33.

Ball, S.J. (1994) *Education Reform: A Critical and Post-structural Approach.* Buckingham, UK: Open University Press.

Ball, S.J. (1999) *Educational Reform and the Struggle for the Soul of the Teacher!* Hong Kong: The Chinese University of Hong Kong.

Barrett, A. (2005) Teacher accountability in context: Tanzanian primary school teachers' perceptions of local community and education administration. *Compare,* 35(1), March, 43–61.

Bernstein, B. (1996) *Pedagogy, Symbolic Control and Identity.* London: Taylor & Francis.

Broadfoot, P., Osborn, M., Gilly, M. and Bucher, A. (1993) *Perceptions of Teaching: Primary School Teachers in England and France.* London: Cassell.

Campbell, J. (1996) *Professionalism in the Primary School,* papers presented at ASPE Conference.

Campbell, J., Emery, H. and Stone, C. (1993) *The Broad and Balanced Curriculum at Key Stage 2: Some Limitations on Reform,* paper given at the BERA Annual Conference, University of Liverpool, Liverpool, UK.

Croll, P., Abbott, D., Broadfoot, P., Osborn, M. and Pollard, A. (1994) Teachers and educational policy: Roles and models. *British Journal of Educational Studies,* 42(2), 333–347.

Darmanin, M. (1990) Maltese primary school teachers' experience of centralised policies. *British Journal of Sociology of Education,* 11(3), 275–308.

DfEE (1997) *White Paper: Excellence in Schools.* London: Stationery Office.

Elliott, J. (1996) Quality assurance, the educational standards debate, and the commodification of educational research. *Curriculum Journal,* 8(6), 63–83.

Galton, M., Hargreaves, L., Comber, C., Wall, D. and Pell, A. (1999) *Inside the Primary Classroom: 20 Years On.* London: Routledge.

Gipps, C.V., Brown, M., McCallum, B. and McManus, S. (1995) *Intuition or Evidence? Teachers and National Assessment of Seven-Year-Olds.* Buckingham, UK: Open University Press.

Hargreaves, A. (1991) Contrived collegiality: The micro-politics of teacher collaboration, in Bennett et al. (eds.) *Managing Change in Education.* London: Chapman/Open University.

Hargreaves, A. (1994) *Changing Teachers, Changing Times: Teachers' Work and Culture in the Post-modern Age.* London: Cassell.

Hargreaves, L., Cunningham, M., Hansen, A., McIntryre, D., Oliver, C. and Pell, T. (2007) *The Status of Teachers and the Teaching Profession in England: Views from Inside and Outside the Profession, Final Report of the Teacher Status Project.* Nottingham, UK: DfES Publications.

Helsby, G. and McCulloch, G. (eds.) (1997) *Teachers and the National Curriculum.* London: Cassell.

Hoyle, E. (1974) Professionality, professionalism and control in teaching. *London Educational Review,* 3(2), 13–19.

Hoyle, E. (1986) *The Politics of School Management.* Sevenoaks, UK: Hodder & Stoughton.

Hoyle, E. (2000) Teaching: Prestige, status and esteem. *Educational Management and Administration,* 29(2), 139–152.

Hoyle, E. and John, P. (1995) *Professional Knowledge and Professional Practice*. London: Cassell.

Jackson, P.W. (1968) *Life in Classrooms*. New York: Holt, Rinehart & Winston.

Jeffrey, B. and Woods, P. (1996) Feeling deprofessionalised: The social construction of emotions during an OFSTED inspection. *Cambridge Journal of Education*, 26(3), 325–343.

Klette, K. (2002) Reform policy and teacher professionalism in four Nordic countries. *Journal of Educational Change*, 3, 265–282.

Levin, B. (1998) An epidemic of education policy: What can we learn from each other? *Comparative Education*, 34(2), 131–142.

Lorie, D. (1975) *Schoolteacher: A Sociological Study*. Chicago, IL: University of Chicago Press.

McLaughlin, M. and Talbert, J. (1993) How the world of students and teachers challenges policy coherence, in S. Fuhrman (ed.) *Designing Coherent Education Policy: Improving the System*. San Francisco, CA: Jossey-Bass.

McNess, E., Broadfoot, P. and Osborn, M. (2003) Is the effective compromising the affective? *British Educational Research Journal*, 29(2), 243–257.

Menter, I., Muschamp, Y., Nicholls, P., Ozga, J. and Pollard, A. (1997) *Work and Identity in the Primary School: A Post-Fordist Analysis*. Buckingham, UK: Open University Press.

Nias, J. (1989) *Primary Teachers Talking*. London: Routledge.

Nias, J., Southworth, G. and Yeomans, R. (1989) *Staff Relationships in the Primary School: A Study of Organisational Cultures*. London: Cassell.

Nixon, J., Martin, J., McKeown, P. and Ranson, S. (1997) Towards a learning profession: Changing codes of occupational practice within the new management of education. *British Journal of Sociology of Education*, 18(1), 5–28.

Osborn, M. (1996) Teachers mediating change: Key state 1 revisited, in P. Croll (ed.) *Teachers, Pupils and Primary Schooling*. London: Cassell.

Osborn, M., McNess, E., Broadfoot, P., with Pollard, A. and Triggs, P. (2000) *What Teachers Do: Changing Policy and Practice in English Primary Schools*. London: Cassell.

Osborn, M. (1997) Policy into practice and practice into policy: Creative mediation in the primary classroom, in G. Helsby and G. McCulloch (eds.) *Teachers and the National Curriculum*. London: Cassell.

Osborn, M., Broadfoot, P., McNess, E., Planel, C., Ravn, B., and Triggs, P. (2003) *A World of Difference? Comparing Learners Across Europe*. Maidenhead, UK: Open University Press.

Ozga, J. (2000) *Doing Research in Educational Settings: Contested Terrain*. Buckingham, UK: Open University Press.

Pollard, A. and Triggs, P., with Broadfoot, P., McNess, E. and Osborn, M. (2000) *What Pupils Say: Changing Policy and Practice in English Primary Education*. London: Cassell.

Rasmussen, J. (2000) Construction of the Danish teacher on the basis of policy documents, in K. Klette, I. Carlgren, J. Rasmussen, H. Simola and M. Sundkvist (eds.) *Restructuring Nordic Teachers: An Analysis of Policy Texts from Finland, Denmark, Sweden and Norway* (pp. 38–108), Report No 10/2000 University of Oslo, Institute of Educational Research.

Reynolds, C. (2005) No teachers left untested: Historical perspectives on teacher regulation, in N. Bascia, A. Cumming, A. Datnow, K. Leithwood and D. Livingstone (eds.) *International Handbook of Educational Policy, Part One*. Dordrecht, The Netherlands: Springer.

Reynolds, C. and Smaller, H. (1997) *Professionalism as Practice: Past and Present Struggles for Control over Teacher's Work in Canada*, paper given at 8th Conference on International Research on Teacher Thinking, October, Kiel, Germany.

Richards, C. (1998) Curriculum and pedagogy in key stage 2: A survey of policy and practice in small rural primary schools. *The Curriculum Journal*, 9(3), 319–332.

Rowan, B. (1994) Comparing teachers' work with work in other occupations: Notes on the professional status of teaching. *Educational Researcher*, Aug–Sept.

Torrance, H. and Pryor, J. (1998) *Investigating Formative Assessment: Teaching, Learning and Assessment in the Classroom*. Buckingham, UK: Open University Press.

Troman, G. (1996) The rise of the new professionals? The restructuring of primary teachers' work and professionalism. *British Journal of Sociology of Education*, 17(4), 473–487.

Training and Development Agency for Schools (2007) *CPD: National Priorities for Schools.*
van Zanten, A. (2000) L'école de la périphérie. Scolarité et ségrégation en banlieue. Paris: PUE.
Waller, W. (1932) *The sociology of teaching.* New York: Russell & Russell, Inc. Republished in 1965 by John Wiley & Sons, New York.
Webb, R. and Vulliamy, G. (1996) A deluge of directives: Conflict between collegiality and managerialism in the post-ERA primary school. *British Educational Research Journal*, 22(4), 441–445.
Webb, R. and Vulliamy, G. (1996) *Roles and Responsibilities in the Primary School: Changing Demands, Changing Practices.* Buckingham, UK: Open University Press.
Webb, R. and Vulliamy, G. (2006) *Coming Full Circle? The Impact of New Labour's Education Policies on Primary School Teachers' Work.* London: Association of Teachers and Lecturers.
Woods, P. (1995) *Creative Teachers in Primary Schools.* Buckingham, UK: Open University Press.
Woods, P. and Jeffrey, B. (1996) *Teachable Moments.* Buckingham, UK: Open University Press.
Woods, P. and Jeffrey, B. (1997) Creative teaching in the primary national curriculum, in G. Helsby and G. McCulloch (eds.) *Teachers and the National Curriculum.* London: Cassell.
Woods, P., Jeffrey, B., Troman, G. and Boyle, M. (1997) *Restructuring Schools, Reconstructing Teachers: Responding to Change in the Primary School.* Buckingham, UK: Open University Press.

Part II
Teachers and Their Development

Chapter 6
Does the Teaching Profession Still Need Universities?

John Furlong

> It is difficult to say what are the determinants of professional
> status, but university connection(s) ... are certainly not unim-
> portant... The teaching profession has valued the links with the
> universities as an important source of professional standing.
>
> Hoyle, 1982: 165

Throughout his career, a core theme running through Eric Hoyle's writing has been his concern with the development of the teaching profession. Building on the work of classic American sociologists such as Everett Hughes and D.C. Lortie, for over 30 years Hoyle has been an observer, commentator and analyst of the teaching profession in England, highlighting advances, challenges and contradictions in the profession's changing fortunes.

One factor that Hoyle has consistently seen as important in his analysis of the profession is its changing relationship with universities. From his earliest writings (Hoyle, 1974), Hoyle has considered universities important for the advancement of the teaching profession for two, closely interrelated reasons. Firstly they are important because they contribute to the process of 'professionalization'. Drawing his analysis from the sociology of the professions, Hoyle has argued that professionalization is an essentially political process; it is concerned with the advancement of the status of a profession. Because of their own status in society, a close association with universities, for initial training, for continuing professional development and for research, can therefore contribute to the political advancement of the teaching profession, helping to legitimate the status of its professional knowledge.

Secondly, universities are important because of their contribution to the development of what in 1974 he termed 'extended professionality' or later, professional development (Hoyle, 1982). Extended professionality involves teachers in increasing the breadth as well as the depth of their understanding of their own practice. According to Hoyle, extended professionality develops in two ways: it develops both through greater forms of collaboration between individual teachers and other professionals and through the changing forms of professional knowledge that come about when teachers engage with theory and research. Although Hoyle has always acknowledged that there is a highly complex relationship between university based knowledge and professional practice (see Hoyle and John, 1995, in particular), he

D. Johnson, R. Maclean (eds.), *Teaching: Professionalization,*
Development and Leadership,
© Springer Science + Business Media B.V. 2008

argues that it is through engaging with theory and research that teaching becomes increasingly seen as a rational rather than an intuitive activity; it is through such engagement that professional skills and knowledge can indeed become 'extended'.

In reality, the relationship between the teaching profession and higher education has always been fragile and unstable; there have been periods of strength followed by periods of weakness (Gardner, 1996). Nevertheless, for Hoyle, from his earliest writings, the engagement of the university sector has been central to his aspirations for the development of the teaching profession. Because of this commitment, by 1982, following a period of a relatively strong relationship between the two sectors (Wilkin, 1996), with considerable foresight, he was warning of the possible implications of the 'turn towards the practical' that he saw developing in both teacher education and research. He argued that while some sections of the profession, and particularly the government, might welcome such moves, undermining traditional links with the university sector could have considerable negative implications for the long term standing of the profession as a whole. For example, the development of

> *School-based initial teacher training could be taken as a case for actually reducing the period of institution based training. School-focused in-service training could be taken as an indication that there was no need to fund secondments, full time courses and higher degree work. The involvement of teachers in research, particularly action-research, could provide an argument for the reduction of funds for the more fundamental and more detached types of research undertaken by projects currently funded via government agencies.*

> (Hoyle, 1982: 166)

These observations, though at the time merely speculative, were indeed prescient. The intervening 25 years have seen almost all of his predictions realised. Developments in the 1990s, with the establishment of the Teacher Training Agency (now the Training and Development Agency (TDA) for Schools) with its emphasis on competences and 'standards' and the rapid expansion of new routes into teaching, mean that although many courses remain HEI-led (Furlong et al., 2000) universities are no longer seen as 'essential' partners. No longer is engagement with university-based knowledge, and especially theory, research and scholarship, seen as a key ingredient in the early professional development teachers (Furlong, 2005).

The changes to continuing professional development (CPD) were even more rapid: indeed, the reference back to secondments, full time courses and funded higher degree programmes for teachers, really is a reference to a bygone age. By the late 1980s, most of these sorts of opportunities for teachers to engage in-depth with university-based knowledge had been abolished. Today, the vast majority of CPD is provided through schools and often by schools themselves. Again, while universities may well contribute to such programmes on a regular basis (for example, through the TDA's Postgraduate Professional Development (PPD) scheme), their involvement is no longer seen as an essential component for most forms of professional development, even at the highest level – the National Professional Qualification for Head Teachers. As a consequence, we are now in the strange position where there is a flourishing demand from teachers for part time masters and doctoral degrees, often funded by teachers themselves. But full time courses have largely become the province of international students and the handful of ESRC (Economic and Social Research Council) students being trained to work as educational researchers; this now seen as a quite different profession.

The position in relation to research is more complex but no more positive. Interest in forms of applied and practice-based research, including action research, has certainly increased, although unlike Scotland (Scottish Executive, 2002) and Wales (General Teaching Council for Wales, 2007) it has yet to find a consistent place in professional development frameworks in England. But despite the growing popularity of forms of action research amongst teachers, links with universities have been piecemeal and largely voluntary in nationally sponsored schemes such as the Best Practice Scholarship Scheme (Furlong and Salisbury, 1995) and Networked Learning Communities (Campbell and Keating, 2005). As a result, there has been considerable debate about the quality and generalisability of the outcomes of such research and development work (Foster, 1999). Other pressures, most particularly from the RAE, have served to undermine the research capacity of many universities in the UK. While the numbers of higher education institutions designated as universities has expanded substantially over the last 30 years, the concentration of research funding means that now only about one third of university departments of education have the financial underpinning to support a vibrant research culture (Dadds and Kynch, 2004). One result of this and the collapse of the full time CPD market described above has been the current demographic crisis in university departments of education recently highlighted by the ESRC (Mills et al., 2006); now over 50% of current educational researchers are over the age of 50. Moreover, the government-led emphasis on 'the practical' in initial training and in CPD since the 1990s has done little to support the professionalization of research itself; as a result, criticisms of the quality of educational research in this country continue.

Overall, this formal exclusion of higher education from so many dimensions of professionalism is well captured in the TTA's 2005 document outlining their extended remit. As the renamed Training and Development Agency for Schools, they took on responsibility for overseeing all forms of initial and in-service education of teachers, and the wider school workforce. In many ways, therefore, their vision can be seen as encapsulating current national policy on the development of the teaching profession.

Our stakeholders and customers

Starting from what schools need, we will work in partnership with a range of organisations, including:

Schools, to be their first point of reference for guidance on all aspects of training and development. Head teachers and school leadership teams will be key customers

Providers of initial teacher training, to ensure the availability of good quality training that prepares teachers to join school teams

---

(continued)

> (continued)
> **New and existing contractors and suppliers,** to help us deliver the best
> possible services and achieve value for money
> **Local partners,** including local education authorities and training providers
> so that our plans and proposals support school and local priorities
> **Government and national organisations,** to coordinate existing initiatives and
> bring coherence to the introduction of new products and services

TDA (2005)

Setting aside comments on the language ('customers', 'providers', 'suppliers', etc.) what is clear is that there is no explicit reference here either to individual teachers (apart from head teachers) or to universities. The structured links between the teaching profession and the university sector that Hoyle looked for have, over the last 30 years, been almost expunged.

Given this turn of events, one is forced to ask – does it matter? Has the fact that, today, the teaching profession has a less systematic engagement with the university sector than Hoyle might aspire for, in reality undermined the development of the profession – either its professionalization or the development of individual teachers' professionality?

Of course it can be persuasively argued that the recent past has seen teachers' professionalism seriously undermined – indeed Hoyle (1995) himself has argued that being professional has been reduced in scope to being an 'effective service deliverer'. We have seen new forms of managerialism including the dramatically increased emphasis on institutional and personal performativity (Ball, 2003) that comes about with increased specification of service demands and ever more sophisticated forms of performance data; the growing balkanization of teachers where teachers' traditional outward orientations to 'the profession' are replaced by narrow, more inward looking forms of competition (Hargreaves, 1994); and growing intervention by the Government into pedagogy itself through a range of different prescribed 'national strategies' – for literacy, for numeracy and for Key Stage 3.

On the other hand, while it remains the case that teaching is no nearer being recognised as a 'full profession' than in the past, on a par with say medicine or law, one could argue that the status of teaching, particularly in recent years under New Labour, has increased significantly. Certainly the popularity of teaching as a career has improved: current concerns are about the oversupply of newly qualified teachers rather than about crises of recruitment. In addition, the conditions of teaching have improved substantially: staff student ratios have been reduced with over 20,000 additional teachers in post in England since 1997; there is higher pay, for beginning teachers and especially for senior teachers; and workforce remodelling has meant far more classroom support than in the past with teachers taking on new responsibilities for managing classroom assistants and, with the Every Child Matters agenda, working directly with a range of other professionals.

In addition, there are now substantial opportunities for new forms of extended professionality through networking. Virtually every government-led initiative (from Training Schools to Trust Schools, from Advanced Skills Teachers to the Excellence in Cities programme) now includes the requirement that teachers themselves will work collaboratively with others in their own school and beyond in order to support the development and dissemination of good practice (Reid et al., 2004). And schools themselves are expected to take lead responsibility in assessing and responding to their staff's professional development needs, where appropriate 'purchasing' professional development opportunities from a wide range of providers – Local Authorities, private consultants and universities. On the surface at least it would seem that government policy has taken seriously David Hargreaves' plea for the development of the 'knowledge creating school', where schools take the lead in their own development, where there is a high volume of internal debate and professional networking, where there are regular opportunities for reflection, enquiry and dialogue and where there is a culture of 'no blame' experimentation and challenge (Hargreaves, 2003).

Teachers certainly experience a very different world from the one that Hoyle was commenting on in the early 1980s and most of these developments have been achieved in ways that specifically exclude the university sector in any systematic way. Does this then mean that the teaching profession does not need the university sector any more, either politically in terms of professionalization or in terms of developing teachers' professionality? Has teaching, through strong and detailed government intervention, started to find a different way of increasing its professional standing in society? I, and I suspect Hoyle himself, would suggest not.

In the remainder of this paper I will argue that, while there have been some improvements in the professionality of some teachers and indeed in the standing of the profession as a whole, overall, its position remains deeply contradictory; there are still significant barriers to teaching being seen as a full profession, barriers which a proper engagement with higher education could assist in overcoming. A proper engagement with higher education offers, I will suggest, not merely political advantage in terms of some kind of reflected status, but a genuine status, derived from extended professionality both at the individual and at the collective level of teaching as a whole. And I will also argue that now, following two decades of 'the turn to the practical', despite the real challenges involved, the opportunity is there for the teaching profession to engage with universities in new and more productive ways than in the past.

Research

At the most general level, teaching needs good research to support good policy and practice. Although there is widespread scepticism that research findings can be used directly to guide the action of policy makers or practitioners, there is now a growing commitment to the view that research should be part of a 'policy cycle', entering into that cycle in a number of different ways. Different forms of research can, for example, be used as part of policy planning: putting issues on the policy agenda; helping policy makers recognise their current and future information requirements; reviewing what is already known. It can also be part of policy development: piloting new initiatives; developing specialised policy instruments, for example, new forms of assessment, specialised curriculum materials. And it has a role in policy evaluation: finding out what worked, what did not work; linking past experience back to further policy planning.

As Selby-Smith (2000) demonstrated in his study of policy making in vocational education in Australia:

> The policy process is characterised by a number of stages (and) research of different types can potentially play a part at each stage. (research can be used in)...problem identification and agenda setting, (or) linked with the subsequent policy formulation phase...Research can also contribute at the evaluation phase, which provides opportunities for programme fine-tuning and adjustment to changing circumstances
>
> (Selby-Smith, 2000: 3)

The role of the universities remains essential here although, as has already been indicated, there are major challenges in terms of research capacity, training, demography, etc. Moreover, despite significant improvements, there remain concerns about the quality of some educational research. What is clear, however, is that the production of high quality, policy-oriented research does serve to increase the professionalism of teaching. It does this both through its contribution to the status of the field – its professionalization – and by increasing the depth and breadth of knowledge available to individual teachers – to their professionality. At the broadest level, therefore, the teaching profession does have an interest in the maintenance and development of high quality research in the field of education.

School-Led Research and Development

But despite the importance of educational research, the truth is that, for the most part, the development of educational policy, and particularly the development of practice, does not happen through formal research. As I have already indicated, contemporary policy to a significant degree sees schools themselves as the power-houses of innovation and development – working within national frameworks, but increasingly taking responsibility for their own development.

But is it true that school-led research and development does not need higher education? Or, to put it more modestly, does higher education have nothing to offer here? A number of different initiatives have been piloted in recent years to support school-led research and development, most notably the Networked Learning Communities initiative (2002–2006) in which 134 school networks took part, and the Best Practice Research Scholarship Scheme (BPRS). The BPRS scheme, sponsored by the DfES, ran from 2000 to 2004 during which time over 3,000 teachers were awarded a small grant of up to £3,000 to undertake research and development in relation to their own teaching. The grant money was to be spent on a range of activities in support of their research, including the opportunity to buy mentoring support. They could if they chose purchase mentoring support from higher education, but that was not mandatory.

In 2002–2003, I and colleagues from Cardiff University (Furlong and Salisbury, 2005) undertook an evaluation of the BPRS scheme on behalf of the DfES. During our evaluation, we were struck by the similarities between what we saw happening and what Michael Gibbons and colleagues (Gibbons et al., 1994) characterise as 'the new production of knowledge'. Very much in line with the concept of the 'knowledge creating school', they argue that universities, for so long the home of science, are no longer the only places in modern societies where knowledge is produced. Rather, Gibbons et al argue, the growing demand for specialist knowledge in our increasingly technical society and the expansion of the numbers of potential knowledge producers (as a result of the massification of higher education) mean that in many sectors of society (including schools), conditions are now set for the emergence of a new model of knowledge production – what they call Mode 2.

Mode 2 knowledge, they suggest, will be more transitory, more context specific, more frequently located within individuals themselves and their particular working context than in scientific journals. In short, it is, at least in part, 'embedded' knowledge. The criteria for judging its quality, they argue, must also be different; they must include judgments about its impact on practice and its impact on practitioners themselves.

During our evaluation we witnessed many impressive school-based initiatives which took on the characteristics of 'Mode 2' knowledge production; teachers were undertaking exciting and valuable research and development projects, many of which had a real impact on their own practice and that of others in their schools.

But however exciting the scheme was, we also noticed that projects were hugely variable in quality. Too many teachers, we observed, did not read or read too narrowly or uncritically before designing their studies; as a result, they were constantly reinventing the wheel. Another common weakness was that many teachers were not sceptical enough about their own research findings. Too often, relatively modest findings from very small scale interventions were taken as justifications for quite significant changes in practice. A further tension was that, because of the commitment to context specific development, in many respects a real strength, the opportunities for dissemination and the accumulation of knowledge were severely restricted.

What we came to recognize during our evaluation was that, despite the obvious strengths of school-led research and development, if it was to be of good quality, and to contribute to knowledge beyond its specific context, it should not happen alone. If we are to be confident in this approach to research and development, teachers and schools not only need linking with each other; they also need linking with those in higher education and elsewhere who are themselves experienced researchers, who have a wide knowledge and experience of using of high quality research strategies and a breadth and depth knowledge of current research studies that are relevant to practice. This is not to suggest that as, perhaps in the past, those in universities should be in the lead; one of the great strengths of the BPRS and similar schemes is that it puts teachers themselves in the driving seat. It is however to suggest that a proper national system that supports school-led research and development does need to develop supportive partnerships between teachers, schools and those in higher education. One of the weaknesses of the BPRS scheme and indeed the much larger Networked Learning Communities scheme was that this was not mandatory (Campbell and Keating, 2005). Whether those weaknesses are now being addressed by the TDA's more recent Postgraduate Professional Development programme remains to be seen, although there are some positive signs (TDA, 2007a).

Professional Education – Initial Teacher Training

Another dimension in the 'turn to the practical' noted by Hoyle concerns initial teacher education, or what is now in England firmly called initial teacher training. Here there have been major changes. In the course of one generation we have moved from a position where universities and university-based knowledge dominated training to a position where practical training in schools is now virtually the exclusive focus of the professional preparation process. In many ways, schools are now in the lead in initial teacher training and rightly so. Even in courses formally provided by universities, students spend a majority of their time in school; and the current curriculum, which is strongly centrally prescribed, means that the focus of courses is almost exclusively on practical work in schools, even when students are based in the university. For the universities, the transition to this school-based model of training was a painful one with the sector having to learn to be much more modest about its potential contribution. Personally, I believe that in broad measure the transition has been right.

But do we now need universities at all here? As indicated above, the government does not appear to think so. The establishment of the Graduate Teaching Programme (where schools can recruit and train their own teachers) now accounts for about 13% of training places a year and the continuing role of entirely schools-led schemes (School Centred Initial Teacher Training schemes) makes it clear that they do not see universities as essential. Universities might be practically useful in terms of organising training programmes but they do not add anything distinctive; they have nothing 'essential' to offer. And after 15 years of the school-based model, and the designation of more than 240 schools as specialist Training Schools, more and more teachers might well agree with them (Brooks, 2006). Moreover, the development of standards, which now in their latest iteration (TDA, 2007b) have been written so that they are compatible with 'the whole school workforce', further marginalises university-based knowledge. The standards, although apparently common, can be achieved in so many different ways on different types of training programme, and by different sorts of professional, that the distinctive knowledge base of teachers as professionals is obscured, marginalised.

I would suggest that what schools contribute to initial training is vitally important; it is central. But however good it is, on its own it is not enough in the launching of a new professional in his or her career. Indeed, to think so is to fall prey to a peculiarly narrow form of English pragmatism. Such an approach would be unthinkable elsewhere in Europe – where it is assumed that before even entering professional training students must have high level academic qualifications. In many countries – Italy, Denmark – a Masters degree in a curriculum subject is necessary before candidates can even apply for training; and in France, trainees take the equivalent of a Masters in education – studying theories of pedagogy and the didactics of their subject – before they begin their year's highly practical training. The fact that the teaching profession is held in higher regard in these countries than in England is perhaps no coincidence. I would not suggest that these more academic models are themselves perfect, but are we so confident that we think we have nothing to learn from them? Can genuinely professional initial preparation really be achieved entirely 'on the job'?

As Hirst (1996) has argued, however important practical work in school, however central it must be in the design of our programmes, new teachers also need to be exposed to 'the best that is known' in terms of teaching and learning in their area of specialism. Surely that is our duty as professionals ourselves involved in preparing those who are going to follow us? That must imply some role for professional preparation that goes beyond the specifics of working in this school with these pupils on this scheme of work.

I would also suggest that young professionals need to ask not only how to do something but also 'why'. Schools are not necessarily the best places to ask 'why' questions; they are not seminars, they are about taking action. Asking 'why', questioning, challenging, critiquing – these activities are central to what a university is. Just as universities never could provide effective practical training in learning to teach – it was not their essential purpose – so I would argue that schools are not the best place for introducing new teachers 'to the best that is known' and to the critique of current practice. All of these elements are essential, I would argue, in the highest quality professional education; that is why the notion of partnership is so important. But for this to be achieved, the notion of 'partnership' needs to be seen not as it has become for the TDA, a mere organisational principle. Rather it needs to be seen as an epistemological principle which recognises the different forms of knowledge – some of which are indeed contradictory and in tension – that young professionals should master (Furlong et al., 2006).

Professional Education – Continuing Professional Development

One might make similar arguments about CPD. The development of school-based and school-led CPD over the last generation has been hugely important. It has allowed schools to take the leading role in further professional training. In my view this has strengthened the profession significantly, made the teaching profession and individual schools more confident that they are able to contribute to the development of their own profession instead of simply relying on others. The linking of CPD to national strategies also makes sense. We have moved a long way in the last generation from a position when CPD was something that was defined and led by the university sector and from when the learning needs of individual teachers were always put before the learning needs of schools. As the incoming Labour Government stated over 10 years ago: 'The time has long gone when isolated unaccountable professionals made curriculum and pedagogical decisions alone, without reference to the outside world' (DFEE, 1998:14). We cannot and should not return to those earlier times. As Elmore (2002) reminds us, the demands of institutional accountability will not go away; it is because of this that professional education and indeed professional responsibility must be aligned at the personal, institutional and formal level. The emergence of schools as the key focus and provider of contemporary CPD is no coincidence; it is a natural and appropriate response to increased forms of institutional accountability.

But again one must ask, is CPD offered by schools themselves, by local authorities and by private training providers all that the profession needs? Surely teachers, at some points in their career, have a right to opt for forms of CPD on their terms, not on terms defined by the government or by their head teachers. One of the reasons that the BPRS and the current PPD schemes are so popular, and unleash such energy, is precisely because they have encouraged teachers to define their own learning needs within school and national priorities. In addition, just like students in initial training, experienced teachers also need to do more than share their experience with fellow practitioners; they also need opportunities to engage with 'the best that is known' and on some occasions to step outside what they are doing and ask the question 'why?'

What is needed in CPD is something equivalent to the best partnerships we have established in initial training. Schools, rather than universities, need to be centrally in control of defining their own learning needs. They also need to be key contributors to training itself: focusing training in the specific context of the school; sharing good practice through networking – these are all extremely valuable strategies for making CPD worthwhile both for individual teachers and for schools. But schools also need to be able to draw on what universities have to offer – not merely as a service provider, not merely on a piecemeal, voluntary basis – but in the systematic and structured way that can only come about through formalised partnerships. Again, this is not to put universities in the lead. Far from it. Rather it is to recognise the critical if partial role they can play in supporting the highest quality in-service education that can lead to a genuine extended professionality. Moreover, there are growing numbers of examples of this approach to CPD internationally – the Australian 'Innovative Links Project' (Sachs, 1999) scheme, Huberman's (1992) work notions of 'outsiders' and 'insiders' in professional development, and closer to home the Scottish Chartered Teacher Scheme. England of course continues to experiment with such approaches, currently through the PPD programme but, like so many initiatives under New Labour, these experiments are seldom institutionalised as a right for all teachers and are often short lived. As such they seem to imply the deep ambivalence on the part of government about a form of professional education that prioritises the needs of individual teachers over those of the central state.

Conclusion

I opened this paper by referring to Hoyle's concerns, expressed in 1982, about the implications of 'the turn to the practical' in teacher education and research, and how it might serve to undermine the link between the teaching profession and universities. What I have tried to show is that Hoyle was right to be concerned; those links were and continue to be seriously undermined in a whole range of different ways. However, I have also tried to acknowledge that the turn to the practical has not been all negative in its consequences. Over the last 25 years, the teaching profession has grown substantially in terms of its confidence as a major contributor to professional learning – in initial teacher education, in CPD and in forms of school based research. Moreover, everything that we now know about the complexities of professional knowledge insists that we should indeed place 'the practical' at the heart of professional learning and development.

In comparison with other countries, this reifying of the practical in professional learning can be seen as constituting a huge 'English experiment', an experiment that, without the involvement of universities, has enhanced teachers' own sense of their professionality. While in many other arenas of professional activity, ordinary teachers have seen their opportunities for agency and professional development closed down, in the area of professional education itself there have indeed been important new opportunities.

But despite the value of this 'experiment' and despite its evident popularity with many teachers, I have also tried to demonstrate that it is not sufficient in itself. For all the possibilities of extended professionality that have come about through new responsibilities and new forms of networking, the severing of systematic engagement with universities has served to curtail what Hoyle, back in 1974, identified as the other important factor for developing extended professionality – engagement with theory, research and scholarship.

It may be that, in the long march of the profession, a 25 break away from its previous subservient relationship with those in universities was necessary for the teaching profession. Whether or not that is the case, I would suggest that the last 25 years have now put us in a position where it is possible to imagine a proper more adult relationship between the universities and the profession; a relationship that recognises and values the complexity and partiality of different forms of professional knowledge but that sees 'the practical' as needing to be in the lead. Are we ready to live with those complexities and uncertainties; are we now ready genuinely to value different forms of professional knowledge? I think so.

However, for that to happen, it is clear to me that teachers in England do need to be given the opportunity, once again, to engage in systematic and sustained ways with universities – in their initial training, in their CPD and in forms of school-based research and development. Not, as I have tried to argue, in old ways, where universities take the lead, but in new collaborative partnerships where those in schools can draw effectively for themselves on the forms of knowledge and can critique that which universities have to offer.

What an adult and systematic engagement with universities could now give the teaching profession is help in increasing professionalization in genuine ways – not merely, as in the past, through reflected status, but through the development of new, richer and deeper forms of profession knowledge; knowledge that is genuinely grounded in the practice of teaching. It is this, I would suggest that would help to extend teachers' professionality; it is this, I would suggest that would help to raise the status of the teaching profession as a whole even further.

References

Ball, S.J. (2003) 'The teacher's soul and the terrors of performativity', *Journal of Education Policy*, 18(2), 215–228

Brooks, V. (2006) 'A 'quiet revolution'? The impact of Training Schools on initial teacher training partnerships', *Journal of Education for Teaching*, 32(4), 379–393

Campbell, A. and Keating, I. (2005) *Shotgun Weddings, Arranged Marriages or Love Matches: An Investigation of Networked Learning Communities and Higher Education Partnerships*. BERA Conference, University of Glamorgan, Wales, UK

Dadds, M. and Kynch, C. (2004) *The Impact of RAE 3b Rating on Educational Research in Teacher Education Departments*, British Educational Research Association. www.bera.ac. uk/publications/op.php

DfEE (1998) *Teachers: Meeting the Challenge of Change*. London: DfEE

Elmore, R. (2002) *Bridging the Gap Between Standards and Achievement: Report on the Imperative for Professional Development in Education*. Albert Shanker Institute. http://www. shankerinstitute.org/Downloads/Bridging_Gap.pdf

Foster, P. (1999) 'Never mind the quality, feel the impact: a methodological assessment of teacher research sponsored by the Teacher Training Agency', *British Journal of Educational Studies*, 47(4), 380–398

Furlong J. (2005) 'New labour and teacher education: the end of an era?', *Oxford Review of Education*, 31(1), 119–134

Furlong, J. and Salisbury, J. (2005) 'Best practice research scholarships: an evaluation', *Research Papers in Education*, 20(1), 45–83

Furlong, J., Barton, L., Miles, S., Whiting, C. and Whitty, G. (2000) *Teacher Education in Transition: Re-forming professionalism?* Buckingham, UK: Open University Press

Furlong, J., Campbell, A., Howson, J., Lewis, S. and McNamara, O. (2006) 'Partnership in English initial teacher education: changing times, changing definitions. Evidence from the Teacher Training Agency National Partnership Project'. *Scottish Educational Review*, 37(1), 32–45

Gardner, P. (1996) 'Higher education and teacher training: a century of progress and promise' in Furlong, J. and Smith, R. (eds) *The Role of Higher Education in Initial Teacher Training*. London: Kogan Page

General Teaching Council for Wales (2007) http://www.gtcw.org.uk/documents/framework/ Strand_3–4_Framework.pdf

Gibbons, M. et al. (1994) *The New Production of Knowledge: The Dynamics of Science and Research in Contemporary Societies*. London: Sage

Hargreaves, A. (1994) *Changing Teachers, Changing Times*. London: Cassell

Hargreaves, D. (2003) *Education Epidemic: Transforming Secondary Schools Through Innovation Networks*. London: Demos

Hoyle, E. (1974) 'Professionality, professionalism and control in teaching', *London Educational Review*, 3, 3–19

Hoyle, E. (1982) 'The professionalisation of teaches: a paradox', *British Journal of Educational Studies*, 30(2), 161–171

Hoyle, E. (1995) 'Changing concepts of a profession' in Busher, H. and Saran, R. (eds) *Managing Teachers as Professionals in Schools*. London: Kogan Page

Hoyle, E. and John, P. (1995) *Professional Knowledge and Professional Practice*. London: Cassell

Huberman, M. (1992) *Linking the Practitioner and Research Communities for School Improvement*. Address to the International Congress for School Effectiveness and Improvement, Victoria, BC.

Hirst, P. (1996) 'The demands of professional practice and preparation for teachers' in Furlong, J. and Smith, R. (eds) *The Role of Higher Education in Initial Teacher Training*. London: Kogan Page

Mills, D. et al. (2006) *Demographic Review of the Social Sciences*. Swindon, UK: ESRC

Reid, I., Brain, K. and Comerford Boyes, L. (2004) 'Teachers or learning leaders? Where have all the teachers gone? Gone to be leaders everyone', *Educational Studies*, 30(3), 251–264

Sachs, J. (1999) 'Using teacher research as a basis for professional renewal', *Journal of In-Service Education*, 25(1), 39–53

Scottish Executive (2002) http://www.scotland.gov.uk/Publications/2002/12/15833/14074

Selby-Smith, C. (2000) 'The relationship between research and decision-making in education: an empirical investigation', in Department of Education, Training and Youth Agency (eds) *The Impact of Educational Research* Canberra, Australia: DETYA http://www.detya.gov.au/highered/respubs/impact/overview.htm

TDA (2005) *Making a Difference to Every Child's Life: The Teacher Training Agency's Extended Remit*. London: TDA

http://www.tda.gov.uk/upload/resources/pdf/t/ttacorescript-layout2copy.pdf

TDA (2007a) *Postgraduate Professional Development Programme –Impact Evaluation Report*. London: TDA

http://www.tda.gov.uk/upload/resources/pdf/p/ppd_impact_report_march_2007.pdf

TDA (2007b) *Draft Professional Standards for Teachers in England*. London: TDA http://www.tda.gov.uk/upload/resources/pdf/d/draft_revised_standards_framework_jan_2007.pdf

Wilkin, M. (1996) *Initial Teacher Training: The Dialogue of Ideology and Culture*. London: Falmer

Chapter 7
Professional Development for School Improvement: Are Changing Balances of Control Leading to the Growth of a New Professionalism?

Agnes McMahon

Introduction

The main purpose in this chapter is to reflect on the strategies that have been adopted by successive governments in England to encourage, support and provide continuing professional development (CPD) for teachers and headteachers and to consider whether these strategies have led to the emergence of a new teacher professionalism. Policy makers have been increasingly concerned to identify and use mechanisms to influence practice in schools and classrooms in order to raise standards in education. Teacher professional development has been seen as one of the key levers for change and over the years questions have been raised on a regular basis about what are appropriate processes and content for CPD and whether these issues should be decided by the teachers, Local Education Authorities or the Government. The balance of influence between these stakeholders has shifted back and forth from a position where all parties had an input into policy making to one of more central government control, which in turn has implications for teacher professionalism.

The discussion is structured in three sections corresponding to three periods in which differences in educational ideology, approaches to educational policy, and strategies of implementation can be discerned. The three sections are labelled: Partnership, New Public Management and Modernisation. These divisions and labels are somewhat arbitrary and one can argue about the boundaries between sections but I have found them a useful organising device. Partnership refers to the period when the main stakeholders all had input into educational decision-making and there was a broad consensus about the direction of policy. Typically this led to systems of structuring and managing schools which enabled teachers to have "*a degree of freedom in the exercise of professional practice*" (Hoyle, 1986: 170) and to enjoy relative autonomy. The distinction between New Public Management and Modernisation is less clear since both are rooted in a belief in the market and the value of choice and competition as a means of improving provision. The term associated with New Public Management and sometimes used interchangeably with it is managerialism. The defining features of managerialism are a strong central regulatory framework, and devolved decision

D. Johnson, R. Maclean (eds.), *Teaching: Professionalization,*
Development and Leadership,
© Springer Science + Business Media B.V. 2008

making to organisational level, a focus on measurable outputs and a willingness to rely on quasi-market forces. Levacic (1999) has argued that in the late 1980s and 1990s the UK Government increasingly adopted a rationalistic approach to school management emphasising the importance of strategic planning and objective setting, financial control, monitoring implementation and reporting outcomes of activities, one consequence of which was to strengthen the role of the headteacher as chief executive rather than professional leader. Simkins (1999) suggested that managerialism assumes that techniques for achieving better management are knowable and generally applicable so managers must be given freedom to manage. For Hoyle and Wallace managerialism is *"leadership and management to excess"* (2005: 68). They argue that the emphasis on control, although not wholly negative, has led to an intensification of staff work loads, lowered job satisfaction and may have distracted headteachers and teachers from their core task centred on teaching and learning. Although many features of managerialism continued in the period I have labelled Modernisation, these years are associated with a move away from strict market principles and some change in focus, less concern about the structure and organisation of schools and more emphasis on teaching and learning (DfEE, 1997). The Government's expressed wish was that this would lead to the emergence of *"a new professionalism for teachers"* (DfES, 2004: 5, 39).

(a) Partnership – promoting professional development and school improvement prior to 1988

The period from the 1970s to the 1988 Education Reform Act is referred to here as a time of "Partnership". Although the term was not widely used at the time, retrospectively it does reflect the broad consensus that appeared to exist between the Department of Education and Science (DES), the local education authorities (LEAs) and the teachers about a range of educational issues. Throughout this period the DES was the major initiator of policy but implementation was largely devolved to LEA and school levels. McNay and Ozga commented that:

> *The existence of the broad consensus permits a division of labour: the DES promotes particular policies and establishes the general direction of policy, the LEAs make provision, and the teachers interpret the word within their own classrooms....* (1985: 2)

The DES position could be characterised as a "hands off" approach, teachers were generally regarded as autonomous professionals, the curriculum was controlled by schools and teachers rather than the government thus headteachers and their staff had considerable freedom to select the changes that should be introduced and how they should be implemented. Teacher autonomy involved teachers taking responsibility for their individual professional development, although not all teachers made the most of the opportunities that were available. Educational policy was not a high national priority. However, in the late 1970s and 1980s this situation changed and teacher autonomy was progressively challenged as successive Governments sought to introduce central controls and regulations which culminated in the 1988 Education Reform Act. Two key documents which helped to shape the policy context during this period were The James Report (DES, 1972) and the Ruskin College Speech (Callaghan, 1976).

The 1972 Report on Teacher Education and Training (The James Report) was a wide-ranging and influential report which reviewed arrangements for the education, training and probation of teachers in England and Wales. Teacher education and training was conceptualised as falling into three cycles: first, personal education, second, pre-service education and induction, and, third, in-service education and training. The recommendations about in-service education are especially pertinent to this discussion in that they emphasised the importance of continuing education for teachers. In-service education was said to include,

> ... *the whole range of activities by which teachers can extend their personal education, develop their professional competence and improve their understanding of educational principles and techniques.*
>
> (DES, 1972: 2.2)

It was anticipated that teachers would need to deepen their knowledge and understanding of teaching methods and educational theory as well as their areas of special expertise. The underlying presumption was that individual teachers would identify their own development needs although it was noted that: "*Sometimes the acquisition of new subjects and skills may be dictated not so much by the inclinations of the teachers as by the needs of the schools*" (DES, 1972: 2.9). The continued training of teachers was said to be an essential task for every school.

If the James Report had highlighted the importance of continuing professional development for teachers this was reinforced by the so called "Great Debate on Education" sparked by Prime Minister Callaghan's 1976 speech which called for a broad debate about the future of education, a debate which should involve parents, professional bodies, representatives from higher education and industry as well as the teachers. Although he praised the work undertaken by many in the teaching profession, some concerns about student achievement were noted and teachers were warned that they were accountable for outcomes:"... *you must satisfy the parents and industry that what you are doing meets their requirements and the needs of their children*" (1976: 156). Becher and Maclure (1978) argued that this speech marked a change in the political climate and opened up a debate about standards of achievement, the content of the curriculum and the governance and management of schools. Trust in the professional expertise of the teachers began to erode.

Looking back now at educational policies in the 1980s it can be seen how the consensus between the DES, LEAs and Teacher Associations was beginning to fragment. Experience with school self evaluation, teacher appraisal and management training serve as illustrations.

(i)   School self evaluation

The push for greater professional accountability did not lead initially to an increase in school inspections by Her Majesty's Inspectorate (HMI) or by local education authorities. However, a government publication on the school curriculum exhorted schools to set out their aims in writing and to assess how far these aims were being achieved in the education they provided (DES, 1981). In turn LEAs encouraged schools to engage in self evaluation: Elliott (1984) reported that 90 of the then 104 LEAs in England and Wales had initiated discussions on school self evaluation and 44 authorities had produced some form of guidance for schools. Clearly, these developments could be interpreted as ways of strengthening professional accountability. The Schools Council, which was jointly funded by the LEAs and the DES but with teachers forming the majority membership, decided to sponsor the Guidelines for Review and Internal Development in Schools (GRIDS) project (McMahon et al., 1984) with a brief to develop some procedural guidelines for school self evaluation. The GRIDS project was part of the accountability movement but also a response to it in that one of its key purposes was to achieve internal school development rather than produce reports for formal accountability purposes. Headteachers and their staff could use the guidelines to help them assess the effectiveness of their school independent of controls exercised by their LEA or by national government.

(ii) Teacher appraisal

No formal systems for teacher appraisal were in place in the 1980s when the Government began to argue that the teaching profession needed to be more tightly controlled. In several DES publications suggestions were put forward that teachers' tasks should be more clearly specified, that their performance should be assessed, and that judgements about performance should be linked to salary. For example, the Government White Paper *"Teaching Quality"* reiterated the importance of in-service training but also drew explicit links between a teacher's training and deployment and made a connection between performance and pay (DES, 1983: paras 89 and 90). A further suggestion was that each teacher's performance should be formally assessed, this assessment to be based on classroom visits and an appraisal of *"both pupils' work and of the teacher's contribution to the life of the school."* (DES, 1983: para 92). These proposals challenged the notion that teacher professional development was an intrinsic "good" by suggesting that it should be linked much more explicitly to the assessment of teacher performance and to identified school priorities. This was reiterated in the 1985 White Paper, *Better Schools* (DES, 1985a) which signalled a move away from the concept of teachers as autonomous professionals taking individual responsibility for their professional development to the notion of teachers as employees guided in their development by a managerial assessment of their needs. Professional and career development and salary were to be *"largely determined by reference to periodic assessment of performance"* (para 181).

However, these proposals were strongly resisted by the teacher unions. As Secretary of State for Education, Keith Joseph was keen to introduce a teacher appraisal scheme, but could not gain the cooperation of the teacher and head teacher associations and, realising that the proposal to link appraisal and salary rewards was a major stumbling block, he withdrew this suggestion in a speech in November 1985. The issue of performance related pay for teachers did not reappear on the policy agenda for a number of years.

(iii)   Funding for in-service education

These early, but unsuccessful, moves to introduce teacher appraisal can be interpreted as the beginnings of a more managerialist approach to the profession and this trend is also evident in the provision of professional development. In 1983, Government began to shape the content of in-service teacher education by allocating funding for what it identified as specific national priority areas: £7 million was allotted to courses on management training for heads and other senior staff; mathematics teaching; teaching the 16–19 age group; special educational needs in ordinary schools; and bilingual needs in Wales. Of course, this earmarked funding largely determined who received training as well as shaping the training content. As part of the management initiative, the DES and the Welsh Office funded a National Development Centre (NDC) for school management training initially for three years (1983–1986), later extended until 1988. The NDC had a development rather than a research brief (Bolam, 1986), its main role being to promote the provision of high quality school management development and training for headteachers and senior staff in schools. Various strategies were used to promote quality in provision: a resource bank of information about good practice in management training was established; rigorous evaluation of training course provision was encouraged; management training materials were developed; and workshops, fellowships and attachments were used to facilitate the sharing of ideas and expertise. Experience of coordinating the management training courses in the first year led NDC staff to widen the Centre's brief to focus on management development as an underlying concept (McMahon and Bolam, 1990). In retrospect, this too can be seen as part of the managerialist trend.

Over the next few years the DES increased its central control over the content of in-service education by requiring LEAs to submit bids for funds for teacher professional development. This approach was piloted in 1985 though the Technical and Vocational Educational Initiative (TVEI) scheme, followed by the Local Education Authority Training Grants Scheme, first known as GRIST (Grant related in-service training) and later as LEATGS (Local Education Authority Training Grants Scheme) which was intended to"... *promote the professional development of teachers; to promote more systematic and purposeful planning of in-service training; to encourage more effective management of the training force; and to encourage training in selected areas, which are to be accorded national priority*" (DES, 1986). The practice of the DES holding a central pool of funds that LEAs could draw upon to support the secondment of teachers to long courses (e.g. MEd programmes) also ended. Reflecting later on this period Williams commented:

> *The trend ... for central bodies to define the agenda and predominant funding arrangements for INSET has distanced the individual teacher from the source of funding, de-emphasising the needs of the individual and asserting the importance of national priorities. The emphasis has been increasingly more upon the teacher as someone to be trained to meet current requirements and less upon the teacher as a professional who has his or her own personal agenda for professional development.*
>
> (Williams, 1993: 15)

Challenging Professional Autonomy?

Hoyle has argued that one reason why teachers enjoyed a relatively high level of autonomy for many years was: "... *the sheer difficulty of exercising control ... since their work is carried out in private settings and is hard to evaluate, especially in the short term.*" (Hoyle, 1986: 85) If this was true at the start of these "Partnership" years by the late 1980s the DES's control over teachers was much more apparent. The strategy of centralising funding for professional development and identifying priority areas for training was a powerful influence. Yet, it would be wrong to assume that the DES had taken complete control or indeed, that government policy makers wished to do so. Undoubtedly, the climate had changed, there had been a shift in the balance of control towards the DES and with this came a wider recognition that teachers and other educational professionals needed to be accountable for student learning. Nevertheless, agreement among the different stakeholder groups, DES, LEA and Teacher Associations, about the direction of policy could still be identified. LEAs and schools engaged with school self evaluation rather than argued against it; the earmarked funding for priority areas did not provoke teacher opposition to professional development; headteachers participated in management training; only the proposals for performance related pay met with strong resistance.

(b) Promoting professional development and school improvement in the era of New Public Management

The period from 1988 to 1997 is characterised here as the era of New Public Management although, as already noted, the boundaries between one period and another are permeable. The 1988 Education Reform Act has been taken as a starting point as it is widely regarded as a watershed in educational policy in England and Wales. Maclure (1992) argued that it was the most important piece of legislation since the 1944 Education Act because it instituted a major shift in power, from the local education authorities back to the Department for Education. In the late 1980s and 1990s, features of new public management, which had profound implications for the maintained school system, were introduced in England and Wales. Two powerful contextual factors influenced these developments. First, was the pressure from the DES for schools to become more managerial in their approach (Levacic, 1999), and second, the growing influence of research on school effectiveness and school improvement (Reynolds and Farrell, 1996) which highlighted, among other factors, the importance of strong leadership for effective schools (DfE, 1992a, para 1.33). The Government was keen to raise educational standards and policy makers became much more interventionist, pushing through reforms that promised improvement. Central government control was increased through the introduction of a national curriculum and national systems of testing and assessment. Local authorities were required to delegate substantial financial responsibility to schools, including for staffing costs, and governors were given increased powers in the selection, appointment and management of staff. The concept of parental choice of school was introduced and, since school budgets were linked to the number of students on roll, many schools were put in a position where they had to compete with one another to attract pupils. Governors and parents could also vote for their school to seek Grant Maintained status thereby taking it out of local authority control and rendering it qualified to receive direct Government funding. All these reforms are consistent with, indeed may be used as indicators of, the rise of the managerial state (Clarke and Newman, 1997).

The significant increase in the number of Government education policies and the quantity and scope of the changes required of teachers and schools meant that the pressure was relentless and schools struggled to implement multiple innovations (Wallace and McMahon, 1994). Control of education was progressively removed from the local education authorities and centralised in the DES although the size and complexity of the education system made it difficult to supervise and some tasks were delegated to quasi autonomous non-governmental organisations (quangos), one example being the schools inspection system (OFSTED). The powers of the Secretary of State for Education were considerably increased. There are numerous topics and issues that could be explored to illustrate change during this period but I will focus on three themes: teacher appraisal; continuing professional development; effective leadership and leadership development for school improvement.

(i)   Teacher and headteacher appraisal

As noted above, there were several unsuccessful policy initiatives on appraisal in the early and mid 1980s. Eventually, these culminated in a national pilot scheme for teacher and head teacher appraisal, funded by the DES from January 1987 to July 1989. Considered in retrospect, the experience of the teacher appraisal scheme provides a fascinating illustration of a change process at a point of transition from partnership in policy making to a more centralist, managerialist approach. First, it is important to note that there were no agreed procedures for teacher appraisal until Government Regulations making appraisal compulsory were introduced in 1991 (DES, 1991a). Despite this, interest in teacher appraisal had increased in the 1980s, the DES had been developing an argument in support of appraisal (e.g. DES, 1983 and 1985a) and surveys by James and Newman (1985) and Turner and Clift (1987) revealed that there had been an ad hoc growth of schemes developed by individual schools. Despite Government messages about the need for teacher accountability, the majority of the school schemes had a developmental purpose and were designed to facilitate staff development and identify INSET needs. 1986 was marked by acrimonious disputes between the DES and the teacher unions about salary and conditions of service which culminated in teachers losing their salary bargaining rights and the Government deciding what should be the teachers' conditions of service. During this dispute the Advisory Conciliation and Arbitration Service (ACAS) was called in to assist negotiations between the teacher unions, the LEA employers and the DES and, though the negotiations as a whole were not successful, a working party set up to discuss teacher appraisal did agree on a set of principles that the members felt should underpin any appraisal scheme. These principles emphasised teacher professional development, made no reference to pay and explicitly stated that disciplinary procedures would be separate:

… what the Working Party has in mind is a positive process, intended to raise the quality of education in schools by providing teachers with better job satisfaction, more appropriate in-service training and better planned career development based upon more informed decisions.

(ACAS, 1986: 3)

A pilot scheme was set up to develop and trial procedures for implementing appraisal following the principles agreed in the ACAS report. The pilot project was not unproblematic, nevertheless, in 1989 a report on the scheme signed by all three stakeholder groups (teacher representatives, LEAs and the DES), was published (DES, 1989a). The framework presented in the report conceptualised appraisal as a professional school-based process. It was recommended that appraisal statements should be treated as *"personnel documents of a particularly sensitive kind"* and should be kept by the headteacher and the appraisee and made available, on request, only to officers authorised by the LEA Chief Education Officer (and not to school governors). Information about professional development needs could be recorded separately and given to those responsible for planning training and development. At a comparatively late stage questions had been raised by the DES about the criteria for appraisal. This proved to be a very sensitive issue and the statement about criteria was carefully worded.

… it is clear that appraisal cannot and should not be designed to provide a simplified account of the appraisee's performance against a set of fixed criteria of good practice. We would therefore strongly oppose the mechanistic use in appraisal of standard check lists of performance.

Clearly, however, if appraisal is to be meaningful, it must be conducted against the background of certain expectations about teachers and teaching, and in the case of headteachers, the management and leadership of schools. Indeed it must be conducted against the background of sound professional criteria if it is to lead to improved learning for pupils. Furthermore, teachers and headteachers have a right to know what these criteria are.

(DES, 1989a, para 61 and 62)

All the stakeholder groups felt able to commit themselves to the NSG report which included the comment that:"*… we believe that the experience of the pilots provides a sound basis for the development of appraisal throughout England and Wales*" (DES, 1989a, para 6). Plans had been made for a national appraisal scheme to be implemented from Autumn 1989. In the event this didn't happen. The main explanation given by the DES was that schools already had a heavy innovation load following the 1988 Education Act. However, the costs of providing release time for classroom observation and appraisal training, as well as a concern that the framework had too strong an emphasis on development as opposed to accountability, could also have been reasons for delaying implementation (McMahon, 1995).

Nevertheless, the national scheme for teacher appraisal that was introduced in 1991 was very similar to the scheme recommended by the NSG at the end of the pilot project. A significant difference was that the accountability aspect had been strengthened by the inclusion of a clause in the regulations that information from the appraisal statement could be used "*… in advising those responsible for taking decisions on the promotion, dismissal or discipline of school teachers or on the* *use of any discretion in relation to pay*" (DES, 1991a). The scheme was to be phased in for all teachers over a four year period. Initial implementation went smoothly but in many schools teachers were appraised once and then appraisal was quietly abandoned, despite being a legal requirement. The extent of DES commitment to the scheme must be questioned as it continued to press for performance-related pay. In its evidence to the School Teachers Review Body in 1992 the DES comment was that:

> *The Government has made clear its belief that regular and direct links should be established, across all public services, between a person's contribution to the standards of service provided and his or her reward. The development of performance related pay (PRP) is an essential component of the Government's strategy for raising standards in the public sector.*

> (DES, 1992: para 1)

The appraisal project is an instructive illustration of the transition from partnership to a more managerial approach to policy design and implementation. Although the framework for appraisal had been developed through a partnership of DES, LEA employers and teacher associations the DES finally lost faith in the agreement that had been reached.

(ii)   Continuing Professional Development (CPD) for Teachers and Headteachers

During this period the Government also adopted a more coercive and directive approach to professional development, one which challenged teachers' autonomy in the classroom and seemed to signal a reduction of trust in their professionalism. Policies were developed to make explicit the expectations held of teachers and to try and ensure that they all participated in professional development which was viewed as a key strategy for school improvement. Several policies had direct implications for the teacher's role. One example was the School Teachers' Pay and Conditions Document (DES, 1988) which set out for the first time a generic job description for teachers and prescribed their hours of work. These included five non-teaching days which could be used for teacher professional development. The mission to clarify objectives for teachers progressed further with the introduction of a privatised inspection force coordinated by the Office for Standards in Education (OFSTED) following the 1992 Education Act. The inspection framework set out criteria for practice against which the schools and individual teachers would be assessed (see OFSTED, 1993). As pupil results at the different Key Stages and OFSTED school inspection reports were published, data about the perceived outcomes of teachers' work entered the public domain. In 1994 the Government established a Teacher Training Agency (TTA) with a brief covering teacher supply and recruitment, initial teacher training and induction and continuing professional development and research. The TTA was a Government quango, the purpose of which was to: "*improve the quality of teaching, to raise the standards of teacher education and training, and to promote teaching as a profession, in order to improve the standards of pupils' achievement and the quality of their learning*" (TTA, 1996: 12). A key component of this strategy was to develop a national framework of standards for professional development which would set out the knowledge, understanding, skills and attributes required for the job at different levels as well as the key tasks and expected outcomes. The standards for Qualified Teacher Status (QTS) and the National Professional Qualification for Headship (NPQH) were developed into formal assessed qualifications (TTA, 1998).

As Government expectations of teachers became more explicit these in turn influenced the content and methodology of teacher professional development programmes. The 1988 Act had introduced a major reform agenda, and many of the reforms, particularly the national curriculum and the national testing programme, required many teachers to modify their approach to teaching and learning. The five "professional development" days included in the teacher's contract were typically used for one-day, school-based training events which all members of staff were expected to attend. At the risk of over generalisation, it can be said that the greater part of this training focused on briefing staff about the reforms. External training courses were typically short, not more than one or two days in duration and often less. A "cascade" model was adopted whereby teachers with a specific responsibility for an area would receive training "first hand" and then would be expected to teach the same material to their colleagues in school. Arrangements for funding in-service education changed and a quasi-market was introduced in professional development as INSET funding was progressively delegated to the schools within a framework of DES designated priority areas. Schools were expected to select and buy-in training provision, either from their LEA or from independent consultants. The requirement for schools to draw up a development plan (DES, 1989b) had, at least in theory, simplified the task of identifying organisational needs and schools were encouraged to develop school based staff development programmes. Bolam suggested that the emerging model for CPD was "*based on the idea of self-developing professionals working in self-managing schools which have access to diverse forms of internal and external CPD provision*" (1993: 21). However, the thrust of DES advice was that priority should be given to meeting school needs with the result that a teacher of a priority subject (e.g. maths) might have more CPD opportunities than say, a music teacher.

This approach did have consequences; although the number of teachers engaging in professional development undoubtedly increased they did not necessarily feel that what they received was contributing to their individual professional growth. Subsequent research on secondary teachers' perceptions of CPD (McMahon, 1998) led me to conclude that teachers' understanding of professional development was rather instrumental; essentially they saw it as the training and experiences needed to enable them to do their job. Few of them spoke of engaging in CPD for its intrinsic value: they saw it being linked to their immediate job or to future career development. Where there were no obvious opportunities for career development motivation could be adversely affected. Teacher workloads were heavy, there were relatively few opportunities to participate in any training or education courses and day-to-day tasks had priority. Opportunities to reflect more broadly about their professional values and to engage in challenging intellectual study rather than skill training were rare.

(iii)   Effective leadership and leadership development for school improvement

Given the ideology of new public management, it is not surprising that considerable attention was focused on management training for headteachers and senior staff in schools. The DES-funded National Development Centre (NDC) for school management training in the 1980s (1983–1988) had been university-based and was essentially a research and development project, although the DES did nominate the chair and members of the Steering Committee. The successor body to the NDC was the School Management Task Force (1989–1992), again government funded but under much tighter control as it was located in the DES. The brief for this body was to work with regional consortia of LEAs to support the introduction of delegated budgets and to promote more effective management of schools. Appraisal for headteachers was introduced as part of the national appraisal scheme in 1991. In 1992 support was provided for newly appointed headteachers through the, admittedly short lived, government-funded pilot schemes on mentoring for new headteachers (Bolam et al., 1993). In 1995 the TTA introduced the Headlamp scheme for supporting new headteachers. Hoyle and Wallace (2005: 105) argue that these policies were moves to increase the professionalization of school leaders, aimed at underlining the importance of leading and managing in relation to teaching and learning, and thus that one consequence was to curb teacher professionalism.

Strengthening Central Control?

In the years 1988–1997 the former "Partnership" between the DES, LEAs and the schools was replaced by a system in which policy was developed by the DES, considerable responsibility was devolved to schools and the LEA role was weakened. Ostensibly schools had greater power but in reality responsibility was devolved within a strong regulatory framework in which governors and head teachers were held accountable for the implementation of the reform agenda and for pupil achievement. The balance of control rested firmly with the DES and it drove through a series of reforms relating to the curriculum, assessment and testing, and school inspection which, though intended to raise standards, were not wholly supported by teachers. Was there a reduction in teacher professionalism? It is difficult to make any clear judgement about this but professional autonomy was certainly challenged as teachers' freedom to shape the curriculum they taught, their patterns of work and their opportunities to select the forms of professional development that met their individual needs were constrained. It is also questionable whether the stronger central control imposed by Government actually led to school improvement. Research evidence about school effectiveness and improvement underlined the importance of a school culture in which staff had shared vision and goals and relationships were collegial and collaborative. It is difficult to build such a culture when the context in which the school is operating emphasises target setting and accountability, performance management and performance related pay for staff, measures which often focus on the work of individual teachers and are more likely to promote competition than collaboration. (McMahon, 2001). In these years of new public management teacher workload increased and the profession came under greater control and scrutiny, some negative consequences were a reported reduction in teacher morale (DfEE, 1999) and growing concern about recruitment into the profession and the difficulty of filling senior school management and headteacher posts.

(c) Modernisation – promoting professional development and school improvement after 1997

The label used for the third section, which is roughly the period from 1997 to 2006, coinciding with a "New Labour" government, is Modernisation. This term, although used by government ministers and in policy documents, has not been widely adopted in educational circles. A 1999 paper titled *Modernising Government* presented this rather vague definition:

> *Modernising government means identifying, and defeating, the problems we face. It means freeing the public service so that it can build on its strengths to innovate and to rise to these challenges. It means raising all standards until they match the best within and outside the public service, and continue improving. It means transforming government, so that it is organised around what the public wants and needs, rather than around the needs or convenience of institutions.*

(Cabinet Office, 1999: 1.18)

Newman has suggested that the Labour government worked to build a consensus around, "*an agenda of modernising reforms designed to remedy deep-seated social problems such as poor schooling, ill health*" (Newman, 2001: 2) and she argues that this was a partial retreat from the ideological commitment to market mechanisms as the driver of reform in the public sector. However, she also noted that in practice the modernisation project led to an intensification of the reforms and a steady flow of targets, performance indicators, audits and inspection. The Government's ambitious aims for education were outlined in the White Paper, Excellence in Schools,"… *to change attitudes towards education and foster a realisation that education matters to everyone.… We must replace the culture of complacency with commitment to success*" (DfEE, 1997: 3). Clearly, earlier educational reforms were not judged to have produced satisfactory outcomes. Raising standards in schools was still the core aim, teachers were recognised as being central to achieving this aim and they were to be valued, provided with extensive in-service training and their success celebrated.

Initially the proposed methods for raising standards outlined in the report did not differ significantly from those introduced by successive Conservative governments, although it was implied that they would be more rigorous. OFSTED inspections would continue and failing schools would have to improve, make a fresh start or close. A Standards and Effectiveness unit was to be set up in the re-named Department for Education and Employment (DfEE). There was to be a push to raise standards of literacy and numeracy. More data about pupil and school achievement were to be published, the focus was to be on outcomes rather than process. However, there were some changes in language, fewer references were made to management and more emphasis was placed on leadership. Improvement was to be achieved through a partnership of schools, LEAs, OFSTED and the DfEE. But, in this partnership the DfEE pre-decided what should be the role of each party.

> *The main responsibility for raising standards lies with schools themselves. But they will be more effective in doing so if they work in active partnership with LEAs, OFSTED and the DfEE. The LEAs' role is to help schools set and meet their targets. OFSTED's role is to inspect performance by individual schools and LEAs, and provide an external assessment of the state of the school system as a whole. The DfEE's role is to set the policy framework, promote best practice, and to provide pressure and support in relation to LEAs as LEAs themselves do for their schools.*
>
> (DfEE, 1997: para 3.16)

Since 1997 education reform has stayed top of the political agenda. Numerous initiatives and innovations have been introduced, the majority, if not all, have been driven by a determination to raise standards of achievement. Schools and teachers are constantly challenged to improve. Newman (2001) argued that the Government was attempting to control both the outputs and processes of professional work. This could be problematic as demonstrated in policies for performance management and continuing professional development including leadership development.

(i)   Performance management and continuing professional development

An early step in the push to raise standards was to re-introduce a tougher scheme for teacher appraisal. The existing appraisal scheme had effectively ceased in many schools and was criticised in the 1997 White Paper as being an inadequate means of checking on teacher performance and failing to lead to increased teacher effectiveness. (DfEE, 1997, 5.23). The requirements for the new system of appraisal, henceforth known as performance management (DfEE, 1998 and 1999) not only introduced performance related-pay for the first time but also directed that salary rewards should be linked to measurable improvements in pupil performance. This was in sharp contrast to the earlier appraisal framework (DES, 1989a) which had emphasised teacher professional development. At the same time a new system of Threshold Assessment was introduced. This was effectively a salary bar at nine points on the salary scale (since reduced); teachers had to demonstrate their competency against national standards to pass the threshold and so get access to higher pay ranges. The re-introduction of appraisal with threshold assessment meant that teachers had to demonstrate, and convince their assessors, that their work was contributing in measurable ways to raising standards of learning and teaching. The push was to use evidence based criteria rather than, or as well as, professional judgement to assess the quality of a teacher's contribution.

The policy position on professional development for teachers was also rather different, not least because more money was allocated to support CPD. The principles outlined in the paper, *Professional Development* (DfEE, 2000), show how thinking about CPD was changing. Three of the principles that were especially important were: the view that individual teachers should take ownership of and give priority to their own professional development; the strong recommendation that CPD should be focused on raising standards of pupil achievement; and an acceptance that a wide range of development opportunities should be available to suit different needs. In some respects, this strategy seemed to move back to a recognition of teacher autonomy in CPD. The DfEE appeared to respond to the criticism that professional development opportunities had focused too much on national and school priorities and that individual teacher needs had been neglected. Earmarked funding was provided for a number of CPD initiatives, for example, Best Practice Research Scholarships; International Exchanges and Study Visits; Business Placements; Teacher Sabbaticals. All of these provided opportunities for individual teachers and headteachers to engage in CPD activities which met their individual needs and would also address the raising standards agenda in some way. Nevertheless, research indicated that it remained difficult to achieve a balance between individual and organisational needs (Hustler, 2003; Bolam and Weindling, 2006; OFSTED, 2006). Despite positive evaluations of many of these initiatives their specific funding was not renewed and there was a change in Government policy in 2004. In future, decisions about CPD provision and specific professional development activities were to be taken by schools and teachers themselves, informed by performance management reviews and linked to plans for school improvement. Funding for CPD would be included in the school budget and there was to be a greater emphasis on in-school and across-school activities such as coaching and mentoring, classroom observation, training and other forms of collaboration. The importance of subject knowledge for teachers was emphasized and teacher appraisals were to be refocused to become teaching and learning reviews intended to stimulate demand for high quality training and encourage teachers to take more responsibility for their own development. Significantly, professional development was described as a key element in a new form of teacher professionalism:

> *a new professionalism for teachers, in which career progression and financial rewards will go to those who are making the biggest contributions to improving pupil attainment, those who are continually developing their own expertise, and those who help to develop expertise in other teachers.*

> (DfES, 2004: 5, para 39)

Teachers were to be encouraged to be more proactive in their own professional development and would be rewarded if this was judged to have contributed to raising pupil attainment, although how such judgements would be made was unclear.

(ii)   Leadership development and professional learning communities

Government belief in the importance of training for headteachers and senior staff (school leaders) continued after 1997. Significant funding was provided to establish a National College for School Leadership (NCSL) which opened in November 2000 with a brief to provide a single focus for research and training in school leadership. The NCSL's achievements in a relatively short period of time have been impressive (Bush, 2004): a number of leadership development programmes have been developed; the college has invested in online learning, web-based learning, and is promoting electronic means of communication and learning for school leaders; it commissions, undertakes and disseminates research on leadership. The NCSL also set up the Networked Learning Communities Group which facilitated staff from different schools working together in partnership with other educational organisations and individuals to promote learning and share good practice (Southworth, 2004).

A further development was the establishment of the General Teaching Council (GTC) for England which began work in September 2000. Set up by government legislation in 1998, its brief was to act as a voice for the teaching profession and give advice to the Secretary of State on professional matters about teachers, including their professional development (Saunders, 2004). In practice, in establishing the GTC, the government provided a channel for the teachers' voice into the policy making arena bypassing the local authorities and teacher associations. The pattern of staffing in schools has also changed through the "Re-modelling the Workforce" initiative which led to a big increase in numbers of support staff (e.g. teaching assistants, technicians). Theoretically this would free teachers from many bureaucratic tasks and enable them to concentrate on raising standards in classrooms although there would clearly be implications for their role, not least some additional responsibility for the management and training of support staff.

It is significant that the concept of the school as a professional learning community (PLC) (Bolam et al., 2005) has become central to the government's strategy for raising standards. For policy makers, interest in a learning community stems from the belief that when teachers and other school staff work together collaboratively with a clear focus on learning, the school's overall capacity to raise standards is enhanced. Clearly, if school staff are working to establish themselves as a PLC then it is more likely that teachers, support staff, parents, governors, etc. will have a shared understanding about what can be done to maximise learning and how they can contribute to this.

A Focus on What Works?

In a number of respects the "Modernisation" period can be seen as a continuation of managerialism rather than a move away from it, certainly there has been no diminution in central government control. The core educational policy goal has continued to be to raise educational standards yet there have been some changes in approach. In policy development the focus has been on finding "what works" and on the implementation of policies that seem to promise the desired results. Spending on education has significantly increased and the emphasis on competition seems to have diminished slightly. Use of the web and electronic mail has made it much easier for the DfES to disseminate information directly to schools and consult teachers without recourse to the LEA. But the pressure to implement reforms continues unabated and, although teachers are expected to be more proactive about their own CPD, this is within a clear framework of national standards of good practice and expectations about pupil learning outcomes.

Conclusion

What conclusions might be drawn from this review of practice and policy in continuing professional development? Certainly there have been considerable changes since the 1970s. Most notable is the increasing centralisation of policy-making as demonstrated in the changing relationships between the Department for Education (the precise title of the department has changed over the years), the local education authorities and the teachers as represented by their professional associations. This has moved from the notion of partnership to a position where the roles of the LEA and the teacher associations are considerably weaker, schools are self-managing and there is a more direct relationship between the individual school and central government. But centralisation of policy making has not been accompanied by a growing certainty about the strategies that are most likely to promote teacher learning and growth and school improvement. Questions about appropriate forms of appraisal/performance management, school self-evaluation/inspection and headteacher/leadership training reoccur on a regular basis. Policy on CPD has shifted from a situation where the teacher was seen as an autonomous professional, responsible for the development of their own knowledge and skills, someone who should be supported and encouraged but not directed in their development, to a position where the headteacher and senior staff are expected to make provision for the CPD of school staff within the context of a framework of national standards for the profession, performance management and school improvement planning.

Does this represent the emergence of a new teacher professionalism? For Hoyle and Wallace new professionalism means that "... *practitioners [are] required to demonstrate competence in delivering an externally-determined service*" (2005: 167). This is an accurate description of what is happening given the current policy framework for teachers' work. The expectation of the DfES is that a characteristic of new professionalism is that teachers will be continually developing their own expertise and helping other teachers to develop (2004). It is questionable whether there is enough flexibility in the system to enable this growth of expertise as regulations and guidelines about the curriculum, pedagogy and teaching and learning priorities coupled with a rigorous assessment and performance management system leave little scope for individual teacher innovation and creativity. Indeed the core tasks may be so prescribed that there is risk of the job becoming boring. As Hoyle and Wallace note, the new professionalism approach is, "... *in danger of impoverishing the quality of professional practice and inhibiting the very incremental innovation that is vital for improving its effectiveness*" (2005: 167). If teachers are to acquire the knowledge and skills needed to cope successfully with the current pace of educational change they will require opportunities for reflection and challenging study to help them become independent thinkers and problem solvers. Successive governments have clarified expectations for teachers and have set standards for professional practice which are monitored and assessed through pupil outcomes and OFSTED inspections. But is this the correct balance of power and influence? There are likely to be unique features in every school context, a common national solution cannot be applied for every problem that arises. A more productive interpretation of new professionalism would be one which allowed headteachers and their staff more space for creative problem solving and developing their professional skills albeit within a regulatory framework. Hoyle and Wallace make a plea for temperate leadership and management which nurtures teachers and supports them to "*do things professionally*" and "*act professionally*" (2005: 190). If policy makers were to place more trust in teachers and a greater reliance on their professional judgement, if they were to re-balance the policy making process so as to facilitate a greater input from Local Authorities and Associations for Headteachers, Teachers and other staff, then we might witness new shared understandings of professionalism which are about creativity and innovative problem solving as well as competency.

References

ACAS (1986) *Teachers' Dispute ACAS Independent Panel: Report of the Appraisal/Training Working Group*. London: Advisory, Conciliation and Arbitration Service

Becher, T and Maclure, S (eds) (1978) *Accountability in Education*. Windsor, Berks: NFER

Bolam, R (1986) The ND Centre for School Management Training, in Hoyle, E and McMahon, A (eds) *The Management of Schools: World Yearbook of Education 1986*. London: Kogan Page, pp. 252–271

Bolam, R (1993) Recent developments and emerging issues, in Williams, M and Bolam, R (eds) *The Continuing Professional Development of Teachers: Papers prepared for the General Teaching Council England and Wales*. GTC, England: Department of Education, University College of Swansea

Bolam, R, McMahon, A, Pocklington, K and Weindling, D (1993) *National Evaluation of the Headteacher Mentoring Pilot Schemes*. London: DfE

Bolam, R, McMahon, A, Stoll, L, Thomas, S and Wallace, M with Greenwood, A, Hawkey, K, Ingram, M, Atkinson, A and Smith, M (2005) *Creating and Sustaining Effective Professional Learning Communities Research Report 637*. London: DfES

Bolam, R and Weindling, D (2006) *Synthesis of Research and Evaluation Projects Concerned with Capacity-Building Through Teachers' Professional Development*. London: General Teaching Council for England

Bush, T (2004) The National College for School Leadership: Purpose, Power and Prospects. *Educational Management, Administration and Leadership* 32, 3:243–249

Cabinet Office (1999) *Modernising Government*. London: Government Cabinet Office

Callaghan, J (1976) Speech at Ruskin College printed in Maclure, S (1992) *Education Re-formed (third edition)*. London: Hodder & Stoughton

Clarke, J and Newman, J (1997) *The Managerial State*. London: Sage

Department of Education and Science (DES) (1972) *Teacher Education and Training (The James Report)*. London: HMSO

Department of Education and Science (DES) (1981) *The School Curriculum*. London: HMSO

Department of Education and Science/Welsh Office (DES) (1983) *Teaching Quality* (Cmnd 8836). London: HMSO

Department of Education and Science/Welsh Office (DES) (1985a) Cm 9469 *Better Schools*. London: HMSO

Department of Education and Science/Welsh Office (DES) (1985b) *Quality in Schools: Evaluation and Appraisal*. London: HMSO

Department of Education and Science (DES) (1986) *Circular 6/86 Local Education Authority Training Grants Scheme: Financial Year 1987–88*. London: DES

Department of Education and Science (DES) (1988) *School Teachers Pay and Conditions Document*. London: HMSO

Department of Education and Science (DES) (1989a) *School Teacher Appraisal: A National Framework Report of the National Steering Group on the School Teacher Appraisal Pilot Study*. London: HMSO

Department of Education and Science (DES) (1989b) *Planning for School Improvement*. London: DES

Department of Education and Science (DES) (1991a) *The Education (School Teacher Appraisal) Regulations 1991*. London: DES

Department of Education and Science (DES) (1991b) *Circular 12/91 School Teacher Appraisal*. London: DES

Department for Education (DfE) (1992a) *Choice and Diversity: A New Framework for Schools*. London: DfE

Department for Education (DfE) (1992b) *School Teachers Review Body: Written Evidence from the Department for Education: Performance Related Pay*. London: DfE

Department for Education and Employment (DfEE) (1997) *Excellence in Schools*. London: The Stationery Office

Department for Education and Employment (DfEE) (1998) *Teachers Meeting the Challenge of Change*. London: The Stationery Office

Department for Education and Employment (DfEE) (1999) *Teachers Meeting the Challenge of Change – Technical Consultation Document on Pay and Performance Management*. London: The Stationery Office

Department for Education and Employment (DfEE) (2000) *Professional Development: Support for Teaching and Learning*. London: DfEE

Department for Education and Skills (DfES) (2004) *Five Year Strategy for Children and Learners Cm 6272*. London: HMSO

Elliott, G (1984) *Self-evaluation and the Teacher: An Annotated Bibliography and Report on Current Practice Part 5*. London: School Curriculum Development Committee

Hoyle, E (1986) *The Politics of School Management*. Kent, England: Hodder & Stoughton

Hoyle, E and Wallace, M (2005) *Educational Leadership: Ambiguity, Professionals and Managerialism*. London: Sage

Hustler, D, McNamara, O, Jarvis, J, Londra, M, Campbell, A and Howson, J (2003) *Teachers' Perceptions of Continuing Professional Development*. Research Report 429 London: DfES

James, C R and Newman, J C (1985) Staff appraisal schemes in comprehensive schools: A regional survey of current practice in the South Midlands and the South West of England. *Educational Management and Administration* 13, 3:155–164

Levacic, R (1999) Managing resources for school effectiveness in England and Wales: Institutionalising a rational approach? In Bolam, R and van Wieringen, F (eds) *Research on Educational Management in Europe*. Munster, Germany: Waxmann

McMahon, A, Bolam, R, Abbott, R and Holly, P (1984) *Guidelines for Review and Internal Development in Schools: Secondary School Handbook*. London: Longman for the Schools Council

McMahon, A and Bolam, R (1990) *Management Development and Educational Reform: A Handbook for LEAs*. London: Paul Chapman

McMahon, A (1995) Teacher appraisal in England and Wales in Duke, D (ed) *Teacher Evaluation Policy*. Albany, NY: SUNY

McMahon, A (1998) Secondary School Teachers' Perceptions of Continuing Professional Development: Final Report for the Leverhulme Trust

McMahon, A (2001) A cultural perspective on school effectiveness, school improvement and teacher professional development in Harris, A and Bennett, N (eds) *School Effectiveness and School Improvement: Alternative Perspectives*. London: Continuum

McNay, I and Ozga, J (1985) *Policy-making in Education: The Breakdown of Consensus*. Oxford: Pergamon

Maclure, S (1992) *Education Re-formed*. London: Hodder & Stoughton

Newman, J (2001) *Modernising Governance: New Labour, Policy and Society*. London: Sage

OFSTED (1993) *Handbook for the Inspection of Schools*. London: HMSO

OFSTED (2006) *The Logical Chain: Continuing Professional Development in Effective Schools*. London: Ofsted

Reynolds D and Farrell, S (1996) *Worlds Apart? A review of International Surveys of Educational Achievement Involving England (OFSTED reviews of research series)*. London: HMSO

Saunders, L (2004) *Grounding the Democratic Imagination: Developing the Relationship Between Research and Policy in Education*. Professorial lecture London: Institute of Education, University of London

Simkins, T (1999) Values, power and instrumentality: Theory and research in education management. *Educational Management and Administration* 27, 3:267–281

Southworth, G (2004) A response from the National College for School Leadership. *Educational Management Administration and Leadership* 32, 3:339–354

Teacher Training Agency (TTA) (1996) *Corporate Plan 1996: Promoting Excellence in Teaching*. London: TTA

Teacher Training Agency (TTA) (1998) *National Standards*. London: TTA

Turner, G and Clift, P (1987) *A Second Review and Register of School and College Based Teacher Appraisal Schemes*. Milton Keynes, England: Open University Press

Wallace, M and McMahon, A (1994) *Planning for Change in Turbulent Times: The Case of Multiracial Primary Schools*. London: Cassell

Williams, M (1993) The continuing professional development of teachers in Williams, M and Bolam, R (eds) *The Continuing Professional Development of Teachers: Papers Prepared for the General Teaching Council England and Wales*. GTC, England: Department of Education, University College of Swansea

Chapter 8
Teacher Professionalism and Teacher Education in Hong Kong

Paul Morris*

Introduction

The development and status of both teacher education and the teaching profession are strongly interlinked because, as Furlong et al. (2000) has argued, the key elements of teacher professionalism and the fundamental nature of teachers' work can be most directly influenced by changing the knowledge, skills and values required of new teachers. Accordingly attempts to redefine teacher professionalism and the nature of teachers' work have been primarily pursued through policies designed to construct 'a new generation of teachers with different forms of knowledge, different skills and different professional values' (Furlong: 2000, 6). Similarly, the location of teacher education provision in an education system is a powerful barometer of the status and nature of teacher professionalism in a society. Where teacher education is provided in post-secondary institutions, which are perceived to be outside the higher education sector, the status and level of teacher professionalism would be relatively weak.

In examining teacher education, the focus is on the Hong Kong Institute of Education (HKIEd) and its forerunners – the Colleges of Education which is/were the main provider of teacher education in Hong Kong. The government is the most powerful single influence on both the requirements of new teachers and the location and status of teacher education providers. In examining teacher professionalism, the focus is on one of its key manifestations, namely the processes for regulating and holding teachers accountable which, in the final analysis, are determined or delegated by government. Therefore it is necessary to understand the influences and constraints which have affected the government – the most pertinent ones being its degree of legitimacy, the changing nature of policy making processes and its relationship with those elements of civil society that are most directly linked to schooling.

This paper initially reviews the situation prior to the return of Hong Kong's sovereignty to the People's Republic of China in 1997 as this has provided the

*Prior to mid 2007 the author was the President of The Hong Kong Institute of Education, Hong Kong, China

D. Johnson, R. Maclean (eds.), *Teaching: Professionalization, Development and Leadership,*
© Springer Science + Business Media B.V. 2008

119

antecedents from which the current situation has developed. Subsequently the post-handover situation is analyzed. Before proceeding, it is necessary to undertake a brief clarification of the key concepts central to the paper. Professionalism/professionalization and one of its key manifestations – the locus of accountability – are concepts which have been extended in a variety of directions and sometimes in ways beyond their core meanings.

Professionalism and Teacher Education

Professionalism is a contested term with a variety of meanings – pest control firms, armies and crime syndicates have appropriated it as a euphemism for efficiency, the provision of specialist services or the possession of a body of specialist knowledge.

Hoyle (1975) has argued the existence of a continuum of teacher professionality ranging from the 'extended' to 'restricted'. He also distinguished professionality from professionalism. The former refers to the knowledge, skills and procedures which teachers use in the process of teaching. Professionalism refers to the various factors which affect the status, salary and conditions of the profession. The process of trying to improve the level of professionalism (status, pay, self-regulation, etc.) is defined by Hoyle as professionalization. Other critical issues have emerged from the literature. Hargreaves (1994) and Elliott (1991) argue the emergence of a 'new professionalism' and others (e.g. Evans, 1998) dispute the suggestion that a single teacher culture exists. Often these meanings are combined, or conflated, with the result that the goal becomes to simultaneously enhance *teacher professionalism* (in terms of its status), *teacher professionality* (the behaviour of individual actors) and *teacher education*. It is important to distinguish between these three dimensions, as failure to do so results in a tendency to ignore both their interconnections and possible tensions. For example, teachers may operate as extended professionals but work in a context in which teaching is not perceived within the wider community to be a profession, or the community may expect teachers to act with high levels of professionality but they still do not have the features of a profession.

Similarly, the struggles to improve the professionalism of teaching around the world are matched by the ongoing struggle to improve the status of teacher education. However, teaching and teacher education have a long history of what the Holmes Group (1986: 6) termed 'mutual impairment'. Teacher education has been seen as academically weak in universities or has been located outside the university sector, and this undermines the status of teaching. This has served to reinforce its relatively low social status and made it difficult to recruit the most able students to join the teaching profession.

There is, according to Larson (1977), agreement that professions are characterized by a combination of the following general dimensions: a body of knowledge and techniques which professionals apply in their work; training to master such knowledge and skills; a service orientation; distinctive ethics, which justify the privilege of self regulation that society grants them; and an implicit comparison with other occupations, which highlights their autonomy and prestige. Eraut (1994) stresses that the key features of a profession involve a strong moral commitment to the needs of the client. Similarly, Hoyle and John (1995) argue that debates about what it means to be a professional revolve around three key elements: knowledge of a specialist field, autonomy to make professional judgements and the responsibility to act ethically. Shulman (2005) identifies similar elements when he defines a professional education as 'a synthesis of three apprenticeships – a cognitive apprenticeship wherein one learns to think like a professional, a practical apprenticeship where one learns to perform like a professional, and a moral apprenticeship where one learns to think and act in a responsible and ethical manner that integrates across all three domains.'

The Context Prior to Reunification with China

Within Hong Kong there is ample evidence (Cheung, 2001; Lo, 2000) indicating the high level of professionality of individual teachers despite the fact that the profession itself has few of the characteristics associated with a strong level of professionalism. It is the latter sense which is the primary concern of this chapter. However, overall if we compare teaching to other professions (e.g. medicine and law, which require high standards of entry and exit, and are self-regulatory) or to the experience in countries with high levels of teacher professionalism (e.g. Finland, Sweden and Japan), it is difficult to view it as possessing the characteristics of a strong profession (Morris and Williamson, 2000). Teaching in Hong Kong could, until recently, be defined in Etzioni's (1969) terms as a 'semi-profession':

> *Their training is shorter, their status is less legitimated, their right to privileged communication is less established, there is less of a body of specialized knowledge, and they have less autonomy from supervision or social control than the 'professions'.* (p. v)

The specific features of teaching in Hong Kong that have served to define its status and level of professionalism prior to 1997 were:

- There were no minimum entry requirements for people to obtain employment as teachers (except for kindergarten and Physical Education teachers). Thus, even in 2001 over 40 percent of those who obtained jobs as teachers had no professional qualifications (Lai et al., 2001).
- In some subject areas, most notably English and Art, a very high proportion of teachers of those subjects had no background in studying the subject as a major within their degree programmes.
- Most teacher education courses were sub-degree programmes provided in government post-secondary colleges that were outside the mainstream university sector. Following the expansion of the university sector in the late 1980s, they had increasing difficulty in competing to recruit students.
- There was a very strong distinction between the status and qualifications of secondary school teachers of academic subjects and that of both primary teachers and secondary teachers of non-academic subjects (such as Art, Music and PE). Prior to the establishment of the HKIEd in 1994, their training took place in

Colleges of Education run by the Civil Service. Primary teachers and secondary teachers of cultural subjects were trained through sub-degree Certificate courses that involved either three years of study after Secondary 5 or two years after Secondary 7. Therefore, many primary teachers had not themselves completed secondary school and when they emerged from a three-year college certificate course, they had been trained to teach four school subjects, namely Chinese, English, Mathematics and General Studies. In reality, the level of subject depth for many teachers in each of these areas had only reached that of A-level equivalence, and for many teachers their level of English language proficiency was extremely low but they were expected to teach English. In contrast, teachers of most secondary school academic subjects (all subjects except PE, Art, Music and Technology) were university graduates and paid on a higher scale than the Certificate teachers. This situation only began to change from the late 1990s.

- There has been no agency that serves to represent teachers professionally or to regulate teachers' professional behaviour. There are two significant bodies that represent the interests of teachers in Hong Kong, but these are both unions that are distinguishable by their affiliation to major political groupings. The largest and probably the strongest single union in Hong Kong is the Professional Teachers' Union (PTU), which was born as a result of a strike by Certificate teachers in the early 70's when the government attempted to reduce their salaries. During the 1970s and 1980s, the PTU was a major source of opposition to the colonial government and since 1989 has strongly been aligned with the Democratic Party. The other major body, the Federation of Education Workers, is far smaller in terms of its membership but is aligned with pro-Communist and mainland political groupings and perceived therefore as more pro-government. The outcome of this scenario is that the relationship between government and the teachers has often been highly politicized, especially given the absence of any body that focuses on promoting or protecting teaching as a profession.

The above conditions all contributed to maintaining teaching as an occupation with few of the characteristics associated with a strong degree of professionalism. These same conditions have also been the primary reasons put forward by the government to justify its increased role in monitoring and evaluating teachers. Some of these features are now changing and these are addressed in a later section.

Similar conditions relating to the training and qualifications of teachers have previously operated elsewhere, especially in countries that were former British colonies. However, unlike the situation elsewhere, it was not until the 1990s that overt attempts were made in Hong Kong to enhance the status of teaching. The comparatively late actions to raise the status of teaching (e.g. by requiring minimum entry requirements and a degree) seem to arise from a number of factors:

- There was a signal failure in the policy making process to anticipate the impact on teacher education and the teaching profession of the shift from an elite to a mass education system and the resulting sudden growth of the university sector. This failure seems to be *more* a product of oversight and the fact that the Colleges were outside the higher education policy making system than of strategic planning.

Prior to the rapid expansion of higher education in the late 1980s, the former Colleges of Education were able to attract highly qualified school leavers as only around 2 percent of the relevant age group could secure places in local universities. This situation changed drastically when, by the early 1990s, the university sector, which excluded the colleges, had expanded to recruit 18 percent of the relevant age group and about another 10 percent went on to study overseas. The result was that the attractiveness and academic standards of the intake to the Colleges declined markedly. As a former Director of Education (HKIEd Alumni Newsletter, Jan. 2006) describes the situation of the former Colleges:

their golden years were between the end of World War II and the 1960s, when they had no shortage of good students seeking admission. However, over time, as more higher education places became available in other institutions in Hong Kong, their popularity began to decline. By the early 1990s, it became clear to the then Education Department that if the colleges were not made autonomous and their standards not significantly upgraded, their inability to attract good students could seriously affect the quality of the teaching force in the long run.

- There was in Hong Kong, as elsewhere, a strong view, especially among the policymaking elite, that teaching was a type of work that required no specialist expertise but merely required a knowledge of the subject and the technical skills of transmitting information to prepare pupils for public examinations. Kindergarten and primary school teaching in particular were characterized as 'women's work' that primarily involved caring for and minding young children. Further, many of those who were making decisions about education policy were reluctant to see the government lose its control of those institutions.
- Most importantly, in all areas of education policy the colonial government's overriding concern was to ensure that the system did not encourage any activities that might be subversive or destabilizing. Thus school curricula were depoliticized and focused on far away places and times (Morris, 1997). Also the teachers' strike of 1972 threatened the stability of the colonial government. Control of the colleges allowed government to both determine the curriculum and ensure the demand for and supply of teachers was matched.

The outcome of these influences was a form of reverse or benign accountability insofar as the colonial government seemed unwilling to encourage the emergence of a more unified, professionalized and potentially subversive teaching force, and more accepting of a situation in which teachers were compliant, disunited and uncritical. Through inaction it effectively allowed the status quo to continue. Primary teachers were prepared through short sub-degree programmes in government-run colleges with a very strong technical orientation, while secondary schools were staffed by graduates, who often took a teaching job when the labour market was tight or while they searched for other employment. The government ensured thus that it was not faced with a more organized and professionalized teaching force.

The observation of the Visiting Panel (1982) was accurate and prescient:

... we are concerned with the lack of cohesion and indeed the absence of a sense of there being a teaching profession in Hong Kong as distinct from groups of teachers who work in particular schools. (p. 96)

Professionalism, Accountability and Self-Regulation

The government's desire to avoid the emergence of a stronger teaching profession was most evident in its response to the attempts in the 1980s and 1990s by external advisors and some members of the teaching community, led by university academics, to develop a self-regulating and accountable profession in Hong Kong. (For a full account, see Cheng and Wong, 1997).

Brown (1990: 159) defines accountability as having to answer for one's actions, and particularly for the results of those actions. Jones' (1992) definition of accountability, as the process of being called to account to some authority for one's actions, captures the essence of the concept. Mulgan (2000) comments on the shifting meaning of the term 'accountability' and underlines the need for conceptual clarification.

> *That 'accountability' is a complex and chameleon-like term is now a commonplace of the public administration literature. A word which a few decades or so ago was used only rarely and with relatively restricted meaning .... now crops up everywhere performing all manner of analytical and rhetorical tasks and carrying most of the major burdens of democratic 'governance' (itself another conceptual newcomer).* (p. 555)

Mulgan argues that if the concept has at its core the idea of being 'called to account', then this necessarily requires both some form of external scrutiny and the possibility of sanctions. The implications of this are that concepts of accountability based on an individual scrutinizing their own performance do not represent forms of accountability, but are more accurately described as forms of 'professional responsibility'.

Therefore, central to the debate about accountability is not the need for its existence, but rather its locus of control, as the critical question that arises is to whom teachers are expected to be accountable for their actions. If one views accountability as an obligation for any profession, then it would essentially involve an ongoing process undertaken by the professional community. If, however, there is not widespread trust in the competence and overall professionalism of teachers, and/or if the profession does not, or is not permitted to, hold its members accountable, then their performance will be increasingly monitored and judged by agencies established outside the profession – specifically and most notably by the state. Even where the process of accountability is undertaken within a profession, the power to both scrutinize members of the profession and use sanctions is ultimately delegated by the state. Throughout this article, the focus is on the former aspect of accountability, that is external scrutiny.

The Visiting Panel recommended in 1982 the setting up of a teaching service (akin to a General Teaching Council) independent from the government that would promote and monitor the profession and hold members accountable through the power of registration and deregistration. The Education Commission, which operates as the main advisory body on education policy, in its second Report (ECR2, 1986) rejected this proposal and instead recommended the establishment of a Teachers' Centre and publication of a voluntary Code of Practice, which would be designed to foster a sense of professionalism. These were implemented and a large committee elected by teachers and other education workers undertook the latter task. The *Code for the Education Profession of Hong Kong* (1990) was published after an extensive public consultation process, and was used as another opportunity to recommend the establishment of an independent professional entity, called a General Teaching Council, as a body to implement the code and maintain professional discipline. A proposal to this end was subsequently made, but again rejected by the Education Commission in its fifth Report (ECR5, 1992).

Instead the Commission counter-proposed that a Council on Professional Conduct in Education be established by the government's Education Department and recommended that its main role would be to advise the Director of Education in cases of dispute concerning misconduct. This body was established and recently criticised by government officials (South China Morning Post dated 9 May 2006) for failing over two years to substantiate any of the complaints against teachers. The Commission Report also recommended setting up the Advisory Committee on Teacher Education and Qualifications (ACTEQ). This is the only formal body empowered to support the process of professionalization of teaching. However, it is a classic example of the government's instinct to rely on a top-down, bureaucratic and paternalistic approach. The government controls the Committee's membership and agenda, and in 2002 the representatives of the teacher education providers were excluded from the membership as they were too argumentative. The Committee's work has been characterized by a lack of focus and consultation and a failure to address the most critical issues, namely the declining attractiveness of teaching as a career and the low level of professionalism.

The key elements of this saga of proposal and counter proposal were that whilst advocates from the profession desired to create a self-regulating and independent body with powers, the government's goal was to maintain control and avoid either the emergence of a potentially strong professional body or a potentially powerful body that might be taken over and politicized by the PTU. The Education Commission was used to neutralize the quest for self-regulation and was willing to do so for two reasons. Firstly, there was a genuine concern that any representative body would be dominated and politicized by the PTU. Secondly, in the run up to ECR5 in 1992, the Commission was willing to compromise on this issue so as not to jeopardize the progress it had made in other areas of policy, especially that related to disestablishing the Colleges of Education, setting up the HKIEd as an autonomous tertiary institution, and the creation of 35 percent of graduate posts in primary schools. These policies were designed to strengthen the teaching profession and initially were strongly resisted by the government.

In many respects, the core issues and tensions were very similar to those seen elsewhere as governments and the teaching force compete to exercise control over the profession. As Ingvarson (2000) comments with regard to the Australian experience, governments will not relinquish their powers of control easily or voluntarily. In recent years, in Hong Kong, the idea of a General Teaching Council re-emerged on the policy agenda and in 1997 the Education Commission set up a working party to pursue the issue. There has been, to date, no substantive progress on the issue.

The ways in which teachers were held accountable, albeit in its loosest sense of that concept, emerged not from the state or the professional community but from the various charitable and religious bodies that ran most of the schools and regulated them directly within the broader context described earlier (only about 10 percent of schools are directly run by the government). The key aspects of that context were that the government maintained direct control of both the nature of the curriculum and the system of public examinations. Teachers were employed by schools that competed vigorously to recruit and retain the most academically able pupils. The key element within this competition was the school's public examination results and the associated capacity to provide pupils access to higher levels of education, i.e. secondary or tertiary level. The examinations involved pupils studying curricula that had been carefully devised by the government to ensure a focus on matters academic and the avoidance of any content that might be viewed as politically sensitive or questioning the legitimacy of the government (Morris, 1996).

The combination of this highly competitive and exam-oriented system along with the strong central control of school curricula and a weak teaching profession, characterized by the absence of any entry requirements or mechanisms to ensure accountability, resulted in a very effective but instrumental and narrow system of accountability. Teachers and pupils both worked hard in an attempt to secure success in the public examinations, which would decide both the pupil's future in the highly competitive educational system, where the chances of going on to higher education were strongly influenced by the kindergarten, primary and secondary schools attended, and the status of the individual teachers in schools. The resulting definition of the role of the teacher as primarily a coach of pupils preparing for external and decontextualized public examinations was reinforced by the fact that the vast majority of pupils would be taking their examinations in English and many of the teachers and pupils had a poor level of proficiency in that language. In effect teachers, especially those in secondary schools, were primarily judged by reference to and held accountable for the examination results of their pupils.

Whilst there were some post World War II incidents where the government acted to remove teachers who were attempting to promote politically subversive ideas (Sweeting, 1993), on the whole there was no formal system designed to appraise, monitor or regulate teachers. The overall picture was therefore one of an absence of any formal accountability by either the professional community or the government, and this occurred in an environment where there was a weak degree of professional autonomy and a very low level of professionalization amongst teachers. The accountability that did operate was of a generic nature and a by-product of a highly competitive examination-driven system.

The government thus effectively extended its laissez-faire economic policy to its relationships with schools and to the teaching profession except wherever a threat might emerge to its stability. Thus the riots of 1966/67 saw the introduction of a number of measures to strengthen the government's control of schools and to de-register teachers who worked in the pro-communist patriotic schools (Sweeting, 1993). However, with the excesses of the cultural revolution in China, the role of schools in Hong Kong as a proxy for China's political tensions became far less pronounced after the late 1960s, when schools devoted themselves to the task of preparing pupils for public examinations.

The Present

The post-handover government therefore inherited a system that was characterized by a restricted professionality and a low level of professionalism, especially in terms of the absence of any specific processes of either an internal or external nature to promote accountability. The only significant changes accepted and implemented prior to the handover were those recommended by ECR5 to establish the HKIEd (formed in 1994 from the merger and disestablishment of the Colleges of Education) and that 35 percent of teachers in primary schools should be graduates.

Thus, on 1 July 1997, the system continued to prepare teachers for primary schools and cultural subjects through sub-degree courses which officially prepared primary teachers to teach four subjects, accepted students to train as teachers prior to their completing secondary schooling, allowed many teachers to teach subjects they had not previously studied at an advanced level and allowed people to obtain employment as teachers who had received no professional training. Whilst the creation of the HKIEd in 1994 took teacher education out of the hands of the civil service, it was expected to continue to primarily provide sub-degree courses as the policy was that only 35 percent of primary school teachers were to be graduates. It was thus perceived to be operating on the margins of the higher education sector despite being placed under the aegis of the University Grants Committee (UGC) from 1996. This served to maintain the low status of teaching (or as the Holmes Report described it the cycle of 'mutual impairment') and make it difficult for the main teacher education institution to compete with the seven universities to recruit staff and students.

The post-handover period has been characterized by a far greater concern for developing and implementing educational reform policies designed to improve the quality of schooling. To achieve this has required not only a completely new curriculum framework and the implementation of its longstanding policy on medium of instruction, but also a focus on matters of accountability and quality assurance, especially as they relate to the capabilities and qualifications of teachers. Some of the key manifestations of the increased focus on implementing educational reforms include enforcing from 1998 the policy that all but 114 secondary schools use Chinese as the medium of instruction and, from 2002, the reduction of the bandings of pupils' academic abilities from five to three (pupils are allocated to secondary schools based upon their banding).

The period since reunification has also seen a number of significant measures designed to both enhance the status of the teaching profession and/or introduce measures designed to allow the government to regulate both teachers and teacher education. Key measures proposed or the actions taken include the following:

- In 1997 the Chief Executive announced in his Policy Address that in future all new primary and secondary school teachers would be graduates and professionally trained. From 2002 all sub-degree teacher education courses (except in the area of early childhood education) were closed down and thus all future primary and secondary teachers will be graduates. This had an immediate impact on the HKIEd which rapidly phased out its sub-degree courses and replaced them with degree programmes. Now over 70 percent of its students are following degree and postgraduate programmes. However, the requirement that all new teachers be professionally trained has not been implemented and a significant proportion of new teachers have received no professional preparation.

- Whilst all new teachers are now graduates, only 35 percent of the posts in primary schools are at graduate level, and 70 percent in secondary schools. This means that in practice most primary school teachers are on the non-graduate pay scale, regardless of their qualifications, which is about 20 percent lower than the graduate scale. The primary teachers who hold graduate posts are on a pay scale which has a top point which is about 15 percent less than that of graduate secondary teachers.

- In 2000 the government stipulated that all new kindergarten teachers would have to undertake at minimum a Qualified Kindergarten Teacher's course by 2003/04, which involves a period of study of one year. Before 2001/02, the minimum entry requirement was only two passes in the Hong Kong Certificate of Education Examination (HKCEE) taken at the end of Secondary Five, including one language subject. After 2001/02, this was raised to five passes, including two language subjects.

- In 2000 the government introduced a requirement that teachers of English and Putonghua, who were not exempted by virtue of having done a first degree and a Postgraduate Diploma in Education in the language they taught, had to pass a language proficiency attainment test (LPAT). This measures their competency in five areas (Reading, Writing, Listening, Speaking and Classroom Language Assessment). In 2003, out of the 643 serving English teachers who had joined the teaching force in 2001/02 and were required to take the test, 333 failed and their schools have had to redeploy them to teach other subjects or dismiss them. Whilst there are a range of controversies concerning the nature of the assessment – especially with regard to its difficulty level, the need to pass in five discrete areas and the fact that some native English-speaking teachers have also failed the test – it represents the first attempt in Hong Kong to specify and implement a minimum level of competence for teachers of any subject.

- A report in 2003 by the Standing Committee on Language Education and Research (SCOLAR), which advises on language education, addresses problems related to the qualifications and proficiency of language teachers. It recommended that schools be required to only employ language teachers who majored in the language they teach and who are professionally trained. The achievement of this goal will take time, but will eventually make the LPAT unnecessary. The policy will, if implemented, ensure that primary schools recruit nearly exclusively only teachers who have majored in English and Chinese.

- More recently, a range of measures have been introduced to change the mechanism by which teacher education is resourced. Under the mantra of competition, value for money, reducing costs and enhancing reform, both in service and full time teacher education programmes are increasingly being provided through competitive tenders or commissions rather than through the provision of dedicated student places via the UGC. This has initially occurred for teacher education provision in those areas of schooling which are less established such as early childhood and special needs. Whilst this is portrayed as a move to achieve the deregulation and competition of the free market, when examined in detail it does not result in a move to private provision. Rather it involves the state moving away from being a provider of resources for teacher education to being a 'purchaser of services' from the teacher education institutions who are described as 'service providers'. As Elliott (2001) argues, this places the state (as purchaser) and teacher education providers in a new relationship which is based on contractual accountability which is used to determine the "quality" of provision.' The nature of the contracts has been used as a mechanism for the ongoing surveillance and control at a micro level of the curriculum, teaching materials and the teachers. Thus recent contracts issued by the Education and Manpower Bureau (EMB) have required the providers to: video-tape all classroom sessions and provide the videos to government, submit all teaching materials (e.g. handouts and powerpoints) to the government; transfer the ownership of the copyright of all teaching materials used to the government; provide details of all teachers; and allow a government official to sit in on all classes. This is all portrayed as part of a quality assurance process, but the requirement that all classes be video-taped has resulted in some attendees refusing to contribute to any discussions. The contractual terms have also been used to request changes of the teacher and of specific powerpoint slides.[1] In effect, the use of contractual arrangements to provide teacher education programmes is being used to create a powerful mechanism for the surveillance and monitoring of the ongoing delivery of courses by the state. In the final analysis, this arrangement ensures that any differences of viewpoint are only subject to resolution in terms of the nature of the contractual terms.

There are major limitations on the implementation and influences on the development of these policies that arise as a result of the 'legitimacy deficit', which refers to the situation whereby neither the colonial government nor its successor is perceived to possess a strong mandate from the people to govern. Whilst the government is able to control a majority of seats in the legislature, this is done through a series of functional constituencies. Only 24 of the 60 seats in the Legislative Council are directly elected through a system of universal suffrage, and the majority of the directly elected politicians are strongly pro-democracy and anti-government. It is notable that the

---

[1] As a communication to a 'service provider' stated: "*While we respect the professional understanding of the trainers, I have to point out that as discussed in our meeting after the award of the contract and as specified in our quotation document for commissioned course, contractors are to note that the design of the course content should be in line with the existing education policies and with the aim to help the participants to assume the role of school managers more confidently and not to frighten them off the course. As such, taking on the experience in Programme A, I should be grateful if you could revisit the course content and speaker for session one in the coming programmes for the rest of this school year.*"

largest functional constituency is for teachers and this has always elected a leading member of the Democratic Party. What emerges therefore is an elected opposition, which is perceived by the public to have a higher level of legitimacy than the government (Kuan and Lau, 2002). This deficit places limitations on the government's ability to implement unpopular policies, especially in the context of a lively civil society, a free and critical media and, in the educational policy arena, a strong teachers' union. The low level of legitimacy ensures that most new policies in education are highly contested. Whilst the colonial government obtained a form of legitimacy by providing (or at least operating during) a climate where people could pursue their economic self-interest, this option was less evident during the onset of the Asian economic crisis from 1997 up until 2000. The post-handover government has instead attempted to achieve some legitimacy by demonstrating its commitment to reforming/improving key areas of social policy such as education and housing.

The legitimacy deficit, and the associated lack of a popular mandate, encourages the government to promote educational reform by portraying themselves as protecting and promoting the interests of pupils and parents against an out-moded, recalcitrant and self interested education establishment. This strategy has been supported through the use of a number of interconnected tactics. The first involves the fostering of a climate of heavy-duty criticism of the status quo as the rationale for introducing new policies which are based on appeals for essentially rhetorical concepts such as the 'knowledge society', 'life-wide learning' and 'learning to learn'. In parallel, it is implied through constant reference to the need for 'fundamental reform' and 'comprehensive change' that the pursuit of this goal will require radical rather than evolutionary policies. Thus weaknesses and problems in the local school system are highlighted, turned into a policy problem and contrasted with an ideal (Morris and Scott, 2003).

Secondly, features of the local education system are selectively contrasted to those elsewhere (Morris, 1998) and again extensive reference is made to the need for fundamental or revolutionary rather than evolutionary change. This has often involved comparing aspects of public schooling in Hong Kong, especially English language proficiency standards, with those of elite and/or private schools elsewhere. This resonates easily with leaders of the business community and the local policy making elite who have often been themselves educated in private schools and/or send their children to them.

The third tactic involves, as Choi (2005) argues, identifying a set of global trends and developments and suggesting that everyone else is moving in this direction and if Hong Kong does not introduce fundamental reforms, then it will be uncompetitive, be left behind and that these changes are inevitable. The global trends identified have tended to promote the discipline of the competitive market as the solution to educational problems. Thus privatization, managerialism, competition and accountability emerge as solutions and those who question this goal are dismissed as self-interested Luddites determined to stop progress. As the key policy document (EMB, 2000) expresses it:

> To really benefit students, schools, teachers, parents and all sectors of the society should be prepared to show commitment, make contributions and to embrace these changes.

Thus longstanding features of the system, especially its exam-oriented nature, the competitive culture, the focus on discrete academic subjects and the low level of teacher professionalism have all become the object of government-led ridicule and derision within which teachers are often portrayed as unwilling to change and the key source of the problems. The undesirable features of pedagogy, pupils perceived declining language proficiency, and the problems encountered in implementing the curriculum reforms have all been portrayed as the direct fault of teachers and/or the providers of teacher education. The fact that many teachers were untrained, not teaching the subject they specialized in or they only had two or three years of sub-degree level preparation education and that these features were the product of previous government policy is conveniently ignored. The overall negative climate as to the nature of schooling which emerged was also highly conducive to the government introducing the range of measures described above to directly evaluate, monitor and control teachers.

The fourth tactic involves a process of dealing with any perceived criticism of government policy in a way which combines vilification with retribution. The tactic is to publicly portray any criticism or opposition as solely motivated by the pursuit of self-interest or of power and treated accordingly. The response of the Secretary for Education and Manpower to the public concern expressed by the President of Lingnan University to the effectiveness of Associate Degree programmes in Hong Kong is illustrative. He explained "*No doubt, as programme director of the Civic Party's Institute for Public Service, he feels obliged to promote party politics ...... Perhaps it is pointless to argue with him as he may have a separate agenda*" (*South China Morning Post*, June 2006).

Employers of individuals who have criticized policies, especially the education reforms, have been pressured and the HKIEd specifically has been pressured to limit the academic autonomy of staff who have promoted policies, such as smaller class sizes, which contradict EMB's policies. The HKIEd also suffered major budget cutbacks following its organization of a School Principals' Conference which resulted in extensive criticism of the reform agenda.

The government's ambivalence towards the professionalization of teaching is therefore most evident in its treatment of the HKIEd. As noted earlier, this is the sole institution dedicated to teacher education. It was created in 1994 by the government as a mono-purpose institution and was expected to primarily offer sub-degree courses. This changed quickly in 1997 with the introduction of the 'all graduate all trained' policy which required it to upgrade and offer primarily degree and postgraduate level courses. In 2004, after external reviews by the UGC, it gained self-accrediting status. However, there was a great deal of resistance in government to see the HKIEd upgraded to a self-accrediting institution despite recommendations that its current status be upgraded (Report of the Teaching and Learning Quality Process Review Panel, 2003). The motives for this seem to derive from a combination of concerns. If the HKIEd were to become a university-level institution, then this would serve to upgrade the profession, limit the government's capacity to control its activities and perhaps dilute the role it plays as a convenient scapegoat for the low level of teacher professionalism. Ultimately, any upgrading of the HKIEd could also be at odds with the government's preference for promoting the professionality of teachers rather than the professionalism of the teaching force.

In the 1990s, a number of tertiary colleges, including Lingnan, Baptist and the Open Learning Institute were granted university title soon after they gained self-accrediting status and the primary criterion influencing that decision was the achievement of self-accrediting status. It was however made clear that self-accrediting status would not result in the HKIEd being awarded university title. Accordingly, no formal application was made by the HKIEd for university title despite the frequent requests from students who desired a title which reflected their status.

However in November 2005, the Minister for Education stated that he supported the re-titling to university of a private non self-accrediting post-secondary college. Questions were immediately asked as to why the HKIEd could not also be re-titled. The response was that this was not possible as it "only" trained teachers and its mono-disciplinary nature was contrary to the 'world trend'.[2] The EMB's unstated agenda for denying university title was to engineer the merger of the HKIEd with the Chinese University of Hong Kong. Whilst HKIEd was willing to consider a federal arrangement, it was not willing to implement a full merger. Subsequently, EMB, via UGC, moved to further cut undergraduate places which would have resulted in the closure of the only courses in Hong Kong, designed to train secondary Art and Music teachers. It also moved to exclude the HKIEd from a range of developments designed to upgrade opportunities for the upgrading of kindergarten teachers.

The HKIEd was thus placed in a situation where it was faced with a range of disarticulated policies and policy contradictions. Firstly, it was created by the government as a mono-purpose institution and subsequently it has been told by the UGC that its role is to only focus on teacher education and research relevant to the needs of local schools. Now the specialized role for which it was created and is required to maintain is cited as a reason for denying it a change of title.

Secondly, the government has frequently criticized the HKIEd for failing to recruit students with high A-level scores and used this as a reason for reducing its student numbers. At a systemic level, there is a major problem in Hong Kong in recruiting talented school leavers and graduates into the teaching profession. The reasons for this are complex, but key factors are the general climate of negativity towards teachers and the extensive coverage in the media of teacher redundancies, school closures, teacher workloads and suicides. The upturn in the economy has also had a cyclical impact. On top of these systemic factors, the HKIEd has found it difficult to compete as it lacks university title. The Chinese term for 'Institute' (學院) is associated with non-degree awarding institutions and is defined in the Ordinances as of lower status than a university. The HKIEd's 'threatened' situation

---

[2] Previously, in his post as Vice Chancellor of a local university, the Minister had attempted unsuccessfully to implement two other mergers as Secretary for Education and Manpower, The Chinese University of Hong Kong and The Hong Kong University of Science and Technology, and The Hong Kong Polytechnic University and The City University of Hong Kong.

has thus been the result of a convergence of a number of distinct strands: the government's desire to control the debate on educational policies was challenged by the HKIEd; a merger offered, the albeit superficially prospects of reducing costs and of recruiting students with higher 'A' level grades; and, it allowed key personnel in government to pursue their own political agendas. The situation faced by the HKIED became the focus of intense media speculation in early 2007 and this resulted in the Government establishing a Commission of Inquiry to examine allegations of interference in academic and institutional autonomy. The report of the Inquiry was published in June. It concluded, inter alia, that the former Principal Secretary for Education and Manpower had requested the President to curb the criticisms of Government policy by staff of the HKIEd. The commissioners commented "it was unacceptable that she did not express her opinions openly and through proper channels, but instead in a manner with the semblance, if not the substance, of intimidation and reprisal. The Commission disapproves of such behaviour unequivocally" (COI 2007). They also found that two allegations which emerged during the Inquiry did occur despite denials by those concerned. These were that the SEM had threatened to rape the HKIEd if it did not merge with CUHK and that the PSEM had requested a Professor to dismiss one of her colleagues. Following the release of the report the former PSEM resigned from government and the SEM was not reappointed. The Government has not accepted the report and is now undertaking a Judicial Review of it's findings. Notwithstanding, it is likely that the embarrassment of the Inquiry to the Government will result in not being treated in the way it was and being given University title.

Conclusion

Overall, the 'history' of both the proposed General Teaching Council (GTC) and the position of the HKIEd is indicative of a set of fundamental contradictions between the state's desire on the one hand to upgrade the teaching profession and on the other its policy actions to ensure that the GTC was stillborn and that the main institution involved with upgrading teachers remains marginalized. How might this paradox be explained? The potential explanations differ in terms of their emphasis on the changing macro-socio-political context or on specific local conditions. However, these explanations are not mutually exclusive as a range of factors at different levels have interacted and combined to create the scenario described. A comprehensive understanding would involve recognizing the intertwining or convergence of at least three distinctive explanatory strands.

Firstly, that the position of the HKIEd and GTC could be seen as a reflection of a broader global trend which has seen the decline of the welfare state and the emergence of a fundamental paradox in education policies. This has involved both an increasing emphasis on the role of markets and consumer choice (a weaker role for the state) operating in parallel with a far greater involvement of the state through a reliance on regulation, monitoring and surveillance (a stronger role for the state).

Green (1997) suggests that the overall motive for this increase of government intervention is a by-product of globalization which has limited the role of nation states in many areas (especially the economic) which were traditionally their responsibility. Apple (1998) and Whitty and Edwards (1998) argue with reference to the USA and UK respectively that this paradox has developed as a result of the 'conservative restoration' which is portrayed as an alliance of a range of powerful social movements including: neo liberals, neo conservatives, and authoritarian populists. Furlong et al. (2000) describe the different but essentially negative viewpoints of each of these movements towards the specific role of teacher education. It is questionable whether the ideology underlying these movements has been 'restored" in Hong Kong or has always prevailed. However, the post handover period has seen the government increasingly rely on the business elite as their natural political allies which involves a return to the situation that previously operated most ostensibly in the early 1970s. Consequently, policies premised on the primacy of subject knowledge over professionalism and a highly critical view of teacher education have prevailed. In parallel, we have seen the emergence of quasi markets in which contracts and commissions are used to create both a 'market' and to serve as a means of control and surveillance.

Secondly, that the position of the HKIEd and the GTC is primarily a manifestation of the ongoing ideological tension between the state and its teachers as they compete to define who has the power to control the profession. This tension, as Bottery (1998) has argued is evident in other parts of the public sector, such as the Police and Health sectors, as the government attempts to introduce the discipline of the market. Wilding's (1982) analysis suggests that governments are inevitably in tension with all professions who have a natural tendency to restrict entry and raise their members' benefits. Accordingly, governments are inevitably placed in a position where they both promote individual professionality and limit collective professionalism. This tension is exacerbated in Hong Kong where the state has also, as shown above, had a tendency to approach all education policies from the default position of ensuring that any threat to the weak legitimacy of the government by a strong teaching profession was avoided. Consequently, teachers in Hong Kong, as has been shown above, have never achieved the position of being an occupation with a high level of professionalism which had the autonomy and was licensed to act in ways which were in the best interests of the client. Their position has been more akin to what Dale (1989) terms as 'regulated autonomy' within which they have been subject to the direct control and surveillance by the state and of the market in which schools compete for pupils and pupils compete with each other. From this perspective, the government's position towards both the teaching profession and HKIEd can be interpreted as an attempt to ensure that respectively the profession does not achieve a greater level of autonomy and is maintained in a position of regulated autonomy and the HKIEd's status remains marginal.

A third possible explanation emerges from the work of Scott (2001) on the overarching impact in Hong Kong of the government's low level of legitimacy on all aspects of policy making. He argues that the absence of a popular mandate has contributed to a disarticulation of policy making since the handover. This refers to the increasing fragmentation and competition between the various components of the policy making community. Under the colonial government what was presented to the public was a relatively coherent and unified set of policies, which the civil service promoted and defended. This is not to suggest that dissent or conflict was absent but generally, conflicts between within the policy-making community were not open to public scrutiny. This was supported by a policy making process which made extensive use of a wide range of advisory bodies which effectively co-opted many dissenting voices. The political nature of the recent ministerial appointments from 2002 (as non civil servants) has also required them to seek legitimacy and credibility through the media and by maintaining a high public profile. Since 1997 this unity and coherence has disappeared as a range of new centres of power outside the traditional policy making community have emerged and the civil service itself has been portrayed as a policy problem – being deemed insufficiently loyal, over-manned and overpaid. In parallel, advisory bodies have increasingly only included members who are compliant. In 2002, to embrace the idea of public accountability, a set of 11 Ministers were appointed from outside the civil service to head the key ministries. The result is that the source and nature of policies has become fuzzy and contested as various groups attempt to define and redefine policies. The International Monetary Fund (IMF) noted this in June 2003, when it criticised as confusing the system of overlapping ministerial responsibilities. From this perspective, the policy contradictions affecting the HKIEd and the teaching profession are merely a reflection of a wider failure by government to pursue a coherent long-term policy as the various elements of the policy making community are increasingly uncoordinated, competitive and stress short term tactical rather than strategic concerns.

A final range of explanations emerges from those analysts (e.g. Dale, 1989; Salter and Tapper, 1981) who focus on the critical and changing role of the state and bureaucrats in policy making which is described by Neave (1988) as a shift from a 'bureaucratic state' to an 'evaluative state'. This shift in role is a corollary of the decline in the welfare state and the emergence of a strong regulatory state. These explanations focus on the tendency, clearly illustrated in the case of Hong Kong for the state to play an increasingly interventionist role through the active promotion of the role of the market and of contractual relationships. In parallel, the role and behaviour of public servants has changed away from that of the neutral professional whose task was to implement government's policies towards a more personalized, politicized and directive and evaluative role. Others distinguish between the decline of the 'bureaucratic professionals' and the emergence of the 'new managerialists' (Gerwirtz et al., 1995); and between 'social service' and 'commercialized' professionalism (Hanlon, 1998). In the latter, the role of public servants is a powerful and contested one as they design and interpret systems of evaluation and determine the allocation of funding. From this perspective, public servants play an increasingly powerful and politicized role in the implementation of policies and their inputs are increasingly open to charges of partisanship, retribution, self-interest and the tendency to allocate blame elsewhere. This would suggest that a focus on macro-socio/political conditions to explain education policies can be exaggerated and understate the impact of local political conditions.

In the scenario examined in this paper, each of the above explanations has some purchase. Those explanations which are manifested globally have clearly been evident, but they have been powerfully combined with those factors which are more specific to the local context and which have their roots in Hong Kong's distinctive political system.

References

Apple, M. (1998). Review Essay. *Educational Researcher*, Vol. 27, No. 6, pp. 27–28.

Bottery, M. (1998). *Professionals and Policy: Management Strategy in a Competitive World.* London: Cassell.

Brown, D.J. (1990). *Decentralization and School-Based Management.* London: Falmer.

Cheng, K.M. and Wong, S.Y. (1997). Empowerment of the Powerless Through the Politics of the Apolitical: Teacher Professionalism in Hong Kong. In B.J. Biddle (ed.), *International Handbook of Teachers and Teaching*. Dordrecht: Kluwer Academic, pp. 411–436.

Cheung, E. (2001). Hong Kong Secondary School Teachers' Understanding of Their Careers. Unpublished PhD thesis, The University of Hong Kong.

Choi, P.K. (2005). A Critical Evaluation of Education Reforms in Hong Kong: Counting Our Losses to Economic Globalisation. *International Studies in Sociology of Education*, Vol. 15, No. 3, pp. 237–256.

Code for the Education Profession of Hong Kong (1990). Hong Kong: Preparatory Committee, Professional Code for Educational Workers.

COI (2007) Report of the Commission of Inquiry on Allegations relating to the HKIEd. Government Logistics Department, HKSAR.

Dale, R. (1989). *The State and Education Policy*. Milton Keynes, UK: Open University Press.

ECR2 (1986). *Education Commission Report No. 2*. Hong Kong: Government Printer.

ECR5 (1992). *Education Commission Report No. 5*. Hong Kong: Government Printer.

Elliott, J. (1991). A Model of Professionalism and Its Implications for Teacher Education. *British Educational Research Journal*, Vol. 17, No. 4, pp. 309–318.

Elliott, J. (2001). *The Paradox of Educational Reform in the Evaluatory State and its Implications for Teaching and Teacher Education*. Keynote address to the annual conference of the International Council for Teacher Education, Santiago, Chile, July 2001.

Eraut, M. (1994). *Developing Professional Knowledge and Competence*. London & Washington DC: Falmer.

Etzioni, A. (1969). *The Semi-Professions and Their Organization: Teachers, Nurses, Social Workers*. New York: Free Press.

Evans, L. (1998). *Teacher Morale, Job Satisfaction and Motivation*. London: Paul Chapman.

Furlong, J. et al. (2000). *Teacher Education in Transition*. Buckingham, UK: Open University Press, p.6.

Gerwirtz, S., Ball, S. and Bowe, R. (1995). *Markets, Choice and Equity in Education*. Buckingham, UK: Open University Press.

Green, A. (1997). *Education, Globalisation and the National State*. Hampshire, UK: Palgrave Macmillan.

Hanlon, G. (1998). Professionalism as Enterprise: Service Class Politics and the Redefinition of Professionism. *Sociology*, Vol. 32, No. 1, pp. 43–63.

Hargreaves, D.H. (1994). The New Professionalism: The Synthesis of Professional and Institutional Development. *Teaching and Teacher Education*, Vol. 10, No. 4, pp. 423–438.

Holmes Group (1986). *Tomorrow's Teachers*. East Lansing, MI: The Holmes Group.

Hoyle, E. (1975). Professionality, professionalism and control in teaching. In Voughton, V. et al. (eds.), *Management in Education: The Management of Organizations and Individuals*. London: Ward Lock Educational in association with the Open University Press.

Hoyle, E. and John, P. (1995). *Professional Knowledge and Professional Practice*. London: Cassell.

Ingvarson, L. (2000). Teacher Control and the Reform of Professional Development. In H. Altrichter and J. Elliott (eds.), *Images of Educational Change*. Buckingham, UK & Philadelphia, PA: Open University Press, pp. 159–172.

Jones, G.W. (1992). The Search for Local Accountability. In S. Leach (ed.), *Strengthening Local Government in the 1990s*. London: Longman, pp. 49–78.

Kuan, H.C. and Lau, S.K. (2002). Between Liberal Autocracy and Democracy: Democratic Legitimacy in Hong Kong. *Democratization*, Vol. 9, No. 4, pp. 58–76.

Lai, K.C., Ko, K.W. and Li, C. (2001). Profile of the Teaching Profession in Hong Kong in the 1990s (update of Teacher Education Planning Digest, Issue 5). Hong Kong: Office of Planning and Academic Implementation, The Hong Kong Institute of Education.

Larson, M.S. (1977). *The Rise of Professionalism: A Sociological Analysis*. Berkeley & Los Angeles, CA: University of California Press.

Lo, M.L. (2000). Learning Without Tears: The Relativity of a Curriculum Reform and its Impact. In Adamson, B., Kwan, T and Chan, K.K. (eds.), *Changing the Curriculum: The Impact of Reform on Primary Schooling in Hong Kong*. Hong Kong: Hong Kong University Press, pp. 47–80.

Morris, P. (1996). *The Hong Kong School Curriculum: Development, Issues and Policies*. 2nd edn. Hong Kong: Hong Kong University Press.

Morris, P. (1997). School Knowledge, the State and the Market: An Analysis of the Hong Kong Secondary School Curriculum. *Journal of Curriculum Studies*, Vol. 29, No. 3, pp. 329–349.

Morris, P. (1998). Comparative Education and Education Reform: Beware of Prophets Returning from the Far East. *Education 3 to 13*, Vol. 26, No. 2, pp. 3–6.

Morris, P. and Scott, I. (2003). Educational Reform and Policy Implementation in Hong Kong. *Journal of Education Policy*, Vol. 18, No. 1, pp. 71–84.

Morris, P and Williamson, J. (eds.) (2000). *Teacher Education in the Asia-Pacific Region: A Comparative Study*. New York & London: Falmer.

Mulgan, R. (2000). 'Accountability': An Ever-expanding Concept? *Public Administration*, Vol. 78, No. 3, pp. 555–573.

Neave, G. (1988). On the Cultivation of Quality, Efficiency and Enterprise: An Overview of Recent Trends in Higher Education. *European Journal of Education*, Vol. 23, No. 1/2, pp. 7–23.

Report of the Teaching and Learning Quality Process Review Panel (2003). University Grants Council.

Review of Education System: Reform Proposals (Consultation Document) (2000). Hong Kong: Education Commission.

Salter, B. and Tapper, T. (1981). *Education, Politics and the State*. London: Grant McIntyre.

SCOLAR (2003). *Action Plan to Raise Language Standards in Hong Kong – Final Report of Language Education Review*. Hong Kong: Standing Committee on Language Education and Research.

Scott, I. (2001). The Disarticulation of Hong Kong's Post-handover Political System. *China Journal*, Vol. 43, pp. 29–53.

Shulman, L. (2005). *The Signature Pedagogies of the Professions of Law, Medicine, Engineering, and the Clergy: Potential Lessons for the Education of Teachers*. Delivered at the Math Science Partnership Workshop, National Research Council's Center for Education, 6–8 February 2005.

Sweeting, A. (1993). *A Phoenix Transformed: The Reconstruction of Education in Post-war Hong Kong*. New York: Oxford University Press

Visiting Panel (1982). *A Perspective on Education in Hong Kong: Report by a Visiting Panel*. Hong Kong: Hong Kong Government.

Wilding, P. (1982). *Professional Power and Social Welfare*. London: Routledge.
Whitty, G. and Edwards, T. (1998). School Choice Policies in England and the United States: An Exploration of Their Origins and Significance. *Comparative Education*, Vol. 34, No. 2, pp. 211–227.

Chapter 9
The Enablement of Teachers in the Developing World: Comparative Policy Perspectives

David Johnson

Introduction

This chapter argues that the enablement of teachers is probably one of the most important priorities for governments in the developing world. Teachers matter, because as much of the research shows, they have a significant impact on student learning. Thus, while there is little doubt that the development of teachers is perhaps the policy imperative most likely to raise the quality of education (Verspoor, 2008; UNESCO, 2005) and lead to substantial gains in school performance, achieving this has not at all been straightforward.

There is a severe shortage of teachers in developing countries and many of those in school are under-qualified. Recent research suggests that a significant number of teachers are unmotivated (Bennell, 2007), in part because of the difficult environments in which they work, the fact that they are poorly compensated, and that incentives are few and far between.

One of the consequences of this is that some of the best teachers from some countries in the developing world, such as South Africa, Zimbabwe, and Guyana, migrate to Europe or the USA, or from one developing country to another. It is also the case that many good teachers leave the teaching profession to work in the more lucratively paid private sector.

But while the poor remuneration accounts for much of the 'pull' or the so-called 'brain drain', political instability and violent conflict, and the HIV/AIDS pandemic are amongst those factors that account for the 'push'. For those that remain, many feel undervalued due to a lack of teacher participation in the policy process (Poo and Hoyle, 2001), or unsupported because of poor teacher management systems and a lack of continuous professional development. Many of these choose to 'disengage' from the profession, turning up for work - or not - (the rate of teacher absenteeism is very high in many developing countries) neither wanting to teach, nor in many cases, capable of so doing.

D. Johnson, R. Maclean (eds.), *Teaching: Professionalization,*
Development and Leadership,
© Springer Science + Business Media B.V. 2008

There is a general lack of professional support for teachers and a worrying absence of incentives and career path development. Often, those policies adopted by educational systems to redress teacher shortages, such as the 'emergency credentialing' of unqualified teachers, who are paid far less than qualified teachers, leads to anger and resentment. Seen against this background, the enablement of teachers in the developing world can only be described as testing.

This chapter provides an overview of the context of teaching and the status of the profession in developing countries. Then, through comparative analysis, it considers a number of policy options for the enablement of teachers.

Teaching in Developing Countries

It is fifteen years since Farrell and Oliveira (1993) undertook a review of teaching in developing countries and it seems that little has changed. The large majority of teachers in the developing world work under the most challenging conditions. Many schools are located in areas that are very difficult to reach and which are not served by a reliable form of transport. Thus some teachers, and of course children, often walk long distances to and from school. The physical infrastructure of schools is far from adequate. In many countries, where school buildings exist, they are poorly maintained and dangerous. Classrooms are overcrowded, some might argue as a result of the considerable momentum towards achieving 'Education for All' (Avalos, 2000). A recent study undertaken of 60 schools in three states in Nigeria (Johnson, Hsieh and Oniborn, 2007), found that lavatories for staff members were inadequate in 79% of schools. Further, there were no tables for teachers to work on in 75% of these schools. These conditions are compounded by the fact that in many schools, there is an inadequate supply of fresh drinking water, and an erratic supply of electricity. The combination of poor physical conditions and the very large class sizes found in the primary schools of many developing countries (between 40 and 80 children in a class) contributes to the fact that barely one-third of students who start primary schools reach grade 5 (Verspoor, 2008).

Outside of the schools, a combination of social, political and economic factors make the planning of teacher development and professionalization a near impossibility.

The HIV/AIDS pandemic has had a long lasting effect on the teaching profession and on the professional development of teachers. Recent research shows that those teachers living with HIV/AIDS are shunned by their fellow teachers and isolated, which does not augur well for systems in which teacher collaboration is fundamental for building the quality of teaching and learning. In addition to this, there are at least three other areas of concern: first, since teachers form part of a general pool of skilled human resource, AIDS related deaths are likely to result in a further drain on the availability of skilled teachers. Second, there is nothing to suggest that the infection rate amongst teachers is dissimilar to that of the general population and thus the teacher mortality rate is likely to grow over time. Third, the long periods of illness associated with AIDS, reduces teacher contact time, quality, continuity and experience (Badcock-Walters et al., 2003). The effects of AIDS on the teaching force in many developing countries are rapidly becoming clearer. According to UNESCO (2005), Zambia estimated that 815 primary school teachers (equivalent to 45% of those who had trained that year) died from AIDS in 2001. The Teachers Service Commission in Kenya report that the number of teacher deaths rose from 450 in 1995 to 1,400 in 1999, and a survey in four districts in Kenya found that in Kisumu, the district most affected by HIV/AIDS, the primary teacher attrition rate had risen from 1% in 1998 to around 5% in 1999 and had remained at that level since. At that rate, a quarter of the teaching force would disappear within five years (UNESCO, 2005).

Teachers have also been affected by violent conflict in many developing countries, including Rwanda, Sierra Leone, Afghanistan, Uganda, southern Sudan, Timor Leste, Sri Lanka, Cambodia and Angola, to name a few. According to Buckland (2005), some schools in Cambodia and Angola will not be usable for decades because they are in areas where the costs of clearing unexploded mines are prohibitive. More than two-thirds of the teachers in primary and secondary schools in Rwanda were either killed or fled, and in Cambodia and Timor Leste, the impact was even greater. In both countries, schools were left with hardly any trained or experienced teachers, and in the case of Timor Leste, the lack of trained or qualified personnel in its secondary system had a serious effect on access to tertiary education.

In addition to the need to recruit more teachers, improving the quality of the teaching force in terms of qualifications, experience, and competence, is a big challenge for countries in post-conflict reconstruction. Buckland (2005) points out that at the end of the conflict in Lebanon, for example, only 50 percent of its' teachers were qualified, a pattern that can be found in most conflict-affected countries. Further, it is also the case that administrative systems that have faltered when conflict was at its highest levels, remain weak long into the period of post-conflict reconstruction, and have a negative impact on teacher development and professionalization.

To return to the discussion more generally, it is interesting to look at the characteristics of the teaching force in developing countries.

The Characteristics of Teachers in Developing Countries

Large numbers of primary school teachers in developing countries do not have adequate academic qualifications (Hoover and Walforth, 1997; Osei, 2006; Raina and Dhand, 2000). Although there are no agreed benchmarks, becoming a primary school teacher can range from twelve to seventeen years of education. In some sub-Saharan African countries, out of a number surveyed in 2001, less than 10% of the teaching force met even the low minimum standard (lower secondary school education) and many countries fell short of standards set at upper secondary level (UNESCO, 2005). A study of fourteen low income countries, conducted by Schleicher, et al (1995) shows the low levels of education and training among primary-school teachers in these countries: 92% of teachers in Benin, 91% in Uganda and Tanzania, and 89% of teachers in the Maldives have less than nine years of education. By contrast, all teachers in Ethiopia had more than nine years of education. What is interesting is that in most of the countries surveyed, a majority of teachers had received at least some initial teacher training despite their very low levels of academic qualifications. In Benin for example, 92% of primary-school teachers had less than ten years of education but 99% had received training. Also of note is Ethiopia and Uganda. In Ethiopia, although all its teachers have more than nine years of schooling, only 13% have received any formal initial teacher training. In Uganda, this figure was 50%. Since then, it seems that the numbers of new primary school teachers meeting an acceptable norm, has been falling in several countries of the developing world, in all probability because of the pressure for more teachers to cope with increasing levels of enrolment. Increasingly common too, as is the case in China, is the recruitment of low paid, unqualified, substitute teachers as a way of reducing costs on local governments who have to foot the bill for teacher salaries (Jing and Hu, 2007). This highlights a particular problem of an unequal distribution of teachers within countries. Rural and hard-to-reach areas typically have less well-trained teachers (McEwan, 1999; Psacharopoulos et al., 1996).

However, the formal qualifications of teachers are an important, but not sufficient indicator of teacher quality. Perhaps more crucially are teachers' subject and professional knowledge and their ability to understand and make the best use of learning materials. Teacher subject knowledge is crucial and has been shown to be a good predictor of student achievement (Darling-Hammond, 2000). But, as we have seen above, the low number of years that some teachers have in school combined with the short and ineffective cycles of teacher training (Lewin, 2004), constrains their subject knowledge. While there are no formally accepted procedures for assessing the levels of knowledge that teachers do have, a recent study in seven southern African countries found that some primary school mathematics teachers possessed only basic numeracy and actually scored lower than students on the same tests (Postlethwaite, 2004). Johnson, Hsieh and Oniborn, (2007) carried out a rudimentary investigation into the reading and mathematics abilities of a small number of teachers in three states in Nigeria, and found, like Postlethwaite, (2004), reason to be concerned. Many teachers scored lower than the primary aged children that they were teaching. This suggests that pre-service teacher training, which usually combines theoretical and content knowledge with teaching practice in schools, may be ineffective (Lewin, 2004).

But there seems to be little incentive for teachers to improve their qualifications or to develop professionally. Teacher earnings are so poor that many find it hard to maintain a reasonable standard of living (Hedges, 2002; Tekleselassie, 2005). Most teachers have to maintain a household of four to five people on less than US$2 a day. Furthermore, teacher salaries have declined over time, relative to other professional groups. For example, in many countries of Africa, teacher earnings in 2000 were lower in real terms than in 1970. In Sierra Leone, the average monthly salary for government primary school teachers in late 2003 was US$50. This has fallen by over half in real terms since the mid-1990s. To make matters worse, teacher pay often arrives late. Little wonder then that teachers in the developing world take on additional work to make ends meet. In urban areas, teachers earn additional income through private tuition and in rural areas, teachers commonly sell cakes and sweets to their pupils during breaks (UNESCO, 2005). It is claimed that some teachers deliberately do not teach the full syllabus, forcing students to attend private classes. Interestingly, a randomised control trial on teacher incentives in Kenya found that providing teachers with incentives for obtaining higher learning outcomes, increased, rather than decreased the incidence of private tuition and that the gains made petered out over the long term (Glewwe, et al 2004).

The Status of the Teaching Profession in Developing Countries

While the above paints a bleak picture of teachers as low paid professionals, with inadequate knowledge, skills and motivation, it is not the intention here to demonise teachers. Many of them do the best they can, in a profession that has steadily lost its status, and with very little support from the education system. It is to this issue that we now turn.

There is a good deal of research to show that the attractiveness of teaching and its status as a profession is low (Coombe, 1997; Dyer, 1996; Saeed and Mahmood, 2002). So why become a teacher in a developing country? Avolos (2000) argues that there are few other occupational opportunities and Oplatka (2007) in her review of 31 papers in those journals that publish regularly on education in the developing world, suggests that the research additionally points to external reasons rather than internal motives. In India for example, Dyer, 1996 (cited in Oplatka, 2007), found that teaching was a pragmatic option for those in rural areas where there was a shortage of employment, and that becoming a teacher led to a 'settled and secure life' (p. 480). Anecdotal evidence from my own work in Pakistan reveals that those appointed as teachers are recognised as civil servants and as such are entitled to a pension and job security. For Pakistani women, interestingly, a career in teaching was viewed as a noble calling, and one that is encouraged by parents (Kirk, 2004 - cited in Oplatka, 2007; Barrs, 2005). There is also an interesting differences in the way in which teachers in different developing countries viewed the profession. For male teachers in Karachi, Pakistan, teaching was seen as important but was mainly a supplementary form of income. For women, it was seen as a fulfilling profession (Kirk, 2004 - cited in Oplatka, 2007).

Teachers as Professionals in Developing Countries

Let us now turn to the issue of teacher professionalism. It is revealing that the debate on the status of teachers in developing countries first received international attention more than forty years ago when the International Labour Organisation (ILO) and UNESCO published a set of recommendations on the Status of Teachers (ILO/UNESCO, 1966). The issues discussed and the resolutions that were passed have largely, and rather unfortunately, remained on the agenda. One key issue discussed then, and which still appears to be a problem today, is the notion of social dialogue in education. According to CEART (2006):

> 'social dialogue is understood to mean all forms of information sharing, consultation and negotiation between educational authorities, public and private, and teachers and their democratically elected representatives in teachers' organisations. These forms of dialogue variously apply to the major issues concerning the teaching profession: educational objectives and policies; preparation for the profession and further education for teachers; employment, careers and salaries of teachers; rights and responsibilities; and conditions for effective teaching and learning'.

CEART (2006) point out that social dialogue remains illusive, especially in situations where teachers work in isolation. They report the findings of a study which assembled the views of teachers and head teachers in Malawi, Papua New Guinea and Zambia, who feel that they do not have a voice in educational decision-making beyond their immediate teaching or school environment – a view supported by Poo and Hoyle (2001) with reference to South Africa.

Whilst the institutional context in which social dialogue takes place is important, as is demonstrated in the case of South Africa, where the development of the education Labour Relations Council provided a vehicle for bargaining around wages and conditions of service (Ratteree, 2004), there remain unhelpful schisms between educational authorities and teacher professional bodies over policy reform. Avalos (2000) points out that in both South Africa and Bangladesh, educational reforms preceded attention to teachers and this is confirmed by analyses of the history of educational reform in South Africa by both Jansen (2004) and Spreen (2004). More positively, social dialogue has been more successful in Indonesia, Mauritius, Namibia and Nicaragua (CEART, 2006).

A second contentious issue is that of teacher deployment and conditions of service. It is increasingly the case that the deployment of teachers is inequitable, for example, teachers in Ghana with poor linguistic competencies are posted to the rural areas (Hedges, 2002). There are also few incentives that include opportunities for further study or a link between an improvement in qualification or professional development and an improvement in salary. In some countries, poor pension plans and the lack of integration of incentives into these, the personal costs associated with further professional development, and the scarcity of promotion prospects, explain why teachers feel that their professional status is undermined.

The Enablement of Teachers: Comparative Policy Analysis

Given the context in which teaching takes place, the characteristics of teachers, and the status of the teaching profession, there is no doubt that the enablement of teachers, particularly through ongoing professional development, is for many developing countries, a key policy direction. We know that the curriculum in teacher training institutions is weak and the experiences of trainees, unsatisfactory. Lewin (2004) points out that time allocated to the teaching of subject knowledge, methods of teaching, knowledge about how children learn and teaching practice is varied, and that the importance of subject knowledge, given that many trainees lack basic knowledge, tends to be underestimated. Not only do many newly qualified teachers leave initial training institutions with inadequate knowledge of basic subjects or the 'what' of teaching, they are also ill-prepared for the 'how' of teaching. Lewin and Stuart, (2003) and Lewin, Samuel and Sayed, (2003) point out that many teachers do not have the necessary language fluency and capability to teach well and are often unable to engage adequately with in-service training materials. It is also clear that many teachers in developing countries have an impoverished understanding of learners and how they learn and a weak repertoire of strategies for dealing with a wide variety of learning situations. Little wonder then that many newly qualified teachers require a great deal of support from more experienced colleagues during their first year of practice (Lewin and Stuart, 2003; Lewin, Samuel and Sayed, 2003).

But, as I have suggested above, redressing the inadequacies of initial training and compensating for the poverty of the conditions of learning and teaching in developing countries is a testing task. There are many models of teacher professional development and according to Avalos, (2000) they can be conceptualized as strategies aimed at improving teachers' understanding of content, the quality of their instructional strategies, and their capacities to understand how children learn. Indeed, as the global context of education changes and there are increasingly new and different demands on teaching and assessment (Johnson and Kress, 2003; Day and Sachs, 2004), there is an expectation that teachers should be increasingly prepared, not only to implement change but to foresee its need and be imaginative and skillful in providing solutions to problems (Hargreaves, 1999), or in Hoyle's terms, to move from 'restricted' to 'extended' professionals (Hoyle, 1980). This seems to be true for teachers everywhere but the response to this in many countries has been the provision of models of continuous professional development aimed at 'accountability' and 'performativity' (Day and Sachs, 2004). But, while the purposes of continuous profession development in the developing world often mirror those in more-developed countries, i.e., raising the quality of education, the nature of the beast is very different. Christie et al (2004) point out that in several countries of sub-Saharan Africa, continuous professional development is more instrumental and teachers are cast into the role of technicians, in stark contrast to the emphasis on the reflective practitioner in the more-developed world. However, even here the constant drive for accountability undermines teacher 'professionality', encouraging instead a culture of compliance (see Hoyle and Wallace, 2005). But, as I point out below, where systems are so fragile and the possibilities for teacher development so weak, especially in large, heavily indebted poor countries, then more centralist models of teacher development, is perhaps not a bad thing.

The rest of this chapter is organised in three sections, each that deals with a different policy imperative for the enablement of teachers in the developing world. The first of these discussed here is the relatively common policy drive to strengthen educational systems in support of teachers (some would argue, a drive towards accountability). The emphasis here is the reform of inspection and supervision arrangements and I discuss the relative advantages of this below.

The chapter then looks at a less common approach to teacher enablement, but one that has been tried in several developing countries; that is, the potential efficacy of teacher centres. There are at least two variants to this model of professional development, the first a concentration of self contained resources centres close to an identified cluster of schools. The second, which is perhaps a more interesting variant, and one that is less common, is the school-based resource centre.

Teacher centres are aimed at developing and providing resources to assist teaching, the primary purpose being the improvement of pedagogy. More experienced teachers and those that display a propensity for innovation are identified and trained to provide support and 'know-how' to less experienced teachers. There are some criticisms of this approach, mainly that it has only a limited impact on classroom practice and at its' heart is a one-way knowledge transfer mode of professional development (Hoppers, 1998; De Grauwe, 2001). This is a little harsh given the context of teaching and learning in developing countries discussed earlier, and indeed the Sri Lankan and Gambian experiences discussed here, show that teacher centres can be very valuable in enabling teachers.

Finally, the chapter turns to a relatively uncommon approach to professional development. That is the development of teachers through assessment portfolio's. There is the suggestion from some quarters that continuous professional development should enable teachers to collaborate among themselves, to think about their teaching, to reflect on the social and cultural demands and constraints of the context in which they work and should involve networking among institutions, teacher educators, teachers, policy-makers and the community at large (Hargreaves, 1994; Furlong, 2000). Although this may prove illusive in those developing countries with weak national systems of education, it does not rule out a certain degree of experimentation in some developing countries as studies in South Africa (Johnson, 1998) and Malawi and Sri Lanka (Johnson, Hayter and Broadfoot, 2001) demonstrate. This is discussed more fully below.

Teacher Supervision and Inspection

A favoured policy response to redressing poor teacher quality in developing countries is the reform of the school inspection system (many of which have fallen into desuetude because inspectors have no transport to get to schools, particularly those in hard-to-reach rural areas, and which arguably are in greatest need of support). There appears to be a tension between those policy options that favour inspection as a means to ensuring accountability, and those that support the idea of inspection as a mechanism to support the development of teachers. In the latter case, the inspector is seen as a 'critical friend'. In the former, inspection is about ensuring accountability. Certain standards are set and schools are required to meet them. The logic is that accountability will lead to improvement because being accountable implies that if a school underperforms, actions to correct this will follow. In other words, tight inspection and control are essential for success Dalin (1992).

But, research on the effects of school inspection provides a mixed picture. There appears to be little evidence that inspection per se brings about improvement to the quality of teaching and learning within schools (Shaw, et al 2003) and indeed some research has shown that it could even reduce levels of student achievement in the year of the inspection (Rosenthal, 2004). There is however some evidence that inspection can lead to some improvement amongst the weakest institutions (Matthews and Salmons, 2004) and that it can act as an important catalyst for change (Gray and Gardner, 1999). The UK Office for Standards in Education (Ofsted) talk of 'Improvement through inspection', recognising that inspectorates have no direct control over all the factors that might lead to schools improving but that direct interventions such as the feedback provided to the school and the publication of school reports are highly likely to lead to improvement.

Yet, we do know that where there is an absence of an enabling framework, teacher accountability and performance is undermined. Indeed, reforming the arrangements for school inspection and supervision, particularly where it includes clearer job descriptions, seems to have positive effects on the quality of education. In Burkina Faso, for example, policies aimed at improving the guidance for *chefs de circonscription* (district officers) for supervising and supporting whole schools, and the other for pedagogical advisors for supporting individual teachers in their classrooms, have had impressive results on student performance (Samoff, et al 2000). In 2003 the success rate at the end-of-primary school national examination reached 70% for the first time (from an average of 50–60% before). In addition, gross enrolment reached 48%, against 39% 2 years before.

In Senegal, the absence of job performance specifications and a lack of clear guidance in what inspectors should do accounted for a drop in the number of school visits by inspectors from year to year, with enormous disparities in supervision between regions. To address this concern, a system of incentives based on a clear task definition for each of the main groups of personnel (teachers, heads and supervisors) was developed. As a result, learning outcomes improved as did the organisation of schools.

Reforming the arrangements for teacher supervision and inspection appears to be a promising policy option but the caveat here is that it assumes that steps have been taken to ensure the mobility of inspectors and access to most schools.

Developing Teacher Professionalism through Teacher Resource Centres

As pointed out above, many teachers in the developing world have inadequate subject and professional knowledge. Whilst the question of subject knowledge is more objectively assessed, it is worth noting that professional knowledge is not. There are many views as to what makes for the most effective teaching methods in developing countries, especially in those with large classes. One proposition is that whole class teaching, done well, is both realistic and effective. Another view is that teachers in the developing world ought to be more 'learner focussed' and as a result, many national curriculum reform imperatives, particularly those supported through development assistance, have favoured activity-based learning. Whatever the approach, judgements about the professional competence of teachers are difficult to define and to evaluate, especially when seen in the context of the prevailing conditions of many of the schools and classrooms in developing countries. Methodologically too, it is difficult to know whether the external observations of teachers' teaching, often confined to one lesson period, is a sufficient indicator of the quality of teaching (Johnson, 2007). Despite these reservations, it is commonly agreed that teachers who tell children the aim of the lesson, link the topic for discussion to earlier work, use, as far as possible, teaching aids, even those constructed by low cost materials, encourage some student participation (even if it is through a thoughtful approach to questions put to students in a whole-class teaching situation), and allow some time for students to demonstrate what they have learned (a written exercise, solving a problem on the blackboard, displaying a diagram, etc.,) have an acceptable range of teaching competencies. While this is by no means an exhaustive list of features of 'good' teaching, it does provide a starting point for the shaping of in-service professional development programmes.

The development of in-service provision for teachers demands a sound organisational structure and a carefully considered implementation plan. In many countries, cascade models of training, where experts train trainers, who in turn train teachers (often in the local language of the area) have had limited success. Teachers rarely have more than a few days of exposure to training, and from those training sessions that I have observed in Bangladesh and Sri Lanka, the content is much distilled. For these reasons, many governments in the developing world have experimented with the development of teacher resource centres for a more continuous development of teacher professional and subject knowledge. There are a number of variants to the model, and I shall discuss two of these, the impacts of which I have evaluated.

To support its mathematics curriculum reform strategy, the Government of Sri Lanka developed a national system for the provision of in-service education through the creation of 84 Teachers' Centres. Each centre was staffed by 3 mathematics teachers who were selected for their skills and expertise as good classroom practitioners. Those finally chosen, following interviews and classroom observations, underwent rigorous training as in-service advisers.

The main activity for the in-service advisors was the development and piloting of an intensive course over a 10-week period that dealt with many aspects of primary mathematics reform, including knowledge of the subject, effective classroom teaching strategies, and the development and use of low cost teaching resources. The course was modular in design and involved in-service advisors spending some time in schools, to observe the extent to which participants were able to put into practise what they have learned at the resource centre.

An evaluation of participant responses to the training showed high levels of teacher satisfaction (Johnson and Yahampath, 2003). Teachers indicated that they had learned things that they did not know before, and that their knowledge of mathematics had increased considerably. They valued the in-school follow up sessions, particularly the discussion between themselves and the in-service advisors that ensued after their teaching of a mathematics lesson.

School heads and the local community were equally enthusiastic. Many of those interviewed felt that something positive was happening in the school. Teachers seemed to be more motivated and children appeared to enjoy the challenge of more innovative approaches to teaching and learning.

More crucially, in a national longitudinal study of children's learning, we found that in those areas which were serviced by a teacher resource centre, learning achievements of children in classes 1, 2, and 3, improved significantly (over 2 standard deviations) on such tasks as 'sorting', 'conservation', 'measurement' and 'position' (Johnson and Yahampath, 2003).

But, the main drawback for the sustainability of the teacher resource centres in Sri Lanka was the lack of systemic reform of teacher career structures. Those teachers who were deployed to teacher resource centres were frustrated because of a lack of external recognition of their work, and the fact that there was no additional remuneration.

A second example of teacher centres and a different variant to the one just discussed is the school-based teacher resource centre, such as those developed with the support of the British government in The Gambia. In an ambitious professional development programme that aimed to enable teachers to support a national reform of Mathematics, English, Science and Social Studies, a number of enthusiastic and creative teachers were identified across the country and trained in regional resource centres by in-service advisors, who at that stage were drawn from a pool of British teachers attached to the Voluntary Service Organisation (VSO). The training took place a few afternoons a week after school. Once trained, these teachers were deployed into their own schools as Resource Teachers.

The project, which began in 1997 was evaluated in 2000 (Johnson, Hayter and Penny, 2000). In 2002, two years after the end of the project, a post-post evaluation was conducted to look at the extent to which the teacher professional development programme had been sustained (Johnson and Hayter, 2000). Fifteen schools which in 2000 were found to have significant levels of resource teacher activity and which subsequently led to strong continuous support for teachers in schools, which in turn had an effect on their approaches to teaching, were identified and re-evaluated.

The study found that seven schools were rated on average 2 points lower – thus a negative shift. Only two schools made small gains, each achieving a higher rating of 1 point; thus a positive shift. Five schools retained their ratings. On the whole therefore, it seems that the model of in-school professional development in The Gambia was self sustaining. But even so, there a number of factors that may undermine long term sustainability, the same being true for Sri Lanka.

First, policies for the redeployment of teachers are weak. In the case of The Gambia, the redeployment of Resource Teachers was a significant factor in the decline of professional development activity. Second, teachers such as those who have been trained are often deployed within the school to work with those classes preparing for a school leaving examination. They thus have less time to devote to carrying out their role as support teachers. Third, when external support for the resource centres cease, national governments tend not to allocate further finances to keep them running.

However, even with these caveats, teacher resource centres, especially school-based resource centres appear to be a useful policy direction for the enablement of teachers in developing countries.

I now turn to a possible policy direction that is relatively underdeveloped in the developing world; that of teachers' developing their professional knowledge and teaching expertise through developing an understanding of children's learning.

Developing Teachers' Understanding of How Children Learn

Teachers in developing countries are not always aware, and very rarely sensitized through professional development, to how children learn. The policy option below examines the extent to which it is possible for teachers in the developing world to collect concrete artefacts of children's learning, and to learn either individually or collectively from these. Essentially, teachers compile assessment portfolios for their students and in brief, this allows teachers a window through which they can judge their students' work, improve their teaching practice, and document their own progress.

In an interventionist study carried out in Malawi and Sri Lanka (Johnson, Hayter and Broadfoot, 2001) thirty teachers from different locations in each country were asked to collect samples of children's work. They were encouraged to bring a variety of samples such as writing and mathematics worksheets, but also samples of children's talk which was recorded verbatim on a 'teacher record sheet' the latter which was provided. Teachers were asked to select from work that they had broadly judged as 'good', 'average' and 'experiencing difficulties'. They were also asked to make brief written comments on each sample, justifying the broad achievement level awarded. Once this development work had been concluded, teachers went back to their own school and over a two year period began to build up portfolios of their children's work.

Asking teachers to annotate and learn from their children's work produced interesting results. Although teachers cannot be said to have 'uncovered' the learning processes associated with the tasks themselves, it is clear that some teachers were beginning to think about the factors which influenced learning, as well as the processes of learning. Take the following comment by a teacher in Malawi who was looking at the relative performance of a student on a mathematics task:

> 'The performance of this child in mathematics is average because wherever he has been given work to do he tries as much as possible to get it right. At times he manages to do so but at times with difficulties, for example when an example has been given the teacher must repeat it several times before he understands what is expected to do. A number of skills and methods must be used in order for him to grab a thing. For example, if the teacher is to explain about a triangle using bottle tops he/she has to demonstrate, then do practice together with the pupil, then ask him to do by himself. In so doing is able to do it correctly.

> *The problem in understanding is not because the pupil is not intelligent but because he lacks continuous practice at home as well as at school, because of the swollen numbers of pupils in one class. Given a chance to learn in a class where the number of pupils is reasonable and the teacher is able to do individual help probably he can do better than at present'.* (Johnson, Hayter and Broadfoot, 2000: 67)

Of a second child, the teacher has this to say:

> *According to the performance of this pupil, it shows that the girl is able to do a good number of activities with little supervision. For example once she has been given an example in Mathematics, she is able to do the rest on her own. After thorough investigations it was discovered that she is able to grab things fast because before her primary education she had attended nursery school. She has got sisters who are in private schools where English is fluently spoken. Her family is well to do. According to reliable sources her parents once worked outside this country where probably life is a bit advanced...'* (Johnson, Hayter and Broadfoot, 2000: 68)

The big question of course is whether activities of this kind can be scaled up in policy terms. The biggest challenge would be the manageability of task administration as a method of gathering evidence of children's achievements. According to Sheil and Forde (1995) the manageability of a profiling system is vital to its success. They argue that administration of tasks, documentation and reporting procedures are time consuming and when demands on teachers become excessive, the profiling system may be regarded as unmanageable. The study found that administering the learning tasks were indeed demanding of teachers' time. Teachers in Sri Lanka found that using the tasks as assessment tools was not necessarily new to them, but the practice of making notes or recording their findings, was definitely unfamiliar.

The physical size of the classrooms in the schools involved in the study was also a factor. None of the teachers involved in the study were able to use the tasks with all the children in their classes, but this is neither important, nor necessary if the purpose of the exercise is professional development rather than assessment per se. This last point is crucial. Despite the reservations raised here, a more limited exercise in which teachers across a country are trained to look at the artefacts of a small number of children is an excellent means of helping them to understand their own teaching in relation to children's learning. The problems of management not withstanding, this policy direction for the enablement of teachers has much promise.

A second variant of this method of teacher professional development was carried out in a small study in South Africa (Johnson, 1998). This exercise was more limited than the study carried out in Malawi and Sri Lanka (Johnson, Hayter and Broadfoot, 2000) in that it provided teachers with a 'ready made' set of learning criteria which they were expected to apply to samples of children's learning. Here again, thirty teachers from different types of school (at the time they were organised by racial groups) and with vast disparities in resources and resource allocation, were brought into a series of professional development workshops. Teachers were also asked to bring samples of children's work to these workshops but rather than developing their own levels of achievement, they were asked to rate these pieces of work in relation to a set of indicators of achievement and from this to develop a portfolio of evidence. What was different and perhaps more interesting than the Johnson, Hayter and Broadfoot study, was the fact that teachers used a given set of criteria repeatedly over time to chart the learning development and progression of a small number of students (Johnson, 1998). This proved to be very successful for a large number of individual teachers.

But on the whole, the collection of evidence proved to be a challenging task for teachers. Samples of children's work was collected haphazardly and bears out the findings of Gipps et al. (1995) that the systematic collection of evidence is not an easy task for teachers. Some teachers reported that they collected almost everything they could with the intention of finding something that would constitute evidence of achievement.

Additionally, resource limitations proved to be an influence upon the amount and range of evidence of achievement which could have been accumulated. The research recognised that there would be a disparity between schools in the sample in relation to materials used in the classroom, and thus resultant artefacts. In less well resourced schools, even techniques such as marking places in children's exercise books where evidence of achievement was visible, and annotating this into a record of achievement for the pupil, proved to be difficult.

Apart from the problems of collecting evidence physically, it is clear from the data that many teachers had a problem in determining what constituted 'relevant and appropriate' evidence. Some of the samples of evidence examined did not always appear to relate closely or to support the attainment target under consideration. It was also difficult to determine how long it was appropriate to keep evidence of attainment since this soon became dated as children made progress in and across learning areas.

The biggest gain from the professional development exercise is that teachers used the learning indicators for formative, diagnostic and evaluative purposes, and as a meta-language for talking about children's learning. Interestingly, in policy terms, the methods used in this study were incorporated into the professional development framework of the Outcomes Based Education curriculum model adopted in South Africa a few years later. Sadly, the indicators were much more complex and the demands on teachers' time, colossal. So much so, that there was much pressure for the government, even after attempts at revision, to abandon this approach to assessment and teacher professional development. Teachers have never really taken this policy direction to heart and the fact that they had been ignored in its development, accounts for some of their resistance to it. We can do well to learn from Maxwell and Cumming (1998) who comment on this from the Australian experience:

> Change which calls for fundamental reorientation of teachers' thinking and fundamental redesign of teachers' practice, that is change which involves a paradigm shift across the whole teaching profession, requires a process of individual intellectual struggle on the part of all teachers in order for the new paradigm to overthrow the old. For this to be successful, teachers need to perceive some purpose or advantage in engaging in the struggle. (p. 3)

Conclusions

The chapter provided an overview of the context of teaching, the characteristics of teachers and the status of the teaching profession in the developing world. In discussing the enablement of teachers in developing countries, I am reminded of the many discussions I have had with Eric Hoyle, based on his experiences in The

Gambia, South Africa and Zimbabwe. For him, as for me, the very basic conditions in which teachers teach and the very different goals they try to address, renders any model of professional development adopted uncritically destined to failure. It is important we felt, to find a way of addressing the most basic needs of teachers, almost in a Maslovian way, before attempting approaches aimed at their self-actualisation. As we have seen in this chapter, the basic needs of teachers in the developing world are considerable and any policy options for the enablement of teachers must take account of this reality. Of course we live in times where educational policies for the developing world are imposed, negotiated under constraint or literally bought and sold, depending either on the extent to which a country is aid dependent or in a position to experiment within its own policy environment (Johnson, 2006(b)). We know better than to assume a similar level of educational development in all developing countries and thus submit that any of the three models of professional development discussed above are indicative of a spectrum of approaches that might be applied, consequent upon a carefully costed, culturally and socially validated comparative analysis.

References

Avalos, B. (2000) Policies for teacher education in developing countries. *International Journal of Educational Research*, 33, 457–474

Badcock-Walters, P., Kelly, M., Görgens, M. (2004) *Does Knowledge Equal Change? HIV/AIDS Education and BehaviourChange*. Background paper for *EFA Global Monitoring Report 2005*.

Barrs, J. (2005) Factors contributed by community organisations to the motivation of teachers in rural Punjab, Pakistan, and implications for quality teaching. *International Journal of Educational Development*, 25, 333–48

Barrs, M. (1988) *The Primary Language Record: Handbook for Teachers*. London, Hodder & Stoughton.

Bennell, P. and Akyeampong, K. (2007) *Teacher Motivation in Sub-Saharan Africa and South Asia*. London, DFID

Buckland, P. (2005) *Reshaping the Future: Education and Post-Conflict Reconstruction*. Washington, World Bank.

CEART (2006) Joint ILO/UNESCO Committee of Experts on the Application of the Recommendations concerning Teaching Personnel, 9th Session. Geneva, ILO/UNESCO

Christie, P., Harley, K. and Penny, A. (2004) Case studies from sub-Saharan Africa. In C. Day and J. Sachs (eds) *International Handbook on the Continuing Professional Development of Teachers*. Berkshire, Open University Press

Coombe, C. (1997) Unleashing the power of Africa's teachers. *International Journal of Educational Development*, 17, 1, 113–117

Dalin, P. (1992) *How Schools Improve: An International Study*. London, Blackwell

Darling-Hammond, L. (2000) Teacher quality and student achievement: a review of state policy evidence. *Education Policy Analysis Archives*, 8, 1

De Grauwe, A. (2001) School supervision in four African countries. Vol. I, Challenges and Reforms. Paris, UNESCO International Institute for Educational Planning

Day, C. and Sachs, J. (2004) Professionalism, performativity and empowerment: discourses in the politics, policies and purposes of continuing professional development. In C. Day and J. Sachs (eds) *International Handbook on the Continuing Professional Development of Teachers*. Berkshire, Open University Press

Dyer, C. (1996) Primary teachers and policy innovation in India: some neglected issues. *International Journal of Educational Development*, 16, 1, 27–40

Farrell, J. P. and Olivea, J. B. (eds). (1993) *Teachers in Developing Countries: Improving Effectiveness and Managing Costs.* Washington, The World Bank

Furlong, J., Barton, L., Miles, S., Whiting, C. and Whitty, G. (2000) *Teacher Education in Transition.* Buckingham, Open University Press

Gipps, C. Brown, M., McCallum, B. and McAlister, S. (1995) *Intuition or Evidence.* Buckingham, Open University Press.

Glewwe, P., Ilias, N. and Kremer, M. (2004). Teacher incentives. Mimco Harvard University (1996) The relevance of standard estimates of rates of return to schooling for educational policy: a critical assessment. *Journal of Development Economics,* 51, 267–90

Gray, C. and Gardner, J. (1999) The impact of school inspections. *Oxford Review of Education,* 25, 4, 455–469

Hargreaves, D. (1994) The new professionalism: the synthesis of professional and institutional development. *Teaching and Teacher Education,* 10, 4, 423–38

Hargreaves, D. (1999) Helping practitioners explore their school's culture. In: J. Prosser (ed) *School Culture.* London: Paul Chapman

Hedges, J. (2002) The importance of posting and interaction with the education bureaucracy in becoming a teacher in Ghana. *International Journal of Educational Development,* 22, 353–366

Hoover, M. and Walforth, J. (1997) Effects of community-based training on teachers' attitudes in Andrean Peru. *Teaching and Teacher Education,* 13, 4, 383–396

Hoppers, W. (1998) Teachers' resource centers in Southern Africa; an investigation into local autonomy and educational change. *International Journal of Educational Development,* 18, 3, 229–46.

Hoyle, E. (1980) Professionalisation and de-professionalisation in education. In: E. Hoyle and J. Megarry (eds) *World Yearbook of Education: The Professional Development of Teachers.* London, Kogan Page

Hoyle, E. and Wallace, M. (2005) *Educational Leadership: Ambiguity, Professionals and Managerialism.* London, Sage

ILO/UNESCO (1966) Joint ILO/UNESCO Committee of Experts on the Application of the Recommendations concerning Teaching Personnel. Geneva. ILO/UNESCO

Jansen, J. (2004) Importing outcomes-based education into South Africa: policy borrowing in a post-communist world. In: D. Phillips and K. Ochs (eds) *Educational Policy Borrowing: Historical Perspectives. Oxford Studies in Comparative Education.* Oxford, Symposium Books

Jing, Z. and Hu, W. (2007) Country Profile Prepared for the Education for All Global Monitoring Report 2008. Education for All by 2015: Will We Make It?

Johnson, D. (1998) Teacher assessments and literacy profiles of primary school children in South Africa. *Assessment in Education: Principles, Policy and Practice,* 5, 3, 381–412

Johnson, D. (2006(a)) Investing in teacher effectiveness to improve educational quality in developing countries: does in-service education for primary mathematics teachers in Sri Lanka make a difference to teaching and learning? *Research in Comparative Education,* 1, 1, 73–87

Johnson, D. (2006(b)) Comparing the trajectories of educational change and policy transfer in developing countries. Oxford Review of Education, 32, 5, 679–696

Johnson, D. and Hayter, J. (2000) Evaluation of the RESETT Project, The Gambia, Unpublished mimeograph. Bristol, Graduate School of Education

Johnson, D. and Kress, G. (2003) Globalisation, literacy and society: redesigning pedagogy and assessment. *Assessment in Education. Principles, Policy and Practice,* 10, 5–14

Johnson, D. and Yahampath, K. (2003) Primary Mathematics Project: Final Evaluation Report. Sri Lanka: National Institute of Education, Maharagama (ISBN 955-8628-07-7)

Johnson, D., Broadfoot, P. and Hayter, J. (2000) The Quality of Learning and Teaching in Developing Countries: Assessing Literacy and Numeracy in Malawi and Sri Lanka. London, DFID Education Research Papers

Johnson, D., Hsieh, J. and Oniborn, F. (2007) A baseline study of the conditions of teaching and learning, and learning outcomes in Nigeria. Unpublished Research report. Cambridge, Cambridge Education Limited

Kirk, J. (2004) Impossible fictions: the lived experiences of women teachers in Karachi. *Comparative Education Review,* 48, 4, 374–395

Lewin, K. (2004) The Pre-Service Training of Teachers: Does it Meet Its Objectives and How Can It Be Improved? Background paper for EFA Global Monitoring Report 2005

Lewin, K. M. and Stuart, J. S. (2003) Researching Teacher Education: New Perspectives on Practice, Performance and Policy. Multi-Site Teacher Education Research Project (MUSTER) Synthesis Report, London, Department for International Development (DFID Educational Paper 49a.)

Lewin, K. M., Samuel, M. and Sayed, Y. (eds). (2003) *Changing Patterns of Teacher Education in South Africa: Policy, Practice and Prospects.* Sandown, Heinemann

Matthews, P. and Sammons, P. (2004) *Improvement Through Inspection.* London, Ofsted

Maxwell, G. and Cumming, J. (1998) Reforming the Culture of Assessment: Changes in Teachers' Assessment Beliefs and Practices Under a School-Based Regime. Paper presented at the 24th Annual Conference of the International Association for Educational Assessment, Barbados, West Indies

McEwan, P. J. (1999) Recruitment of rural teachers in developing countries: an economic analysis. *Teaching and Teacher Education*, 15, 849–859

Oplatka, I. (2007) The context and profile of teachers in developing countries in the last decade: a revealing discussion for further investigation. *International Journal of Educational Management*, 21, 6, 476–490

Osei, G. M. (2006) Teachers in Ghana. Issues of training, remuneration and effectiveness. *International Journal of Educational Development*, 26, 1, 38–51

Poo, B. and Hoyle, E. (1995) Teacher involvement in decision-making. In D. Johnson, (ed) *Educational Management and Policy: Research, Theory and Practice in South Africa.* Bristol Papers in Education, Comparative and International Studies: 4, Centre for International Studies in Education, University of Bristol

Postlethwaite T. N. 2004. What do International Assessment Studies Tell Us About the Quality of School Systems? Background paper for EFA Global Monitoring Report 2005

Psacharopoulos, G., Valenzuel, J. and Arends, M. (1996) Teacher salaries in Latin America: a review. *Economics of Education Review*, 15, 4, 401–406

Raina, V.K. and Dhand, H. (2000) Reflections on teaching history in the developing world: an Indian experience. *The Social Studies, March/April*, 84–88

Ratteree, B. (2004) Teachers, Their Unions and the Education for All Campaign. Background paper for EFA Global Monitoring Report 2005. Paris.

Rosenthal, L. (2004) Do school inspections improve school quality? Ofsted inspections and school examination results in the UK. *Economics of Education Review*, 23, 1, 143–151

Samoff, J., Sebatane, E., and Dambele, M. (2001) Scaling up by focussing down. Creating space to expand educational reform. Association for the Development of Education in Africa. Working Paper. ADEA, Paris

Saeed, M. and Mohammed, K. (2002) Assessing competency of Pakistani primary school teachers in mathematics, science and pedagogy. *International Journal of Educational Development*, 16, 4, 190–195

Schleicher, A., Siniscalco, M., Postlethwaite, T. N. (1995) *The Conditions of Primary Schools: A Pilot Study in the Least Developed Countries.* Report to UNESCO and UNICEF

Shaw, I., Newton, D. P., Aitkin, M. and Darnell, R. (2003) Do Ofsted inspections of secondary education make a difference to GCSE results? *British Educational Research Journal*, 29, 1

Sheil, G. and Forde, P. (1995). Profiling pupil achievement in language and literacy: current issues and trends. In: B. Raban-Bisby, G. Brooks, and S. Wolfendale (eds) *Developing Language and Literacy.* Stoke-on-Trent: Trentham Books, pp. 147–160

Spreen, C. A. (2004) The vanishing origins of outcomes-based education. In: D. Phillips and K. Ochs (eds) *Educational Policy Borrowing: Historical Perspectives. Oxford Studies in Comparative Education.* Oxford, Symposium Books

Tekeleselassie, A. A. (2005) Teachers' career ladder policy in Ethiopia: an opportunity for professional growth or 'a stick disguised as a carott'? *International Journal of Educational Development*, 25, 4, 618–636

UNESCO GMR (2005) *The Quality Imperative.* Paris, UNESCO

Verspoor, A. (2008) In: D. Johnson (ed) *The Changing Landscape of Education in Africa.* Oxford, Symposium Books

Part III
Leadership and Management in Support of Teachers

Chapter 10
Professional Learning Communities and Teachers' Professional Development

Ray Bolam

Introduction

This chapter takes the overall purposes of this collection as its starting point. It addresses the question of how the quality of teaching might be improved by considering selected theoretical and empirical work on effective approaches to the professional development of teachers and on schools as professional learning communities. In so doing, it also considers issues related to the changing nature of the teacher profession and those patterns of school leadership and management that create conditions for effective teaching while balancing internal and external constraints.

Policies and practices affecting teachers' work, learning and development are necessarily rooted in the particular context of a single educational system and, indeed, are often the product of unique, and changing, sets of circumstances – political, economic, social, cultural, historical, professional and technical – in that system. Nevertheless, many recent changes have much in common across countries in their substance and impact. Thus, there is considerable evidence that national reforms directed at school improvement have resulted in substantial changes in the roles of school teachers and principals. For example, in an OECD survey of school management in nine countries –Belgium, Greece, Hungary, Japan, Mexico, Netherlands, Sweden, the UK and the USA – the writers argued that

> *Schools everywhere are being asked to do more than ever before. They face a complex world and a seemingly endless set of pressures. Those who manage schools must take responsibility for an arduous task.*
>
> (CERI, 2001: 13)

Of course, the nature and impact of such changes also varies between countries. Drawing upon evidence from two European studies – one of primary teachers in England and the other of secondary teachers in England, France and Denmark, McNess et al. (2003), found that

> *Evidence from both projects suggested that teachers in England were concerned that externally imposed educational change had not only increased their workload but also created a growing tension between the requirements of government and the needs of the pupils. A perceived demand for a delivery of performance, for themselves and their pupils, had*

created a policy focus that emphasized the managerially effective in the interest of account-
ability, while ignoring teachers' deeply rooted commitment to the affective aspects of
teaching and learning. (p. 243)

Some commentators (e.g. Olsen, 2002) have argued that these policies were adopted across the public sector as a whole: reforms in health, social services and housing, as well as education, were said to have a common technical/ideological core, and were often referred to as managerialism, rational management or new public management. Within a broad new public management framework, many countries adopted 'steering' strategies, often based on dedicated or categorical funding, to couple professional development tightly to the implementation of their reform policies, an approach that, according to Halasz (2000), has probably become the dominant one in OECD member countries. Good examples in England were the introduction of the national literacy and numeracy strategies. The curricula and pedagogical content of these innovations were specified very tightly by central government agencies as, too, was the associated training, and the outcomes were reported to have been very successful (www.standards.dfee.gov.uk).

In short, school teachers and leaders in many countries have increasingly found themselves working in a political context in which external, 'restructuring' changes, initiated by national, state or local authorities to raise standards of achievement, take priority over their own vision of desirable improvements. These contextual factors pose difficult practical dilemmas for them, perhaps the most significant being that of how to implement an onerous external change agenda while simultaneously promoting school-initiated improvements. Paradoxically, one major conclusion of research on school effectiveness and improvement has been to stress the importance of capacity building and collective learning at the school level. According to Teddlie and Reynolds (2000), teachers in effective schools reportedly work collaboratively to achieve shared goals; they have high expectations of their students, teach purposively, monitor student work and give positive feedback. Similarly, in their historical overview, Hopkins and Reynolds (2001) argued that school improvement research emphasised the need for schools to create an infrastructure, especially collaborative patterns of staff development, to enable knowledge of best practice and research findings to be shared and utilised. However, schools also vary significantly, both within and between countries, along several important dimensions – context, funding, size, structure, functions, staffing and teaching models. For example, Southworth and Weindling (2002) concluded from a study of 26 large (with 401–600 pupils) primary schools in England that, compared to smaller schools, they were characterised by more staff expertise, more opportunity for peer support, more internal communication difficulties, more delegation, more reliance on middle managers and more frequent use of teams.

Against this background, this chapter's central argument is that, where circumstances and constraints permit, it makes sense for school leaders and managers to aim for promoting a professional learning community, using some form of distributed leadership, as the foundation for sustained improvements in student learning, whether the latter are initiated by external authorities or within the school. However, it is also the case that the situations in which they find themselves are distinctive, even unique and that these situations change over time. Hence, given the unavoidably contingent and unpredictable nature of their work, they must necessarily adopt strategies and methods consistent with their own knowledge and skills and appropriate to their particular organisations, tasks, staff and contexts – institutional, local and national.

Two working definitions are adopted although, as we shall see, they are far from being unproblematic:

> ... I take 'educational leadership' to have at its core the responsibility for policy formulation and, where appropriate, organisational transformation; I take 'educational management' to refer to an executive function for carrying out agreed policy; finally, I assume that leaders normally also have some management responsibilities....
>
> (Bolam, 1999)

> ...professional development is the process by which teachers and headteachers learn, enhance and use appropriate knowledge, skills and values. The notion of appropriateness must itself be based on shared and public value judgements about the needs and best interests of their clients. Thus, although this perspective certainly includes staff, management and human resource development directed at raising standards and the improvement of teaching and learning, it recognises that, because these are essentially employer- and organisation-oriented concepts, they should be seen as only a part of professional development, albeit a fundamentally important part. The essence of professional development for educators must surely involve the learning of an independent, evidence-informed and constructively critical approach to practice within a public framework of professional values and accountability, which are also open to critical scrutiny.
>
> (Bolam, 2000: 272)

Although the chapter draws on selected international literature, its principal focus is on experience in England, partly because this is the system with which I am most familiar but mainly because it is so relevant to the chapter's themes. The findings from two recently completed empirical studies[1] are used as running illustrations. The first is the *Creating and Sustaining Effective Professional Learning Communities* study (Bolam et al., 2005), referred to throughout as the EPLC project. Its overall purposes were to identify the main features of a professional learning community (PLC) and to draw out practically useful findings for those wishing to adopt this approach in schools. The second study (Bolam and Weindling, 2006) is referred to throughout as the SRS project. It involved a systematic review and synthesis of 20 research studies of CPD for teachers in England, published from 2002 to 2006, and aimed to contribute to the development of CPD policy by providing a trustworthy overview of what the studies collectively showed (or failed to show) that could inform the policy environment in a time of change.

Following this introduction, the chapter is organised in seven sections.

1. Introduction
2. Teachers' learning and CPD
3. Schools as professional learning communities
4. Reflective professional enquiry and evidence-informed practice
5. Openness, partnerships, networking and external support

---

[1] I gratefully acknowledge my indebtedness to colleagues on both projects for allowing me to draw on the work we did together.

6. Leadership and management
7. Teachers as professionals in a changing policy context
8. Discussion and conclusions

Teachers' Learning and CPD

It is widely accepted by policy makers and practitioners that ongoing professional learning by teachers is a necessary condition for school improvement. In a sample of OECD countries, professional development was said to be

> ... central to the way principals manage schools, in at least two respects: first, as instructional leaders, principals may be expected to coordinate professional progression of their staff; second, they need to manage the learning community as a whole, using development as part of school change.
>
> (CERI, 2001: 27)

However, it is also apparent from the literature there are many different models of professional development in operation (Bolam and McMahon, 2004; McMahon, this volume).

The SRS findings provided evidence confirming that the majority of teachers in England held a traditional view of CPD, largely equating it with short, external, in-service training courses but also that CPD must be much broader than such short courses to be effective; about the value of offering CPD programmes designed for teachers at different career stages; that the more influence teachers have over their own CPD the more likely they are to consider it effective and more generally, about the importance of teachers' professionalism and agency as key components of effective CPD; and about the importance of including support staff, not just teachers, in CPD and in other aspects of professional learning communities. They also provided evidence about the need to focus CPD on teaching and learning; demonstrating that it was actually happening in the schools studied; about the importance of good needs identification; confirming that striking a balance between national, school development and individual needs was problematic; about the value of award bearing courses and other higher education contributions to CPD; about the value of coaching and mentoring as key components of CPD; about the value of sharing of knowledge and practice both within and between schools, of collaborative CPD and of reflective practice. An important feature of these findings concerning CPD processes is that they are likely to apply across all CPD settings – for example, in school-based, course-based and national dissemination activities – regardless of whether they are aimed at all teachers, subject specialists, department heads, headteachers or support staff. Finally, with respect to CPD outcomes and impact, they provided evidence that well-structured and implemented CPD is likely to improve teacher motivation and morale; can have a positive impact on teachers' attitudes, knowledge and skills; can lead to successful changes in teachers' practice, to school improvement; can improve pupils' learning and achievement. However, the synthesis provided only weak evidence that CPD will improve teacher retention.

The EPLC project distinguished between individual and collective learning, and also between external courses and work-based learning opportunities, including those that occur incidentally rather than deliberately. In the survey, although 73% of primary respondents said that teachers *systematically feedback the outcomes of external courses to colleagues*, this was true of only 59% of secondary respondents. The majority (74%+) of all respondents said that most/nearly all teachers in their schools *learn together with colleagues, take responsibility for their own learning* and *use performance management to enhance professional learning*. Over 80% gave these responses in nursery, primary and special, deemed primary, schools. All 16 case study schools used the available external CPD opportunities, but to varying extents. This variation was sometimes for financial reasons (e.g. how much of its own resources a school was prepared to put into supporting staff on external, award-bearing courses: one school was able to fund virtually anyone who made a serious request, while another was unable to provide any such support). Successful practice to promote learning often involved the more focused use of time and internal arrangements: for example, by ensuring that staff meetings dealt with student and staff learning (e.g. discussing a piece of writing or photos of an activity in a primary school); by holding three-weekly meetings of the key staff to review the progress of their common students in a special school; by encouraging staff to teach each other (e.g. ICT skills in a secondary school).

These conclusions were, broadly speaking, confirmed by a recent HMI survey which, in addition, found that:

> In about one third of the primary schools visited by subject inspectors, the arrangements for CPD in the subject they were inspecting were inadequate. This was partly due to the emphasis on literacy and numeracy and partly due to managers' failure to detect important subject-related issues.
>
> (Ofsted, 2006: 5)

and that

> in secondary schools too much emphasis had been placed by some subject leaders on using examination awarding bodies for staff development. The drive in these departments to improve examination results by learning about new course specifications and assessment arrangements had deflected attention from improving the quality of teaching and from developing Key Stage 3.
>
> (Ofsted, 2006: 10)

Several of the findings indicated that most teachers still see CPD largely in terms of short, external courses and training days. As Bierema and Eraut (2004) pointed out, there is an unhelpful prevailing assumption that learning and working are separate activities yet, they argue, most workplace learning takes place independently of CPD. Interestingly, when teachers interviewed for the EPLC case studies were asked questions using the terminology *CPD*, they responded along traditional lines. But when they were asked '*How do you learn?*' they were much more likely to respond in terms of a broader set of experiences that included work-based learning, and learning from their own initiatives outside work, for instance in learning how to use IT. The approach adopted in the *Transfer of Good Practice* project was also illuminating in this context:

.... we are interested not only in the nature of practice itself but also in the ways in which it is acquired. When one examines transfer as a learning process, then the question of what a teacher has to learn in order to competently perform a new practice becomes critical. The focus has to shift from practice as an observable performance to practice as the overt result of experientially acquired understandings and capabilities which remain largely tacit. Understanding the receiving teachers' learning needs and processes is essential for understanding successful or less successful attempts to transfer practice between teachers and between contexts.

(Fielding et al., 2005: 5)

In the same vein, Darling-Hammond and Bransford (2005) offered a framework for teacher learning in the USA which suggested that teachers learn to teach in a community that enables them to develop a *vision* for their practice; a set of *understandings* about teaching, learning, and children; *dispositions* about how to use this knowledge; *practices* that allow them to act on their intentions and beliefs; and *tools* that support their efforts.

Schools as PLCs

For some writers and researchers, these ideas have coalesced around the concept of the school as a learning community, the underpinning rationale for which has several inter-relating strands. Historically, it relates to notions of inquiry, reflection and self-evaluating schools and certain key features were evident in the work of education writers in the early part of the last century. For example John Dewey was committed to the view that:

...educational practices provide the data, the subject matter, which forms the problems of inquiry.

(Dewey, 1929)

A generation or so ago, Stenhouse (1975) argued that teachers ought to be school and classroom researchers and play an active part in the process of curriculum development, while Schön (1983) was influential in advocating the notion of the 'reflective practitioner'. From the school-based curriculum development movement of the 1970s there emerged a series of projects and activities on the 'thinking school', the 'problem-solving school' (Bolam, 1977) and, perhaps most notably, the 'Creative School' (CERI, 1978; Hoyle, 1974). Later, in the 1980s came the shift to the self-reviewing or self-evaluating school (e.g. McMahon et al., 1984). More recent interest stems from the belief that, when teachers work collaboratively, the quality of learning and teaching in the organisation improves (Mitchell and Sackney, 2000; McLaughlin and Talbert, 1993; Barth, 1990).

The progress of educational reform is claimed to depend on teachers' capacity, both individually and collectively (Elmore, 1995; Lieberman, 1995; Newmann and Associates, 1996; Little, 1999) and how this links with school capacity (Stoll, 1999). There also appears to be considerable expectation, although at this point the evidence is still limited (see Louis and Marks, 1998; Wiley, 2001), that schools operating as learning communities will have a positive impact on pupil outcomes.

In the broader context of adult and work-based learning, the idea of a learning community links directly with the concept of community of practice (COP), for which Wenger (1999) proposed the following indicators: sustained mutual relationships, whether harmonious or conflictual; shared ways of doing things together; rapid flow of information; the absence of introductory preambles in conversations because they are assumed to be continuations; knowing what others know and what they can do. He also argued that a whole organisation may be too large a social configuration both for individuals to relate to as a COP and also for analytic purposes. Treating them as a single COP would gloss over discontinuities, which are integral to their structure; they are better viewed as constellations of interconnected practices. Constellations share historical roots, have related enterprises, belong to the same institution, face similar conditions and have members in common. The potential applications to schools and to their departments, teams and groups are self-evident.

The EPLC project (Stoll et al., 2003) suggested that a professional learning community (PLC) is likely to exhibit five broad sets of overlapping characteristics: *shared values and vision* directed towards the learning of all pupils (students); *collective responsibility* for pupil learning, helping to sustain staff commitment through peer pressure and holding to account those who don't do their fair share; *reflective professional inquiry* as an integral part of work including ongoing conversations about educational issues, frequent scrutiny of practice with colleagues, mutual observation, joint planning and applying new ideas and information to problem-solving to meet pupils' needs; *collaboration* in developmental activities directed towards achieving shared purposes, thus easing teachers' sense of isolation and generating mutual professional learning; *group, as well as individual, learning* in that professional learning is more frequently communal rather than solitary, all teachers are learners with their colleagues and, through frequent interaction, individual unspoken, or tacit, knowledge is converted into shared knowledge.

In the light of the literature review, the following working definition was adopted:

> *An effective professional learning community has the capacity to promote and sustain the learning of all professionals in the school community with the collective purpose of enhancing pupil learning.*

Practitioners in the survey and case study schools generally responded positively to the idea of a PLC and to the working definition. Even though few were familiar with the term and none used it in their everyday professional conversations most appeared to find it helpful and, apparently, unproblematic. The findings confirmed the existence and importance of the five characteristics identified in the literature review and, in addition, highlighted three more as being important: openness, networking and partnerships; inclusive membership; mutual trust, respect and support.

It was assumed that being a PLC is not an end in itself. Rather, it is a means to an end and, hence, its 'effectiveness' should be judged in relation to two main outcomes: impact on the professional learning and morale of the staff – teachers, school leaders and other adult workers – and impact on pupils. Some survey findings

demonstrated a positive, though weak, link between full expression of PLC characteristics and pupil outcomes – in particular value-added performance. The case study
findings supported the conclusion that the more fully a PLC expressed the eight
characteristics, the more they impacted positively on pupils' attendance, pupils'
interest in learning and actual learning, and on the individual and collective professional learning, practice and morale of teaching and support staff. Thus, it was
concluded that *effective* PLCs fully exhibit eight key characteristics: shared values
and vision; collective responsibility for pupils' learning; collaboration focused on
learning; individual and collective professional learning; reflective professional
enquiry; openness, networking and partnerships; inclusive membership; mutual
trust, respect and support.

Teachers as Professionals in a Changing Policy Context

Issues to do with the nature of the teaching profession are manifestly culture bound
(Le Metais, 1997) and there can be little doubt that recent policy developments in
England have significant implications for the idea of teaching as a profession.
These developments include the 'Every Child Matters' agenda (DfES, 2004b)
which required schools to work with providers of other children's services and thus
for school staffs to collaborate with people from different professions and backgrounds; the implementation of the Workforce Agreement with its far-reaching
implications for the roles, responsibilities and professional development of *all*
school staff, not just teachers (School Workforce Development Board, 2005); the
Five Year Strategy (DfES, 2004a) which heralded the introduction of a dedicated,
three-year Schools Budget to cover, *inter alia*, CPD costs; a refocusing of teacher
appraisals to become teaching and learning reviews in order to build up teachers'
demand for high quality training, and encourage them to drive their own development; and a considerable emphasis on the so-called *new professionalism*.

A key element of the Workforce Agreement concerned the use of teaching assistants,
the number of whom has risen dramatically from 35,500 in 1997 to almost 100,000
in 2005 whereas in the same period the number of full-time equivalent teachers in
the maintained sector rose by about 4,000 to 430,000 (DfES, 2005a). This was
accompanied by a shift in teaching assistants' roles and responsibilities towards
greater involvement in the actual processes of teaching and learning – including,
for example, in the assessment of pupils' learning. Thus, there has been a blurring
of the distinction between teachers and teaching assistants which the government
argued was part of a legitimate process of different professional groups playing
complementary roles in the interests of children (Morris, 2001). Most teacher
unions accepted this development as helping teachers to focus on teaching rather
than administration or behaviour control but the National Union of Teachers did
not, seeing it rather as diluting teacher professionalism.

Against this background, one key issue in the EPLC project was, inevitably, to do
with who in a school was, or should be, thought of as a member of the professional

community. There were few direct references to support staff in the literature review since most earlier studies assumed, explicitly or implicitly, that membership of the learning community was restricted to teachers. Yet it became apparent that the situation in English schools was changing: in the survey, over half of all respondents said that learning support assistants (LSAs) were *valued by teachers* and *had opportunities for professional development*; 74% of primary and 42% of secondary respondents said 'nearly all' LSAs *share responsibility for pupil learning*; 77% of primary and 57% of secondary respondents reported that 'nearly all' LSAs *actively contribute to the school as a professional learning community*; and more than half of all respondents reported an overall increase in the last two years. In addition, 47% of primary and 35% of secondary respondents said support staff were involved in reviewing pupil outcome and progress data while more than three quarters of all respondents reported that temporary and supply staff were included in CPD activities. Moreover, in all 16 case study schools, the overall PLC was seen as including teachers and those support staff working most closely with them (e.g. LSAs, nursery nurses, technicians) to promote pupil learning. The teachers always led the teaching and learning and may be regarded as constituting the 'core' of the PLC with the most highly trained support staff (e.g. nursery nurses) being generally close to this 'core' and, sometimes actually part of it, especially in nursery, special and primary schools where support staff typically worked most closely with teachers. The demarcation between teaching and support staff was most apparent in secondary schools. Other support staff, parents or governors were sometimes perceived as members of the learning community where they contributed to educational activity. Administrative, cleaning, care-taking and school meals staff were more likely to be regarded as part of an extended school community, often with some pastoral responsibility for pupil welfare and behaviour, though particular, enthusiastic individuals were sometimes closely involved in the plc, especially in the smallest schools. External 'professionals', like educational psychologists or those in higher education, generally made inputs into their sphere of responsibility rather than into the PLC as a whole.

None of the twenty SRS studies directly investigated the *new professionalism*, largely because the idea came to prominence after they had started their work. Since 2001, several policy documents have used the term but with different emphases. Most notably, the Five Year Strategy proposed

> *a new professionalism for teachers, in which career progression and financial rewards will go to those who are making the biggest contributions to improving pupil attainment, those who are continually developing their own expertise, and those who help to develop expertise in other teachers.*
>
> (DfES, 2004, para 39)

The Rewards and Incentives Group (RIG) (2005), which advises the School Teachers' Review Body (STRB), explicitly linked it to CPD and teachers' day-to-day work:

> *Underlying the new teacher professionalism is the aim that professional development is an ongoing part of the everyday activities of a teacher rather than a separate activity which adds to the work load of teachers. The new teacher professionalism espouses a culture of greater openness where all teachers are engaged in effective professional development*

which enhances pupil attainment and teachers' job satisfaction, and supports school improvement and teachers' career progression.

(RIG, 2005, para 9.2)

The STRB itself, which has a national remit for teachers' pay and conditions in England, clearly saw CPD and the new system of performance management as being integrally linked to each other, and by extension to the new professionalism, as succinctly summarised in its explication of an illustration:

Figure 7.1 illustrates this outcomes-based approach, the mutual responsibilities of teachers and managers, and the links between CPD, performance and pay progression. Its purpose is to clarify these relationships, not to prescribe a specific system for direct application in schools. It highlights the importance of a continuous cycle of performance, development and reflection, within which teachers systematically apply their learning to their teaching practice. Teachers' decisions on their CPD will also be influenced by factors including the school's staff development and improvement plans and by the forthcoming framework of professional standards. As teachers undertake and learn from CPD, its benefits should be seen in aspects of their performance. Performance will be assessed through appraisal and linked with pay progression through the school's pay policy... ...

(STRB, 2005, para 7.33)

Since the new professionalism is such a central new policy idea, it will be important to clarify its operational meaning and its implications for teachers, school leaders and, of course, for CPD policy and practice. For example, The School Teachers' Review Body struck a somewhat sceptical note about

... suggestions that the STPCD include references to teachers' having an 'entitlement' to CPD. It is more helpful to view CPD from the viewpoint of mutual responsibilities.

(STRB, 2005, para 7.29)

and the government saw clear links with the proposed national standards:

A clear framework of national standards is essential to our plans for a new teacher professionalism and to stimulate demand for CPD.

(Secretary of State, DfES, 2005b: 3.1)

Reflective Professional Enquiry and Evidence-Informed Practice

In recent years, there has been an increased focus on reflective enquiry or enquiry-based practice and on evidence-informed practice. A major part of the latter's rationale is the belief that teaching should emulate medicine, aiming to be a research-informed profession (Hargreaves, 1996). Three broad, inter-connected approaches are open to school leaders and teachers wishing to promote evidence-informed practice: to engage in systematic research and evaluation in the school, in departments and individual classrooms; to adopt a more systematic approach to the collection, analysis and use of 'routine' data, for example, students' examination results, value-added data and external school inspection reports; to search for and use externally generated research (Stoll et al., 2002). The first mode is well established in action research, but the second is becoming more common, as schools use value-added data to plan specific follow-up action and school improvement projects involving teachers as action researchers. The rationale for the third mode is the belief that practitioners should have access to high quality research, using it to inform their decisions and actions.

Leithwood et al. (1999) saw such approaches as *'creating the conditions for growth in teachers' professional knowledge'* (p. 149). They argued that this is best accomplished by embedding professional development in practical activities, what they called "situated cognition" (p. 151). According to several writers a new form of professionalism is emerging in which teachers work more closely and collaboratively with colleagues, students and parents, linking teacher and school development (e.g. Hargreaves, 1994) while King and Newmann (2001) concluded that teacher learning is most likely to occur when teachers can concentrate on instruction and student outcomes in the specific contexts in which they teach; have sustained opportunities to study, to experiment with and to receive helpful feedback on specific innovations; and have opportunities to collaborate with professional peers, both within and outside their schools, along with access to the expertise of researchers. Similarly, Smylie (1995) drew upon a range of adult learning theories to identify conditions of effective workplace learning, including opportunities for teachers to learn from peer colleagues in collaborative group work settings, together with open communication, experimentation and feedback.

The evaluation of the Best Practice Research Scholarships (Furlong et al., 2003) concluded that in all the sampled 100 schools there was a strong consensus from the 'Research Scholars' (i.e. participating teachers) and their senior colleagues that the Scholarships were a particularly valuable form of professional development. They reported many examples of perceived significant improvements in teachers' confidence in their own professional judgement; much greater use of reading which made teachers more knowledgeable and informed in their discussions of classroom practices; the systematic collection of evidence. These in turn were seen as contributing to changes in the nature of teachers' reflection and a growing understanding, on the part of many teachers, of their own professional learning. Impact on practice was widely reported but the robustness of the evidence varied considerably. There were significant claims that their projects had had a major impact on their teaching; in many cases these claims were corroborated by their senior colleagues. Where projects were undertaken by more senior teachers, there were many examples of a wider impact in the school. In the *Research Engaged School* project (Sharp et al., 2005), which involved fifteen schools, four features were found to be highly inter-related: a research orientation; a concern with investigating pedagogy; the promotion of research communities; a commitment to putting research at the heart of policy and practice. Comments on the initiative's impact emphasised the benefits of the enquiry process which enabled them to develop a 'learning community', with staff taking an active interest in addressing their own priorities for improvement. In particular, staff talked about the benefits of collaborative learning and that the initiative had offered them CPD which was both motivating and relevant.

It seems clear that school leaders and teachers in England are becoming increasingly confident in using these approaches. In the EPLC survey, 50% of all respondents said 'most' teachers were informing their practice through the routine collection, analysis and use of data while 79% of primary and 68% of secondary school respondents reported that these numbers had increased in the past two years. All respondents said they used at least one form of review of pupil outcome and progress data; almost 90% said that pupil outcome and progress data were reviewed by the headteacher and individual class teachers; and over 80% of all respondents said that the SMT and governors reviewed pupil outcome and progress data. Reflective professional enquiry was judged to be high in three of the 16 case study schools, medium in 11 and low in two schools, both 'early starters'. Over the course of one year, the expression of this characteristic was judged to be increasing in six schools and diminishing in none. In over a fifth (22%) of nursery and primary schools half or more of the teachers were reported to be carrying out classroom-based research and in a third of these schools, half or more were seeking out and using external evidence that is relevant and practical to inform their work. This compares with 11% of secondary schools where half or more of the teachers were reported to be carrying out classroom-based research and 16% of these schools where half or more were seeking out and using external evidence that is relevant and practical to inform their work. Some of the case study nursery and special schools had mechanisms for gathering and using data. Early assessment of all children with two weeks of their arrival at one special school set a baseline on which to build. Records (including anecdotal records) were kept on each child's progress file and targets set. One teacher had made videos of children both as a record of their progress over a year, as well as being a source for teachers to review in identifying pupil needs and progress. In a secondary school, reflective enquiry was a common feature and three different types could be identified: first, an assistant head analysed pupil achievement data, which was seen by all staff and used widely across the school to set individual pupil targets, monitor student progress, and agree performance management targets with teachers; second, teachers had opportunities to observe each other teach, including through a so-called Learning Walk; third, internally funded research projects, focused on teaching and learning, were reported back to a Learning Forum. This was a sophisticated programme, developed over a number of years.

Openness, Partnerships, Networking and External Support

The importance of high quality external support and of shared learning opportunities for school leaders and teachers finds support from the international literature and from the SRS and EPLC findings. The SRS studies demonstrated that this can take a variety of forms, including supporting schools' own provision and activities, LEA support for CPD and for partnerships with other schools and external agencies, networking between schools, award-bearing courses and other contributions from universities.

The most familiar form of support is that provided at the district or local authority level. Fullan et al. (2002) argued

that to get large scale reform, you need to establish and coordinate ongoing accountability and capacity-building efforts at three levels – the schools, the district, and the state. (p. 3)

The SRS evidence confirmed that, in England, Local Authorities (LAs) ought to make a significant contribution to CPD and school improvement, that the best LAs do so but that the support available from advisers varied within and between LEAs. The value of high quality external CPD provision and expertise was also confirmed although, in practice, the quality was variable. Similarly, the EPLC literature review concluded that schools look beyond the school boundaries – to external support, networking and other partnerships – in order to promote, sustain and extend their PLC. In the survey, 96% of primary and 98% of secondary respondents said they had at least one formal working link with other schools and 83% of primary and 95% of secondary respondents had at least one teacher involved one or more of nine listed national initiatives.

Given the emphasis on promoting competition between schools that characterised policy in several countries during the 1990s it comes as something of a surprise to find that there has recently been a shift towards collaboration between schools in the form of networking and partnerships. According to Cordingley and Temperley (2006)

.......government departments and agencies are all promoting networks as a means of counteracting the negative effects of competition.... (p. 1)

Several writers have offered a rationale for the networking approach. Lieberman (2000) argued that schools are being asked to educate a growing and diverse population yet school systems that are organised bureaucratically and function traditionally have difficulty adapting to change whereas networks are well suited to making use of new technology and institutional arrangements. They are flexible, borderless and innovative, are able to create collaborative environments, and to develop agendas that grow and change with participants. Jackson (2002) argued that they give teachers the opportunity to create as well as receive knowledge and Hargreaves (2003) that they enable small scale improvements to spread through the system more quickly than top-down initiatives. In England, the National College for School Leadership has actively promoted networked learning communities (http://www.ncsl.org.uk/networked/index.cfm).

That schools look externally for ideas is also consistent with a reflective and enquiring approach. In the EPLC case study schools, *the range of external networks and partnerships* was judged to be high or increasingly high in five schools and low throughout in two schools – both so-called *early starters*. Another key aspect of this characteristic is an open, outward looking and flexible orientation. Evidence for this came from all sources. Significantly more *mature* PLC respondents than *early starter* respondents in both primary and secondary surveys reported that a higher percentage of their teachers *experiment and innovate in their work* and the same was true in relation to *see the school as stimulating and professionally challeng-*

ing. This openness of more *mature* PLCs also appeared to be a sign of confidence about being able to deal with external change. One headteacher said this was connected with:

> *"being able to respond when you have to and being flexible", "standing up to external change – we'll do this when we think the time is right", "taking control"* and *"connecting with 'the great outdoors'".*

While many secondary schools had external connections, only just over a third of the respondents (35%) reported that nearly all/most of their teachers *actively seek ideas from colleagues in other schools.* This contrasted with nursery/primary school peers who also identified a very high level of involvement with other schools (96%), most of which were within or cross phase clusters or both), and where nearly two thirds (62%) reported that nearly all/most of their teachers *actively seek ideas from colleagues in other schools.* Isolation was often cited as a key reason for involvement in networks. The head of a rural secondary school said that e-learning was critical to connect their school with outside ideas. In some cases small, isolated schools made use of links, while others didn't. In one school, staff observed teachers in neighbouring primary schools, while in another school, the travel time between schools make these networks difficult to maintain.

The impact of networks on the PLC generally appeared to be positive; respondents said they benefited from the CPD opportunities and pupils benefited from the wider range of learning opportunities that networks can bring. More generally, and following several research reviews Cordingley and Temperley (2006) concluded that effective networks

> ....*need to have a clear and compelling purpose around which ownership can be built...* .....and to provide evidence that they are.......... *making a difference for adults and especially for young people....* (p. 3)

and also that

> ...*CPD in school networks is more likely to be collaborative than individual and, therefore, more likely to offer learning gains for pupils as well as teachers.* (p. 15)

The *Transfer of Good Practice* Project (Fielding et al., 2005) concluded that the most important single aspects of the transfer process were that both parties should be mutually engaged for a significant period of time and that the process should be, if not learner-led then 'learner-engaged'. The transfer of practice was more likely to be successful when the recipients had been involved from the beginning in the process of agreeing and planning the transfer activity. Certain kinds of trusting relationships were fundamental to the transfer of good practice. They were not an extra or a pleasant accompaniment, but the necessary foundation of the complex, demanding and potentially rewarding process of professional learning across institutional boundaries. Networks were judged to be excellent for distributing and exchanging ideas, and for general intelligence seeking. However, transfer of practice is more intrusive than transfer of information or ideas; and therefore more demanding on the quality of the relationships between those involved in the process.

Leadership and Management

The SSR findings provided evidence: about the important roles of heads, senior staff and CPD coordinators in promoting and supporting CPD; that CPD coordinators need specific training and support, especially in how to evaluate the impact of CPD; that both time and specific funding are needed for effective CPD; about the importance of school culture in the improvement of CPD and, more specifically, about its importance in promoting a research orientation and a professional learning community. There was strong evidence that school staff found it difficult to evaluate the impact of CPD and that cost effectiveness and value-for-money were rarely taken into account when CPD is evaluated either within schools or by external evaluators, findings endorsed by the HMI survey (Ofsted, 2006). The problematic nature of CPD evaluation for researchers is well known (Guskey, 2000); fortunately, at least some policy makers recognise this:

> *Assessments of the impact of professional development need to take into account that it takes time for the benefits of professional development to be realised fully and reflected in improved classroom practice. They should not focus only on immediate results.*
> (Rewards and Incentive Group, 2005, 9.3)

In the EPLC study, the idea that schools might be at one of three hypothetical stages of development as a PLC – starter, developer or mature – was investigated. The survey and case study respondents accepted them as common-sense, pragmatic distinctions but, although there was some empirical support for their validity, it was concluded that the 'stages of development' concept should be used with caution. Four key processes for promoting and sustaining an effective PLC were identified: optimising resources and structures; promoting individual and collective learning; specifically promoting and sustaining the PLC; and strategic leadership and management. The effectiveness of these processes, for example in terms of their impact on the teaching-related practice of individuals and on leadership and management practice, varied between schools and over time in the same school. Accordingly, as well as the impact of the PLC on the professional learning and morale of the staff and on pupils, the extent to which these four processes are themselves carried out effectively was judged to be a third measure of overall PLC effectiveness.

A different mix of facilitating and inhibiting factors, both internal and external, was identified in each of the 16 case study schools, indicating the important influence of both external and site-level contextual factors and underlining both the opportunities and the limitations of headteachers' and staff's capacity to exercise control over factors that were often complex and dynamic. Facilitators included high individual staff commitment and motivation, strong links with other cluster-group schools, focused coordination of CPD and site facilities, like staff meeting rooms, which helped collaborative work and professional dialogue. Inhibitors included high staff resistance to change, high staff turnover, central and local policies that negatively affected resources and budgets and changes in key staff, especially at senior level. Survey evidence also indicated the importance of related inhibiting contextual factors in primary schools, notably the presence in the school of *a high percentage of free school meals* and *a high percentage of students with English as a second language.*

In more developed PLCs, staff adopted a range of innovative practices to deal with the inhibiting and facilitating factors in their setting. For example, innovative methods for making best use of human and physical resources included a competitive 'Learning Leaders' scheme in a secondary school, ensuring that all staff in a nursery school had non-contact time, using regular staff meetings to promote collaborative work and professional learning in a primary school and three-weekly case conferences for all staff working with individual children in a special school. A widely used national human resource development scheme – *Investors in People* – was found to be especially helpful in starting the process of promoting a PLC, but less helpful once a school was quite far along its process of development.

Context and setting were crucial to understanding how the eight characteristics and four processes played out in practice. For example, the survey found that primary schools were generally more likely than secondary schools to exhibit the characteristics to a greater extent, differences broadly confirmed in the case studies. Thus, nursery, primary and special support staff typically worked very closely with teachers whereas the demarcation between teaching and support staff was most apparent in secondary schools where the subject and departmental structures often resulted in small (or sub-) PLCs, with their own distinctive ways of working together; however, one-teacher departments in smaller secondary schools faced quite different issues. Location could also be a crucial influence: for example, staff in relatively remote schools found it difficult to share experience beyond their own school. Accordingly, it was concluded that, although PLCs have common characteristics and adopt similar processes of leadership and management, the practical implications for developing a PLC can only be understood and worked out in the specific conditions – like phase, size and location – of particular contexts and settings.

Discussion and Conclusions

The underlying question that has been addressed in this chapter is what approaches to teacher professional development appear to be effective in improving teaching and student learning. The main conclusion drawn is that these improvements are more likely to occur when school staff are working as a professional learning community and that it would be sensible for school leaders to encourage them in this endeavour. Research on CPD in England has revealed that many teachers still see CPD in terms of short, external courses and training days but that when asked how they learn, teachers are more likely to refer to examples of work based learning, collaboration with professional colleagues, analysis and use of data about student learning, involvement in research, etc. All these learning opportunities and more should exist within a professional learning community. The eight PLC characteristics identified in the EPLC project (Bolam et al., 2005) show the power of the concept: professionals collaborating, learning together and taking collective responsibility for student learning. However, there is no easy formula for establishing a PLC. Although all schools in England have to implement changes arising from the extensive national reform agenda and operate within the regulatory frameworks, school leaders nonetheless work in distinctive contexts which change over time. Accordingly, school leaders will need to draw upon their individual knowledge and skills to select strategies and methods for developing a PLC that are appropriate for their own organisation and context. Implementing the four key processes for promoting and sustaining a PLC identified in the EPLC study: optimising resources and structures; promoting individual and collective learning; specifically promoting and sustaining the PLC and strategic leadership and management, will require leadership skills of a high order. As Hoyle and Wallace (2005) have argued, school leaders who encourage school improvement '... *value teacher autonomy, display trust with acceptance of related risks, and sponsor innovations that emerge from communities of professional practice*' (2005: 197). The task of developing a school as a PLC is challenging and difficult but worth tackling because of the potential benefits in terms of professional and student learning.

References

Barth, R (1990) *Improving Schools from Within: Teachers, Parents and Principals Can Make the Difference*. San Francisco, CA: Jossey-Bass

Bierema, L L and Eraut, M (2004) Workplace-focused learning: perspectives of continuing professional education and human resource development. *Advances in Developing Human Resources* 6: 52–68

Bolam, R (1977) Innovation and the problem-solving school, in King, E (ed) *Reorganising Education: Management and Participation for Change*. London: Sage

Bolam, R (1999) Educational administration, leadership and management: towards a research agenda, in Bush, T, Bell, L, Bolam, R, Glatter, R and Ribbins, P (eds) *Educational Management: Re-defining Theory, Policy and Practice*. London: Paul Chapman.

Bolam, R (2000) Emerging policy trends: some implications for continuing professional development. *Journal of In-service Education* 26, 2: 267–279.

Bolam, R and McMahon, A (2004) Literature, definitions and models: towards a conceptual map, in Day, C and Sachs, J (eds) *International Handbook on the Continuing Professional Development of Teachers*. Berkshire, England: Open University Press

Bolam, R, McMahon, A, Stoll, L, Thomas, S and Wallace, M with Greenwood, A, Hawkey, K, Ingram, M, Atkinson, A and Smith, M (2005) *Creating and Sustaining Effective Professional Learning Communities* (Research Report 637 and Research Brief 637). London: DfES http://www.dfes.gov.uk/rsgateway/DB/RRP/u013543/index.shtml

Bolam, R and Weindling, D (2006) *Synthesis of Recent Policy-Related Research and Evaluation Projects Concerned with Teachers' Professional Development*. London: General Teaching Council for England and Association of Teachers and Lecturers www.gtce.org.uk/policyandresearch/research/gtcsponsored/

Bolam, R, Stoll, L and Greenwood, A (2006) The involvement of support staff in professional learning communities, in Stoll, L and Seashore Louis, K (eds) *Professional Learning Communities: Divergence, Detail and Difficulties*. London: Open University Press/McGraw-Hill

Centre for Educational Research and Innovation (CERI) (1978) *Creativity of the School*. Paris: Organisation for Economic Co-operation and Development

Centre for Educational Research and Innovation (CERI) (2001) *New School Management Approaches*. Paris: Organisation for Economic Co-operation and Development

Cordingley, P and Temperley, J (2006) *Leading Continuing Professional Development in School Networks: Adding Value, Securing Impact*. Nottingham, England: NCSL and CUREE http://www.ncsl.org.uk/networked/networked-a-to-m-publications.cfm#l

Darling-Hammond, L and Bransford, J (eds) (2005) *Preparing Teachers for a Changing World: What Teachers Should Learn and Be able To Do*. San Francisco, CA: Jossey-Bass

Dewey, J (1929) *The Sources of a Science of Education*. New York: Horace Liveright

DfEE (2001) *Learning and Teaching: A strategy for professional development*. London: DfEE

DfES (2004a) *Five Year Strategy for Children and Learners*. London: HMSO

DfES (2004b) *Every Child Matters: Change for Children*. London: HMSO

DfES (2005a) *School Workforce in England (including pupil teacher ratios and adult teacher ratios) January 2005 (Provisional)* http://www.dfes.gov.uk/rsgateway/DB/SFR/s000575/index.shtml

DfES (2005b) *Response to the TTA from the Rt Honourable Ruth Kelly, MP, Secretary of State March*

Elmore, R (1995) Structural reform and educational practice. *Educational Researcher* 24, 9: 23–26

Fielding, M, Bragg, S, Craig, J, Cunningham, I, Eraut, M and Gillinson, S (2005) *Factors Influencing the Transfer of Good Practice*. London: DfES

Fullan, M, Rolheiser, C, Mascall, B and Edge, K (2002) Accomplishing Large-Scale Reform: A Tri-Level Proposition Unpublished Paper. Toronto, Canada: OISE/UT

Furlong, J, Salisbury, J and Coombes, L (2003) *Best Practice Research Scholarships*. London: DfES

Guskey, T R (2000) *Evaluating Professional Development*. New York: Corwin

Halasz, G (2000) System regulation changes in education and their implications for management development. Unpublished Keynote Paper for the Annual Conference of the European Network for the Improvement of Research and Development in Educational Management (ENIRDEM) September 23. The Netherlands: Tilburg University

Hargreaves, A (1994) *Changing Teachers, Changing Times: Teachers Work and Culture in the Postmodern Age*. London: Cassell

Hargreaves, D H (1996) *Teaching as a Research-Based Profession: Possibilities and Prospects: The Teacher Training Agency Annual Lecture 1996*. London: TTA

Hargreaves, D H (2003) *Education Epidemic: Transforming Secondary Schools Through Innovation Networks*. London: Demos

Hopkins, D and Reynolds, D (2001) The past, present and future of school improvement: towards the third age. *British Educational Research Journal* 27, 4: 459–476

Hoyle, E (1974) Innovation and the social organisation of the school, in CERI (ed) *Creativity of the School, Technical Report Number 1: Position Papers by Member Countries*. Paris: OECD/CERI

Hoyle, E and Wallace, M (2005) *Educational Leadership: Ambiguity, Professionals and Managerialism*. London: Sage

Jackson, D (2002) *The Creation of Knowledge Networks: Collaborative Enquiry for School and System Improvement*. Nottingham, England: NCSL (mimeo)

King, M B and Newmann, F M (2001) Building school capacity through professional development: conceptual and empirical considerations. *International Journal of Educational Management* 15, 2: 86–93

Leithwood, K, Jantzi, D and Steinbach, R (1999) *Changing Leadership for Changing Times*. Buckingham, England: Open University Press

Le Metais, J (1997) Continuing professional development: the European experience, in Tomlinson, H (ed) *Managing Professional Development in Schools*. London: Paul Chapman

Lieberman, A (1995) Practices that support teacher development: transforming conceptions of professional learning, *Phi Delta Kappan* 76, 8: 591–596

Lieberman, A (2000) Networks as learning communities: shaping the future of teacher development. *Journal of Teacher Development* 51, 3: 221–227

Little, J W (1999) *Teachers professional development in the context of High School Reform: Findings from a three year study of restructuring schools.* Paper presented at the annual meeting of the American Educational Research Association, Montreal, April

Louis, K S and Marks, H (1998) Does professional community affect the classroom? Teachers' work and student experience in restructured schools. *American Journal of Education* 106, 4: 532–575

McLaughlin, M W and Talbert, J E (1993) *Contexts that Matter for Teaching and Learning: Strategic Opportunities for Meeting the Nation's Education Goals.* Palo Alto, CA: Centre for Research on the context of secondary schools

McMahon, A, Bolam, R, Abbott, R and Holly, P (1984) *Guidelines for Review and Internal Development in Schools: Secondary School Handbook.* London: Longman for the Schools Council

McNess, E, Broadfoot, P and Osborn, M (2003) Is the effective compromising the affective? *British Educational Research Journal*, 29, 2: 243–258

Mitchell, C and Sackney, L (2000) *Profound Improvement: Building Capacity for a Learning Community.* Lisse, The Netherlands: Swets & Zeitlinger

Morris, E (2001) *Professionalism and Trust: The Future of Teachers and Teaching.* London: DfES/ Social Market Foundation

Newmann, F M and Associates (1996) *Authentic Achievement: Restructuring Schools for Intellectual Quality.* San Francisco, CA: Jossey-Bass

Olsen, J (2002) Towards a European Administrative Space? Advanced Research on the Europeanisation of the Nation-State (ARENA) University of Oslo: Working Paper No. 26

Ofsted (2006) *The logical chain: continuing professional development in effective schools.* HMI Document 2639 www.ofsted.gov.uk

Rewards and Incentive Group (RIG) (2005) *The Joint Evidence of the Rewards and Incentives Group (RIG) to the School Teachers Review Body*

Schön, D A (1983) *The Reflective Practitioner.* New York. Basic Books

School Workforce Development Board (2005) *Building the School Team: Our Plans for Support Staff Training and Development 2005–06.* London: Teacher Training Agency

School Teachers Review Body (STRB) (2005) *Fifteenth Report.* London: The Stationery Office

Sharp, C, Eames, A, Sanders, D and Tomlinson, K(2005) *Postcards from Research Engaged Schools.* Slough, England: NFER

Smylie, M A (1995) Teacher learning in the workplace: implications for school reform, in Guskey, T R and Huberman, M (eds) *Professional Development in Education: New Paradigms and Practices.* New York: Teachers College Press

Southworth, G and Weindling, D (2002) *Leadership in Large Primary Schools.* England: University of Reading and Create Consultants. www.ncsl.org.uk

Stenhouse, L (1975) *An Introduction to Curriculum Research and Development* London: Heinemann Educational Books

Stoll, L (1999) Realising our potential: building capacity for lasting improvement, *School Effectiveness and School Improvement* 10, 4: 503–532

Stoll, L, Bolam, R and Collarbone, P (2002) Leadership for and of change: building capacity for learning, in Leithwood, K and Hallinger, P (eds) *Second International Handbook of Educational Leadership and Administration.* Dordrecht, The Netherlands: Kluwer

Stoll, L, Wallace, M, Bolam, R, McMahon, A, Thomas, S, Hawkey, K, Smith, M and Greenwood, A (2003) *Creating and Sustaining Effective Professional Learning Communities.* DfES Research Brief RBX12-03 Nottingham, England: DfES

Stoll, L, Bolam, R, McMahon, A, Thomas, S, Wallace, M, Greenwood, A and Hawkey, K (2006) *Professional Learning Communities: Source Materials for School Leaders and Other Leaders of Professional Learning.* London: DfES Innovation Unit http://www.ncsl.org.uk/networked/ networked-o-z.cfm#p

Teddlie, C and Reynolds, D (eds) (2000) *The International Handbook of School Effectiveness Research*. London: Falmer
TTA (2005) The TTA's Role in the Future of CPD: Response to the Secretary of State London: TTA
Wenger, E (1999) *Communities of Practice: Learning, Meaning and Identity*. Cambridge, England: Cambridge University Press
Wiley, S (2001) Contextual effects of student achievement: school leadership and professional community. *Journal of Educational Change* 2, 1: 1–33

Appendix

The first study – the *Creating and Sustaining Effective Professional Learning Communities* (EPLC) project (Bolam et al., 2005) – was funded by the Department for Education and Skills (DfES), the General Teaching Council for England (GTCE) and the National College for School Leadership (NCSL) from 2002–06 (**www.eplc.info**). Its overall purpose was to draw out credible, accessible and practically useful findings for policy makers, coordinators/providers of professional development and school leaders (managers) about schools as professional learning communities and also for teachers and other adults working in schools about the cultures, behaviours and structures that might enable them to play an active role in the creation and sustenance of learning communities. To achieve this purpose, a range of research methods was adopted: a literature review; a questionnaire survey of headteachers or continuing professional development (CPD) coordinators from a national sample of almost 400 nursery, primary (elementary), secondary and special schools in local authorities across England; examining links between characteristics of professional learning communities and student progress through factor analysis and multilevel models; case studies of sixteen different schools in each phase of schooling (nursery, primary, secondary, special) and at each of the three stages of development (i.e. early starter, developer, mature); workshop conferences to share experiences and research findings with representatives from the case study schools. The project concluded with the production of a set of dissemination and training resources (Stoll et al., 2006). The project's overall, general conclusion was that the idea of a plc was one well worth pursuing as a means of promoting school and system-wide capacity building for sustainable improvement and pupil learning.

The second study (Bolam and Weindling, 2006) was funded, from 2005–06, by the General Teaching Council for England (GTCe) and the Association for Teachers and Lecturers (ATL). It involved a systematic review and synthesis (SRS) of twenty research studies of CPD for teachers in England, published from 2002 to 2006. The review was intended to contribute to the development of CPD policy for capacity building in schools. The design of the study was quite different from a conventional systematic review in that the studies to be included were largely specified beforehand, on the grounds that they had been commissioned by, or for, a policy-maker audience. The sponsors wanted there to be a trustworthy overview of what the studies collectively showed (or failed to show) that could inform the policy environment in a time of change. All the studies were funded by national agencies and all had been published within the previous four years. The twenty selected studies, fell into three broad, and not entirely discrete, methodological categories – five were systematic reviews of research, six used surveys and case studies and nine were evaluations. They differed widely in their focus, aims and scope covering such topics as the impact of collaborative CPD on classroom teaching and learning; postgraduate professional development programmes; teachers' perceptions of CPD; teachers' work and lives and their effects on pupils; developing teacher leadership; schools as professional learning communities (summarised above); research-engaged schools; the transfer of good practice; inter-LEA collaboration on CPD; and several major CPD programmes (e.g. Induction; Best Practice Research Scholarships, teachers' sabbaticals, London Leadership Strategy). Each study was independently reviewed, analysed and assessed by two researchers, using a *'Weight of Evidence'* approach in making judgements about their quality (www.eppi.ioe.ac.uk). The findings, grouped under twenty factors, were compared with policy and practice in 2001 and 2005, using three documents (DfEE, 2001; TTA, 2005 and DfES, 2005) as key indicators, together with some supplementary documents. The overall conclusion, based on the evidence from the synthesis of all twenty studies, was that the large majority of findings supported recent and current CPD policy and practice and offered a sound basis for developing future policy and practice in England.

Chapter 11
Towards Effective Management
of a Reformed Teaching Profession

Mike Wallace

Britain Leads the World – In an Unwise Direction?

The purpose of this chapter is to argue that effective leadership and management of the education profession requires a shift of direction away from current orthodoxies of radical transformation, promoted by reform policies, towards a more temperate approach. Temperance would serve a less ambitious but more realistic endeavour to bring about incremental improvement in students' education. It would encourage and enable teachers to operate as professionals, exercising the judgement necessary to do their best for their students in their classroom and school settings. Conversely, it would embody the expectation that teachers should act professionally in their relationships with colleagues, students and parents, within broad consensually defined limits of acceptable practice.

Ideally, more temperate organizational leadership and management would be supported by more temperate central government policies than the raft of reforms designed literally to 're-form' the education profession by tightening central government control over the scope of practice. They embrace both indirect control measures, as in the national specification of the curriculum, and direct, as in the 'remodelling' of the education profession itself. Recently a senior government official commented to me, with some pride, that Britain leads the world in driving the 'delivery' of public service transformation through its target-setting regime. In the absence of a political U-turn, effective leadership and management of the education profession would imply protecting the capacity of teachers, as far as was possible, to mediate the contextually insensitive central government reforms connected with this control thrust, for the sake of effective educational provision – in spite of, rather than because of, UK government policy-makers' well-intentioned efforts.

Signs that the wisdom of such reformist zeal may be questionable are not difficult to detect. Three examples will suffice. First, at the international level. Between 1991 and 2001 the UK dropped from 13th to 20th place in the league table published by the Organization of Economic Cooperation and Development (2003), charting the proportion of students from 30 countries achieving good qualifications at the end of their secondary school education. Improvement in the UK according to this measure was outstripped by greater improvement in other countries with less ambitious

D. Johnson, R. Maclean (eds.), *Teaching: Professionalization,*
Development and Leadership,
© Springer Science + Business Media B.V. 2008

reform movements. Could the comprehensiveness of UK reforms have contributed to the unintended consequence of slipping down the international league table?

Second, at the national education system level, chronic overload of teachers and headteachers built-up from the onset of central government reforms in the late 1980s. By 2002, teachers in a national survey (GTC, 2003) identified the three factors that most demotivated them as: 'workload (including unnecessary paperwork)' (56%), 'initiative overload' (39%), and the 'target-driven culture' (connected with performance and improvement targets imposed by central government). Some 35% indicated their intention to leave the profession within the next 5 years – and only just over half were expecting to retire. Could the endeavour to drive up standards through multiple reforms encompassing 'tough targets' have contributed to the unintended consequence of driving out experienced professionals on whom implementation depends, and generating a chronic teacher shortage?

Third, at the school organization level, 'superheads' – experienced and superlatively successful headteachers appointed under a central government policy to turn round failing English secondary schools – have experienced mixed fortunes. Three of the first nine superheads appointed to schools in socially deprived areas resigned in the same week (TES, 2000). Could the assumption that leadership success in one context was automatically applicable to another have contributed to the unintended consequence of perpetuating problems for staff in some of our most challenging school settings?

Each instance reflects – however indirectly – the good educational improvement intentions of policy-makers or leaders and managers coming unstuck, consistent with what Fink (2003: 105) dubs the 'law of unintended consequences...for every policy initiative there will be unpredicted and unpredictable results'. Occasionally the results may be fortuitous, exceeding expectations without deleterious side-effects. But more often they amount to an 'own goal', revealing that the reality of implementation falls far short of policy-makers' envisioned improvement goals. Either way, there is intrinsic ambiguity over how things will turn out until after the implementation effort.

Reforms have long been driven by the attempt to tighten political control: ultimately to reduce the diversity of 'progressive' and 'traditional' professional practices emerging by the 1970s, proximally to minimize ambiguity over the change required for that reduction. It seems ironic that this endeavour is the root cause of such debilitating unintended consequences alongside many intended improvements. For there is little evidence to suggest that most policy-makers and, in their turn, organizational leaders and managers act other than in good faith in their genuine quest to improve education. If we are to move towards more effective educational improvement strategies, we need to deepen our understanding of irony and to learn to live with it as an integral feature of professional practice, rather than continue trying haplessly to eliminate it through ever-tighter political or leadership and management control.

Accordingly, a case for temperate leadership and management of the education profession will be made, using an ironic perspective on organizational life and change developed by Eric Hoyle and myself (Hoyle and Wallace, 2005). This is neither a theory nor a model, merely a heuristic tool for exploring ambiguity and the propensity for unintended consequences of actions. But it does offer a new platform for thinking about how to improve education through loosening central controls enough to facilitate the bounded expansion of professional practice. Most ideas underpinning this perspective are scarcely novel. But they have been marginalized in the educational leadership and management literature.

The Analytical Advantage of Combining Traditions

The ironic perspective draws eclectically on several traditions of enquiry driven by different and partially incompatible 'intellectual projects' (Wallace and Wray, 2006):

- Exploring organizational practices and their underlying ideologies to develop 'knowledge-for-understanding' of more academic than practical interest (e.g. March, 1999; Rowan and Miskel, 1999; Weick, 2001).
- Focusing on individual and collective professional learning from a positive standpoint towards practice and policy to develop prescriptive 'knowledge-for-action' that will inform policy and professional development interventions (e.g. Leithwood and Louis, 1998; Wallace, 1996).
- Examining practice and policy from a sceptical standpoint to develop 'knowledge-for-critical evaluation' that exposes their underlying ideologies and negatively judged unintended consequences, through sociological studies of teachers' workplace (e.g. Woods et al., 1997; Helsby, 1999; Osborn et al., 2000).

Eric Hoyle and I are engaged in a hybrid intellectual project, harnessing ideas from each tradition towards our ends: to build our critique of current orthodoxies of school leadership and management and policy, from which flows our rationale for advocating a more temperate approach. We seek to deepen understanding through the ironic perspective to inform efforts to improve practice and policy. But we stop short of prescription. The ironic perspective implies that whatever may turn out to work will vary with contingent and partially unpredictable local circumstances. So the more detailed any prescription, the more insensitive it becomes to contextual contingencies, and the more it is vulnerable to the irony of unintended consequences – creating more problems than it solves.

The case for temperance is developed in the remaining sections via the ironic perspective. First, the perspective itself is outlined. Conceptual tools are offered for focusing on the extent of ambiguities that are endemic to organizational life and their inherent exacerbation by change, within broad structural parameters – economic and ideological – delimiting what is considered to be doable and what is even thinkable (see Wallace and Pocklington, 2002: 47–51).

Second, ironies of managerialism are explored. Managerialism is stipulatively defined as excessive leadership and management, threatening to become self-serving rather than serving education, and to inhibit the professional practice that they purport to transform. Belief in managerialism results in overestimating the capacity of policy-makers to control organizational leadership and management, and the capacity of organizational leaders and managers to control teaching and learning for effective student education.

Third, evidence is considered, primarily from the teachers' workplace literature, of the diversity of responses to managerialism in schools. Far from entering into the spirit of reforms, many (perhaps most) teachers go through the motions where required to meet external accountability requirements. Simultaneously, they adapt contextually insensitive reforms wherever possible to make them work in the contingent circumstances of their classrooms and their schools. The hypothesis is offered that they subscribe to a sceptical view of government policies, a pragmatic orientation towards their implementation, and a constructivist and collaborative approach towards teaching and learning. Finally, this approach is endorsed as an effective way of meeting irony with irony. It is argued that such an approach should be embraced by leaders and managers and policy-makers in developing a more temperate approach towards incremental improvement. This will reduce external pressure and expand the scope for teachers to serve education as responsible and creative professionals, while monitoring to ensure that their practices remain acceptable.

The Ironic Perspective

The connotations of irony range from coincidence, through the literal meaning of words contradicting someone's intention, to unanticipated outcomes despite one's best efforts. All highlight the limited capacity of people to make sense of the social world and to control it to suit their interests. Irony offers scope for a new perspective because it neatly captures the phenomenon of limited human capacity which is intrinsic to organizational life and to change, especially that flowing from policy initiatives. Connotations of irony with most analytic potential are selectively employed in the perspective, since there is no canonical definition of irony.

This perspective offers a sensitizing device for exploring the empirical gap between intention and outcome or between concept and experienced reality, and the conceptual gap between declared and implied meaning, which together contribute to the limited manageability of organizational life and change (Wallace, 2003). It provides one starting point for considering how to cope as effectively as possible with relative unmanageability. Two forms of organizational irony may be distinguished. *Situational irony* refers to those ironies that are constitutive of social reality. The key manifestation is the unintended consequence: most commonly when good intentions have unfortunate consequences, but potentially where apparently unfortunate occurrences bring unexpected benefits.

Semantic irony refers to irony in language – whether intended, or unintended but observable. Intentional irony includes wordplay where the meaning conveyed contradicts the words used, as when an organizational mission statement is invoked cynically to underscore its transgression in practice. Intentionality can be difficult to ascertain, especially where, say, organization members feel pressurised to adopt visionary terminology. Some may employ it with unreflective sincerity. But others may employ it with intentional but covert insincerity, because they perceive that their career prospects depend on the appearance of sincerity. Visionary rhetoric is especially vulnerable to semantic irony. There is a designed-in disjunction between the lofty aspirational rhetoric and the mundane organizational reality that is experienced.

Preconditions for irony are created by various sources of *ambiguity*, or uncertainty in meaning. Practices, organizational structures and language may all be interpreted differently, causing some degree of dissonance or unpredictability. Doubt over what is actually happening, vacillation between alternative interpretations of the same event, or equivocation over what should be done are often reducible, but can never be eliminated.

Change is an intrinsic feature of organizations, even in a relatively stable policy environment. It contributes to ambiguity through generating uncertainty relating to the learning entailed in putting the change into effect. As time unfolds, turnover of organization members arises sooner or later and responsibilities are reallocated. Incomers are faced with learning to operate in their new organizational setting, while longer-serving colleagues must adjust to them. Most learning required to fulfil novel tasks involves tacit, incidental learning through the job experience (Wallace, 1996). It may be augmented by conscious reflection on action and by preparatory or ongoing training. Planned changes add temporarily to the intrinsic level of ambiguity while further learning is necessitated to implement the shift in practice. Even modest improvement efforts imply some challenge to habitual practices and assumptions.

Initially, the meaning of planned change will be ambiguous. Organization members cannot wholly understand the new practice before they have individually (and often collectively) experienced it and integrated it into their repertoire. Equally, how to implement the change will be ambiguous before the implementation attempt is made. Preparatory training cannot provide implementers with what they can learn consciously or tacitly only by modifying their practice in the normal work setting, ideally with feedback (Joyce et al., 1999). Knowing precisely how to make a change in practice can emerge only from trying to do so, however well informed by others' advice. Full sense can be made of a significant change only when it becomes assimilated into normal practice and its initial degree of ambiguity diminishes.

Attempts to change practice across multiple organizations generate ambiguity of a different order of magnitude. Innovations may accrete, forming an evolving profile for every organization. Each innovation may be at a different point of implementation, and may compete for priority with the other innovations, alongside responses to unplanned contextual pressures or temporary crises, and the rest of ongoing practice. Greatest ambiguity is likely where a programmatic sequence of linked reforms is applied across multiple systems of organizations, as with the UK central government's public service modernization strategy (OPSR, 2002). A set of political principles (itself embodying ambiguity in advocating national standards alongside devolution) underpins a broadly consistent programme of reforms for every public service, of which education is but one.

Normal practice in such organizations is affected by myriad factors associated with organization members' characteristics, the system of which their organization is a part, and their social milieu. To the extent that they possess agency, they have some capacity to choose their course of action in the light of their interpretation of the situation (Giddens, 1984). This capacity to act in alternative ways according to alternative beliefs which cannot be directly controlled creates a permanent degree of ambiguity. Change piles on further complexity. Expression of agency amongst implementers inevitably creates potential for ambiguity through the possibility of different responses, including covert or overt resistance, or even subversion by hijacking a change to achieve incompatible goals (e.g. Wallace, 1998a; Moore et al., 2002). Since policy-makers cannot achieve total control over implementation, they cannot escape generating preconditions for irony.

Sources of Ambiguity

A chronic gap between the ambition of official goals proclaimed for many organizations and their realization has often been noted. It is widely institutionalized through vision and mission statements designed to give organization members something to aim for which is beyond their immediate reach. A variable degree of endemic *organizational pathos* (Hoyle, 1986) ensues, where goals promise more than the reality experienced.

Planned change across a system of organizations is equally characterised by endemic *policy pathos*, a chronic gap between policy-makers' stated goals and the extent to which they are achieved. Policy-makers can have only limited knowledge of the contextual detail of the organizations which are the target of their initiatives, and cannot predetermine change outcomes. The greater the ambition of policy changes, the greater the learning required of implementers, and the greater the scope for less-than-faithful implementation. Hence the long-established notion of 'mutual adaptation' between policy-makers' vision for change and implementers' practice (McLaughlin, 1991). Scope for infidelity derives from the capacity for agency which limits the manageability of change. Implementers may pursue various operational goals, perhaps extending to covert subversion.

Organizational and policy pathos result not only from consciously proclaimed ambitious goals. They also result from all the other ongoing activity in each organization into which the policy change is launched. The range of official and unofficial goals being pursued is likely to be both *diverse and diffuse*. Today's policy change overlays yesterday's improvement strategy, itself added to routine work across the organization or system.

The diversity of supplementary goals, rather than the diffuseness of a particular goal, generates ambiguity. Narrowing the focus of any goal and measuring its achievement cannot remove the ambiguity connected with pursuing this goal alongside all the other goals also being pursued. Some goals may be incompatible with others (as with enforcing national standards and promoting devolution). Once there are multiple goals, it becomes impossible to pursue them all with equal vigour. Prioritising some means that others get subordinated. Many goals are not amenable to operationalizing in terms of measurable performance. (How can, say, 'developing a lifelong love of learning' be determined until students reach the end of their lifecourse – when they will be in no condition to confirm or deny that love?)

Inherent *limits to rationality* of organizational life and policy implementation are a perennial source of ambiguity. As March and Simon (1958) long ago demonstrated, rationality is always bounded because it is impossible to weigh up all possible consequences of all possible decision choices before selecting the optimal course of action. Satisficing is the best that can be achieved, using whatever evidence is available to inform a hunch about which way to go.

Limits to rationality come in several forms. First, *cognitive* limits flow from the impossibility of predicting future outcomes of decisions and an inevitably restricted awareness of what is happening inside and outside any organization. The more complex and programmatic a change, the less comprehensive an overview is feasible, since no individual can share the experiences of everyone involved. Consultation, surveillance and outcome measurement can provide only limited evidence of the interaction between the change and other aspects of organizational contexts. The greater the effort to gather information, the more likely it is to precipitate the irony of distracting implementers who are the sources of this intelligence from dealing with the change itself.

Second, *logical* limits apply where individuals' pursuit of a particular goal can prevent it being achieved when others also pursue it. A classic education example is promoting greater consumer choice in a context of restricted resources. Collective choices will be delimited by the pattern of alternatives in the marketplace. Where more people make the same choice than the capacity of provision, they collectively inhibit each other from attaining what they have individually chosen. Marketization risks the irony of frustrating choice because the aggregate of individual choices cannot be reliably manipulated to ensure that demand matches supply.

Third, *phenomenological* or interpretive limits are imposed where the same event or change process is construed in incompatible ways. As a social institution, a school may be viewed very differently by senior staff and class teachers. The diversity of possible constructions is limited by widely held assumptions about what schools are and what counts as professional practice. But there is always scope for incompatible perspectives which will be regarded as 'rational' by their protagonists. The frames of reference governing social constructs may relate to contradictory beliefs, norms (rules about how people should behave) and values. Witness the pursuit of organizational efficiency by minimizing the resources required to achieve given outcomes alongside the pursuit of greater effectiveness, for which additional resources may be needed.

Fourth, *control* limits flow from the probability that nobody, of whatever authority, can achieve absolute control over others. Control ambiguity flows from the interdependence of all organization members: power is distributed – however unequally – within and between organizations. Even those with most authority depend ultimately on the cooperation of those whom they lead, and their support can never be wholly predicted. Any individual has some capacity to resist or subvert working to achieve official goals.

Unresolvable *dilemmas* (see Ogawa et al., 1999) add another perennial source of ambiguity for individuals, groups, organizations or multi-organizational systems. Action oriented towards one pole of the dilemma triggers negative consequences, building pressure for action towards the opposite pole. No stable, cost-free middle ground is achievable between both poles. What is good for system-wide reform may not be good for those whose additional effort is necessary to make it happen, as indicated by the irony mentioned earlier of overloading teachers for the best of educational reform intentions. Intrinsic reform dilemmas arise over what balance to strike between pace of change and sustainability of envisioned new practices, and between central direction of a universal form of change and nurturing local innovation which is more sensitive to local circumstances.

Such sources of ambiguity generate potent preconditions for reforms to generate the situational irony of unintended consequences, inhibiting policy-makers from achieving their goals. Even more ironic, those unintended consequences that they judge negatively tend to stimulate them into ameliorative policy-making, bringing the situational irony of more change with its accompanying ambiguity. Favourable conditions for further unintended consequences are thus created, and so the likelihood of yet further amelioration. Take the instance of teacher overload brought on by reforms. Government ministers' ameliorative response was more reform: compulsory workforce remodelling that includes restricting teachers' duties and the formal integration of learning support assistants into classrooms. More change, more ambiguity – and the irony of further restricting the scope for teachers' professional discretion.

Ironies of Managerialism

Leadership and management have a vital part to play in supporting organizational activity and improvement. Effective leadership and management of schools create structures and processes and establish relationships enabling teachers to engage as fully as possible with teaching and learning. The term 'managerialism' is normatively and critically conceived as *excessive* leadership and management, reaching beyond an appropriate educational support role and threatening to become an end-in-itself. Managerialism is underpinned by an ideology which assumes that all aspects of organizational life can and should be controlled. In other words, that ambiguity can and should be radically reduced or eliminated. The ironic perspective helps explain why this assumption is false.

It was noted earlier how an underlying thrust of UK education reforms has been to delimit much more tightly the boundaries of teachers' professional practice, curbing the extremes that by the 1970s were causing public and political disquiet.

Increasingly these reforms have been designed to channel teachers' agency towards achieving instrumental goals driven by economic interests. The irony of well-intentioned government policies inhibiting as well as enhancing educational achievement is an unintended consequence of an over-optimistic belief in the comprehensiveness of potential control over teachers' professional work. Delimiting unacceptable extremes of practice implies, appropriately, control at the edges where practices would be condemned by most people (say gross incompetence, negligence or indoctrination). But reformist zeal has gone much further towards educational micromanagement, attempting comprehensive control of teaching and learning and their leadership and management. This is too much of a good thing. The content of reforms and the change process invoked to implement them have exacerbated the endemic ambiguity they were implicitly designed to eliminate, enhancing the preconditions for irony.

Many reforms have focused on direct control of teaching and learning, including the national curriculum, the literacy and numeracy strategies, national assessment, league tables and inspection. A complementary programme of reforms has focused on tightening control over leadership and management as a means of indirect control of teaching and learning. Ostensibly, freedom to express agency at the organization level has been opened-up through local management and the establishment of trust schools. But other reforms have delimited this freedom to ensure that leaders and managers act as conduits for the teaching and learning reforms and assist government policy-makers in reducing the scope for teachers' professional judgement. Development planning and school self-evaluation are linked to external inspection whose criteria relate to other reforms. Performance management is linked to nationally prescribed and locally negotiated student attainment targets. National leadership training – some compulsory for aspiring headteachers – is linked to responsibility for 'delivering' central government education reforms and sustaining the new practices required. A key tenet of managerialism is thus that the agency of teachers can and should be channelled within narrow limits delimited by central government policy-makers, or by leaders and managers acting on their behalf. Empowerment to express agency lies solely within the bounds of predetermined policy.

Indicative ironies of managerialism include, first and foremost, the over-restriction of teachers' scope for professional judgement in the classroom, which fails to allow sufficiently for contextual contingency. Every classroom is like all other classrooms, some other classrooms and no other classroom. Teaching and learning are highly contextualised and replete with endemic ambiguity. What works with one student or class may not work with another, and teachers soon develop a repertoire of strategies on which they draw according to their ongoing diagnosis of each teaching situation. This repertoire is never complete, as new classroom challenges, collaborative working and planned professional learning opportunities stimulate further practical experimentation. Mandatory reforms focused on teaching and learning, for whose faithful implementation school leaders and managers are held accountable, tend to be couched in terms of a relatively untested 'one size fits all' strategy aimed at tightening the boundaries of teachers' discretion. The insensitivity of the reforms to contingent classroom circumstances exacerbates the endemic level of ambiguity, as teachers try to make them work in detailed contexts for which they could never be designed. Yet within broad limits of acceptable practice, teachers' discretion is essential for educational improvement because of their need to adapt to contingent and relatively ambiguous circumstances. Policy-makers have apparently failed to comprehend the nature of professional practice. The drive to halt its unacceptable extremes has been over-applied, generating the irony of halting much necessary experimentation within these extremes on which the success of educational reforms depend.

Second, managerialism operates ironically as a 'weapon of mass distraction'. Reforms have brought a huge increase in the quantity of leadership and management which sap the time devoted to teaching and learning. Not just temporarily to implement particular reforms, but permanently once they have been put in place. Yet schools used to be run with far fewer specialised leadership and management roles, and research has consistently shown that what happens in the classroom is far more important for educational outcomes than leadership and management. At best they can create favourable conditions for teachers' professional practice. At worst, they can get in the way of teaching. For leadership and management tasks extend to class teachers. Distributed leadership is generally advocated as empowering teachers as leaders. But time spent leading is time spent not teaching, a key contributor to the intensification of work that, as indicated earlier, has demotivated so many in the profession. Additional leadership and management tasks for headteachers have precluded their involvement in the leadership of teaching and learning.

Third, managerialism amounts to an unhelpful 'solution in search of a problem' (March and Olsen, 1976), creating conditions that encourage leaders to generate problems to solve because they are expected to demonstrate proactivity. Leadership has been distinguished from and given primacy over management as the more proactive aspect of coordinating teachers' work. Pressure from agencies linked to central government (e.g. DFES, 2004; OFSTED, 2003) is increasingly placed on staff with leadership responsibilities to express proactivity as a moral imperative, whether through inspiring colleagues or providing innovative leadership of teaching and learning. Speculatively, identifying and solving problems legitimates new leadership roles, underpins career advancement opportunities, and justifies special pleading for resources. Conditions are ripe for leaders to overcomplicate existing problems or manufacture new ones in the name of innovation for greater effectiveness. The epithet 'if it ain't broke, don't fix it' has no place in educational transformation.

Fourth, leadership and management have been partially professionalized as part of the government strategy to halt the gradual professionalization of teachers. By the 1970s the extent of teachers' classroom autonomy had allowed extremes of practice to emerge which brought on the reforms. The irony here is that giving leaders and managers the 'right to manage' is nominal, so increasing the level of ambiguity they experience because their increased autonomy under local management is belied by their obligation to follow government policy – 'the right to manage on our behalf'. The National College for School Leadership is instrumental in giving leadership and management the hallmarks of a profession through its training programmes, research reviews contributing to the specialist leadership knowledge base, and articulation of national standards embodying an implicit ethical code (DFES, 2004).

Fifth, the rhetoric of radical transformation of education to be nurtured by transformational leadership is mythical, producing semantic irony where language belies experience. The isomorphism between supposedly local community-driven school vision statements reflects the success of government reforms in prescribing most of their visionary content. What is described as transformational leadership is more accurately expressed as *transmissional leadership* – 'any vision you like as long as it fits with central government's vision for you'. The major irony here though is situational: central government reforms heralded as transformational (e.g. OPSR, 2002: 2) systematically inhibit any potential for radical transformation at school level. They narrowly delimit the boundaries for experimentation through the curriculum specification, target and accountability regime. A further irony is that conditions for transformation were greater when teachers had much more professional autonomy, and the reforms have systematically removed that capacity.

Further, it is questionable whether state education, essentially a conservative institution for social reproduction, could realistically take the lead over economic institutions for transforming society. What is being sought of school leaders and managers is faithful transmission of political goals and promotion of activity to implement them, not transformation of their schools according to their own diverse beliefs and values and those of local community members. The ambition of transformational goals belies the limited capacity of any public service to spearhead radical social change. Much stronger structural economic social forces ensure that state education remains more responsive than revolutionary.

Ironic Response

Perhaps the ultimate irony is that most headteachers and teachers appear not to have embraced managerialism, retaining their allegiance to teaching above their allegiance to leading and managing. Behavioural change can be enforced through surveillance and sanctions. Cultural change cannot. Research evidence from teachers' workplace studies suggests that maybe the dominant response is to cope with the excesses of managerialism, keeping up appearances of faithful implementation for accountability purposes, while seeking ways of mediating reforms to make them work in the contingent circumstances of individual schools and classrooms. Enduring ambiguity remains over how far the appearance of centrally directed reform is matched by the reality of professional practice. Here lies an obverse of the irony for policy-makers that their well-intentioned reforms bring negative unintended consequences. It is that implementers retain sufficient agency to meet irony with irony through their partially covert buffering responses as leaders and managers, and as teachers.

Research on development planning in the 1990s (Wallace and McMahon, 1994; Wallace, 1998b) illustrates how this chronically raised level of ambiguity has been generated. School development planning was a managerial innovation for supporting school staff with implementing reforms. The lock-step annual planning cycle and typically pre-specified limit to the number of priorities that could be addressed each year was insensitive to the diversity of school contexts and – more ironically – to the incremental imposition of further central government reforms. Ameliorative adjustments had to be made as existing reforms proved either unworkable in themselves, or to clash with other reforms. The annual cycle was over-rigid for the relatively turbulent planning environments into which it was introduced, but it must be seen to be followed. The form this intervention took did not allow for incremental updating of plans. It exacerbated the endemic ambiguity for school leaders and managers flowing from their dilemma over long-range direction-setting versus retaining short-term flexibility to adapt to unpredictably evolving circumstances.

A common response was to compile the development plan as required, especially once the inspection regime came to include examining each school's development plan document. But then informal incremental planning, conducted alongside development planning, actually guided practice. It offered needed flexibility that the annual development planning cycle did not. Adaptation was required for coping with a reform that might have been well matched to relatively stable pre-reform school contexts when it was developed, but was ill suited to the more turbulent programmatic reform contexts in which it was to be implemented.

Overall, research into the impact of reforms on the experience and practice of professional staff suggests that they respond differently. These responses may be categorized as compliance, non-compliance, or mediation. Compliance connotes that reform goals are accepted, whether enthusiastically (implying belief in these goals), or resignedly (implying belief that behavioural acquiescence is prudent). Compliance reduces ambiguity for policy-makers as long as reforms are workable. Non-compliance connotes anything from retreatism, covertly perpetuating present practice in the hope of not being detected, to overt resistance. This response generates ambiguity for policy-makers over determining the extent of non-compliance and over how to increase compliance.

Mediation is different. It can comprise an ironic form of response where staff try to adapt reforms to make them work according to their existing professional values in their circumstances. Workplace studies imply that such mediators are principled, sincerely endeavouring to work around externally imposed requirements. They express what may be termed *principled infidelity*. 'Infidelity' follows from not adhering fully to policy-makers' expectations. 'Principled' follows from attempting to sustain their professional values instead of embracing the alternative values under-girding reforms.

Bending agency towards mediating reforms adds ambiguity where superficially dutiful compliance covers divergent practices. Insofar as reforms like development planning are contextually insensitive, covert adaptation by mediators may make them work better than if mediators had been more compliant. Principled infidelity may undermine the achievement of policy-makers' reform goals to the letter while contributing to the spirit of these goals by making a related but more realistic practice work (as with development planning). Mediators may thus reduce negative unintended consequences of reforms by giving priority to the interests of staff and the local community over those of policy-makers.

Principled mediators may be regarded as committed 'ironists' whose infidelity should be endorsed in coping with reforms that are not of their making. Speculatively, such ironists express an *ironic orientation* towards professional practice and change. They appear to be sceptics, committed to improving educational practice. Their scepticism is born of their familiarity with endemic ambiguity and the ironies that often arise, and their reservations about the impact of 'one size fits all' reforms on their practice and on the interests of their students. They are likely to adopt the position which Moore et al. (2002) labelled 'principled pragmatism'. This term was applied to headteachers who seek to square reforms with their personal educational beliefs and values. Mediators are likely to be reflexive about their successes and failures with a view to improving, and to adopt a perspective on change which, while open to new ideas, features a strong sense of contingency. Externally initiated reforms or other changes are assessed against the perceived needs of staff and students, scrutinized for their workability in this local setting, and compromises sought where necessary to cope with policy-makers' unrealistic expectations.

The ironic orientation hypothesized here has affinity with the relatively indeterminate, inherently ambiguous nature of professional practice. Traditional claims for professional autonomy have long lost political and public support. Arguments for the exclusive entitlement to apply esoteric knowledge learned through lengthy training in making inferential diagnoses and administering treatments (Abbott, 1988) in uncertain situations has been widely interpreted as merely protecting professionals' self-interests. Reforms have undermined teachers' autonomy and rendered them more accountable to central government and to parental preferences (Dale, 1989). But the unrealistic endeavour behind managerialism to eliminate ambiguity in teachers' professional practice has misread the ineradicable core of ambiguity that is endemic to it. An ironic orientation is therefore appropriate in accepting the inevitability of ambiguity and irony and pragmatically seeking ways of coping as effectively as possible in contingent circumstances.

Wise Moves: Towards Effective Management of a Reformed Teaching Profession

Any educational improvement strategy carries risks, and endemic ambiguity coupled with its exacerbation by change mean that there can be no guarantees of success. But learning to live with irony is a good risk. It offers considerable potential for enhancing teaching and learning, supported by temperate leadership and management and temperate policy-making. This potential rests on harnessing the ironic orientation towards educational ends through moderation rather than missionary zeal, the cautious pursuit of incremental improvement rather than transformation, and coping with ambiguity and irony rather than attempting to eliminate them through hyper-control.

Moderation, incrementalism and coping may sound politically unattractive. The UK electorate has long been groomed to expect visionary rhetoric and rapid results. But the electorate has also been groomed for cynicism about broken political promises where the rhetoric has ill-matched their experience of education and other public services. Ministers can ill afford the bad risk of adding further to the growing sense of public disenchantment.

Effective management of a reformed teaching profession entails most significantly the policy-makers who exercise overall responsibility for the national state education system and leaders and managers in the schools themselves, supported less directly by staff in intermediate administrative organizations and government agencies. Lets us consider the contribution of the former two groups to managing the teaching profession effectively by maximizing the potential for educational improvement.

Temperate Policy-Making

The international comparison mentioned earlier suggests that there is ample room for greater educational effectiveness. Future policy-making therefore needs to be directed towards realistic improvement. First, when setting the political agenda more extensive consultation with representatives of leaders and managers and class teachers on whom implementation depends could offer a reality-check for politicians' ideas and foster implementers' cooperation. The risk for politicians of 'provider capture' to suit professionals' interests over those of students and parents is set against the risks of non-compliance, ameliorative policy-making to address problems created by unrealistic reforms, unfulfilled public expectations and further decline of electoral support.

Second, an incremental strategy for evolutionary improvement with allowance for problems to emerge could maximize the capacity for fluent adjustment, and even rethinking the strategy itself in the light of any ironic consequences. The political risk of appearing to have run out of big ideas by eschewing visionary rhetoric and tight control is balanced against the risks of undeliverable promises, of sunk investment in unworkable reforms whose retraction may be judged a political U-turn, and of demotivating and burning out implementers on whose efforts policy-makers depend.

Third, building flexibility into reforms could deliberately foster the principled infidelity necessary for implementers to make generalized practices work in specific settings. The risk of unacceptable mediatory responses is set against the risk of central direction that is too rigid to provide this vital element of integral adaptability.

Fourth, promoting the development of school staff capacity to cope with endemic ambiguities and those added by change could help teachers and headteachers to pre-empt the ironies that striving for impossible certainty can precipitate, and to deploy routine strategies for coping with the ironies that slip through. The risk of imprecision and opacity is set against the risk that implementers will be completely thrown whenever negative unintended consequences arise despite their best endeavours.

Fifth, developing unobtrusive monitoring and mild accountability mechanisms that make maximal use of new technology could pre-empt or otherwise alert policy-makers to any unacceptable extremes of professional practice in schools. Focusing on surveillance of extremes could minimize unproductively diverting the attention of the conscientious and competent majority of staff from their core purpose of education. The political risk of having insufficient information to prove system-wide quality of educational performance to the electorate is set against the costs of strong surveillance and heavy information demands in terms of staff distraction.

Temperate School Leadership and Management

Temperate policy-making has important implications for temperate school leadership and management. First, the nature of professional practice, consistent with the ironic orientation, implies that teachers could be more effective if they were given greater (though not unlimited) scope to exercise responsible professional judgement. Overall, more effective leadership and management mean less leadership and management. Since teachers have become caught up in specialised managerial roles and distributed leadership, relieving them of non-teaching tasks where possible would enable them to concentrate more on their teaching. The role of headteachers and other senior staff is to be exemplary practitioners of principled infidelity, whether in giving enthusiastic support to implementing policy changes, adapting them, protecting teachers from them, or promoting local innovation. The risk of confusion over the coordination required to promote coherence and progression in teaching and learning is set against the risk of leadership and management becoming self-serving at the expense of the educational activity it exists to serve.

Second, for headteachers, as the formal 'top' school leader, a key strategy for coping with further reforms is *orchestration*. A stipulative definition of this concept is 'coordinated activity within set parameters expressed by a network of senior leaders at different administrative levels to instigate, organize, oversee and consolidate complex change across part or all of a multi-organizational system' (see Wallace and Pocklington, 2002: 207–209). Orchestration encompasses considering whether and how to respond to externally initiated change. It extends to active promotion and organization to get change under way, and continual monitoring and adaptive action to cope with the unfolding consequences of ambiguity. Headteachers as orchestrators could take the strain off their colleagues and absorb some of the stress induced by reforms through the three subthemes of flexible planning (for rapid adaptation while attempting to sustain a broad direction), culture-building and communication (for fostering a sense of communal commitment to high quality educational provision), and differentiated support (for helping other staff to learn how to cope with their tasks). The managerial risk of being held to account for colleagues' unfaithful implementation of externally instigated changes is offset by the risk of overloaded and overstressed staff, and so an impoverished educational experience for students.

Third, temperate leadership implies fostering good professional practice in all areas of work. It could include encouraging staff and ensuring that they both operate professionally through exercising the judgement that is necessary for the assiduous performance of their tasks, and act professionally through developing and sustaining appropriate relationships with colleagues, students and parents. It could run to fostering continual individual and collective professional learning within the 'professional learning community' (Bolam et al., 2005) in each school, protecting the degree of autonomy needed to make reforms work in every teacher's classroom. The managerial risk of losing control over colleagues' practice in implementing change is set against the risk of inhibiting their capacity to express principled infidelity in making change work for the sake of high quality service provision.

Fourth, leaders and managers could actively encourage the generation of ideas, techniques and procedures from professional practice (within the boundaries of acceptability), through identifying, supporting and achieving congruence between experimental practices and externally shaped requirements. They could expand the scope for distributed leadership focused on teaching and learning, creating favourable conditions for emergent practice among different specialised groups. The risk of unworkable innovation or unacceptable divergence from regulatory norms is set against the risk of failing to develop improved, context-sensitive ways of doing the things that matter most to staff, students and parents.

Finally, promoting a climate of 'high trust-with-verification' could set the expectation that staff will take responsibility for operating professionally and so not abuse the autonomy accorded them to foster local innovation and emergence. An initial presumption of trust, rather than the mistrust that strong surveillance and accountability mechanisms signify, stands to maximize capacity for coping with the increased ambiguity accompanying reforms or locally initiated change. It carries the risk that staff might betray this trust (hence the need for verification through accountability mechanisms), balanced against the risk that a low-trust climate marked by obtrusive surveillance may militate against staff taking responsibility for their professional conduct.

A more temperate approach to managing the education profession offers politicians and school leaders and managers the least-worst prospect of failure, since in a world of endemic ambiguity success cannot be guaranteed. Temperance is practically realistic in not promising more than can be delivered with any certainty. A temperate approach accepts the wisdom of risking mildly ironic consequences: giving teachers back the 'right to teach' is likely to produce moderate diversity of incrementally changing practices and outcomes. But it minimizes (though it cannot eliminate) the risk of generating serious ironic consequences. Intemperate approaches promise much more, but they inherently increase the risk of debilitating irony because of their ambition: whether the mandating of new practices inhibiting local experimentation needed to find what works in different contexts, raised expectations that cannot be met, or perverse side effects such as appearance taking precedence over the reality experienced by students and parents. And where is the wisdom in that?

References

Abbott, A. (1988) *The System of Professions: An Essay on the Division of Labor*. Chicago, IL: University of Chicago Press

Bolam, R., McMahon, A., Stoll, L., Thomas, S. and Wallace, M. (2005) *Creating and Sustaining Effective Professional Learning Communities*. Research Report 637. London: Department for Education and Skills

Dale, R. (1989) *The State and Educational Policy*. Milton Keynes, UK: Open University Press

Department for Education and Skills (DFES) (2004) *National Standards for Headteachers*. London: DFES

Fink, D. (2003) The law of unintended consequences: The 'real' cost of top-down reform, *Journal of Educational Change*, 4, 105–128

General Teaching Council (GTC) (2003) Keynote speech by Carol Adams to the North of England Education Conference. http://www.primaryheands.org.uk/documents/doc9html (Accessed 2nd March 2006)

Giddens, A. (1984) *The Constitution of Society*. Cambridge: Polity

Helsby, G. (1999) *Changing Teachers' Work*. Buckingham, UK: Open University Press

Hoyle, E. (1986) *The Politics of School Management*. London: Hodder & Stoughton

Hoyle, E. and Wallace, M. (2005) *Educational Leadership: Ambiguity, Professionals and Managerialism*. London: Sage

Joyce, B., Calhoun, E. and Hopkins, D. (1999) *The New Structure of School Improvement*. Buckingham, UK: Open University Press

Leithwood, K. and Louis, K. S. (eds) (1998) *Organizational Learning in Schools*. Lisse, The Netherlands: Swets and Zeitlinger

March, J. (1999) *The Pursuit of Organizational Intelligence*. Oxford: Blackwell

March, J. and Olsen, P. (1976) *Ambiguity and Choice in Organizations*. Bergen, Norway: Universitetsforlaget

March, J. and Simon, H. (1958) *Organizations*. New York: Wiley

McLaughlin, M. (1991) The RAND change agent study: Ten years after, in Odden, A. (ed) *Education Policy Implementation*. Albany, NY: SUNY

Moore, A., George, R. and Halpin, D. (2002) The developing role of the headteacher in English schools: Management, leadership and pragmatism, *Educational Management and Administration*, 30(2), 175–188

Office for Standards in Education (OFSTED) (2003) *Leadership and Management: What Inspection Tells us*. Document No. HMI 1646. London: OFSTED

Office of Public Service Reform (OPSR) (2002) *Reforming our Public Services: Principles into Practice*. London: OPSR

Ogawa, R., Crowson, R. and Goldring, E. (1999) Enduring dilemmas of school organization, in Murphy, J. and Louis, K. S. (eds) *Handbook of Research on Educational Administration* (2nd edn). San Francisco, CA: Jossey-Bass

Organization for Economic Cooperation and Development (2003) *Education at a Glance 2003*. Paris: OECD

Osborn, M., McNess, E., Broadfoot, P. with Pollard, A. and Triggs, P. (2000) *What Teachers Do. Changing Policy and Practice in Primary Education*. London: Continuum

Rowan, B. and Miskel, C. G. (1999) Institutional theory and the study of educational organizations, in Murphy, J. and Louis, K. S. (eds) *Handbook of Research on Educational Administration* (2nd edn). San Francisco, CA: Jossey-Bass

Times Educational Supplement (TES) (2000) Whatever happened to the heroes? 5th May

Wallace, M. (1996) When is experiential learning not experiential learning? in Claxton, G., Atkinson, T., Osborn, M. and Wallace, M. (eds) *Liberating the Learner; Lessons for Professional Development in Education*. London: Routledge

Wallace, M. (1998a) A counter-policy to subvert educational reform? Collaboration among schools and colleges in a competitive climate, *British Educational Research Journal*, 24(2), 195–215

Wallace, M. (1998b) Innovations in planning for school improvement: Problems and potential, in
    Hargreaves, A., Lieberman, A., Fullan, M. and Hopkins, D. (eds) *International Handbook of
    Educational Change*. Dordrecht, The Netherlands: Kluwer
Wallace, M. (2003) Managing the unmanageable? Coping with complex educational change,
    Educational Management and Administration, 31(1), 9–29
Wallace, M. and McMahon, A. (1994) *Planning for Change in Turbulent Times: The Case of
    Multiracial Primary Schools*. London: Cassell
Wallace, M. and Pocklington, K. (2002) *Managing Complex Educational Change: Large-Scale
    Reorganization of Schools*. London: Routledge
Wallace, M. and Wray, A. (2006) *Critical Reading and Writing for Postgraduates*. London:
    Sage
Weick, K. (2001) *Making Sense of the Organization*. Oxford: Blackwell
Woods, P., Jeffrey, B., Troman, G. and Boyle, M. (1997) *Re-structuring Schools, Re-structuring
    Teachers: Responding to Change in the Primary School*. Buckingham: Open University
    Press

Chapter 12
Organization and Leadership in Education: Changing Direction

Ron Glatter

The purpose of this chapter is to raise some issues about the current direction of the field of study and training that is now commonly referred to as 'educational leadership and management' (ELM). It is intended as an agenda-setting chapter, opening up a number of more or less connected topics which the author considers worthy of debate by members of the field's academic community and their collaborators in the worlds of policy and practice. The discussion will lead to a number of proposals for refocusing and reorienting our work. The issues will be discussed under three broad headings, the first of which will receive most attention.

1. Does the field need a change of direction towards organization?
2. What are some key features of the current context?
3. How might we move forward?

Should there be a Change of Direction Towards Organization?

A Brief Backward Look

The present writer undertook postgraduate work in the mid-1960s under a remarkably knowledgeable and insightful political scientist, W. J. M. ('Bill') Mackenzie, author of, among other texts, *Politics and Social Science* (1967). He introduced his students at Manchester University to the then new writing on organizations, such as March and Simon's *Organizations* (1958), Amitai Etzioni's *Complex Organizations* (1961) and Blau and Scott's *Formal Organizations* (1963). Along with these works from the U.S.A. came landmark U.K. studies such as Burns and Stalker's (1961) work on mechanistic and organic forms of innovation and Joan Woodward's (1965) exploration of socio-technical systems.

The theory was generic and applications were to be made to specific fields such as education. At the same time in the same university Eric Hoyle (1969) was presenting this literature, together with other work on organizations that had a more explicitly educational focus, to teachers and other students of education who recognised its salience by their acclaim of his lectures. The appreciation of Hoyle's large professional audiences was not just for his deep understanding of this new field but also for the clarity and wit of his presentations. As a young researcher I was privileged to attend these memorable occasions. It seems to me highly appropriate that the case being made in this chapter for a revival of interest in organization studies should appear in a volume dedicated to the scholar who has done more than anyone else in the U.K. to promote and develop this area of academic enquiry within education.

Later work of great significance included Charles Perrow's *Complex Organizations: a critical essay* (1972) from the U.S.A. on the dangers of reifying organizations and, from the U.K., David Silverman with his 'action' frame of reference in his *The Theory of Organizations* (1970). In view of my later discussion it is worth noting how prominent, even in book titles, the word 'complex' was as an adjective in relation to organizations already at that time. These works tended not to focus on leadership in a major way. There was significant work on leadership of course, for example, by Chester Barnard (1938), Philip Selznick (1957) and Fred Fiedler (1967), but it appeared almost as a sub-set of organization theory.

Restoring an Organizational Perspective

My intention here is not to present an analysis or review of this early work but to see it as a backdrop to more recent developments. I was forcibly reminded of it by an article by Johnson (2004) entitled 'Where have all the flowers gone? Reconnecting leadership preparation with the field of organization theory'. He argued that an organizational perspective had virtually disappeared from academic debate and preparation programmes in North America and that it was time to put it back again.

In this country within education the dominant concepts have been, first, 'management' and, later, 'leadership'. It is relevant to consider how leadership has in recent years come to dominate the field. In this context I am reminded of Bolman and Deal's outstanding work on reframing organizations in which they argue when discussing leadership that we have come to "focus too much on the actors and too little on the stage on which they play their parts" (1991: 408).

A key work, at least in the U.K., was Gerald Grace's 1995 book *School Leadership* with its challenging first sub-title *Beyond Education Management*. 'Management' had been the dominant concept almost since the origin of the field in the U.K. (unlike in North America where the more lofty 'educational administration' clung on (Brundrett, 2000)) and had spawned a seemingly ever-growing array of preparation programmes and research projects. Grace however considered the discourse of management to be inextricably associated with a narrow technicist orientation, hierarchical approaches and a market ideology. By contrast leadership was thought more capable of foregrounding the moral, professional and democratic dimensions of running educational institutions. By promoting the idea of leadership rather than management he also hoped to secure a new emphasis on scholarly approaches based on critical sociology.

What Grace may not have foreseen, and certainly I did not anticipate it, was that the government would adopt 'leadership' so quickly and so strongly. Leadership soon became a regular feature of ministerial speeches and in 1998 Prime Minister Tony Blair announced that a National College for School Leadership (NCSL) would be established. The College opened its doors at Nottingham in 2000 and was followed by the Centre for Excellence in Leadership (CEL), focusing on the so-called 'learning and skills' sector, in 2003. So Grace's incursion into the field of educational management had an ironic and paradoxical aftermath (Hoyle and Wallace, 2005). A significant factor here may have been Blair's almost mystical belief in the power of leadership, encapsulated in a speech on 'Leadership in the Modern World' to News Corporation employees in California in 2006 which concluded with these exhortations to leaders: "Don't let your ego be carried away by the praise or your spirit diminished by the criticism... But for heaven's sake, above all else, lead" (Blair, 2006: 3).

The role of government in promoting leadership is highly ambiguous, as Wallace and Hoyle (2005) note. On the one hand there is a rhetorical emphasis on pro-activity and transformation while on the other the structural conditions established, for example, through tight accountability regimes and curriculum specifications, often inhibit leadership that is other than transmissional – any vision you like so long as it fits with ours.

I want to suggest in this chapter that leadership and management may be too restricting as labels for defining the scope of our field and that we should seriously consider adopting (or re-adopting) organization as our core concept. Perhaps 'leadership', like 'choice' (another term beloved by politicians for its rhetorical value), has been oversold. The difficulty of establishing a direct empirical connection between leadership and student effects may be indicative in this regard (Leithwood and Levin, 2005). Indeed according to Pfeffer and Sutton (2006) studies in a range of types of organization indicate an ambiguous connection between leadership and performance – the effects are "modest under most conditions, strong under a few conditions and absent in others" (p. 192). The data indicate that organizational performance is determined largely by factors outside the control of individuals and the authors consider that "leadership effects are overstated" (*ibid*.: 257, note 22). I am not of course arguing that leadership and management do not matter or that they should be displaced, simply that it may be time for a re-orientation or re-focusing towards ideas associated with organization more broadly.

Organization remains a central concept in the wider field of management studies (for example, Clegg et al., 2006; Grey, 2005) so its near-disappearance from studies within education should raise concerns of a theoretical nature.[1] Academic posts

---

[1] It is noteworthy that only one of the 30 chapters in the new edition of Clegg et al.'s well-known collection *Handbook of Organization Studies* (2006) has 'leadership' in the title.

outside education regularly have titles such as 'Senior Lecturer in Organizational Behaviour' and 'Lecturer in Public Sector Organization'.[2] Such posts in education almost invariably have 'leadership' but not 'organization' in the title.

In addition however the devaluing of organization has major *practical* implications which I will illustrate in a somewhat unconventional way. The distinguished journalist Peter Preston successfully edited *The Guardian* for some 20 years, and therefore has a good understanding of leadership from a practitioner perspective. Writing a few days after the Asian tsunami disaster of late 2004, he commented that pouring in doctors, nurses and medicines without proper planning "is merely to leave hope piled in open boxes at some bemused local airport... It makes effective bureaucracy the greatest friend of those in need" (Preston, 2005). He went on to look at other examples closer to home, including from the health and education services, and concluded that "organization matters". Reading that made me recall that I came into the field because of a similar perception and a belief that nothing worthwhile on any scale can be achieved without organization, whether in the sense of an activity (as Preston was using the term) or an entity.

The mention of bureaucracy may remind us that the term 'organization' has what might be described as an image problem. To many people it has a strongly mechanistic flavour and carries a sense of impersonality. This is somewhat strange as the word's etymological link is to organism rather than mechanism, and of course much writing about organization presents a sharply contrasting picture. A good example is a chapter called 'Life and Leadership in Organizations' in a book by the physicist, ecologist and systems theorist Fritjof Capra (2003). He talks about an organization's 'aliveness' being under threat from the mechanistic approach which he sees as one of the main obstacles to organizational change. This approach also promotes the illusion of control. He argues that machines can be controlled but living systems can only be influenced through impulses. Survival depends on creating "a boundary of meaning and hence of an identity among the members of a social network, based on a sense of belonging, which is the defining characteristic of community" (*ibid.*: 95). His conclusion is not optimistic. He sees today's organizational environments as increasingly life-destroying rather than life-enhancing.

Of course 'leadership' and 'organization' are connected. Ogawa and Bossert (1997) argue that leadership is a quality of organizations. They criticise views of leadership "that treat it as a quality that individuals possess apart from a social context" (*ibid.*: 16) and say that studies of leadership should have the organization as their unit of analysis. In my view that offers much potential. It would enable us to 'go up a level' in order to see the interconnections more clearly. Bottery (2004: 116) has recently offered us a very helpful multi-level model of trust. In this, if you look out from the meso level of the organization rather than from the micro level of the individual you get a clearer picture of the forces at work, for example, of how what Bottery calls the paradox of simultaneous control and fragmentation (control

---

[2] These examples are taken from actual advertisements, the first from Warwick Business School and the second from King's College London, which appeared adjacent to each other in *Education Guardian* on 31 January 2006.

from the state, and fragmentation from the market) is playing itself out. What is particularly noticeable about that type of paradox is its great complexity, and therefore the challenge for leaders in dealing with it. This type of analysis is very close to Wallace and Pocklington's (2002) notion of "orchestration" in their study of complex organizational change in education. It is significant in the context of this discussion that when Ogawa and Bossert say that leadership is an organizational quality they are treating leadership as "a systemic characteristic" (1997: 9).

Complex Adaptive Systems

Indeed it is arguable that the concentration on leadership has resulted in the applicability of systems thinking, of viewing organizations (for example) as complex adaptive systems, and the related ideas of complexity theory being seriously neglected in our field. Concepts such as non-linearity, self-organization, design, emergence, requisite variety, attractors and paradox have considerable and largely untapped potential (Chapman, 2002; Glatter et al., 2005; Raynor, 2004). More widely, systems approaches feature strongly in more politically-oriented forms of analysis which themselves have had little currency in our field (see, for example, Newman, 2001). At least one of these, new institutionalist theory (Scott, 2001), could be very fruitful in such a 'political' area as education and has indeed been applied to the study of local government (Lowndes and Wilson, 2003) and, in North America, to education (Crowson et al., 1996). This theoretical approach is concerned among other things with developing "an understanding of the complex, diverse and multi-level nature of institutional environments" (Lowndes and Wilson, 2003: 280).

Whereas leadership tends to emphasise the individual, complexity theory and institutional theory focus more on the context. Attempts have been made to mute the emphasis on the individual in leadership studies through concepts such as distributed leadership (Gronn, 2000; Harris, 2005) and democratic leadership (Woods, 2004, 2005). These ideas undoubtedly raise extremely important issues about the theory and practice of leadership, including moral and ethical dimensions. Crucial though these are, it is important that the connection between leadership and organization is firmly established analytically (Ogawa and Bossert, 1997; Robinson, 2001) otherwise we are in danger of continuing to be trapped within the ideology of the 'can-do' culture (Glatter, 1996) whereby agency is always considered capable of overcoming structure.

Gunter (2004) has explained that, despite having found the ideas of complexity theory valuable in her early thinking, she had moved on from them because they did not focus on power explicitly enough. In a detailed review, Wallace and Fertig (2006) are not as dismissive as Gunter but make broadly the same criticism. It seems a valid one, though as I have illustrated above power is by no means neglected by systems theorists. For example, Capra (2003: 79) says that "Social organizations such as businesses or political institutions are designed specifically to distribute power". The criticism raises the question however whether complexity theory and theories of power must necessarily be regarded as mutually exclusive alternatives. Could we, for example, attempt an integration between them, along the lines advocated by Heck and Hallinger (2005) in their critique of the field today (to which this chapter returns later)?

Hoyle hints at the possibility of such integration in his thought-provoking review of Morrison's (2002) book on complexity theory and school leadership. He suggests that "there are aspects of organization theory which are *cognate* to complexity theory" (Hoyle, 2003: 214; my emphasis) and refers to work on unintended consequences, ambiguity, sense-making, coupling theory and endemic dilemmas in educational organizations. These ideas seem very compatible with a complexity perspective. However as Hoyle implies, language other than that directly associated with complexity theory can be, and has been, used to express similar ideas: its language is not to everyone's taste. For example, Crow (2004) talks more conventionally of the dilemmas for school leaders in balancing complexity and rationality without using the concepts of complexity theory directly. Only limited use of them is made by Wallace and Pocklington (2002) in their work on managing complex educational change. Grey, in a book which argues that ethical and political issues should be central to studying organizations, also puts similar ideas in alternative language:

> In the natural sciences… predictability is possible because we can design out unintended consequences and we are dealing with objects which don't have agency. In social things, including obviously organizations, this is not true because people do have some degree of agency, the variables surrounding their behaviour are too many and too varied to be designed out and so predictions will not be reliable.
>
> (Grey, 2005: 129)

Thus the important point is not the precise language used but that such systemic issues of power, context and complexity are more likely to be addressed if the focus is on organization than if it is on leadership.

Hoyle (*ibid.*: 216) also argues "that it is unrealistic to assume that the 'natural' unrolling of complexity will somehow trump the state's power to pursue its policies". That seems correct but it is unlikely that things will go according to plan because of the limits to the control of human systems to which complexity theory draws attention. Again using somewhat different language Grey addresses this paradox: "When I say that organizations will always defy management control, I do not mean that they will totally do so". Even in the Nazi death camps there were recorded instances of subversion and survival. So an emphasis on control and efficiency "leads at one extreme to horror and at the other extreme to failure" (Grey, 2005: 131). More empirical work is needed in this area, to examine exactly how the limits to control operate in real contexts of educational policy and practice. Even at this stage however a complexity approach provides indications about appropriate leadership and management strategies (Raynor, 2004). It suggests that "temperate" leadership and management, moderate and incrementalist rather than 'transformational' in character, is frequently likely to be most effective (Wallace and Hoyle, 2005). Innovation should be seen in terms of a 'discovery' rather than a 'machine' model, in other words as essentially evolutionary rather than revolutionary (Glatter et al., 2005; Hargreaves, 2003).

In terms of power such a gradualist approach should not be identified with *compliance* (as distinct, for example, from non-compliance or mediation: see Wallace and Hoyle, 2005: 12–13). A striking comment on the linkage between power, purpose and complexity was made by the late U.S. political journalist I. F. Stone in reflecting on a long and distinguished career spent observing powerful people and great events:

> You cannot understand events without understanding that power is a prison… [T]here are very severe limits: if you have no power, you're free. But in every prison there is some leeway – someone with courage and ingenuity can do more than one who's lazy or a coward. Find out what can be done and judge on that: you must always have a sense of the possible.

> (quoted by Lloyd, 1986: 19)

In Praise of Problem-Solving

A re-orientation towards systems thinking and organization (as well as 'temperate' leadership) would put a strong focus on problem-solving. Some writers (for example, Thrupp and Willmott, 2003) denigrate the idea of problem-solving because they see it as a purely technical 'maintenance' activity rather than as a core task that must take full account of context and values. In this connection Robinson's (2001) sophisticated yet practical analysis of leadership as embedded in task performance and problem-solving seems particularly insightful. She regards leadership as occurring "when ideas expressed in talk or action are recognised by others as capable of progressing tasks or problems which are important to them" (*ibid.*: 93). Her perspective is centred on context, relationships and personal values and preferences – very far removed from a narrow technicist viewpoint.

Another helpful approach to problem-solving is provided by Raynor (2004). He draws on Schon's (1983) classification of organizational situations as either 'high ground' – fairly straightforward ones requiring mainly technical solutions – or 'swamp' – messy, 'wicked', highly confusing ones. Raynor sees problem-solving in schools as addressing 'swamp' situations and requiring skills of perception, cognitive complexity and reflection. He suggests that the complex information processing needed for problem-solving requires what Claxton (1997) calls 'slow thinking, "where a large database of experience gradually 'settles into' a solution" (Raynor, 2004: 182). An organizational perspective would give full recognition to the significance of problem-solving processes.

A related area is that of the management of paradox and contradiction (Glatter, 1996; Lewis, 2000; Morgan, 1997). This is a prominent feature of modern organizations, including educational ones, but is scarcely mentioned in official documents such as school leadership standards, perhaps because they seek to sustain a myth that solutions to organizational problems are always clear and self-evident. For instance, in a context of complexity schools are expected both to be creative and innovative and also to 'deliver' dependable performance and guaranteed effectiveness – to be 'high reliability organizations' (Leithwood et al., 1999). They must also seek to reconcile the ever-growing political emphasis on autonomy and independence with the prescription to collaborate for the benefit of all the pupils in a geographical area (Woods et al., 2005b). These examples indicate again that a systems approach requires a multi-level perspective. As Ed Balls, a key U.K. Treasury adviser before he became a Member of Parliament and Secretary of State responsible for schools in England, is reported to have said in connection with public sector reform: "One of the things we've learnt is that we need to get systems, rather than individuals, right" (quoted in Caulkin, 2004). It is unfortunate that, despite this important insight, there is still so much system dysfunction, mostly arising from inappropriate command-and-control and quasi-market models and that, when problems inevitably arise with these, blame is often incorrectly placed on individuals and groups.

Thus, if we are to overcome the tendency to over-attribute success and failure to individuals, we need, as Pfeffer and Sutton argue (2006: 99), to focus on "locating and dealing with systemic causes of performance issues". A good example of this in education is provided by Lupton (2005) who examines empirically the problem of how to improve the quality of schooling in the poorest neighbourhoods. She draws attention to the need for contextual changes, for example, in national policies relating to accountability and school admissions, and also for different organizational designs that would significantly enhance organizational capacity in these highly fragile settings in which individuals are constantly under pressure and trading competing objectives. It is not enough just to motivate and develop staff because "...there is a limit to which better management, monitoring and training can secure good practice in the face of systemic constraints" (*ibid.*: 602).

Three Key Features of the Current Context

A major challenge currently facing the field in the U.K., the first of three such challenges that I want to identify, is the Research Assessment Exercise (RAE), in my view a prime example of the kind of dysfunctional arrangement referred to above. The eminent political scientist David Marquand recently castigated social scientists and humanities academics for copying those in the natural sciences so that

> the academic profession became a secular priesthood, preoccupied by its own, increasingly arcane, internal arguments, all too often expressed in a rebarbative and inaccessible jargon and developed in obscure journals whose editorial practices aped those of the natural sciences. The public culture was impoverished, and the academy cut itself off from the living forces of the outside world.
>
> (Marquand, 2004: 76)

To the extent that this is an accurate picture – and it appears at least recognisable – it could be argued to follow directly from the pressures of misguided incentive structures like the RAE which impact negatively on more practical and policy-oriented fields like our own and Marquand's (Levačić and Glatter, 2003). As Anthony Hopwood, director of Oxford's Said Business School has written: "At times it is as if the very act of publishing in journals has become more significant than the additions to knowledge that result from this" (quoted in MacLeod,

2005). From a background in the humanities MacCabe (2005) has argued that "Future ages will look back on the amount of wasted labour involved in the production of unread academic work with astonishment and contempt". Our own field has undoubtedly suffered in a similar way. Fortunately there seems at the time of writing to be an impetus, including even from those who have seen some merit in the RAE, to make 2008 the last one and replace it with a much lighter touch and more continuous system (see, for example, MacLeod, 2005; Wiggans, 2005). However the initial government proposals appear to have had a cool reception (see, for example, Corbyn, 2006).

The RAE is an example of the ever-growing power of the central state in England, the second key feature of the current context to which I want to refer (Foster, 2005). This power was already strongly evident by the conclusion of the last Conservative government (Glatter, 1997) and it has grown apace under New Labour. Local democracy has been a particular victim. We have far fewer and very much larger units of local government than other comparable countries. We also have far fewer elected officials and very many more appointed members of 'quangos' than do other major European countries (Jenkins, 2004). We are perhaps becoming what Kogan (2002) called "the compliant society" in which values are imposed rather than negotiated and in which evidence and analysis hold little sway when they conflict with particular pre-ordained 'directions of travel'.

The last feature of the context I want to mention is one where, by contrast, diversity reigns: the much more pluralistic supply side in research that now exists. Here are a few examples. Some 25 years ago a major research project on the selection of headteachers for secondary schools – the 'POST' project – was begun at The Open University for the then Department of Education and Science (Morgan et al., 1983). The first large-scale study since then, 'Recruitment and appointment of headteachers', is being undertaken at the time of writing for the NCSL by the management consultancy the Hay Group in a consortium which includes one university (Cambridge) along with the Eastern Leadership Centre and the National Association of Headteachers (NAHT). The evaluation of the controversial academies programme is being undertaken for the Department for Education and Skills (DfES) by the management accountancy firm PriceWaterhouseCoopers (PwC). The first annual report, which was unpublished until journalists requested it under the new Freedom of Information Act, indicated that the DfES had commissioned PwC "in association with the University of York" to undertake the evaluation (PriceWaterhouseCoopers/DfES, 2003: 1). The second annual report (PriceWaterhouseCoopers/DfES, 2005) made no mention of York University and indicated that PwC alone was commissioned to do the work. Another DfES project, a *Follow-up Research into the State of School Leadership in England* (Stevens et al., 2005), was commissioned from the MORI Social Research Institute. The initial study had been conducted by the Institute of Education, University of London (Earley et al., 2002). A report on extended schools was done by the think tank Demos working with the Hay Group (Craig et al., 2004).

There appears therefore to be a growing involvement of non-academic bodies such as management accountants, consultancies, think tanks and polling organizations in research on educational policy and organization. This seems a significant development. SCRELM (the Standing Conference on Research into Educational Leadership and Management) and other relevant bodies should urgently consider its implications and appropriate strategic responses.

Some Possible Ways Forward

In thinking about ways forward we might consider first the fairly radical critique of where we are as a field recently offered by Heck and Hallinger (2005). Although I suspect that their analysis will not be universally shared, it is arguably powerful enough to merit a serious response, even if it is rejected in which case it must be replaced by defensible alternatives. Essentially they accuse the field of self-indulgence, specifically of:

- Fostering an excessive diversity of perspectives without sufficient integration
- Over-emphasising normative issues
- Paying inadequate attention to studying how educational problems may be alleviated

For example, they argue that:

> In recent years, the field has been long on intellectual critique, but short on sustained action (and demonstrated results) about alternatives that will enhance schooling for children. This has created a crisis of credibility.
>
> (*ibid.*: 239)

Many of us would assert that the field has a wider scope than is indicated by the phrase "schooling for children", but leaving that aside there is a case for SCRELM and other bodies to debate whether such a crisis of credibility exists, and if it does whether the causes are those claimed by Heck and Hallinger or whether there are others, and what might be done to overcome it.

A second suggestion derives from considering the purpose of organization and leadership in education. It has become commonplace to assert that we need to bear in mind constantly that they are not ends in themselves but that their ultimate purpose is to promote learning. A prominent conclusion from the ESRC seminar series on "Redefining Educational Management and Leadership" (Bush et al., 1999) was that the field needed to give more explicit attention to the connection between leadership and learning. So, for example, the concept of 'learning-centred leadership' has been promoted by the NCSL. However, there is a question about whether this takes us far enough. As Lumby et al. (2003) have put it: "The recent shift towards conceptualising leadership as primarily concerned with learning may have lost sight of the fact that learning is not solely an end in itself, but may serve other purposes also..." (*ibid.*: 9). In other words: if leadership is for learning, what is learning for? Is that issue a proper concern of our field? Should we deal explicitly with the core issues about learning, which we have tended not to do, or is that outside our remit, and if it is, on what or whose judgement? This issue has recently been considered by Bottery (2004) in his discussion of the different paradigms that can drive learning purposes, such as cultural transmission, social reconstruction, economic productivity and so on. Surely debate about these cannot be separated from issues of leadership and organization.

This suggests that we might make connections, for example, with the continuing debate between the 'traditionalists' and the 'progressives' over structure and curriculum following the Tomlinson report (DfES, 2004) and, associated with this, the more general characteristic of the English school system that has been referred to as "privileging of the academic" (Woods et al., 1998: 175). A related topic is the debate over so-called Mode 1 and Mode 2 knowledge production, as defined by Gibbons et al. (2000) – Mode 1 being discipline-centred and largely scholarly and Mode 2 transdisciplinary and concerned with application. This debate is clearly relevant to the specific domain of leadership development, even at doctoral level (Andrews and Grogan, 2005), but it extends well beyond that to encompass a broad spectrum of educational activity.

A conclusion for research in the field is that it might focus more than at present on how educational aims and purposes connect with leadership and organization. We appear often to imply that they are connected but it is not evident that we have sought to establish how. In turn such a focus might take us to quite topical issues that teachers, students and parents are much concerned about today, such as classroom behaviour, school buildings – or more generally environments for learning (Glancey, 2006) – and even school meals. Following the enormous impact of the television chef Jamie Oliver's Channel 4 series *Jamie's School Dinners* on policy (Shaw and Luck, 2005) and practice, it can fairly be suggested that food is an educational leadership issue. In fact the series was as much a demonstration of leadership as a polemic about food.

Clearly work in this vein already exists. Woods et al.'s (2005a) study of Steiner schools in England provides an example of how an inquiry into a particular form of schooling can lead to wider and quite fundamental questions about the curriculum and the purposes of education. It gives an indication of the kind of directions in which thinking more deeply about the question "If leadership is for learning, what is learning for?" might take us.

This is not an appeal for a parochial, introspective approach focused on education alone. Such an approach would be entirely inappropriate, not least following the publication of *Every Child Matters* (2003) and its implications for education including extended services based on schools. We should consciously seek to contribute to the wider literature of organization and leadership, in at least two directions:

1. In relation to the public and not-for-profit sectors, whose academics still tend to be separated from those undertaking studies in educational organization and leadership, to our disadvantage and theirs.
2. In the broader field of organization and management studies, in which, as Johnson's (2004) article to which I referred earlier pointed out, schools and universities can be viewed – along, for example, with churches, counselling agencies, hospitals and prisons – as *human service organizations* whose core task is transforming humans. That is not the core task of (for example) either

H.M. Revenue and Customs in the public sector nor of Tesco in the private sector. Only very rarely have we contributed to this broader literature (for example, Glatter, 2004). The recent translation of Mike Wallace from a Professor of Education at Bath University to a Professor of Public Sector Management at Cardiff University appears significant in this regard, not least in the context of this volume as he entered academic life from school-teaching, joining the School of Education at Bristol University at a time when Eric Hoyle was its leader.

Conclusion

I have argued that, after a period of intense concentration on ideas connected with leadership and management, we should consider changing the direction of the field in order to renew its concern with ideas associated with organization, which include viewing organizations as complex adaptive systems and taking an institutional perspective. The suggestion is to effect a re-orientation, not to replace leadership and management by organization. However it carries the implication that ELM – educational leadership and management – may be too restrictive a label to capture adequately the dynamics of the complex human and adaptive systems which we know as educational organizations.

Some key features of the current context for research in the field were briefly considered, specifically the RAE, the growing power of the central state in England and the much more pluralistic supply side in research, and it was argued that the latter in particular merited discussion and consideration of strategic responses. Finally some possible ways forward were proposed: addressing the charge of a 'crisis of credibility'; becoming more involved with issues of educational strategy and purpose and of the day-to-day learning environment; and contributing more frequently to the wider field of organization and leadership.

The suggested re-orientation towards organization might raise a concern that there would be less focus on the *practice* of leadership and management. This should not arise since the shift would provide a more holistic and systemic perspective, which would give better insights for practice. We should be aware however that the term 'practice' may hold dangers. Does it, for example, encourage us to become excessively centred on educational professionals, so that we may fail to give proper attention to the perspectives of students, parents, employers and 'society'? Is there a risk of becoming caught in a version of 'producer capture'?[3] Should we ask not just *what* the field is for, but also *whom* it is for?

---

[3] Ranson et al., 2005, provide one example of a study that avoids this, by focusing on governance.

References

Andrews, R. and Grogan, M. (2005) 'Form should follow function: removing the EdD from the PhD straight jacket', *UCEA Review*, Spring, 10–13.

Barnard, C.I. (1938) *The Functions of the Executive* (Cambridge, MA, Harvard University Press).

Blair, T. (2006) Speech to News Corporation Employees, Pebble Beach, CA, 30 July, downloaded from www.number-10.gov.uk, accessed 1 August 2006.

Blau, P.M. and Scott, W.R. (1963) *Formal Organizations: A Comparative Approach* (London, Routledge/Kegan Paul).

Bolman, L.G. and Deal, T.E. (1991) *Reframing Organizations: Artistry, Choice and Leadership* (San Francisco, CA, Jossey-Bass).

Bottery, M. (2004) *The Challenges of Educational Leadership* (London, Paul Chapman).

Brundrett, M. (2000) *Beyond Competence: The Challenge for Educational Management* (Dereham, Norfolk, UK, Peter Francis).

Burns, T. and Stalker, G.M. (1961) *The Management of Innovation* (London, Tavistock).

Bush, T., Bell, L., Bolam, R., Glatter, R. and Ribbins, R. (1999) *Educational Management: Redefining Theory, Policy and Practice* (London, Paul Chapman).

Capra, F. (2003) *The Hidden Connections: A Science for Sustainable Living* (London, Flamingo).

Caulkin, S. (2004) 'Take aim: You'll always miss' *The Observer*, 14 November.

Chapman, J. (2002) *System Failure: Why Governments Must Learn to Think Differently* (London, Demos).

Claxton, G. (1997) *Hare Brain, Tortoise Mind: Why Intelligence Increases When You Think Less* (London, Fourth Estate).

Clegg, S.R., Hardy, C., Nord, W.R. and Lawrence, T. (2006) *Handbook of Organization Studies*, Second Edition (London, Sage).

Corbyn, Z. (2006) 'Metrics is such a blunt instrument', *The Guardian*, 12 September.

Craig, J. with Huber, J. and Lownsbrough, H. (2004) *School's Out: Can Teachers, Social Workers and Health Staff Learn to Live Together?* (London, Demos/Hay Group).

Crow, G.M. (2004) 'The national college for school leadership: A North American perspective on opportunities and challenges', *Educational Management, Administration and Leadership*, 32(3), 289–307.

Crowson, R.L., Boyd, W.L. and Mawhinney, H.B. (1996) *The Politics of Education and the New Institutionalism: Reinventing the American School* (London, Falmer).

DfES (2004) *14–19 Curriculum and Qualifications Reform: Final Report of the Working Group on 14–19 Reform* (London, Department for Education and Skills).

Earley, P., Evans, J., Collarbone, P., Gold, A. and Halpin, D. (2002) *Establishing the Current State of School Leadership in England* (London, Department for Education and Skills, Research Report 336).

Etzioni, A. (1961) *A Comparative Analysis of Complex Organizations* (New York, Free Press of Glencoe).

Every Child Matters (2003) *Cm. 5860* (London, The Stationery Office).

Fiedler, F.E. (1967) *A Theory of Leadership Effectiveness* (New York, McGraw-Hill).

Foster, C. (2005) *Why Are We So Badly Governed?* (London, Public Management and Policy Association).

Gibbons, M., Limoges, C., Nowotony, H., Schwartzman, S., Scott., P. and Trow, M. (2000) *The New Production of Knowledge: The Dynamics of Science and Research in Contemporary Societies* (London, Sage).

Glancey, J. (2006) 'A classroom with a view', *The Guardian*, 20 June.

Glatter, R. (1996) 'Managing dilemmas in education: The tightrope walk of strategic choice in more autonomous institutions' in S.L. Jacobson, E. Hickox and R. Stevenson (eds.), *School Administration: Persistent Dilemmas in Preparation and Practice* (Westport, CT, Praeger).

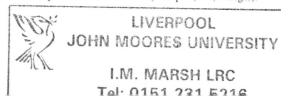

Glatter, R. (1997) 'Context and capability in educational management', *Educational Management and Administration*, 25(2), 181–192.

Glatter, R. (2004) 'Leadership and leadership development in education' in J. Storey (ed.), *Leadership and Leadership Development in Education* (London, Routledge), 203–221.

Glatter, R., Castle, F., Cooper, D., Evans, J. and Woods, P.A. (2005) 'What's new? Identifying innovation arising from school collaboration initiatives', *Educational Management, Administration and Leadership*, 33(4), 381–399.

Grace, G. (1995) *School Leadership – Beyond Education Management: An Essay in Policy Scholarship* (London, Falmer).

Grey, C. (2005) *Studying Organizations* (London, Sage).

Gronn, P. (2000) 'Distributed properties: A new architecture for leadership', *Educational Management and Administration*, 28(3), 317–338.

Gunter, H. (2004) 'Rethinking education: The consequences of chaos theory', paper presented to the British Educational Leadership, Management and Administration Society Annual Conference, Stone, Staffordshire, October.

Hargreaves, D. (2003) *Education Epidemic: Transforming Secondary Schools Through Innovation Networks* (London, Demos).

Harris, A. (2005) *Crossing Boundaries and Breaking Barriers: Distributing Leadership in Schools* (London, Specialist Schools Trust).

Heck, R. H. and Hallinger, P. (2005) 'The study of educational leadership and management: Where does the field stand today?', *Educational Management, Administration and Leadership*, 33(2), 229–244.

Hoyle, E. (1969) 'Organization theory and educational administration' in G. Baron and W. Taylor (eds.), *Educational Administration and the Social Sciences* (London, The Athlone Press), 36–59.

Hoyle, E. (2003) Book review (2002), *Educational Management and Administration*, 31(2), 213–216.

Hoyle, E. and Wallace, M. (2005) *Educational Leadership: Ambiguity, Professionals and Managerialism* (London, Sage).

Jenkins, S. (2004) *Big Bang Localism: A Rescue Plan for British Democracy* (London, Policy Exchange).

Johnson, B.L. (2004) 'Where have all the flowers gone? Reconnecting leadership preparation with the field of organization theory', *UCEA Review*, 16–22.

Kogan, M. (2002) 'The subordination of local government and the compliant society', *Oxford Review of Education*, 28(2/3), 331–342.

Leithwood, K., Jantzi, D. and Steinbach, R. (1999) *Changing Leadership for Changing Times* (Buckingham, UK, Open University Press).

Leithwood, K. and Levin, B. (2005) *Assessing School Leader and Leadership Programme Effects on Pupil Learning* (London, Department for Education and Skills, Research Report 662).

Levačić, R. and Glatter, R. (2003) 'Developing evidence-informed policy and practice in educational leadership and management: A way forward' in L. Anderson and N. Bennett (eds.), *Developing Educational Leadership: Using Evidence for Policy and Practice* (London, Sage).

Lewis, M. (2000) 'Exploring paradox: Towards a more comprehensive guide', *The Academy of Management Review*, 25(4), 760–776.

Lloyd, J. (1986) 'Busy Izzy in search of truth', *New Statesman*, 15 August, 18–20.

Lowndes, V. and Wilson, D. (2003) 'Balancing revisability and robustness? A new institutionalist perspective on local government modernization, *Public Administration*, 81(2), 275–298.

Lumby, J., Foskett, N. and Maringe, F. (2003) 'Restricted view: School leadership and the "choices" of learners', presented at the Annual Conference of the British Educational Management and Administration Society, Milton Keynes, October.

Lupton, R. (2005) 'Social justice and school improvement: Improving the quality of schooling in the poorest neighbourhoods', *British Educational Research Journal*, 31(5), 589–604.

MacCabe, C. (2005) 'Set our universities free', *The Observer*, 13 March.

MacLeod, D. (2005) 'The hit parade', *The Guardian*, 14 June.

Mackenzie, W.J.M. (1967) *Politics and Social Science* (London, Penguin Books)

March, J.G. and Simon, H.A. (1958) *Organizations* (New York, Wiley).

Marquand, D. (2004) *Decline of the Public: The Hollowing-out of Citizenship* (London, Polity Press).

Morgan, C., Hall, V. and Mackay, H. (1983) *The Selection of Secondary School Headteachers* (Milton Keynes, Open University Press).

Morgan, G. (1997) *Images of Organization* (London, Sage).

Morrison, K. (2002) *School Leadership and Complexity Theory* (London & New York: Routledge Falmer).

Newman, J. (2001) *Modernising Governance: New Labour, Policy and Society* (London, Sage).

Ogawa, R.T. and Bossert, S.T. (1997) 'Leadership as an organizational quality' in M. Crawford, L. Kydd and C. Riches (eds.), *Leadership and Teams in Educational Management* (Buckingham, UK, Open University Press), 9–23.

Perrow, C. (1972) *Complex Organizations: A Critical Essay* (Glenview, IL, Scott Foresman).

Pfeffer, J. and Sutton, R.I. (2006) *Hard Facts, Dangerous Half-Truths and Total Nonsense: Profiting from Evidence-based Management* (Boston, MA, Harvard Business School Press).

Preston, P. (2005) 'Bureaucracy is fine for them, not us', *The Guardian*, 3 January.

PriceWaterhouse Coopers (2003) *Academies Evaluation Annual Report November 2003* (London, Department for Education and Skills).

PriceWaterhouseCoopers (2005) *Academies Evaluation 2nd Annual Report* (London, Department for Education and Skills).

Ranson, S., Farrell, C., Peim, N. and Smith, P. (2005) 'Does governance matter for school improvement?' *School Effectiveness and School Improvement*, 16(3), 305–325.

Raynor, A. (2004) *Individual Schools, Unique Solutions: Tailoring Approaches to School Leadership* (London, Routledge/Falmer).

Robinson, V.M.J. (2001) 'Embedding leadership in task performance' in K. Wong and C. W. Evers (eds.), *Leadership for Quality Schooling: International Perspectives* (London, Routledge/Falmer).

Schon, D.A. (1983) *The Reflective Practitioner* (New York, Basic Books).

Scott, W.R. (2001) *Institutions and Organizations*, Second Edition (London, Sage).

Shaw, M. and Luck, A. (2005) 'Kelly lays down food law' *The Times Educational Supplement*, 7 October.

Silverman, D. (1970) *The Theory of Organizations* (London, Heinemann).

Stevens, J., Brown, J., Knibbs, S. and Smith, J. (2005) *Follow-up Research into the State of School Leadership in England* (London, Department for Education and Skills, Research Report 633).

Thrupp, M. and Willmott, R. (2003) *Education Management in Managerialist Times: Beyond the Textual Apologists* (Maidenhead, UK, Open University Press).

Wallace, M. and Fertig, M. (2006) 'Applying complexity theory to public service change: Creating chaos out of order?' in M. Wallace, M. Fertig and E. Schneller (eds.), *Managing Change in the Public Services* (Oxford: Blackwell).

Wallace, M. and Hoyle, E. (2005) 'Towards effective management of a reformed teaching profession', paper presented at the fourth seminar of the Economic and Social Research Council (ESRC) Teaching and Learning Research Programme thematic seminar series 'Changing Teacher Roles, Identities and Professionalism', King's College, London, July.

Wallace, M. and Pocklington, K. (2002) *Managing Complex Educational Change: Large-scale Reorganization of Schools* (London, Routledge/Falmer).

Wiggans, K. (2005) 'Should the research assessment exercise be scrapped?' *The Independent*, 26 May.

Woods, P.A. (2004) 'Democratic leadership: Drawing distinctions with distributed leadership', *International Journal of Leadership in Education*, 7(1), 3–26.

Woods, P.A. (2005) *Democratic Leadership in Education* (London, Sage).

Woods, P.A., Bagley, C. and Glatter, R. (1998) *School Choice and Competition: Markets in the Public Interest?* (London, Routledge).

Woods, P.A., Ashley, M. and Woods, G.J. (2005a) *Steiner Schools in England* (London, Department for Education and Skills, Research Report 645).

Woods, P.A., Castle, F., Cooper, D., Evans, J., Levacie, R. and Glatter, R. (2005b) 'Deep collaboration? Developing new collaborative relationships amongst schools in a time of specialization and diversity', paper presented at the Annual Conference of the British Educational Research Association (BERA), University of Glamorgan, Wales, September.

Woodward, J. (1965) *Industrial Organization: Theory and Practice* (Oxford, Oxford University Press).

Chapter 13
The Development of Educational Leaders in Malaysia: The Creation of a Professional Community

Ibrahim Ahmad Bajunid

This chapter tells the story of national development in Malaysia from the perspective of the development of the middle class, the professions and professional leadership. It focuses on the intellectual leadership provided by the professions, with particular reference to the teaching profession. In Malaysia, the teaching profession had always produced leaders who were the early freedom fighters and who now provide intellectual leadership in contemporary society. The chapter argues that the teaching profession, with approximately 400,000 teachers serving under the Ministry of Education and thousands more serving in other Ministries, State Governments and in private sector educational institutions, constitute the basis of the growth of the salaried middle class in Malaysia. The chapter evaluates the capacity and willingness of the teaching profession to provide foundational leadership values for itself as well as for other professions.

The Malaysian Context

At the height of its influence, the indigenous Malacca Sultanate fell to the Portuguese in 1511, then to the Dutch in 1641, to the British in 1824, and to the Japanese in 1945. Malaysia thus has a history of colonialism. In the early years of Independence, Malaysian leaders attributed many of the problems of the nation to the colonial policy of "divide and rule" and to exploitation of the riches of the land and the mobilization of the efforts of the people in the interest of the colonialists. In recent decades the maturity of national sovereignty is evidenced by the fact that leaders are taking responsibility for current policies without blaming the colonial past, although some blame is still attributed to the forces of neo-imperialism.

When Malaya became independent in 1957 it had approximately 6 million people comprising Malays, Chinese, Indians and other races. The rural Malays were predominantly agriculturalists, fishermen, teachers and civil servants (Stevenson, 1975). The urban-based immigrant populations became traders, artisans and business people. The Chinese, in particular, were involved in tin mining, in small urban-based industries, and in entrepot trade. Since the time of British colonial administration, Indians worked in the rubber estates and public works and social

D. Johnson, R. Maclean (eds.), *Teaching: Professionalization,*
Development and Leadership,
© Springer Science + Business Media B.V. 2008

services departments. Before Independence there were cottage industries but few manufacturing industries. The economic system of indigenous people was essentially one of subsistence economy The various races were separated geographically, occupationally, linguistically and culturally (Loh, 1975). After independence, the country embarked on the process of diversifying economic activities and on the policy of Malayanization (Gullick, 1988; Harper, 1999). Manufacturing industries like Fraser and Neave, Nestle, and Bata expanded their businesses and new ones emerged, creating jobs in urban centres. The government embarked on the Development Plan for Malaya which focussed on tackling the two-pronged challenges of eradicating poverty and fostering national unity. In 1963 Singapore, Sabah and Sarawak joined the Federation of Malaya and formed the Malaysian state, but Singapore seceded and became and independent State in 1965. In 2007 Malaysia has a population of over 27 million with over 50% under 20 years old (Malaysia, 2006b).

Fifty Years of Incremental Changes and Quantum Leap Mindsets

From the early days of national independence, Planned National Development was set in motion in all sectors and Educational Development was regarded as a priority. Embedded in successive Malaysia Development Plans has been the objective of creating a middle class through the creation of a wide range of economic opportunities in the public and private sectors. This objective is to be achieved principally through all levels of the education sector, especially higher education, seen as the sector which drives socio-economic mobility (Archer et al., 2003; Shiraishi, 2004). The University of Malaya moved from Singapore to Kuala Lumpur in 1959 and the Engineering, Medical, Arts and Agriculture Faculties, and with a School of Education offering a Diploma in Education and a Bachelor of Education as Postgraduate degrees, were among the earliest established. The Law Faculty as well as other professional Faculties, were established later. The establishment of these Faculties became the basis of the national capacity for the education and training of professional leaders. The Malaysian Foreign Affairs Ministry began recruiting university graduates to join the expanding Foreign Service as professional diplomats, while the Health Ministry began to recruit people for the medical profession and for nursing. In the 1960s, there were few university graduates teaching in schools except for foreign university teachers from Britain, India, and Indonesia who were on short-term contracts. Holders of the Diploma in Education became the first graduates posted to serve in schools throughout the country. In the 1990s, the Ministry of Education articulated a policy agenda whereby by 2010 all secondary school teachers in approximately 2,000 secondary schools, and half of the teaching force in the 8,000 primary schools, would be university graduates, and, eventually, all teachers will be university graduates (Ministry of Education, Malaysia 2006a). This policy decision ensures that all teachers will be socio-economically in the middle class. Being in the middle class, however, is to be distinguished from being in the professional class (Fantasia et al., 1991; Savage, 2000).

By the twenty-first century, many villagers saw their sons and daughters go to universities. The establishment of the Multi Media Super Corridor (MSC), the e-sovereignty initiative, and other electronic developments are creating the possibility of "one home one computer" and "knowledge at the fingertips". This has opened the possibilities of access to education "anywhere, anytime". Even in the remotest villages and community centers, there will be "electronic cottages" in the future in the Digital Era (Ariff and Chuan, 2000; Ahmad Sarji, 1993). Today, too, many senior members of society who missed early opportunities for further education are now engaged in continuing education through the policy of lifelong learning (Bajunid, 2001, 2002). In the early years of independence, the dominant values were loyalty, respect and gratitude to the extended family in the context of traditional occupations in the setting of rural life. However, with urbanization over the last 50 years, new values are adopted and there is now an unleashing of Malaysian imagination and the emergent generation is encouraged to adopt the credo "*Malaysia Boleh*" – "*be all that you can be*", thereby breaking away from time-honoured traditions. Slowly, the values, norms and meanings of "profession" have begun to reside in the societal psyche and become embedded in family culture and values.

Among the 20 public universities and 36 private universities and university colleges, there are, for instance, a University College of Design, Creativity, Technology and Innovation and the Kuala Lumpur Infrastructure University College. Several medical, engineering and business university colleges were also established in order to meet the social demand for higher education and for professional preparation.

The Professions and the Emergence of the Middle Class in Malaysia

With population increase and higher levels of education there are rising aspirations and expectations for better occupational and economic opportunities, higher standards of living and better quality of life. Comprehensive and rapid changes are occurring in all sectors. In the economic sector, for instance, small family businesses, especially Chinese small businesses, must now compete with hyper-markets (Tan et al., 2005). In these hypermarkets, particularly in the bigger towns, school children are exposed to thousands of products and related services, thus increasing aspirations and expectations. In the past, there were few bookstores and outlets for general books, but today, in the bigger towns there are the large bookshops of the international chains as well as national ventures such as the Malayan Publishing House (MPH). Malaysians are beginning to use computers to buy on-line from e-Bay, from Amazon and from airlines such as Air Asia, and they increasingly utilize various facilities of e-learning, e-government and e-commerce which are now expanding in Malaysia and elsewhere in the world. Clearly, in the era of digital and knowledge revolution, educational leaders cannot just think of the world of school children within the confines of classrooms because the classrooms with walls are becoming the open classrooms and the borderless classrooms of e-learning and blended learning. University leaders cannot simply maintain the position of 'knowledge for knowledge's sake' for education is expected to give focus to human resources, talents, competencies and human capital closely related to business and industry and employability through new job creation and entrepreneurship. (Ministry of Higher Education, 2006; 2007; and see also, [Website] http://www.mohe.gov.my/,).

The expansion of higher education institutions has led to an increase in the number of people with first degrees and higher degrees. This expansion has provided the leaders for the public and private sectors. These leaders have been the drivers for the transformation of Malaysian society. Planned changes covering all sectors have been implemented based on nine Malaysia Development Plans. The National Vision articulated in 1991 has consolidated policy ideas and ideals, development programmes and projects to achieve the goal of a "psychologically liberated" citizenry, resilient, democratic, and with the passion for justice, including economic justice. In the wake of current development, educational leadership in Malaysia must now function in the context of a dynamic learning society informed by the image of a developed nation where the quality of life will be comparable to the most developed society anywhere in the world (Mahathir, 1991; National Institute of Public Administration (INTAN), 1994).

The Professions and Elites in the Context of National Occupations

The Malaysian Occupational Classification is based on International Labour Organization's International Standard Classification of Occupations. Typically the Classification System consists of 509 specific occupational categories of employment arranged into 23 major occupational groups. The hierarchical structure shows the 23 major occupational groups divided into 96 minor groups, 449 broad groups and 821 detailed occupations. The major groups include legislators, senior officials and managers, professionals, technicians and associate professionals, clerks, service workers and shop and market sales workers; skilled agricultural and fishery workers, craft and related trades workers, plant and machine workers and assemblers; elementary occupations and armed forces (Greenwood, ILO, 2000). The Malaysian Occupational Classification focuses on Professional, Technical and related workers; Administrative and Managerial Workers; Clerical and Related Workers; Sales Workers; Service Workers; Agricultural, Animal Husbandry & Forest Workers, Fishermen and Hunters; Production and Related Workers, Transplant Equipment Operators and Labourers. In 2007, in Malaysia, there are over 11 million jobs. Of existing jobs over 12% are in the Professional, Technical and related workers; Administrative and Managerial Workers Category. There are approximately 200,000 doctors, 85,000 engineers, 12,500 practicing lawyers, 1,700 architects, 1,400 veterinary doctors. Planned projections have been made for the increase of graduates in the areas of shortage of professional personnel. Typically, professional and managerial groups are the elites in society, who, in their various leadership roles, influence the entire population. Members of the professions tend not only to focus on leadership in their specialized areas but become legislators and political and community leaders. In a centralized educational system, collectively, those from the teaching profession, have the capacity to influence almost 6 million school children and over 800,000 university students in current enrollment. Teachers also directly and indirectly influence every family with school or university students and they also influence adult learners. These realities have not been fully understood by the profession itself which, hitherto, has been inward looking, holding local micro-perspectives, focusing on the development of individual teachers and individual institutions and their particularistic concerns. A strategic mind shift is required: what Senge (1992) referred to as *"new assumptions and values, new action rules, and new linguistic and cognitive structures."* To date, the teaching profession, stuck in the policy-making and practice quagmire, has failed to define and lead in the areas of "leadership for learning". All 27 Teachers Colleges and the dozen or so Faculties of Education have been training teachers for teaching but have not captured the language register, contents and methodologies of "leadership for learning" (see MacBeath, 2002).

Of the 1 million classified as being in the top professional and managerial group, over 50% are in the teaching profession. This means that the teaching profession is the backbone of the Malaysian middle-class and of the professional class. Notwithstanding the analytic or empirical debates on the notion of how class is conceptualized, for our purpose, drawing on the conventional literature, we can assume that to a greater or lesser extent, teachers may adopt middle class and professional class values. (Day et al., 2000). The middle class values which drive the modernising values of society include the value/importance of education, the equality of individuals, personal freedom, choice of useful leisure activities, a focus on the future, change and progress, a high regard for achievement, action and societal stability, being the consumer and promoter of the arts, fostering of good manners and cultural refinements. The shared values of the professional class, include, professional mission, professional accountability, code of ethics, continuous professional learning, identity as members in the communities of practice, collegiality and professionalism (McKenna and Maister, 2002). The values which are inherent in sociological notions of the middle class and professionalism, would become the increasingly dominant and cherished values in Malaysian society.

Teaching as the Strategic Profession for National Development

It is a reasonable assumption to make that national development is strategically linked to leadership development in the professions. At the centre of this professional leadership has been the teaching profession for *"teaching is the profession upon which all professions rest..."* as aptly stated by Linda Darling-Hammond. While social and intellectual capital exists in the population as a whole, formal knowledge and intellectual capital are generated and disseminated through educational and memory institutions. However, such knowledge is actually applied to the whole range of human activities by the professionals in their respective domains. Academics and professionals are also bridges to global communities of professional practitioners. Knowledge transfer occurs through the thousands of Malaysians studying in universities or working abroad and through the overseas scholars who study, teach conduct research or work in Malaysia.

The contributions to national development are not just from the "pure or true professions," of medicine, engineering or law and architecture, but from the semi professions, of nursing and other para professionals, and from aspiring professions and other self advertised notions of being "professionals." The business sector with a very large retail and trading community and with the business leaders who are professionals in their own right, do contribute significantly to the development of the middle and upper socio economic classes. The business community has broad business acumen and business intelligence which are learned formally and from experience.

Teaching remains at the centre of national development. A strong education and training system has developed with the capacity to generate and disseminate knowledge and skills to a large proportion of the populace (Bajunid, 2007a). In the wake of the Ninth Malaysia Plan (Malaysia, 2006b) and the National Mission, the Educational Development Plan 2006 focusses on the development of human capital and the agenda to raise the prestige and status of the teaching profession. Three of the thrusts of the National Mission are related to the knowledge professions. These are (i) To drive the Malaysian economy up the value chain; (ii) To raise national knowledge and innovation capacity and to foster the development of 'first-class mentality' (iii) To address the recurring socio-economic gaps and imbalances in constructive and productive ways.

Reaffirming the various National Development thrusts, the Ministry of Higher Education (Ministry of Higher Education, 2007) sets out to turn Malaysia into a world class education hub.

To this end, the following issues are included in the agenda of providing (i) Wider access to higher education. (ii) Improvements of Teaching-learning Methods, (iii) Strengthening of research and innovation and promotion of life-long learning. It is evident that the teaching profession and other professions have to rise to the challenges of new benchmarks set in national development agenda (Malaysia, 2003; 2006a; 2007). The teaching profession is not just critical for the development of other professions, but it is actually the focal profession for the development of intellectual, cultural and social capital in the society.

Understanding the Leadership in the Profession: Broader Based Leadership and Educational Development

People who exercise influence on educational matters of policy and practice come from diverse backgrounds, and, therefore an inclusive definition of educational leadership is necessary in order to make sense of the drama of educational development.

For our purpose, educational leaders in Malaysia are not confined to those who work in schools, colleges and universities but include influential and significant others whose range of various leadership roles have direct impact on education: politicians, civil servants, teacher educators, teacher union leaders, business leaders, leaders of non-governmental organizations, community leaders, and opinion leaders.

Among the most significant contributors to educational development, other than teachers, are those leaders from politics and the educational bureaucracy. Contributions from such domains may focus primarily on education policies or on the broader domain of social and national concerns which impact on education, for instance, Consumer Education or Environmental Education or the prevention of social ills. Each leader uses all available resources to structure national psyche in the mould of their particular definition of reality and development. Educational leaders have many opportunities to learn useful lessons from those who have lived long and who have wide experiences. Through mentoring and coaching by older and experienced leaders, younger educators could learn to construct their own understanding of the nature of leadership and define their own construct harmony and values frames. There are, for instance, useful lessons to be learned from political leaders at the level of Prime Ministers, Ministers of Education and Director Generals of Education for the Substance/Contents of educational and school leadership development in Malaysia. Typically, politicians contribute to leadership development by propagating policies which become overarching development frameworks for national development. Tunku Abdul Rahman was the Father of the Nation and ensured that enshrined in the Malaysian Constitution was the recognition of Islam as the official religion, the Malay language would be the national language and that the indigenous people would have Special Rights. All other citizens were to have the basic freedoms of language, religion, culture and property. As national leader, the First Prime Minister focused on the critical importance of education and has said that "What is important for the country are books, not bullets." (Tengku, 1980). For 50 years the focus of the nation has been educational development rather than over military might.

The second Prime Minister, known as the Father of Rural Development, paid particular attention to education in the rural areas and established educational institutions to provide education for the rural population. He also established relations with Communist China and promoted the Association of Southeast Asian Nations (ASEAN) and the concept of the Zone of Peace, Freedom, and Neutrality (ZOFPAN) in the ASEAN region and the National Ideology of Rukunegara. The third Prime Minister focused on the supremacy of law and the realm of justice. The fourth articulated what became known as Vision 2020 whereby Malaysia would become a fully-developed society by the year 2020 and thereby increasing Malaysian self-confidence. In the wake of international conflicts and terrorism when Islam is perceived pejoratively in the international arena, the fifth Prime Minister, Abdullah Badawi, has focussed on civilizational Islam, *Islam Hadhari*, and human capital (Hng, 2004). It is important to note that in the 1980s, the Minister of Education, Musa Hitam, initiated curriculum reform from the primary school right through the secondary school. This was the most wide sweeping curriculum policy and practice reform in the history of Malaysian education which provided indigenous perspectives on the knowledge worth knowing for transmission to future generations.

The second Prime Minister, Tun Abdul Razak, was the one who was the Chairman for the 1956 Education Report outlining the establishment and development of the Malaysian Educational system. The other three Prime Ministers, namely, Hussein Onn, Mahathir Mohamad and Abdullah Badawi were former Ministers of Education. Almost all former Deputy Prime Ministers had previously been Ministers of Education. Of the five Prime Ministers, three were from the legal profession; one was from the medical profession and one from the professional Public and Civil Service. Evidently, leaders at the highest level in Malaysian society are people with understanding of what being a professional means because of their professional education and training. While these people may not have been school leaders, their influence on educational policies and on the impact of policy has been considerable. One difference between educational leaders and school leaders is that educational leaders are typically involved in the macro-dimension of leadership, internationally, in Parliament and in the community, while school leaders are more classroom and institution-based. School leadership is founded on instructional leadership but the demands on school leaders are such that they are expected to provide civic leadership using their educational knowledge as an important source of knowledge for their communities. There is, however, an area of overlap of policy and practice when school leaders have to lead beyond the school and become involved in national policy making and when educational leaders at the macro level as policy-makers question and challenge the diverse range of educational practices and even provide possible solutions or directions for solutions of teaching-learning paradoxes (Prawat, 1999; Harris, 2001). It was not school leaders who ensured the adoption of the agenda of the UN Millennium Goals, or the goal of Asia-Europe Meeting [ASEM] Lifelong Learning Agenda or the Information Communications Technology [ICT] policies as national and educational policies and priorities. Such championing has often been undertaken by political, public service, including foreign affairs. Officials, ambassadors, and even business leaders. Typically too, when these various policies are debated there are sector, system, district, institutional and classroom levels of championing, as the occasions demand. The contributions of political leaders exemplify the complex, multilayered and interrelated nature of educational development in a centralized educational system.

The Development of Leadership Programmes for Educational Leaders

Malaysia has had to confront the same dilemmas that have confronted other educational systems which have sought to develop specific programmes for the preparation of educational leaders and managers. These dilemmas arise basically from the fact that, before the emergence of the need to prepare educational administrators, managers and leaders, in Special Training Institutes or Staff Colleges, teacher preparation had been largely carried out in teachers' colleges and universities. The programmes of academic institutions were primarily concerned with developing a broad understanding of the problems and issues of education, as well as with providing them with the foundational knowledge and skills needed for effective classroom practice and for the broader issues of curriculum, grouping, assessment and so forth. In the past, teachers who were to become future school leaders had not had administrative or leadership training. Until the early 1980s, specific programmes for school leadership training tended to take the form of relatively short in-service courses provided by central or local administrative bodies (Levine, 2005; Bajunid, 1999).

Typically, university lecturers are expected to teach, conduct research, publish, provide consultancy services and serve the community. Schoolteachers are typically expected to teach, provide counselling to students and parents and serve the community. Teachers engage in local community work considerably more than university lecturers whose contributions are in the field of academic research and consultancy and often of a global or international nature. It is clear that there are distinct differences in focus between the leaders at different levels of education, specifically, academic university leadership and school-level leadership (Leithwood and Hallinger, 2002). Whatever the differences in scope and focus, ideally, leaders are expected to invest thought, knowledge, time, and energy and make various kinds of sacrifices towards individual and national character building, community building, advancement of the profession and to promote global peace. As a matter of practice, university lecturers contribute more to the generation of knowledge, considered as their core business, whereas for school leaders and school teachers, teaching and student character building are considered their core business.

In the early years of the development of the School of Education (which then became the Faculty of Education) of the University of Malaya, academic staff were sent abroad to specialize in the areas of Sociology of Education, Educational Statistics, the History of Education, Educational Psychology, Curriculum, Educational Evaluation, Educational Counselling, Educational Technology, Science Education, the Teaching of Mathematics, Languages and the Social Sciences. The Ministry of Education itself conducted weekend courses for secondary and primary school heads for educational administration and management competencies. In the 1970s, the first academic programme in Educational Administration offered in the University of Malaya was taught by Ee Tiang Hong. Programmes on the Sociology of Education with reference to educational leadership were offered by T. Marimuthu. Beyond the University of Malaya, Malaysians went abroad to study. On their return, those who specialized in educational administration, policy and curriculum were typically posted to positions where they could apply their advanced professional knowledge to educational practice, within their leadership domains. Typically, at the system level, the educational leaders are administrators, curriculum, instructional and assessment leaders, and, experts and teachers in specialized fields of education. The generic leadership skills to be acquired through leadership training covered issues of public interest and national educational development.

Towards Edupreneurship in the Teaching Profession

In 1979 the Malaysian Education Staff Training Institute (MESTI) (later, renamed the National Institute of Educational Management) was established as a Professional Division of the Ministry of Education, Malaysia. Its brief was to respond to the need to advance the professional growth and development of educational administrators and improve educational management and planning practices. Initially the priority was on the training of primary and secondary school principals but it also provided courses for educational administrators and support staff in central, state, and district levels (Chew Tow Yow, 1986; Bajunid, 2005). During the early years of its establishment, MESTI conducted a seminal country-wide National Training Needs Assessment Study of the educational and training needs of school leaders. The information gathered pertaining to actual duties and responsibilities of principals and the required competencies became the baseline data and provided important input in the formulation of training courses. The overarching conceptual frameworks as well as the categorizations of competencies continue to be used in the Educational Management Information System packages for Malaysian Smart Schools. (Multimedia Development Corporation, 2005).

The Institute relocated to the Genting Highlands and was re-designated Institut Aminuddin Baki (IAB, 1999). Under the Directorship of the present author, IAB sought to encourage commitment to improving educational leadership and the quality of education generally in the context of multi-cultural multi-ethnic, and multi-faith Malaysia. It was also committed to generate the corpus of knowledge on educational management and leadership from the indigenous as well as from international perspectives. To this end, beginning in 1993, twinning programmes were established with Houston, Bristol, Tasmania and Vandervelt Universities. The Joint Masters' programmes which were established with the University of Houston and the University of Bristol created strong professional benchmarks and exciting and mutually beneficial professional exchanges. Howard Jones who was a highly influential member of the Houston Academic Team brought to bear on the courses he taught a wide-ranging philosophical perspective which encouraged students to be reflective about their work and to dare think outside of conventions. Similarly, Eric Hoyle, who was the leading member of the Bristol team, encouraged students to adopt a variety of perspectives in seeking to better understand the institutions in which they worked and to apply powerful educational and sociological concepts to the social and educational systems and the teaching profession. Scholars who were exposed to the minds of Jones and Hoyle experienced exciting and rare synergistic intellectual insights. (By coincidence, Howard Jones and Eric Hoyle had, some years previously, worked together on a leadership development programme in Indonesia.)

One of the dilemmas facing institutions which seek both to train and educate future leaders lies in the ambiguous relationship between administration, management and leadership. The notions of administration and management were in contestation from the earlier years of the development of the field and to some extent continue to remain so. The field of management, in fact, overlaps considerably with the field of leadership, and increasingly with entrepreneurship In the 1990s, during his tenure of office, the then Minister of Education (who is now the Deputy Prime Minister) continually emphasized the importance of "leadership" and not simply "management" in the training of educators and educational leaders. This emphasis was emphasized particularly with reference to the training of principals. Coming from the political domain and being formerly the Minister of Defence and the Chief Minister of the State of Pahang, as well as being engaged in the Asian Leadership Forum and other strategic thinking initiatives, it was understandable that he gave due importance to "leadership" of principals and not just "administration" and "management.". The Director of IAB at that time had also emphasized the significance of leadership beyond the demands of administration and management. It was at that time that IAB adopted the change which ensured significant emphasis on "leadership" and the National Institute of Educational Management became the National Institute of Educational Management and Leadership. This significant change is not only symbolic but is also substantive. With the increasingly important role of private sector education with its own ethos and challenges, the notion of educational entrepreneurship, specifically edupreneurship, has emerged in the wake of related notions of edutourism, ecotourism.

During the last 50 years there was gradual and incremental growth of private education, but the last fifteen years saw the rapid and phenomenal expansion of private education, especially at tertiary level. Educational leaders in private education have had to raise their own funds, establish international linkages, ensure that their institutions are the preferred providers of education, and create a market for their products, programmes and services. Among the private providers of education are Tuanku Jaafar College, Kolej Yayasan Saad, Sri Chempaka, Sri Inai and Prime College. At the higher education level are INTI International University College, Lim Kok Wing University College of Design, Technology and Innovation, Cosmopolitan, HELP and Sedaya University Colleges and others. These various colleges compete among themselves and also maintain or go beyond the standards set by public institutions and their international partners so that they are also leaders in their own right. These private institutions have become the income earners for the nation and have created the education industry. In order to be competitive with neighbouring countries, including with those whose education systems are mature, such as Australia and New Zealand, these colleges have to ensure that their standards of teaching and learning meet all international quality assurance requirements. In addition to maintaining and raising standards, they have to keep fees low, manage their finances, keep investors and stakeholders happy, and, most of all, satisfy students as their direct customers, and, parents as the indirect customers, always " positively surprising" their clients beyond expectations. Private educational institutions and their leadership have demonstrated that for Malaysia to be a Centre of Excellence, educational entrepreneurship is required. The potential of educational entrepreneurship is currently being explored by leaders in the private sector. Leaders in the tourism industry, for instance, have begun to understand and market the idea of educational tourism, ecological tourism, cultural tourism and health tourism. Clearly then, entrepreneurship is highly valued in private sector education and it has to be noted that the development of educational leaders must now take into account the increasingly entrepreneurial aspects of their roles. Training organizations responsible for curriculum development and training programmes for educational leaders from the private sector must (and the increasingly competitive the public sector) must necessarily address the meaning and implications of "edupreneurship" or entrepreneurship in education. For scholars of educational leadership, there are interesting discourses to engage in with regards to defining and finding relevant practical examples of educational administration, management, leadership and entrepreneurship.

Indigenous Educational Knowledge Generation and Culturally Unique Modes of Knowing

There are today several books on educational policy, history, administration and education written in the Malay language which is considered one of the world's leading and growing languages (Collins, 1996). These books have contributed significantly to meet the challenge of a dearth of indigenous educational materials. Typically, these materials are descriptive and analytic but not critical since the tradition of criticism, publicly or openly expressed, is not yet acceptable to politicians, bureaucrats or even some academics. It seems that at this stage of strategic development of intellectual culture in Malaysia, works in the tradition of critical inquiry as is common in the western world (Freire, 1970; Goodman, 1973) are not well supported by various stakeholders and constituencies. Under these circumstances, and in the context of the dominant indigenous culture at a particular stage of development, it would be appropriate to develop a culture of appreciative inquiry within which there may be embedded critique and the subtle persuasive mode may render criticism more palatable and change, more acceptable. Appreciative inquiry suggests a more balanced and more creative mode of criticism than just outright negative criticism based on some ideological or personal positions (Cooperrider et al., 2001). In terms of educational criticism in Malaysia, Bakri Musa's and Kua's works, although critical, seemed to be welcomed by the community of scholars (Kua, 2002; Bakri, 2003; 2004).

The training and development of educational leaders and school leaders needs to address the issue of educational critiques in such modes as ideological critiques or appreciative inquiry, moving towards educational connoisseurship and professionality. Educational connoisseurship matters if educational leaders have to achieve clarity in the contents and direction of their leadership in terms of epistemology, ontology, axiology and practice. The argument of "dynamic inaction" of doing nothing while waiting for something to happen and problems will take care of themselves may not be appropriate or acceptable in a lively, dynamic educational environment. Educational leaders find themselves involved in the Character Education Movement, the Great Books Movement, the Genius of Mankind Movement, and the Leadership for Learning and the Educational Wisdom Movements. In fact, the field of education provides vast opportunities for explorations of all knowledge fields. Educational connoisseurship invites the exploration of servant leadership, thought leadership, timeless leadership in multicultural contexts and many other kinds of knowledge and leadership perspectives. (Toffler, 1974; Hofstede, 1994; Trompenaars and Hampden-Turner, 1997). That, to date, there are no such visible and robust movements at local, state or federal levels, indicates that teaching as a profession and teachers as members of the professional class, have not made their impact within their circles, and indeed very little impact on other professions. Being called a profession does not make the occupational group professional. While the idea that "teaching is the profession on which all other professions rest" is inspirational and provides the direction for professional leadership, there is a wide chasm between the ideal and the reality. It is robust professional knowledge, hard work, and will, that fosters professionalism and professionality. The teaching profession in Malaysia has a long way to go to play a knowledge leadership role, leading, and setting the highest standards of professionalism, as exemplar to other professions. Educational leaders will have to develop profound understanding of educational philosophy within the contexts of educational and linguistic rights and religious rights. Educational and school leaders have the responsibility of becoming champions of such significant causes as Values and Civics Education or Special Needs Education, for, in Malaysia, these domains are short of champions. However, cruel and unjust the outside world, within the school and classroom, school leaders have the responsibility and the opportunity to ensure that that there is justice in classrooms and schools, and there is hope and there are good people and there are ideals worth fighting for and there are timeless inspiring ideas. Other ideas discussed and launched as programmes in other societies (which need to be explored and redefined for indigenous relevance), include the notion that every child matters, every teacher matters, and every citizen matters. No child, whether normal or gifted or with special needs should be left behind but should have the right to attain the development of their fullest potentialities. At the institutional levels, there are other ideas of schools without failures and schools as happy places. School leaders have immense opportunities to move educational development from the realm of rhetoric to the realm of reality by exercising effectively the leadership of practice, based on mature professional knowledge. Educational and School Development can be driven by ideas and ideals generated from the education sector itself and not merely by ideas from the political, economic, cultural or public service domains. While the paradigms of 'middle class' and 'profession' should not be overstated and turned into ideological doctrine, the teaching profession could be enhanced by exploring profoundly and employing the best of the cultures of the 'middle-class' and 'professions' to advantage.

Examining Possibilities for the Strategic Positioning of the Profession

Educational leaders can exercise educational imagination of the "futural imagery" to ensure that their students will be members of the educated and learned class, the middle class, the class of knowledge workers, the professional or the creative class and members of a democratic and participative citizenry. Educational imagination for the transformation of society can move from the quest to develop a "middle class" to the quest to develop a "creative class" in the context of the knowledge economy, knowledge entrepreneurs and the service industries coupled with the ideas of innovations, designs and creativity (K Economy Master Plan) (Bajunid, 2006). The challenge for educators is to understand and give due regard to such subtle differentiae as 'critical' and 'creative,' 'cosmopolitan' and 'global,' 'creative class' and 'professional class,' for, such efforts of refining mental categorizations are marks and examples of intellectual character (Ritchhart, 2002).

Leadership development programmes should be exciting, dynamic and lively and should draw materials not just from sources such as academic texts, exploring the ideas of thinkers, but should also study actual cases, and have conversations with practicing educational leaders from different domains, across the spectrum of concerns, eliciting understanding of their accomplishments, their successes and failures, their strategies, their dreams, ideals and disappointments, their wisdom and follies (IAB, 1999). While exploring the Great Books on ideas and leadership there should be the exploration of the great movies [and even songs], particularly those movies on the drama of life in classrooms and schools and homes, involving students, teachers, parents and leaders and their passions. Such popular and inspiring works like *To Sir with Love, Ghandi, Do the Right Thing, Stand and Delive, Dead Poet's Society, Dangerous Minds, Akeela and the Spelling Bee,* should not be trivialized or diminished by applying academic criteria, but they should be assessed for edutainment value, for at the very least, they may be inspiring. While they constitute non-traditional sources of materials and knowledge, these works do have messages. Underlying the messages is the notion of "professionality" in teaching.

Visiting schools identified as the best and most successful and examining the best practices and visiting difficult schools to attempt at understanding root causes of problems and failures are all part of the holistic development of teacher leaders, for many of the educational and leadership ideas have to be grasped, mastered at the individual levels and the relevance and appropriateness of the ideas and issues have to be examined in contexts. Visiting and studying the best institutions and organizations beyond schools to understand the embedded educational management excellence in terms of policies, practices, and continuous improvement imperatives are also strategies which should not be dismissed. Leadership development requires not just the mastery of the academic texts but also sensitive understanding and empathy for the diverse scripts of life. Variations of the meaning of profession, professionalism and professionality in education (Hoyle,1974,1982; Hoyle and John, 1994) need to be further explored in relation to the Malaysian context. The struggle to ensure that the teaching profession becomes a dynamic knowledge-based profession, beyond the mere attestation of the Professional Code of Teaching certainly demands more serious meta-analysis, examining and synthesizing of concepts, theories and anecdotal evidence.

Members of the teaching profession with its own socio-educational hierarchy from those who teach in primary schools to those who teach in universities are essentially in the middle class. Also teachers are essentially in the professional class as members of the communities of practice in the professional grouping. Being at once members of the middle class and the professional class enables teachers to move out from what is traditionally considered a conservative profession. As members of the middle class teachers have the potential and capacities to exercise the values of the middle class such as social stability, respectability, family values, stability based on income, wealth and education. As members of the professional class teachers have the capacities and responsibility to contribute to the advancement of the profession as they continue to develop their acumen of experiences and expertise and repertoire of mature knowledge. It is the professionals with their code of ethics, their methodologies, and their contributive contents that provide the legal, rational, ethical, disciplinary and content base logic, processes and ideals of development. If these two realities are understood and accepted, then the roles and visions of teachers can take on new substance and spirit (Bajunid, 2008).

Conclusion

For 50 years the nation has focussed development efforts on national unity, nation-building, establishing infrastructures and infostructures, wealth creation and the equitable distribution of opportunities and improving the quality of life of its people. It has moved from the mentality of the feudalistic and anti-colonial mindset towards nationalism and patriotism, and first-world mindsets, dealing with emerging issues like e-sovereignty, fostering regional cooperation and exercising a participative and constructive role in the global community. With its National Mission focussing on knowledge, innovation and first world mindset, and with a critical mass of professionals and intellectuals, and a large base of enlightened citizenry, the nation is now set on the path of the next phase of development in the sweep of forces of globalization, liberalization and internationalization (Oakley and Krug, 1994; United Nations, 2007).

De Pree (1989) noted that the first responsibility of the leader is to define reality, but an equally significant responsibility is to define a vision (Davis and Davidson, 1991). To date, no individual or group has defined the reality of the teaching profession as the largest profession in the country which, when mobilized and empowered, has the capacity to effect deep, strategic change. Nor has the fact that members of the profession are actually the builders of intellectual, knowledge, cultural, values and social capital, been fully articulated in the language of "visioning". Re-conceptualizing what educators have been doing in the language of management development will revitalize the profession and identify new directions embracing greater societal responsibilities. It is clear that the phenomenon of educational leadership should receive due attention in holistic perspectives and educational leaders need to have self knowledge and confidence in the strategic importance of the teaching profession for the development of knowledge capital, intellectual capital and social capital and human capital. A middle class which is a consumer class but not a creative class, without a critical mass of its members does not ensure the advancement of society. In the same way, a teaching profession whose members are mere consumers of knowledge and not generators of knowledge does not ensure the sustained advancement of the profession and its potentialities for leadership.

References

Ahmad Sarji (ed.) (1993). *Malaysia's Vision 2020: Understanding the Concept, Implications and Challenges*. Petaling Jaya, Malaysia: Pelanduk.

Archer, L., Hutchings, M., and Ross, A. (2003). *Higher Education and Social Class: Issues of Exclusion and Inclusion*. London: Routledge/Falmer.

Ariff, I. and Chuan, G. C. (2000). *Multimedia Super Corridor*. Kuala Lumpur: Leeds.

Bajunid, I. A. (1999). Megashifts in the training of educational administrators/managers: Strategic plans for the realization of Malaysia's 2020. In Bajunid, I. A., Amer Hamzah Jantan, Syed Putra Syed Ali, and Balasandran, A. Ramiah (eds.) *Looking at the Practices of Educational Management and Administration*. Genting Highlands, Malaysia: Institut Aminuddin Baki.

Bajunid, I. A. (2001). The transformation of Malaysian Society through Technological advantage: ICT and education in Malaysia. *Journal of Southeast Asian Education*, 2(1), 104–146.

Bajunid, I. A. (2002). Changing mindsets: Lifelong learning for all. In Amer Hamzah Jantan et al. (eds.) *Integrated Approaches to Lifelong Learning*. Kuala Lumpur: Asia-Europe Institute University of Malaya.

Bajunid, I. A. (2005). "Revisiting indigenous perspectives of educational management and leadership," *Current Issues and Concerns: Proceedings of the National Colloquium on Educational Management and Leadership*, Asian Centre for Research on University Learning and Teaching (ACRULeT), Universiti Teknologi Mara, 2 June 2005, pp. 56–92.

Bajunid, I. A. (2006), 'Towards the Development of an Achieving and Creative Class in Malaysia', Paper presented at the Human Capital Conference, Malaysian Institute of Human Resource Management and Universiti Sabah Malaysia, Kota Kinabalu, 22–24 November.

Bajunid, I. A. (2007a). "Not Scions of Lesser Heritage and Ancestry: The Reawakening of Educational Leadership in the Emerging World Order and the Reshaping of Educational Landscapes," Keynote Address, 5th ASEAN/Asian Symposium on Educational Management and Leadership on the Theme 'the Challenges and Changing Landscapes of Educational Management and Leadership'. Kuala Lumpur, Universiti Utara Malaysia, August 18–19, 2007.

Bajunid, I. A. (2008) (ed.). *From Traditional Schools to Smart Schools: The Malaysian Educational Odyssey*. Kuala Lumpur: Oxford Fajar.

Bakri, M. M. (2003). *An Education System Worthy of Malaysia*. Petaling Jaya, Malaysia: Strategic Information Research Development (SIRD).

Bakri, M. M. (2004). *Seeing Malaysia My Way*. Petaling Jaya, Malaysia: Strategic Information Research Development (SIRD).

Chew Tow Yow (1986). The National Institute of Educational Management. In Hoyle, E. and McMahon, A. (eds.) *The Management of Schools: World Yearbook of Education 1986*. London: Kogan Page, pp. 283–294.

Collins, J. T. (1996). *Malay World Language of the Ages*. Kuala Lumpur: Dewan Bahasa dan Pustaka.

Cooperrider, D. L., Sorensen Jr. Yaeger, T. F., and Whitney D. (eds.) (2001). *Appreciative Inquiry: An Emerging Direction for Organizational Development*. Champaign, IL: Stipes.

Davis, S. and Davidson, B. (1991). *2020 Vision*. New York: Simon & Schuster.

Day, Christopher, Fernandez, Alicia, Hauge, Trond E, and Moller, Jorunn (2000). *The Life and Work of Teachers: International Perspectives in Changing Times*. London: Falmer.

De Pree, M. (1989). *Leadership is an Art*. New York: Bantam Doubleday Dell.

Fantasia, R., Levine, R. F., and McNall, S. G. (eds.) (1991). *Bringing Back Class in Contemporary and Historical Perspectives*. Boulder, CO: Westview.

Freire, P. (1970). *Pedagogy of the Oppressed*. Harmondsworth: Penguin.

Goodman, P. (1973). *Compulsory Miseducation*. Harmondsworth: Penguin.

Greenwood, Adriana Mata (2000). International Labour Organization. Bureau of Statistics. Updating the International Standard Classification of Occupations, ISCO-08.

Gullick, J. M. (1988). *The Indigenous Political System of Western Malaya*. Rev. edn. London: Athlone.

Harper, T. N. (1999). *The End of Empire and the Making of Malaya*. Cambridge: Cambridge University Press.

Harris, J. (2001). *The Learning Paradox*. Oxford: Capstone.

Hng H. Y. (2004). *Five Men and Five Ideas*. Subang Jaya, Malaysia: Pelanduk.

Hoyle, E. (1974). Professionality, professionalism and control in teaching. *London Education Review*, 3(2), 13–19.

Hoyle, E. (1982). The professionalization of teachers: A paradox. *British Journal of Educational Studies*, 30(2), 161–171.

Hoyle, E. and John, P. (1994). *Teaching: Professional Knowledge and Professional Practice*. London: Cassell Education.

Institut Aminuddin Baki (IAB) (1999). *Ikhtibar Pemimpin Pendidikan* (*Lessons from Educational Leaders*). Genting Highlands, Malaysia: Ministry of Education.

IKSEP (2004). *Institut Kajian Sejarah dan Patriotisme Malaysia* (*Malaysian Institute of Historical and Patriotism Studies*). Melaka, Malaysia: IKSEP. (http://www.iksep.com.my)

Hofstede, G. (1994) *Cultures and Organizations*. London: HarperCollins.

Kua, K. S. (2002). *Malaysian Critical Issues*. Petaling Jaya, Malaysia: Strategic Information Research Development (SIRD).

Lee, M. (1999). *Private Higher Education in Malaysia*. Penang, Malaysia: Sinaran.

Leithwood, K. and Hallinger, P. (2002). *Second Educational Handbook of Educational Leadership*. Boston, MA: Kluwer.

Levine, A. (2005). *Educating School Leaders*. New York: The Education Schools Project.

Loh Fook Seng, P. (1975). *Seeds of Separatism: Educational Policy in Malaya 1874–1940*. Kuala Lumpur: Oxford University Press.

MacBeath, J. (2002, January 3–6). *Leadership for Learning; The Cambridge Network*. Paper presented at the 15th International congress for School Effectiveness and Improvements (ICSEI), Copenhagen.

McKenna, P. J. and Maister, D. (2002). *First Among Equals: How to Manage A Group of Professionals*. London: Simon & Schuster.

Mahathir, M. (1991). *Malaysia: The Way Forward*. Kuala Lumpur: Centre for Economic Research and Services, Malaysian Business Council.

Malaysia (2003). *Education Development Plan 2001-2010*. Kuala Lumpur: Ministry of Education.

Malaysia (2006a). Education Development Master Plan 2006-2010. [*Pelan Induk Pembangunan Pendidikan 2006-2010*]. Putrajaya: Government of Malaysia.

Malaysia (2006b). *The 9th Malaysia Plan 2006–2010*. Putrajaya, Malaysia: Government of Malaysia.

Malaysia (2006c). *Malaysian Educational Statistics, 2006*. Putrajaya, Malaysia: Ministry of Education.

Malaysia (2007). *Strategic Plan for National Higher Education Beyond 2020*. Putrajaya, Malaysia: Ministry of Higher Education.

Ministry of Higher Education, (MOHE) Malaysia (2006), *Report by the Committee to Study, Review and Make Recommendations Concerning the Development and Direction of Higher Education in Malaysia*. Shah Alam: University Publication Centre (UPENA).

_____ (2007), [website] http://www.mohe.gov.my/, accessed 6 February 2007.

Ministry of Higher Education (MOHE), Malaysia (2007) National Higher Education Strategic Plan: Laying the Foundation Beyond 2020. (Kementerian Pengajian Tinggi Malaysia (2007).

Pelan Strategik Pengajian Tinggi Negara Melangkaui Tahun 2020), Putrajaya. Government of Malaysia. (See also, www.mohe.gov.my)

Multimedia Development Corporation (2005). The Smart School Roadmap 2005–2020; an Educational Odyssey. (A consultative paper on the expansion of the Smart School initiative to all schools in Malaysia). Cyberjaya, Malaysia: Multimedia super Corridor.

National Institute of Public Administration (INTAN) (1994). *Malaysian Development Experience: Changes and Challenges.* Kuala Lumpur: Ampang Press Sdn. Bhd.

Oakley, Ed and Krug, D. (1994). *Enlightened Leadership: Getting to the Heart of Change.* New York: Fireside Book/Simon & Schuster.

Prawat, R. S. (1999). 'Dewey, Peirce, and the learning paradox'. *American Educational Research Journal,* 36(1), Spring, 47–76.

Ritchhart, R. (2002). *Intellectual Character.* San Francisco, CA: Jossey-Bass.

Savage, M. (2000). *Class Analysis and Social Transformation.* Buckingham-Philadelphia: Open University Press.

Senge, P. (1992). *The Fifth Discipline: The Art and Practice of the Learning Organization.* New York: Random House.

Shiraishi, T. (2004). The Rise of New Urban Middle Classes in Southeast Asia: What is its national and regional significance? Research Institute of Economy, Trade and Industry (RIETI) Discussion Paper Series 04-E-011. 37pp.

Stevenson, R. (1975). *Cultivators and Administrators.* Kuala Lumpur: Oxford University Press.

Tan Teong Jin, Ho Wah Foon, and Tan Joo Lan (2005). *The Chinese Malaysian Contribution.* Kuala Lumpur: Centre for Malaysian Chinese Studies.

Tengku A. R. (1980). *Looking Back.* Kuala Lumpur: Star Publications.

Toffler, A. (ed.) (1974). *Learning for Tomorrow.* New York: Vintage Books.

Trompenaars, F. and Hampden-Turner, C. (1997) *Riding the Waves of Culture.* London: Nicholas Brealey.

United Nations (2007). *Millennium Development Goals (MDG).* New York. United Nations Publications.

Part IV
Teaching as a Profession: Personal Perspectives

Chapter 14
Professional Freedom: A Personal Perspective

William Taylor

Teaching in the 1950s

In the second half of the first decade of the twenty-first century, with writing and talk about education full of references to the national curriculum and assessment, league tables, inspection and school effectiveness, it is not easy to appreciate the strength of feeling that sixty years earlier attached to the freedom of teachers to determine their own content and teaching methods.

I began work in a secondary modern school just after half way through the twentieth century. There were no detailed prescriptions as to what and how I should teach. There were no examinations for which pupils needed to be prepared. At staff meetings the curriculum was not high on the agenda. Most beginning teachers had acquired their knowledge of what was customary and what worked from one or two years of training, and before that, thirteen years experience as pupils. Local authority advisors and members of Her Majesty's Inspectorate appeared from time to time, more often in advisory rather than inspectorial mode. Informal advice from colleagues offered support and guidance, which I certainly needed.

The freedom that teachers in schools such as mine enjoyed had official support. In November 1946, nearing the end of his time as Permanent Secretary of the Ministry of Education, Sir John Maud had given it as his opinion that 'Freedom is what the teacher needs more than anything…perhaps the most essential freedom of the teacher is to decide what to teach and how to teach it' (quoted Lawrence, 1992: 13).

The emphasis on freedom had its roots in two aspects of the history of the previous fifty years.

First, memories of the hated system of 'payment by results' by means of which in the second half of the nineteenth century governments controlled the work of public elementary schools.

Second, revulsion at the ideological totalitarianism of the German, Italian and Japanese dictatorships, against which Britain, the United States and their allies had recently won a war immensely costly in lives and hopes. The Soviet Union had been our ally in that war. But as the realities of life in a communist dictatorship emerged, it became clear that the threat of totalitarianism had not gone away. To the

still fresh memories of 'payment by results' and the Second World war were added
fears generated by communism and by the prospect of allowing politics to influence
what went on in the classroom.

The Legacy of 'Payment by Results'

'Payment by results' described the system of public support for education introduced by the infamous 'Revised Code' of 1862. Expressly in the interests of economy in public expenditure, the Code tied grants to schools to the proficiency of
pupils as assessed by school inspectors. The teachers' associations and other bodies
campaigned to free schools and teachers from this system, and to give more attention to the needs and potentialities of children.

Modified in 1867, 1875, 1882 and 1890, 'payment by results' was brought to
an end in 1898. The 'battle between the teachers and the central authorities'
(Lawton, 1978 in Gordon (1980) 312) about who should control the curriculum
appeared to have been won by the teachers. But as Lawson and Silver (1973: 329)
remind us –

> The consequences of [the abolition of payment by results] must not be exaggerated. A long
> process of conditioning had been taking place. Men who grew accustomed to semi-darkness,
> explained Edmond Holmes, formerly chief inspector for elementary schools, were blinded
> on being brought out into the daylight; for thirty-three years the teachers were 'treated as
> machines and they were suddenly asked to act as intelligent beings'.

It would be a mistake to assume that the end of payment by results was immediately
followed by a period of *laissez faire*.

> It has to be admitted that the idea of complete freedom of the teacher to teach whatever he
> likes is a myth, and so.....is the idea that this tradition of teacher autonomy has a long tradi-
> tion in this country. Elementary schools were controlled by regulations until 1926; the cur-
> ricula in secondary schools were controlled until the 1944 Education Act.
>
> (Lawton, 1978 in Gordon, 1980: 309)

Eric Hoyle and Peter John (1995: 78.) make the point that, in every field in which
professionals operate,

> Professional autonomy is a limited form of autonomy [and]...is always constrained.
> Practitioners do not have licence, but do have *a* licence. The licence to practice is based upon
> demonstrated competence and is conditional. [It].....is variable over space and time. In England
> and Wales perhaps the apotheosis of teacher autonomy was attained in the 1960s.....

From Prescriptions to Suggestions

From 1905 the Board of Education issued a series of *'Handbooks of Suggestions'*
for teachers. The spirit in which these suggestions were offered was summarised in
the preface to the 1927 edition of the *Handbook*

The only uniformity of practice that the Board of Education desire to see in the teaching of public elementary schools is that each teacher shall think for himself and work out for himself such methods of teaching as may use his powers to the best advantage and be best suited to the particular needs and conditions of the School. Uniformity in detail of practice is not desirable, even if it were attainable.

The preface to the *Handbook* also quotes from the Board's Circular 1375 to make clear the context in which suggestions were being offered (italics added)

Certain subjects of the curriculum are required by statute, as, for instance, the provision of 'practical instruction' under Section 20 (1) of the Education Act, 1921. The list of additional subjects hitherto included in the Code probably represents a general consensus of opinion throughout the country as to the subjects suitable for children of elementary school age, but it is, and has long been, open to an Authority to vary the curriculum and there seems to be no sufficient reason for retaining in Grant Regulations a list which derives its authority from general agreement rather than from any exercise of the Board's statutory powers. *The curriculum of a school will remain subject to the general approval of the Board, but detailed comment or advice on the syllabus will in future be confined to the volume of 'Suggestions for Teachers and Others concerned in the work of Public Elementary Schools.*

More then 350 of the 454 closely printed pages that follow this statement at the beginning of the 1927 *Handbook* are taken up with subject-specific advice. Much of this is very detailed. Although the emphasis is indeed on methods and approaches, there is also a great deal that defines content. In history, for one example, it is suggested that by the time the pupil leaves the Elementary school

….he should have gained a connected and definite knowledge of the story of Britain and of the British Commonwealth of Nations, and have begun to realise the bearing of this study on everyday life……This is the ideal, but it is recognised to attain it fully may be beyond the reach of many schools…..In any case, the course should always be continued to modern times. In small schools were classes are grouped, it is too common to find children spending two or even more years on a single "period" of history, with the result that their knowledge stops short, for example, at Tudor or Stuart times. This should in all cases be avoided.

(Ibid.: 122–123)

And in English lessons:

The different parts of speech and their functions in the sentence should gradually be taught, and the children should have practice in recognising them. They will be able to perceive that every sentence has a structure and will appreciate the meaning of such terms as subject, predicate, object, complement. Later they should be taught to analyse the complex sentence and to distinguish the different types of phrase and subordinate clause according to the parts of speech which they represent. They will also perceive that variation in the function and meaning of certain words is accompanied by variation in their form, and they should then learn certain facts of English Accidence and certain rules of Syntax, coming to understand what is meant, e.g., by concords, inflexions, moods, tenses etc.

(Ibid.: 98)

The category 'Elementary education' disappeared with the Education Act of 1944. Young children were to be educated in *primary* schools. 'Secondary education for all' was established for those over 11. Dent (1944) with the exception of Religious education, the 1944 Act had almost nothing to say about the school curriculum. All that was required was that children should be educated according to their age, ability and aptitude.

In succeeding decades professional freedom for teachers continued to be emphasised in official policies. But already in the 1960s there were signs that the post war consensus was weakening and the balance of power over the curriculum changing. As Pateman put it in 1977, the

> ....notion of professional freedom is acceptable so long as the ends or different ends being pursued are not generally contested, and can co-exist, if diverse, without creating a pressing awareness of incompatibility. If there was no consensus on the meaning of health and cure, then doctors would not be able to make the claims to professional freedom which they do. The same applies to teachers. More strongly, once the ends are agreed it is rational to institutionalize professional freedom, for that is only to grant what is the due of expertise, and professionals are simply experts in the means required to achieve given ends....

As consensus weakened, so the movement towards greater central control accelerated. Whilst the 1930s to the 1960s may be seen as a brief interval in which teachers, and those responsible for their education and training, enjoyed a much greater measure of professional freedom than either before or since, the formal position remained until the 1980s that the curriculum was a matter for the schools, not the Government. But the national curriculum, national standards and testing of attainment and rigorous inspection regimes that followed the Education Act of 1988 did not simply represent a sudden and unexpected exercise of political power. Even in the 1950s many teachers had made plain that they would support a more structured approach to the curriculum than that officially favoured – an example of what Hoyle and Wallace (2005: 55) see as 'policy pathos'.

The Secondary Curriculum

To a considerable extent, the freedom of secondary (grammar school) teachers up to and beyond 1944 to determine their own curriculum had been limited by the requirements of the examination boards responsible for the ubiquitous School Certificate examinations. The new secondary modern schools after 1944 were initially free of these requirements (indeed, were dissuaded from basing their curricula on any form of externally imposed test). But they soon began to offer their pupils opportunities to take examinations for the awards of a variety of examining bodies, a situation only resolved by the introduction of a new Certificate of Secondary Educations (CSE) at a lower level than the General Certificate of Education which had replaced the former School Certificate (Taylor, 1963).

How and why did this happen?

With no immediate reorganisation of secondary education along non-selective, comprehensive lines in prospect, and the academic orientation of the Grammar schools maintained, the secondary modern school became in the immediately post-war period a focus of social idealism concerning equality and the encouragement of motives higher than profit and personal gain.

The new secondary education offered teachers the freedom

> ....to plan the curriculum of the school on purely educational lines, to provide their pupils with the best possible conditions for growing up, and to ensure that their leave school with interests thoroughly aroused and a determination to continue their education throughout their lives.
>
> (Ministry of Education Pamphlet No 9, 1947: 31)

The Ministry favoured internal rather than external incentives. Whilst grammar school experience 'need not, of course, prove any obstacle to being a good teacher in a modern school', teachers in such schools were urged to avoid thinking that what had suited them might suit their pupils. But the professional freedom that heads and teachers enjoyed also enabled them to take decisions about the curriculum in response to local and personal pressures. These included pupils' interests in the world of 'real' work, the desire of parents to strengthen their children's employment prospects and, not least, teachers' wishes to raise their own status.

With the exception of some of those who qualified through the immediately post-war Emergency Training Scheme, most secondary modern teachers had received their own education in grammar schools and were familiar with a curriculum structured along academic lines. During their training they may have been encouraged to think of the possibilities of synthesizing traditional subjects within projects or themes and to alter their focus from the subject to the pupil. But most training college courses remained subject centred, and as examination pressures grew, there was pressure for teachers to demonstrate higher levels of subject competence.

In the absence of national directives, the task of reconciling all these influences fell to heads and teachers. Their local decisions reflected their own social and educational experience; their perception of the criteria that would influence their reputations and prospects for promotion and the esteem in which their schools were held; the curriculum content most likely to interest and to motivate their pupils, and the expectations of parents, employers and the local community.

Given the wide variations between local authorities in the proportions of grammar school places available, secondary modern teachers were also aware that some of their pupils, if they had lived elsewhere, would have been following an academic course. For many heads and teachers, these considerations pointed to a structured, subject-focused curriculum along more traditional lines than those officially considered appropriate.

So by the 1960s external examinations had come to play a much more important part in the work of secondary modern schools than had been the case twenty years earlier. Examinations were not imposed on the staff of such schools. On the contrary, their development from the mid-1950s had initially been resisted by officials and the inspectorate. Much of the stimulus for the introduction of examinations had come from the schools themselves.

Government Takes a Hand

As the importance of education for the economy and for the promotion of social mobility grew, it became increasingly difficult for Government to be seen to be leaving curriculum and examinations to the teachers. (Lawton, 1980: 13). In 1960 the Minister (Sir David Eccles) expressed regret that parliamentary debates on education were usually about 'bricks and mortar' and system organization, rather than what was taught in schools:

Of course, Parliament would never attempt to dictate the curriculum, but, from time to time, we could, with advantage, express our views on what is taught in schools and in training colleges. (Quoted Chitty, 2004: 116)

Within two years a Curriculum Study Group was established in the Ministry of Education. The move aroused great suspicion among local authorities and the teachers' organisations, who saw danger in the possibility of political intervention in what was taught and learned in schools, such as had not existed since the nineteenth century. The Department responded to the disquiet by setting up a working party under the chairmanship of Sir John Lockwood which recommended a new body be established to oversee curriculum and examinations. The government accepted the recommendation and the *Schools Council* held its first meeting in October 1964.

Anxieties were expressed both within and beyond the Ministry about the potential effects of setting up a body which contained such a large proportion of teacher representatives (the difficulties encountered in working with the National Advisory Council for the Training and Supply of Teachers were in many minds). However, the membership of the Schools Council was typical of its time – a large representative body with a complex set of subsidiary committees and boards. Starting with 55 members, by 1970 the Council had grown to 75. To help ensure it would not be seen as the creature of any of the interest groups involved it was to be run by no fewer than three Joint Secretaries.

Nationally, the centre of authority on curriculum matters during the 1960s was not easy to define. *De facto* and *de jure* positions diverged. The Ministry of Education's Administrative Memorandum number 25, issued in 1945, had stated:

The Local Education Authority shall determine the general educational character of the school and its place in the local educational system. Subject thereto, the governors shall have the general direction of the conduct and curriculum of the school.

Barnes, who quotes this statement, suggests it is significant in two ways.

First, the autonomy of the school in curricular matters is clearly asserted. Secondly, 'the general direction of the ...curriculum' is placed firmly in the hands of laymen.....' All proposals and reports affecting the conduct and curriculum of the school shall be submitted formally to the governors. .....De facto, what happens in meetings of managers and governors is not often in close accord with the articles....

The direct legal powers of the LEA with regard to the curriculum are somewhat obscure. ...LEAs are by tradition extremely reluctant to confront either governors or heads on curricular matters ....

(Barnes, 1977: 18)

In the mid 1970s UNESCO undertook an international study of professional freedom, the report on which was written by Professor Ben Morris of the University of Bristol (Morris, 1977) The response to the UNESCO enquiry from the Department of Education and Science in London included the following statement. (italics added):

The *contents* of the school curriculum, and the teaching *methods* appropriate, are not prescribed centrally. *In principle* it is up to the schools – the Heads and their assistants – *what* they teach and *how* they teach it. Of course they are *influenced* by their governors and local education authorities. And here are obvious practical constraints of which the most important are the demands of external examinations. But the general principle is an achieved fact, *and is not in jeopardy*.

(Morris, 1977: 76)

In practice, however, *content* and *method* ('what' and 'how') are difficult to separate. Content defined in terms of prescribed texts, or whole class understanding of mathematical principles and proofs graded by difficulty, or chemical elements, or the rules of grammar, or who ruled and what wars and battles they won, all of which is assessed and ranked, does not encourage teaching methods likely to be regarded as 'progressive', ' personalised' or 'child centred'. Absence of freedom in respect of the 'what' inevitably constrains freedom in determining the 'how'.

Looking at society as a whole, the 1960s is widely regarded as a decade of freedom and opportunity when many traditional restraints on individual behaviour and social change were removed (for a balanced view see Sandbrook D., 2005). The following decade has acquired a very different reputation. In education generally, the 1970s are now seen as marking what Booker (1980) called 'The End of the Twentieth Century Dream'. Especially so for many staff in colleges of education, whose careers in teacher education were to come to an abrupt halt with the closures and mergers that took place in the sector throughout the decade and into the early 1980s.

Nineteen seventy six saw a step change in the involvement of politicians, officials and inspectors in decision making about what and how to teach. 'The Yellow book' and 'The Ruskin Speech' of that year have come to symbolise what was to be a new area in relations between Government and the schools.

The document which came to be known as the Yellow Book was a compilation of HMI opinion about the state of education prepared by civil servants following a request from the Prime Minister, James Callaghan. It was never published, but copies were circulated within the education community, and edited extracts appeared in the press. (*Times Educational Supplement* 15 October 1976). The paper was interpreted as a bid by the Department to regain control over the direction of educational development which had been lost to the – increasingly politicised – teachers' unions and to bodies such as the School Council. It was critical of the Council's role in examinations and assessment. The Schools Council had had 'little success in tackling examination problems'. Its performance both on curriculum and examinations had been 'generally mediocre'. It was thus 'open to question whether the constitution of the Schools Council strikes the right balance of responsibility for the matters with which it deals…' (Quoted Lawton, 1980: 76).

On 18 October 1976 the Prime Minister, James Callaghan, delivered a speech at Ruskin College, Oxford, which reiterated many of the themes of the Yellow Book. It did not, however, concede 'the enhanced opportunity to exercise influence over curriculum and teaching methods' that it had been suggested officials and HMI would find useful. What it did do was to initiate a nation-wide 'Great Debate' on education, in the form of a series of large-scale regional meetings on four main topics: the curriculum, the assessment of standards, school and working life and the education and training of teachers.

Over the next few years it became clear that Government intended to take an approach to the curriculum radically different from that expressed in the statement by

Sir David Eccles quoted above. HMI publications, whilst supporting the idea of a 'common curriculum' continued to emphasise the desire to avoid centralized control and to continue to give teachers discretion as to choice of content and methods. (DES, 1977) But Departmental officers and their advisors were already beginning to pursue a separate agenda (Chitty, 2004: 122). In due course, and under a different government, this was to lead to the Education Act of 1988, the National Curriculum, the reform of inspection, the introduction of national standards of attainment and regular testing of pupils throughout their school lives. The events of this period have been extensively and valuably documented and commented upon (e.g. Chitty (1989, 2004), Lawton (1980, 1984, 2004) Lawton and Chitty (1988), and will not be discussed further here. Sufficient to say that by the end of the 1980s, and in sharp contrast to the position four decades earlier, teachers were left in little doubt about what they should teach, what their pupils were expected to learn, and how that knowledge should be tested. This is the context within which much of the contemporary discussion of teachers' professional freedom takes place.

Policy and Practice

Many of the problems that teachers confront today arise from social and economic factors outside their control. Breakdowns in social integration and control and in family support; problems of intergenerational and intercultural relations; the pressures of a consumerist and litigious society; anxieties associated with increased awareness of threats of environmental damage and resource depletion; the increasingly visible behaviour and attitudes of an underclass that has difficulty in coping with the complexities of modern life, including the assessment of risk; the widespread use of drugs and their association with crime – all these can impinge upon work in the classroom. Yet even when collaboration with other agencies in minimising their impact is exemplary, teachers' scope for effective action is limited. This poses problems that either did not exist or were less evident in earlier decades, and places many more demands on teachers than those I experienced more than half a century ago.

Recent surveys, however, suggest teacher's concerns focus on their work in the classroom rather than on their role in society. For example, a large-scale survey of teacher opinion undertaken by MORI for the General Teaching Council for England and the Guardian newspaper in 2003 (Guardian, 2003) showed that:

> Teachers by and large feel respected by their colleagues, parents and students. They enjoy working with young people, feel a sense of personal achievement and believe they are good at their jobs.
>
> But many feel ground down by paperwork and the target-setting culture to the point where they are ready to leave… Asked to list the three factors which most demotivated them, 56% plumped for this one. The teachers were prompted by a range of options and could have offered their own suggestions.
>
> …the other factors most often cited – initiative overload and the target-driven culture – suggest that many are unhappy about their treatment by the government and employers…

Studies of teacher professionalism have multiplied in recent years. Hall (2004) offers a very useful summary and bibliography, focusing upon what worries and concerns teachers. Along with longstanding issues such as pressure on time, absence of effective sanctions in dealing with difficult pupils and lack of political and public respect for their efforts, have been added the demands of curriculum prescription, testing, examinations and inspection, and the increased stress to which all these give rise. There is widespread concern about loss of freedom, increased manageralism and bureaucracy.

When the pace of educational innovation leads to a stream of new educational initiatives from governments over a relatively short period, conflicting and inconsistent objectives and priorities can arise. For example, teachers may deem actions which produce better test results more important than the achievement of broader educational objectives. It was just this outcome that policy makers were seeking to avoid when in1947 the Ministry of Education's Pamphlet No. 9 stated that secondary modern teachers would be free '....to plan the curriculum of the school on purely educational lines' (Ibid.).

In 2006 the results of a study of several hundred teachers undertaken within the Economic and Social Research Council's *Teaching and Learning Research Programme* (ESRC, 2006) showed that teachers were conscious of tensions existing between the objective of helping students to be more effective learners and that of ensuring the best test results.

> ....only about 20 per cent of [the]...sample of teachers felt able to put effective teaching for learning before teaching to targets and tests. Those who were able to give priority to helping students to become independent learners were usually teachers who had a strong sense of their own responsibility and believed that they could make a difference. One school in which the majority of teachers held this view was also a school where exam results were exceptionally good. This suggests that if teachers concentrate on good learning, the results will follow without teaching to the test.

Teachers value freedom of decision and action as much as practitioners in other fields, and many feel constrained by the present focus on accountability and compliance. With well-chosen shots of 'activists' at teacher's annual conferences and carefully selected quotations from their speeches, critics of the professions continue to feed public and political anxieties about the risks of 'producer capture', the danger that schools, hospitals, public transport and universities will be run for the benefit of their staff rather than students, patients or clients. But there is a growing body of opinion, both within and beyond the professions, that although 'producer capture' must indeed be guarded against, excessive regulation may impinge upon the flexibility, creativity and innovation which are needed to provide services which respect the differing needs of individuals and recognise the absence of consensus as to outcome that characterises plural societies.

This perception has already begun to influence the organisation and conduct of inspection, the availability of opportunities for continuing professional development, the way in which bodies such as the Teacher Development Agency fulfil their role, and an emphasis on collaborative professionalism. On the basis of a survey of primary teachers, the Association of Teachers and Lecturers was able to report in early 2006

> ... [the survey] illustrates that there have been more changes in teachers' attitudes and practices in the last 5 years than in the previous 20 years. Despite criticisms of over-prescription, *Coming full circle?* demonstrates widespread endorsement by teachers and headteachers of the changes in teaching methods developed through the national literacy and numeracy strategies. Teaching methods have also been enhanced by ICT and the role of teaching assistants. Teachers perceive that the way in which they have responded to the reforms has contributed to their professionalism. The primary national strategy is welcomed as acknowledging teachers' professional judgement by enabling them not only to innovate but also to put back into the primary curriculum that which had been lost. A recurrent theme in the research was the perception that education policy is "coming full circle".
>
> (ATL, 2006)

It may be, of course, that teachers have, *faute de mieux,* simply come to terms with the loss of freedom suffered in comparison with earlier decades and with the inevitable restrictions of the 'compliance culture'. Few still serving will have had first hand experience of what teaching was like before governments stepped in. More significantly, as Hoyle and Wallace (2005) make clear, heads and teachers have also learned how to exercise the opportunities that still exist to display personal initiative and make choices as to content and methods in their classroom practice. To do so is not to subvert democratically enacted policies and practices, but to take into account local realities that are inevitably difficult to reflect in overall legislation.

The problems teachers encounter today in interpreting and mediating official policies and practices are not new. The processes involved are now more self-conscious and complex than was once the case, but have affinities with how Victorian school masters and mistresses dealt with payment by results, and secondary modern teachers in the 1950s worked round regulations that forbade the use of public funds to pay examination entry fees.

Hoyle and Wallace (2005) document how teachers, in order to mediate and work round policy ambiguities and conflicting external demands in ways not inconsistent with their own professional values and commitments, respond to officially mandated initiatives by adopting an *ironic* stance. Their analysis is focused on recent and contemporary events but has wider applications.

In every society, requirements set by governments are exposed to interpretation and mediation. 'Implementation slippage' is a familiar reality. In democratic societies it can and does lead to policy change if it is realized that to maintain consent and avoid damaging conflict requires, not rigid adherence to rules and regulations, but the careful exercise of judgment.

Matthew Arnold, the Victorian poet and school inspector, knew this when in the in the context of 'payment by results', he wrote the following commentary on the extension of the number of subjects in which students could be presented for examination:

> More free play for the inspector, and more free play, in consequence, for the teacher, is what is wanted.......In the game of mechanical contrivances the teachers will in the end beat us; and as it is now found possible, by ingenious preparation, to get children through the Revised Code examination in reading, writing, and ciphering, without their really knowing how to read, write, or cipher, so it will with practice no doubt be found possible to get the three-fourths of the one-fifth of the children over six through the examination in grammar, geography, and history, without their really knowing any one of these three matters.
>
> (Annual Reports, 1867–68: 297, quoted Rappell, 1994)

Rappell (1994) also quotes evidence from other contemporary reports on the extent to which both pupils and teachers employed a variety of devices to 'work round' the examination process

> The propensity of schoolchildren to copy during tests was certainly not dampened during the period of payment by results. Indeed, many inspectors complained of a high incidence of copying or "looking over" during the examination ....Mr. Tremenheere, for example, in 1879 declared that he had detected such dishonesty in no fewer "than 46 of the 210 'adolescent' departments" visited by him during the year. Mr. Pennethorne wittily advised in 1875 that the authorities should take especial care that they appoint no short-sighted Inspectors ......ploys to fool the inspector were not confined to the pupils. There were frequent complaints that teachers sometimes endeavored to obtain copies of the arithmetic questions set by the H.M.I.s in other schools and then drilled their pupils in them in the hope that the same or similar questions would be asked in their own schools. Spencer relates that when he was a teacher he and his colleagues used to copy down the arithmetic questions from the inspector's cards and to forward them.
>
> "....to friends in other schools not yet examined in order that they might put in some quite useful practice. 'This was quite fair, so it appeared to us. Towards our colleagues in other schools it was, indeed, chivalrous, for it gave them a chance of outdoing us; towards the inspectors we also considered it to be cricket: they were our examiners, and it was lawful to outwit them, if we could, by any device not plainly in the nature of a verbal lie".

Nearly a century later, 1950s Regulations specified that pupils could not be entered for external examinations apart from the General Certificate of Education unless they were 16 at the beginning of September in the year in which the examination was held. Since the school leaving age was still 15, and the examinations for which schools wished to enter their pupils were intended to provide leaving certificates for those who left at this age, the regulation effectively prohibited secondary modern schools from entering pupils and paying their fees. But it did not prevent parents from doing so, with the effect that in the words of the Beloe Committee report of 1960 (Ministry of Education, 1960: 16)

> ....parents have at their own expense with encouragement from the teachers and from the examining bodies, been acting in a manner contrary to the spirit if not to the letter of the Minister's policy.

Here again, the realities of what was happening led to a change policy.

Conclusion

Teachers today do not enjoy the kind of professional freedom I experienced in the early 1950s. They face increased responsibilities, are exposed to more criticism, and are more frequently judged by external standards than was the case in former decades. But the opportunities are there for 'extended professionalism' of the kind that Hoyle advocated in the 1970s (Hoyle, 1974, 1980). Advantage can be taken of well organised support networks and opportunities for continuing professional development such as hardly existed in the 1950s. Teachers can readily access a vast range of materials relevant to their work. There is a clearer structure of professional progression, and of rewards commensurate with responsibilities. Schools are led and managed by men and women who have in most cases undergone systematic preparation for their tasks.

Teachers today, despite all the difficulties they face, are better placed to make informed choices in respect of those not inconsiderable areas of their work still open to individual and group discretion than were many of us who started in the profession in the middle of the last century. As Hoyle and Wallace (2005: 191) wisely put it:

> Virtually all studies of teacher satisfaction indicate teachers' preference not for total autonomy, which is in any case unrealizable, but autonomy within supportive structures and guidelines…..There is really no alternative. As long as the basic technology of teaching remains centred on the teaching-and-learning-group, conceding a substantial degree of autonomy to teachers within the acceptable parameters of surveillance and its costs is inevitable.

References

ATL (Association of Teachers and Lecturers) (2006) Coming full circle: the impact of New Labour's education policies on primary school teachers' work. Retrieved November 14, 2006, from http://www.atl.org.uk/atl_en/resources/publications/research/Coming_full_circle.asp

Barnes, A. (1977) Decision Making on the Curriculum in Britain, in Glatter, R. (ed) *Control of the Curriculum: Issues and Trends in Britain and Europe.* (London: University of London Institute of Education)

Board of Education (London) (1927) *Handbook of Suggestions for Teachers.* (London: HMSO)

Booker, C. (1980) *The Seventies.* (Harmondsworth, UK: Penguin)

Chitty, C. (1989) *Towards a New Education System: The Victory of the New Right* (London: The Falmer Press)

Chitty, C. (2004) *Education Policy in Britain.* (London: Palgrave Macmillan)

Dent, H.C. (1944) *The Education Act 1944* (London: University of London Press)

Dent, H.C. (1977) *Curriculum* 11–16

ESRC (2006) *Testing Time for Teachers as well as Students.* ESRC Press release, 10 August 2006. Retrieved November 14, 2006, from http://www.esrc.ac.uk/ESRCInfoCentre/PO/releases/2006/august/testing.aspx?ComponentId = 16218&SourcePageId = 1

Hall, C. (2004) Theorising Changes in Teachers' Work in *Canadian Journal of Educational Administration and Policy,* July, *32,* 1–14

Guardian (2003) Retrieved 14 November 2006 from http://education.guardian.co.uk/teachershortage/story/0,,870045,00.html

Gordon, P. (ed.) (1980) *The Study of Education: Inaugural Lectures, Volume 2, The Last Decade.* (London: The Woburn Press)

Hoyle, E. (1974) Professionality, professionalism and control in teaching. *London Educational Review 3 2,* 13–19

Hoyle, E. (1980) Professionality and deprofessionalism in education in Hoyle E. and Megarry J. (eds.) *The Professional Development of Teachers, World Yearbook of Education.* (London: Kogan Page)

Hoyle, E. and John, P.D (1995) *Professional Knowledge and Professional Practice.* (London: Cassell)

Hoyle, E. and Wallace, M. (2005) *Educational Leadership: Ambiguities, Professionals and Managerialism.* (London: Sage)

Lawrence, I. (1992) *Power and Politics at the Department of Education and Science.* (London: Cassell)

Lawson, J. and Silver, H. (1973) *A Social History of Education in England.* (London: Methuen)

Lawton, D. (1978) The end of the 'Secret Garden'?, in Gordon, P. (ed.) (1980) *The. Study of Education 2.* (London: Woburn)

Lawton, D. (1980) *The Politics of the School Curriculum.* (London: Routledge)

Lawton, D. (1984) *The Tightening Grip: Growth of Central Control of the School Curriculum.* (London: Institute of Education)

Lawton, D. (2004) *Education and Labour Party Ideologies 1900–2001 and Beyond.* (London: Routledge Falmer)

Lawton, D. and Chitty, C. (eds) (1988) *The National Curriculum.* (London: Institute of Education)

Ministry of Education (1947) *The New Secondary Education.* Pamphlet No 9 (London HMSO)

Ministry of Education (1960) *Secondary School Examinations other than the GCE: Report of a Committee Appointed by the Secondary School Examinations Council.* (Beloe Committee)

Morris, B. (1977) *Some Aspects of Professional Freedom of Teachers.* (Paris: United Nations Educational, Scientific and Cultural Organisation).

Pateman, T. (1977) 'Accountability, Values and Schooling' Retrieved on 14 November 2006 from www.selectedworks.co.uk/accountabilityeducation.html

Rappell, B.A. (1994) Payment by Results: An Example of Assessment in Elementary Education from Nineteenth Century Britain. *Education Policy Analysis Archives 2, 1* Retrieved on 14 November 2006 from http://epaa.asu.edu/epaa/v2n1.html

Sandbrook, D. (2005) *'Never Had It so Good: A History of Britain from Suez to the Beatles.* (London: Little Brown)

Taylor, W. (1963) *The Secondary Modern School.* (London: Faber)

Times Educational Supplement 15 October 1976

Chapter 15
From Loose to Tight and Tight to Loose: How Old Concepts Provide New Insights

David H. Hargreaves

In 1965 I became lecturer in the social psychology of education in the Department of Education at the University of Manchester. Eric Hoyle had been appointed as the lecturer in the sociology of education some months earlier. One of the justifications for our appointment was the urgent need to train college of education lecturers in the basic disciplines of education (psychology, sociology, philosophy and history) that would become the backbone of the newly established BEd degrees in the drive to create an all graduate teaching profession.

Eric and I soon planned courses for these 'students', as well as practising teachers pursuing advanced diplomas and masters degrees. Every Friday evening – what a time of the week!– they listened in huge numbers to an hour of Eric on sociology and then an hour from me on social psychology. Then everyone staggered home or into the local pub. It was easy for the two of us to divide the terrain: Eric was fairly 'macro' in orientation and I was naturally 'micro'. Some of the common ground between us was the school as an organization. Eric played a major role in developing this field within the sociology of education, of course, and perhaps even more so in the adjacent field of the sociology of innovation and its diffusion. My interests, since I was just preparing for publication my ethnographic study of a secondary modern school, were symbolic interactionist rather than functionalist: Goffman's *Asylums*, with obvious parallels to schools, was one of my favourite books.

Over the years Eric continued to introduce me and his students to new writers and ideas in the field of organisations and to particular journals, especially the *Administrative Science Quarterly*. I was reminded of this recently when thinking about how the structures of secondary schools in England are being questioned by some pioneering headteachers. Since the Manchester days I have consistently tried to read books on organisations, but books about business organisations rather than the school as an organisation – a field that for some strange reason seems to have become almost deserted. I had been reading John Roberts's *The modern firm: organisational design for performance and growth* (2004), which attracted me to

D. Johnson, R. Maclean (eds.), *Teaching: Professionalization, Development and Leadership,*
© Springer Science + Business Media B.V. 2008

his conviction that successful business leaders need to see themselves as organisational designers. This struck me as apposite to the role of headteachers who, in the light of developments in personalisation and building schools for the future, need to become organisational re-designers. In particular, Roberts's idea of 'complementarity' seemed to illuminate work being done by schools on developing student voice, assessment for learning and learning to learn.

In the course of his discussion, Roberts (1994) refers to the notion of 'loosely coupled' organisational designs. He writes that a

> loosely coupled design may offer flexibility and be favoured when changes in the environment or autonomous change in the organisation are likely. Then adjustments can be made where needed and performance maintained, without incurring the costs of massive restructuring of the whole system.

I had not thought much about the concept of loose coupling for some time, but recalled that back in the 1970s, James G March and Karl E Weick, two leading American organisation theorists of the time, questioned a common assumption that the interdependence of the parts of organisations were a constant, rather than a variable. The effect of the assumption of constancy is to treat organisations as much more coherent, unified and stable than they in fact are. The alternative is to treat organisations as loosely-coupled systems in which the constituent elements are autonomous rather than inter-dependent. Some differences between tightly-coupled and loosely-coupled organisations may be listed.

Loosely-coupled organisations have the following features:

- Flat, with distributed leadership
- Poorly co-ordinated but autonomous sub-units
- Difficult to control or change from the top
- Lack standardised operating procedures
- Sub-units are weakly monitored
- Failure in one sub-unit does not spread to damage the rest of the organisation
- Tolerate diversity, creativity and experimentation in sub-units
- Sub-units may be innovative in spite of senior management
- Rely on contagion and informal networks to transfer innovative practice
- A shared culture to create the coherence and cohesion needed for success

Tightly-coupled organisations have the following features:

- Hierarchical, with leadership concentrated at the top
- Inter-dependent or integrated sub-units
- Easier to control or change from the top
- Standardised operating procedures
- Sub-units are closely monitored
- Failure in a sub-unit can imperil the whole organisation
- Sub-units have little freedom to be innovative or experimental
- Punish or expel deviant sub-units
- Rely on top-down direction and instructions to implement new ideas
- A leader with a clear sense of purpose and direction

Weick was fascinated by educational organisations, which he described as 'simultaneously unique, neglected, plentiful and puzzling'. In his famous article in the *Administrative Science Quarterly* (Weick, 1976), he interpreted educational organisations that, like other organisations such as hospitals, are staffed by professionals, as loosely coupled, a state of affairs that he believed to be broadly beneficial. John Roberts used Weick to propose a similar line for the modern firm.

Traditionally in England, the professional autonomy of teachers meant that classrooms were loosely-coupled, for what went on there hinged on the judgment of the teacher and in any event was usually weakly monitored by senior management. Indeed, the term 'loosely coupled' when applied to schools usually refers to teacher autonomy and the insulation of each classroom for external interference, even by colleagues and superiors. Both Eric and I began our teaching careers when this professional autonomy was exceptionally high. The content of what we taught, the curriculum, was a matter for our professional judgement when not constrained by the demands of public examinations; and the same was true for our assessment practices. No colleague would have thought it appropriate to tell us how to teach, even if we were patently in need of help: that would be to infringe our professional autonomy.

In England during the 1970s many teachers and headteachers made their reputation by innovating but moving to a new post before the effects of the innovation could be judged. After their departure, the innovation usually disappeared without trace. Since some of these innovations were of dubious value, this was no bad thing. But it also meant that some of the best innovations were also fated to a short life.

Richard Elmore (2000), an American expert on school reform, sees this as one of the causes of failure to improve school and raise student achievement. Loose-coupling, he argues

> explains why most innovation in schools, and the most durable innovations, occur in the structures that surround teaching and learning, and only weakly and idiosyncratically in the actual processes of teaching and learning... Loose-coupling also explains why manifestly successful instructional practices that grow out of research or exemplary practice never take root in more than a small proportion of classrooms and schools.

With the advent of national curriculum and national testing in the late 1980s, when combined with a much stronger inspection system and other forms of accountability, it seems that both the individual school and the education system as a whole have become much more tightly-coupled. Any teacher who entered the profession after 1980 and the introduction of the national curriculum in England has little conception of the professional autonomy exercised by an earlier generation of teachers over curriculum and assessment.

In 1997 the new Labour government tightened the system yet further. Whereas under previous Conservative governments central control of the curriculum and assessment had been increased, curriculum organisation and pedagogy were still a matter for the professional judgement of teachers. But the new government quickly moved to the national literacy, numeracy and key stage three strategies that unquestionably sought to tighten central control over pedagogy as well as curriculum and assessment.

One of New Labour's educational principles was that intervention would be in inverse proportion to success. 'Where schools are evidently successful,' asserted the White Paper, 'we see no benefit in interfering with their work.' Some would dispute whether this apparent promise was ever kept. Michael Barber, who acted as the main ideas man for education ministers, thought that tighter coupling was an essential step to get the education service back on track before allowing a new era of loose coupling. He did not, of course, express it is such sociological terms. His neat account was a movement from informed prescription from the centre to informed professionalism when young teachers had earned their new autonomy (and older teachers regained some of their old autonomy).

Reflection on these matters made me realise that in fact there are three forms of loose-coupling that must be distinguished. There is *professional loose-coupling* that refers to high levels of teacher autonomy. There is also *institutional loose-coupling* that refers to the nature of the coupling between administrative structures. I specify just three of the latter.

- In almost every secondary school – and not just in England – students are divided into age-cohorts, and usually into year groups. This is not, of course, based on any theory or model of learning. It is rooted in administrative convenience, since it is easier to admit students just once a year and keep them together as they pass through the system.
- The school year in divided into terms (usually three, but more recently in some areas into five or six) with set holidays in between them. Each term is divided into weeks and days, and each day is divided into lessons (usually between five and seven). This schedule for units of teaching and learning is ubiquitously referred to as a *timetable of lessons*.
- Since the establishment of the comprehensive system, schools have been administratively divided into an academic (or curriculum) side and a pastoral side. Both are usually grounded in the year group.

Clearly these are examples of very tight institutional coupling. These are hardly noticed in the literature, or by practitioners, because they are so common and have been part of schooling for such a very long time. These are so basic to the notion of school that it is hard to imagine a school without them – not least for parents as they look back on their own schooldays. Indeed, it is hard to imagine a more tightly-coupled system.

There is also a third form of coupling, namely *inter-institutional loose coupling* that refers to the autonomy a school enjoys in relation to other schools and organizations. Traditionally inter-institutional couping has been very loose. Individual schools have guarded their autmy jealously, and this has been reinforced whenever governments have encouraged competition between schools.

The nineteenth-century imaginary and model of schooling, then, is characterised by institutional tight-coupling but also by professional loose-coupling. Yet it is precisely this institutional tight-coupling that schools are now challenging in response to the demands of personalisation. Such school leaders are asking whether these features are designed to serve the interests of the school and the staff or those of the students and their learning needs. Their answer is to try alternative forms that might better meet students' learning needs. Thus a few schools are moving to a 'stage not age' structure, in which children are not grouped into streams, sets or mixed-ability groups within a year cohort, but are grouped by achievement and aptitude within three age cohorts. In other words, most classes contain students from what are conventionally three distinct and separate year groups.

Similarly, a small number of schools are now moving towards a 24/7/364 model to replace the conventional school day, school term and school year. The school will be open for much longer hours and on most days. Teachers and students do not put in any more hours, but both staff and students work on a flexi-time basis.

Traditional pastoral systems are also being abolished. Most practitioners do not know or remember why the pastoral systems, mainly year groups, were created with the establishment of comprehensive schools. It was then argued that large comprehensives would need much more student support than had been provided in the small grammar schools and secondary moderns that they replaced. But it was also essential to find decent posts for the ex-secondary modern teachers, whose career structure collapsed when head of department posts in the new comprehensives were seized by former grammar-school teachers. Today these pastoral systems are giving way to student support systems that are much more focused on learning, and vertical tutor groups that mix students of different ages are replacing year groups.

With regard to inter-institutional coupling, schools are becoming much more closely linked with other schools under a variety of terms – clusters, collaboratives, federations (hard and soft), trusts, families of schools. In some cases this new coupling is very tight indeed, as governing bodies of several schools in a cluster or federation are merged into a single entity, and one headteacher becomes the 'executive priniciple' of several schools. Arrangements for post-14 vocational education and the new specialist diplomas are leading headteachers to forge new forms of collaboration between secondary schools and with colleges of further education.

Such headteachers are following Peter Drucker's advice (Drucker, 1995) that organisations should question their practices and abandon those that inhibit the innovation essential to meeting changed demands.

> Every three years, an organisation should challenge every product, every service, every policy...with the question: If we were not in it already, would we be going into it now? By questioning accepted policies and routines, the organisation forces itself to think about its theory. It forces itself to test assumptions... Without systematic and purposeful abandonment, an organisation will be overtaken by events. It will squander its best resources on things it should never have been doing or should no longer do... In other words, it will be unable to respond constructively to the opportunities that are created when its theory of the business becomes obsolete.

Thus these school leaders question long taken-for-granted structures, since it is these structures that are inhibiting the teacher led innovation and structural flexibility for students that personalisation demands. They use personalisation to frame the school's strategic intent, which requires the abandonment of some traditional practices and the establishment of groups of teachers who are not autonomous, but work collaboratively in teams and so in a new form of professional tight-coupling. In short, they reject the nineteenth-century combination of professional loose-coupling with institutional tight-coupling in favour of a twenty-first century educational model with its organisational design that combines professional tight-coupling with institutional loose-coupling and inter-institutional tight-coupling.

It is thus that schooling is being given a new shape. With luck this revolution will demand from social scientists new work on the fields of educational organisations and educational innovation whose foundations Eric Hoyle so brilliantly established a generation ago.

References

Peter Drucker, *Managing in a time of great change*, Oxford, UK, Butterworth Heinemann, 1995.

Richard F Elmore, *Building a new structure for school leadership*, Washington, DC, The Albert Shanker Institute, 2000.

John Roberts, *The modern firm: organisational design for performance and growth*, Oxford, Oxford University Press, 2004.

Karl E Weick, 'Educational organizations as loosely coupled systems,' *Administrative Science Quarterly*, vol. 21, pp. 1–19, 1976.

Chapter 16
The Place of Theory in the Professional Training of Teachers

Harold Entwistle

In the literature on professionalization, it used to be assumed that one of the necessary criteria for an occupation to be categorized as a profession is that its practitioners should have a command of some form of esoteric knowledge. From time to time however, this assumption that a profession requires an esoteric cognitive base has been called into question from both ideological ends of the political spectrum. From the Left, the distrust of specialized knowledge has been rooted in its equalitarian ideology: arguably, no-one has any right to exclusive knowledge which gives access to either social or economic privilege; or, in an educational context, which has the effect of defining learners as essentially ignorant and utterly subservient to 'authoritarian' teachers. This assumption that a practitioner's knowledge should be exoteric – available to anyone – is tantamount to the conclusion that anyone ought to be able to practise any occupation. Logically, it also seems to entail that anyone is competent to teach in schools.

From the neo-conservative Right, the objection to esoteric professional knowledge has been economically motivated. Such cognitive pretensions allegedly get in the way of the proper functioning of the market, especially the labour market, by setting an artificial obstacle to the movement of people between occupations in response to free market economic forces. Familiarly, it was one of Mrs. Thatcher's ambitions to impose the same economic discipline upon the professions by attacking their restrictive practices that she had effectively succeeded in inflicting upon the trade unions. The claim that esoteric knowledge is a necessary requirement for practising a profession amounted to one such restrictive practice.

Both of these objections, from the Left and the Right, are in the spirit of Bernard Shaw's conclusion that "all professions are a conspiracy against the laity".

Historically, however, there has also been resistance from many practising teachers to the view that theoretical knowledge of educational principles makes any significant contribution to classroom practice. And, occasionally, this view has been underlined by educational theorists themselves. I recall a Senior Professor at an English

D. Johnson, R. Maclean (eds.), *Teaching: Professionalization, Development and Leadership,*
© Springer Science + Business Media B.V. 2008

University where I once taught responding in an examiners' meeting to criticism that our students found nothing practically useful in the educational psychology which he and others were teaching, by claiming that the only relevant 'theoretical' guides to classroom practice are common sense and worldly wise axioms or aphorisms like, 'Praise is better than blame', 'Don't expect them to sit still for too long', 'When they get restive, give them something to do', 'Test them at frequent intervals', 'Give them feedback as soon as possible', 'Open the windows to get a good through draft and help them to keep awake' and so on. So much for the wit and wisdom of R.S. Peters, William Taylor, Basil Bernstein, Brian Simon, Paul Hirst, and other academic worthies who were at the cutting edges of educational theory at the time and who, under the general editorship of William Tibble, edited a series of texts in the Routledge Students Library of Education. Eric Hoyle himself had a best selling text, *The Role of the Teacher*, in this series and it is interesting to speculate whether these short texts on various aspects of educational theory and practice had any significant influence on the work of the schools at that time.

Interestingly, the rather daunting view that practice can only be illuminated by exoteric common sense was not only advanced in relation to education. It focuses a problem faced by theorists in other academic disciplines having an assumed application to some human activity in the 'real' world. For example, Ely Devons, who was Professor of Applied Economics at the University of Manchester, wrote a paper in which he wondered what theory he was applying when businessmen and bureaucrats canvassed his opinion on the economic problems they were facing. He concluded that he was not drawing upon any of the complicated graphs, statistical techniques or theoretical explanations which were taught in the courses in economic theory, but on simple commonsense axioms like, 'You can't have your cake and eat it', 'Don't throw good money after bad' and so on. Other economists have also taken a similar position on the pedestrian origins of their discipline, as have philosophers on theirs. Kant believed that his philosophical theories should agree with common sense and it has been suggested that Rawles's elaborately argued concept of justice is reducible to the commonly understood idea of fairness. Natural scientists have made similar claims that the origins of scientific explanation are to be found in "those formulations in everyday language to deal with everyday situations…it was out of untechnical descriptions that the technical language of science grew" (see Devons, 1961; Robbins, 1949; Rawls, 1971; Harré, 1960).

If these claims by leading scholars that their practical recommendations are rooted in common sense, not in abstract, abstruse theories, are credible, it is clear that something other than a crudely utilitarian justification is required for theoretical studies in many university disciplines. Otherwise, there would seem to be little point in the academic disciplines, other than the provision of employment for academics or as the playthings of intellectuals. The question is what such a non-utilitarian (or differently utilitarian) justification could be, especially for the study of academic educational theory.

My Senior Professor who disclaimed any practical value for the educational psychology he taught went on to say something which suggested a possible value of purely theoretical studies for teachers in the classroom. In his view, the psychology lectures (and, implicitly, the courses in educational philosophy, sociology and history) were offered by the Department only as a furthering of the liberal education of our students. Knowing the dry and statistically oriented presentations that the Ed. Psych. lectures were, my own unspoken 'reply' was, "Well if that's the case, if further liberal education is the aim, wouldn't they be better off studying D.H. Lawrence or Proust, or the history of the French Revolution?". Or, perhaps, if they were graduates in the Humanities, in learning the significance of e = mc² or the structure of DNA.

It has been the conventional wisdom to dismiss liberal education as practically useless, good only for its own sake and, hence, to be pursued disinterestedly without any expectation from the learner of any practical payoff. However, I shall presently argue that, to the contrary, a liberal education does necessarily have practical implications and that it is precisely this utilitarian value of a liberal education which gives theoretical knowledge, whether of Ed. Psych. or history, sociology and philosophy of education, a legitimate place in the curriculum of teacher education.

However, I first want to say something more about the problems of relating theory to practice and the implications which this has for both the teaching of theory and the quality of practice. I proceed from the following assumptions: that a body of esoteric knowledge *is* necessary for the professionalization of teaching; that this knowledge should consist primarily of that aspect of the culture which the teacher is required to teach – usually one of the academic disciplines; and that so far as the teacher's education should encompass some educational theory, this essentially has a role in his or her further liberal education and should not be seen as a collection of recipes for how to cook up a good lesson in the classroom.

There used to be a widespread assumption – which may still exist – that knowledge of an academic subject only gets in the way of teaching because "We teach children, not subjects". Especially, teachers in secondary schools who had good degrees in an academic subject, but no teacher training, were axiomatically assumed to be poor teachers. One's own experience of English secondary education some seventy years ago proves this to have been sometimes true, though as often false. But, oddly, that same pedagogic opinion which believed untrained graduates to be ineffective teachers has also often dismissed educational theory – whether in the educational disciplines of philosophy, psychology, sociology and history or in the pre-discipline synthesized 'mush' of Principles of Education – as "All very well in theory but useless in practice".

There is an extreme child-centred ideology which completely dismisses the notion that, above all, teachers need a culture to teach. This was implicit in the notions which gained popularity, especially three or four decades ago, that schooling is not about transmission of, or initiation into, the various forms of knowledge into which human experience of the natural and social universes has been structured. This assumption has, from time to time, been stated explicitly, as in Ruskin's mid-nineteenth century insistence "that education does not mean teaching people to know what they do not know: it means teaching them to behave as they do not behave". An emphasis on doing, being or feeling has often been substituted in educational rhetoric for knowing. This is acceptable so far as it goes, but it begs the obvious question of how far being, feeling or action of any quality and intelligence can exist without a cognitive core. And despite the extreme anti-intellectual rhetoric, there are few teachers who enter their classrooms without the assumption, however reluctant, that their primary stock-in-trade is some aspect of the culture in which they and their pupils live. It is interesting that a century ago, John Dewey, the authority for much child-centred educational rhetoric, implied that anyone intending to teach mathematical concepts and processes to young children should herself be a skilled mathematician: "Really to interpret the child's present crude impulses in counting, measuring, and arranging things in rhythmic series involves mathematical scholarship – a knowledge of the mathematical formulae and relations which have, in the history of the race, grown out of just such crude beginnings" (Dewey, 1902, 1952). Following Dewey, whether we call it a subject, a discipline, a worthwhile activity, a form of knowledge or a realm of meaning, I take it as axiomatic that a teacher's professionalism depends upon the scope and quality of her own cultural and academic knowledge.

Until shortly after World War II, it was assumed that knowledge of a discipline was the only cognitive capital needed for teachers in secondary schools. But as we have already seen, these were often faulted for being quite incapable of functioning effectively in a classroom, despite their disciplinary erudition: hence the insistence on postgraduate teacher training for all graduate entrants to the profession and the eventual establishment of an all graduate profession with the introduction of the B.Ed. degree.

The discussions which accompanied the institutionalisation of the B.Ed. often reflected a dichotomy between those who favoured a discipline-based initiation into the subject matter which the teacher was probably destined to teach and those who held that a knowledge of how to teach should take precedence, with a focus upon longer internships or teaching practice and, so far as there was to be a theoretical component, an emphasis upon educational theory over subject matter from the school curriculum. But this latter requirement for more practice and an emphasis upon educational theory raised other questions; in particular, if it is simple, commonsense, everyday axioms that are practically relevant in the classroom, what is the point of academic educational theory as a basis for pedagogical practice?

We have already noted a tendency of practitioners to dismiss theory as irrelevant to their daily endeavours in the classroom. There are a number of reasons for this (Hare and Portelli, 1996)[1] but one of them is a misunderstanding of what theory is, especially in relation to practice. There is not room here to explore this point at length, but a quotation from Kant is helpful: "A set of rules presented in a certain generality and with disregard of particular circumstances is called a theory...a practitioner must exercise his judgement to decide whether a case falls under a general rule" (Rubel, 1963).[2] This point has been re-iterated more recently by

---

[1] I have suggested a number of reasons for the difficulties encountered in attempting to relate theory with practice in my essay *The Relationship between Theory and Practice*: *A New Look* (see Hare and Portelli, 1996).

[2] Kant's essay, "On the saying 'That may be all right in theory but is no good in practice'" (see Rubel, 1963).

Schön: "An overarching theory does not give a rule that can be applied to predict or control a particular event, but it supplies language from which to construct particular descriptions and themes from which to develop particular interpretations" (Schön, 1983).

This is to say that the job of a theory is to evoke judgement rather than rote obedience. The application of theory to practice means bringing critical intelligence to bear on practical tasks, rather than merely implementing good advice. Some initiative is required from the practitioner in discovering the pertinence of theory to his or her own peculiar practical situation. But if practitioners do not do this, or do not know how to do it, this may be a fault that we have to lay at the door of teachers of theory, rather than dismissing it as an example of teacher anti-intellectualism. Too often in the past, educational theories have been taught, not as analytical tools, but as ideologies or dogmas which brook no argument. Just as teacher educators should confront students with the fact that compromise is a fact of life in classrooms, so also should they accept the fact that part of the teaching of educational theory must consist of teaching exactly what a theory is, what it can and cannot be expected to do for practice and the various ways in which theories have to be applied, especially by practitioners, in an active, thoughtful and creative sense, not passively as though applying pre-digested instructions or advice. The application of theory to practice, instead of being an exercise in faithfully carrying out good advice, is rather a matter of learning to ask a variety of questions about practical situations with the guidance of relevant axioms or generalizations. This insistence upon the practitioner's responsibility for *actively* applying theories, exercising judgement or critical intelligence, can be summed up in Schön's notion of *the reflective practitioner* in his book of that name.

Schön illustrates his thesis mainly by reference to professions other than teaching: architecture and the law, for example. He devotes only a few pages to teaching. But by inference we can say that with reference to schooling, the notion of the reflective practitioner is the idea of a professional in a practical situation, confronting a problem and the opportunities it affords, asking intelligent, well informed questions about the situation, acting in a manner suggested by the answers to these questions, evaluating the results, reflecting again upon the implications of these, and so on. The result of this interpenetration of theory with practice is to develop what is sometimes called *praxis*. Out of this continuous reflection on practice, one develops one's own *praxis*, one's own practice-relevant theory, one's own characterizations of what one is trying to do in the classroom, why one succeeds or sometimes fails, what has to be done to accommodate to the failure, either by improving one's practice or, perhaps, by redefining the problem. This raises the question of what it is that prompts the practitioner to critical reflection on his or her own practice; and, especially, what, if anything, academic educational theory can contribute to intelligent reflection on the practice of teaching.

We have seen that even for some educational theorists the answer to this question is 'Nothing'. At the end of the day, when a primary school teacher, for example, is reflecting on her day, it is arguable that she is most likely to engage in homespun reflections on the idiosyncrasies and behaviours of individual children; wondering if a particular child had been unwell, or feeling the strain of family breakdown, or is watching too much television too late at night; or whether the class was distracted by interruptions from outside, perhaps a change in the weather; or how some of them did Math last year with Miss Smith who really drills them in the fundamentals, whilst others were with the charismatic Mr. Jones who is a super teacher of the Language Arts but who is bored to distraction by Math and does not do much more than go through the motions. These everyday commonsense reflections on the teacher's own day may be more or less insightful and profitable but they seem to owe nothing at all to a knowledge of academic educational theory. Evidently, what the practitioner reflecting on his or her day does not do is to wonder what Piaget would have said about these things; or whether Plato or Peters might throw some light on his or her dilemmas; or whether, like so many other things, they do it better in Sweden; or whether, according to Bernstein, it is all a matter of direct or elaborated language codes; or whether it all comes down to the correspondence principle, the point being that we shall never get schooling right until we get rid of capitalism and construct an educational system corresponding to democracy. I do not know which discipline from educational theory I have omitted from that list but, if there is one, the reflective practitioner will not draw upon that either in order to explain his or her day or to plan for a better tomorrow.

Now, it may be the case that in reflecting upon her practice, the teacher rarely makes explicit or conscious reference to academic educational theory. But the problem with leaving reflection upon practice to untutored common sense is that not all homespun reflection on the practical situation in the classroom is equally relevant, sufficiently cogent, or sensitive to interpersonal relationships. And mere reflection from out of a teacher's own untutored cognitive resources may fail to come to grips with the complexity of a practical situation or to explore the range of alternative explanations of classroom phenomena, or alternative solutions of educational problems. Nor is all folk wisdom equally sensitive to the moral issues arising in the classroom. Indeed, one's own experience of staffroom reflection suggests that rednecks, racists, sexists and chauvinists are by no means unknown amongst teachers, nor are teachers who expect nothing of students and whose conception of what it means to be an educated person would make a Dickensian schoolmaster look like a liberal progressive.

I want to suggest that intelligent, well-informed, critical reflection on practice can be an outcome of familiarity with educational theory, however tacitly this theory may enter into thinking about practice. Indeed, the tacit contribution of educational theory to practical teaching may be on all fours with the tacit contribution of a liberal education to life in general, or to particular aspects of life, like citizenship, for example. There are those who believe that a liberal education has no utilitarian value but that it has to be undertaken for its own sake, for intrinsic, not extrinsic reasons. This view was espoused by the foremost English educational philosopher of the latter part of the last century, R.S. Peters. But, oddly, along with P.H. Hirst, Peters also articulated a conception of liberal education which saw the disciplines of the school (what they called worthwhile knowledge) as contributing towards personal development in a way which can only be categorised as *useful* for the development of the person (Peters and Hirst, 1970).[3] To be educated, they suggested, is not to have arrived at a destination but to be traveling with a different point of view. One of the things I take this to mean is that the educated person is not merely one who acquires a repertoire of relevant skills and knowledge which satisfies his needs, ministers to his existing interests and assists in solving problems in the here and now; but also that it transforms his perceptions of what the problems are, what opportunities are offered by life, what new interests might enrich his daily experience. Being educated, one becomes aware of new needs and interests. So the relevance of knowledge has to be tested with reference to the possibility of a changing and developing, not a given, static way of life. As an educated, 'different' person, traveling through life with an expanding point of view, one should be more intelligent, sensitive and knowledgeable in all aspects of life – as a worker, a citizen, at home, at leisure and in all one's personal relationships.

As aspects of liberal knowledge, the disciplines which compound educational theory – psychology, philosophy, history, sociology and comparative studies of education – whether taught in a specialized manner or a synthesized tapestry called something like Principles of Education, ought to be able to provide a similar transformation of the teacher's perspectives that a general liberal education does for the person in his other diverse aspects of life. That is, merely because educational theory does not provide recipes or handbooks of advice applicable to particular classroom situations, this does not mean that it cannot transform perspectives such that the teacher confronts educational problems and classroom dilemmas and opportunities from a different point of view. Educational theory can provide a liberal education, such that the teacher's reflection on practice becomes more intelligent, morally sensitive, capable of making finer conceptual distinctions and more subtle analyses of educational issues, as well as being well informed about the various relevant contexts of educational practice. The utilitarian justification for the teaching of educational theory to teachers is the same as the justification for liberal education itself. The teacher, reflecting upon her classroom with more subtle educational theory, is much like the liberally educated citizen reflecting more intelligently upon public affairs (Orteza et al., 1990).[4]

However, this conclusion requires an act of faith. There are those who argue that young people opt to enter teaching with already fixed emotional, moral and intellectual dispositions which are rarely amenable to change. Implicitly, they have entered the profession with inflexible ideas of what teaching entails based upon their own experiences as a student in school. But such a fatalistic conclusion would be sad. We provide public schooling on the assumption that, as R.S. Peters has suggested, education is a process necessarily resulting in improvement: much as the notions of

---

[3] This was one of the volumes in the Students Library of Education series referred to earlier in this paper (Peters and Hirst, 1970).

[4] I have examined the arguments for liberal education as an instrumentally valuable experience, as against the notion that it is valuable intrinsically, providing knowledge only for its own sake, in "Schooling and the Instrumentally Valuable" (see Orteza et al., 1990).

'cure' and 'reform' necessarily entail similar implications for improvement. And it would be especially sad if those who devote themselves to a profession necessarily concerned with the improvement of others should resist the idea that their own professional education is intended to improve their own practice as teachers.

References

Devons, E. *Essays in Economics*, 1961, London, Allen & Unwin.
Dewey, J. *The Child and the Curriculum*, 1902, 1952, Chicago, IL, University of Chicago Press.
Hare, W. and Portelli, J.P. (Ed), *Philosophy of Education – Introductory Readings*, 2nd Edition, 1996, Calgary, Canada, Detselig.
Harré, R. *The Logic of the Sciences*, 1960, London, Macmillan.
Orteza y Miranda, E. and Magsino, R.F. (Ed) *Teaching, Schools and Society*, 1990, London/New York, Falmer.
Peters, R.S. and Hirst, P. *The Logic of Education*, 1970, London, Routledge/Kegan Paul.
Rawls, J. *A Theory of Justice*, 1971, Cambridge, MA, Harvard University Press.
Robbins, L. *An Essay on the Nature and Significance of Economic Science*, 1949, London, Macmillan.
Rubel, G. *Kant*, 1963, Oxford, Clarendon.
Schön, D.A. *The Reflective Practitioner*, 1983, New York, Basic Books.

Chapter 17
Comparative Perspectives on the Changing Roles of Teachers

Patricia Broadfoot

Commentators often remark that schools have changed remarkably little since the 19th century. Unlike say hospitals, in which the paraphernalia of the modern operating theatre means that it would be virtually impossible for a 19th century surgeon to function effectively in it, a teacher in the same situation would immediately recognise the setting, the task and the skills required. They would readily understand the challenge of inculcating a defined body of curriculum content to a classroom group of more or less enthusiastic learners within the parameters of a set timetable and expected outcomes.

But is being a teacher really as standardised as this description implies? Clearly there are more or less significant objective variations in the conditions under which teachers work. In developing countries, there may be no classroom, no equipment and more than fifty pupils in a class. Teachers may be untrained and even unpaid at times. In highly developed countries, teachers will increasingly have access to new technologies – interactive whiteboards, blogs and e-learning platforms that enhance the traditional reliance on 'chalk and talk', books and written work. Some teachers work in highly dirigiste national systems which allow little scope for personal interpretation and professional judgment; others work in the context of intensive testing regimes that drive a results-based culture that also constrains their appetite for innovation and variety of approach.

As this volume makes clear, the enduring legacy of Eric Hoyle's approach to the study of teachers and their work has been to establish the importance of delving beneath the surface of such glib stereotypes; to recognise that as individual professionals, as a staff group within a school and as an occupational group within a particular society, the way teachers take and make their professional practice is subtle, complex and continually changing in response to circumstances and external requirements. Beneath the apparently minor variations from one century to another or from one country to another in the way in which teachers exercise their professional work, lies an enormously significant mix of factors that influence teachers' perceptions of the task in hand, the nature of their engagement in it and consequently, the nature of their impact on the learners in their care. It follows too, that aspirations to improve or change the work of teachers, to make them more motivated and effective or to direct their efforts in new directions, depend for their success on an understanding of the nature of such forces.

D. Johnson, R. Maclean (eds.), *Teaching: Professionalization, Development and Leadership,*
© Springer Science + Business Media B.V. 2008

Hoyle's ground-breaking theoretical work, such as his seminal distinction between 'restricted' and 'extended' professionalism, has inspired an enormous corpus of detailed empirical work designed to identify the influences on teachers' work. His work has informed efforts to evaluate the different professional 'drivers' to which teachers in different settings are subject and hence, to aid in the more general identification of the 'teaching genome'. Such empirical studies have, in turn, provided the foundation for the more recent scholarly focus on the nature of teaching as a profession and what this means for teacher development and leadership in the contemporary educational context. As this book makes clear, Hoyle's work continues to inform a range of international studies designed to illuminate the ways in which the work of teachers around the world today is being shaped by new forces such as intensification and privatisation and what these developments mean for teaching as a profession.

Comparative studies of teachers have proved to be one of the most powerful tools for illuminating the way in which teachers construct their professional identity and the implications of such perspectives for policy implementation and classroom practice. This was the rationale, for example, for a series of comparative studies based at the University of Bristol during the 1980s and 1990s. The first study in the series was a systemically focussed comparison of educational accountability in France and England – two countries regarded at that time at least – as classic examples of centralised and decentralised approaches to the management of educational systems. The enquiry was designed to elicit whether, in practice, these stereotypes of centralisation and decentralisation really were associated with a stronger or weaker experience of central control in practice on the part of teachers. Was it the case in France, for example, that teachers priorities and practices were primarily a response to the directions issuing from the National Ministry of Education as Napoleon had assumed would be the case when he created a strongly centralised education system?

The results of the study suggested a much more complex picture. (Broadfoot, 1985) It found that central directions are inevitably 'watered-down' by the mediation of successive layers of bureaucracy en route to teachers in the classroom as well as the personal interpretation of the intention of these instructions by the many individuals involved in the chain of communication. Thus, in many ways, teachers in France were found to be freer, if they chose to be, than their English counterparts, given that the latter were subject to several additional forms of accountability. The very centralisation of the French system was found to be a protection for teachers against being held to account by parents, head teachers and the local community which was the feeling and experience of the English teachers. Yet, English teachers, by contrast, had a passionate belief in their right to professional autonomy whilst French teachers chose to embrace central control as an ideology as the basis for equality of opportunity and national cohesion. In short, French teachers could have exercised considerable professional discretion but generally chose not to since they believed in the desirability of national consistency. English teachers strove to exercise professional autonomy since this was a defining element of their professional discourse but found themselves heavily constrained by a network of both formal and informal accountability that severely constrained their capacity to exercise such professional autonomy.

Although now somewhat dated, given the very significant changes in both education systems that have since taken place, this study provides powerful testimony to the importance of deconstructing stereotypical interpretations of teacher professionalism and, in particular, the need to understand the reality, rather than the rhetoric of national stereotypes in this light. These important insights into the significant differences between English and French teachers' perspectives and into the gap between rhetoric, and reality in particular, led to the initiation of a much more substantial comparative study of English and French primary teachers' conceptions of their professional responsibility. The 'Bristaix' study, as it came to be called, based as it was jointly on the Bristol and Aix en Provence areas, sought to document through systematic enquiry how primary teachers in these two countries saw their professional priorities and how they thought about key aspects of their work. (Broadfoot et al., 1993).

In seeking to understand the mass of detailed differences identified, Hoyle's concept of 'restricted' and 'extended' professionality emerged as being of critical importance. Hoyle defines 'restricted' professionality as indicating thought and practice that is:

> *intuitive, classroom focussed and based on experience rather than theory. The good restricted professional is sensitive to the development of individual pupils, an inventive teacher and a skilful class manager. He is unencumbered with theory, is not given to comparing his work with that of others, tends not to perceive his classroom activities in a broader context and values his classroom autonomy.*
>
> (Hoyle, 1980: 43)

Extended professionality, by contrast, involves

> being *concerned with locating one's classroom teaching in a broader educational context, comparing one's work with that of other teachers, evaluating one's work systematically and collaborating with other teachers'*. It also involves being interested in theory and current educational developments, reading journals and educational books and *'seeing teaching as a rational activity amenable to improvement on the basis of research and development.*
>
> (Hoyle, 1980: 43)

The Bristaix study found other deep differences in the professionality of teachers in the two countries including 'problematic' versus 'axiomatic' conceptions of teaching and an emphasis on the process rather than the products of learning in England and France respectively. English teachers also tended to hold more 'particularistic' (i.e. individualised) educational goals compared to the more 'universalistic' (i.e. common) goals of French teachers. Not surprisingly, the study concluded that

> *any attempt to at change which fails to take into account the real influences on teachers' professional motivation and practice will be unsuccessful in all respects but one. It may well succeed in eroding the professional commitment inherent in working towards self-imposed goals which is the explicit core of the motivation of both cohorts of teachers in the study reported here. Only then, when it is too late, will the real key to effective educational change be apparent.*
>
> (Broadfoot et al., 1988: 286)

This empirical documentation of the very real differences in the way in which primary teachers in these two countries felt about their work provides some important contemporary lessons of a more general kind in relation to the themes of this book – the professionalization, development and leadership of teachers and the particular issues surrounding teaching as a profession. The Bristaix study demonstrated clearly that teachers' professional perspectives were very different in England and France. It suggested that teachers' professional perspectives were likely to be substantially influenced by the national setting in which they were working and hence, vary significantly from one country to another. It was also possible to hypothesize that variations in teachers' professional perspectives were also likely to be the product of several other social influences in addition to the cultural and institutional traditions of a particular national setting. Significant in this respect is likely to be the teacher's own personal life-history and the 'micro-narrative' of their career experiences.

However, even when the 'Bristaix' study was conducted in the 1980s, there were clear signs that social and political change was beginning to break down national professional stereotypes. Pupils were becoming more diverse in their needs and behaviour; Governments in both countries were becoming more anxious to impose their own educational policy priorities on the education system. During the last two decades, these pressures have strengthened considerably with the intro-duction of considerably greater central control in England with the first ever National Curriculum and Assessment system and the opposite decentralist policy trend in France of trying to empower individual head teachers and schools to enable them better to address the individual circumstances of very different communities. It thus became clear from other comparative studies at this time that the ebb and flow of policy narratives also provide a significant influence on teachers' profes-sional priorities. (Osborn and Broadfoot 1993; Broadfoot et al., 1996) But how best to develop teachers' skills and attitudes in this respect so that they are equipped to respond to the particular and unpredictable challenges of educating children for a rapidly changing world, has become one of the most challenging educational ques-tions of our time. As national educational traditions and assumptions have begun to fragment in response to novel and diverse pressures on the education system, it has become correspondingly more important for Governments in particular to find effective ways of articulating educational priorities in a clear and publicly accepta-ble manner. Even more important, arguably, is policy-makers' capacity to impose these priorities by in turn ensuring that they are incorporated into the professional discourse and priorities of teachers.

Subsequent studies in the Bristol comparative programme, illustrated the scale of this challenge very clearly. In the context of significant policy shifts in both England and France, the 'Quality in Experiences of Schooling Trans-nationally' (QUEST) project, conducted between 1995 and 1997, sought to explore the significance of the differences in *teachers'* perspectives that the Bristaix study had identified for *pupils'* classroom experiences and learning outcomes. Not surprisingly, a comparison of English and French primary school children's achievements revealed that the priorities and tradi-tions of each country were reflected in the profile of strengths and weaknesses identi-fied. French children demonstrated strengths in having mastered taught knowledge and techniques; English children in problem-solving and creativity. (Broadfoot et al., 2000). But which is likely to be more important for the future? How far should national governments be seeking to change the traditional strengths of their education system by seeking to influence teachers to adopt new priorities in response to a rapidly changing world? How can the strength of teachers' professionalism be harnessed to address the implications of such changes when their natural inclination will be to continue to pursue the educational goals and the pedagogic means of achieving these goals that have become enshrined in the national psyche and national tradition?

The complexity of this question is further illustrated by a subsequent study of young secondary pupils in the same two countries but with the addition of Denmark. (Osborn et al., 2003) The ENCOMPASS study confirmed the enduring importance of national traditions and culture in shaping teachers' priorities, their ways of engaging with pupils and their pedagogical approach. The study identified a continuum stretching from 'low distance between teacher and pupil and an emphasis on relationships – the expressive – at one end to high distance between teacher and pupil and an emphasis on cognitive content – the instrumental – at the other. Danish teachers, grounded in the 'Communitarian' tradition, were located at one extreme given their overriding emphasis on relationships and building the social community of the classroom. The 'Cartesian' tradition French teachers were located at the opposite extreme with their contrasting emphasis on cognitive development and intellectual activity in which the pupil as 'person' had little relevance. English teachers, heirs to a 'child-centred' tradition, with their concern for both the social development and happiness of the individual and their intellectual progress, were located between the two extremes. As such, the study confirmed its initial hypothesis derived from the earlier comparative studies discussed above, namely that:

> The policy priorities, institutional arrangements and classroom processes of a national education system are informed by and in turn help to reproduce the deep 'scoio-cognitive' and cultural patterning of a particular nation state.
>
> (Osborn et al., 2003: 215)

It also confirmed that, just as teachers are shaped by the national educational culture and institutional traditions, so too are pupils. This makes it difficult for any generalised 'silver bullet' to be conceived that would help teachers wherever they work, address today's educational challenges despite the fact that these challenges are becoming increasingly similar across different national settings. Despite the fact too, of the increasing evidence to suggest that there are constants – meta-narratives about learning- that are valid beyond the confines of particular cultures. The challenge for teachers, then, in the early 21st century, is to redefine their professional priorities and their pedagogic approach in ways that are in harmony with their deeply rooted, cultural traditions but which are sufficiently innovative to allow them to incorporate a refreshed professional vision that embraces the new challenges and the new educational possibilities of the 21st century.

The ENCOMPASS study concluded that culture must be seen as central to any understanding of education and how it is best delivered in today's world. Comparative studies can show just how important is the culture that defines the features of the national, local, institutional and classroom environment and informs the educational priorities that characterize them. Comparative studies also reveal the importance of the common cultural challenges that globalisation is presenting to schools and teachers – change, diversity and the lack of a clear narrative of tradition or of 'what works'.

At present, teachers in different countries start from very different places in seeking to accommodate the very real pressures associated with globalisation. It is becoming clear internationally that the cultural variants of the familiar model of schools and teaching that 'worked' in the past, is unlikely to 'work' in the future. As Giddens (1993: 268) has argued, the traditional sources of 'ontological security' – trust, predictability and face to face associations which are essential to the 'biographic project' are being eroded. Society is changing in the way that it operates and the skills, knowledge, attitudes and values that it will require of its young people. Yet, paradoxically, government policies derived from anxieties about international competition, have prompted schools across the world to resort to traditional approaches to curriculum, pedagogy and above all, assessment, concentrating on producing human, rather than the desperately needed social, capital. If there is any constant amid the myriad culturally specific factors that influence teachers' priorities and practices, it is that schools are proving very slow to change; that, as suggested at the beginning of this chapter, there is as yet no serious challenge to the familiar 19th century edifice despite the symptoms of educational crisis now manifest in many countries of the world. (Broadfoot, 2007)

The programme of international educational comparisons described here which were conducted over more than three decades, shows how important it is to understand teachers' work as framed by its cultural setting. As such, the studies emphasise the importance of Hoyle's sustained contribution to our understanding of teachers, their work and how they may best be helped to develop over many years. In recent years, the need to understand the interface between teachers and the external pressures they experience as a result of policy changes has become widely recognised. Less widely recognised as yet, is the need to understand teachers' work as a series of interlocking and more or less fluid cultural narratives – individual, institutional, community, national and international. Particularly important is the need to recognise the role of individual agency in cultural production, the need to recognise that teachers are constantly involved in re-shaping their professional perspectives as they engage creatively with the new opportunities and new educational challenges now confronting them.

The ebb and flow of teachers various perceived accountabilities – moral in terms of their duty to their students; professional in terms of their perceived obligation to support colleagues and the head teacher; and contractual in terms of their relationship with the employing authority continues to provide the frame of professional obligations that shape teachers' work. But perhaps most important of all as a professional driver is the impact of personal accountability that mediates and helps to reconcile the sometimes contradictory imperatives that come from these various sources.

Classrooms and schools today may appear superficially familiar to those that first emerged on a mass scale in the 19th century, but in fact they are profoundly different. Indeed, I have suggested that despite appearances, they were already significantly different from each other, even in the 19th century, reflecting as they have always done, the institutional traditions, policy priorities, religious traditions and other cultural features of the different societies that established schools at that time. Equally, despite what may appear to be similarities, the huge number of schools set up around the world during the colonial era are also the product of a unique blend of specific cultural factors. Thanks to the work of scholars such as Hoyle, we now understand much better the dimensions of such differences and the importance of understanding teachers as creators, as well as reflectors of a particular educational culture. We now understand the importance of seeking to understand the 'constants' and the 'contexts' in such responses from a comparative perspective.

Last but not least, we also now understand better the very particular challenges teachers have had to face in asserting their right to be regarded as an autonomous professional group; the struggles they have had in articulating and defending the degree of professional autonomy that is needed if they are to be able to respond adequately to the changing circumstances of those they are required to teach. The recent emphasis on professional development, leadership and the creation of a learning community offers an exciting prospect of greater professional fulfilment for teachers. As the chapter by the late Ray Bolam in this volume documents – the impact of institutional leadership and the scope for enhancing teachers' profes-sionalism that is inherent in the creation of a 'learning community' focussed on professional development offers an exciting prospect for teachers to have much greater scope to create, rather than simply reflect, the cultural currents that will inform their work.

If the long overdue challenge to the 19th century norm of schools and schooling is indeed to materialise, it is likely to come through harnessing the creativity and courage of teachers to think the unthinkable and try the untried. The more we under-stand 'what makes teachers tick', the more means to unlock such energy for change will be identified. These are challenging times for teachers; but they are also exciting times as the real possibility of a refreshed journey of professional discovery begins to open up. Eric Hoyle's work has played a crucial part in launching this journey and in establishing its importance. His work continues to shape the route to be taken and to point to the desired destination. If there are few teachers today whose professional life has not in some way been touched by Hoyle's work, there will be even fewer in years to come whose working life is untouched by his legacy.

References

Broadfoot, P. (1985) 'Changing patterns of educational accountability in England and France', in *Comparative Education*, Vol. 21, No. 3, pp. 273–286

Broadfoot, P., Bruchet, A, Gilly, M. and Osborn, M. (1993) *Perceptions of Teaching: Teachers' Lives in England and France*. London, Cassells

Broadfoot, P. and Osborn, M. with Gilly, M. and Paillet, A. (1988) 'What professional responsibility means to teachers: national contexts and classroom constants', in *British Journal of Sociology of Education*, special issue Vol. 9, No. 3, pp. 265–287

Broadfoot, P. Osborn, M., Planel, C. and Pollard, A. (1996) 'Teachers and change: a study of pri-
    mary school teachers' reactions to policy changes in England and France', in T. Winther-
    Jensen (ed) *Challenges to European Education: Cultural Values, National Identities, and
    Global Responsibilities*. Peter Lang, Europaischer Verlag der Wissenschaften, Frankfurt am
    Main, Berlin
Broadfoot, P., Osborn, M., Planel, C., Sharp, K. and Ward, B. (2000) *Promoting Quality in
    Learning: Has England Got the Answer?* London, Cassell
Broadfoot, P. (2007) *An Introduction to Assessment*. London, Continuum
Giddens, A. (1993) *New Rules of Sociological Method*. Cambridge, Polity
Hoyle, E. (1980) 'Professionalisation and deprofessionalisation in education', in E. Hoyle and
    J. Megarryy (eds) *World Year Book of Education 1980*: *Professional Development of Teachers*,
    pp. 42–54. London, Kogan Page
Osborn, M. and Broadfoot, P. (1993) 'Becoming and being a teacher: the influence of the national
    context', in *European Journal of Education*, Vol. 28, No. 1, pp. 105–116
Osborn,M., Broadfoot, P., McNess, E., Planel, C., Ravn, B. and Triggs, P. (2003) *A World of
    Difference? Comparing Learners Across Europe*. Maidenhead, UK, Open University Press

Chapter 18
The Role of the Private Sector in Higher Education in Malaysia

Thangavelu Marimuthu

Introduction

Malaysia's economic growth since Independence in 1957 has been impressive. The real gross domestic product (GDP) averaged a growth of 6.5% per annum between 1957 and 2005. Malaysia is one of the fastest growing nations amongst the developing countries. It has made great strides in improving the quality of life of its people as well as making advances in the areas of education, health, infrastructure and industry. The country has been transformed from an export oriented economy, which relied mainly on its primary commodities such as rubber, tin and palm oil, a diversified industrial nation.

In 1965, Malaysia was the world's largest producer of both natural rubber and tin, which together accounted for 55% of the country's export and about 30% of GNP. In fact agriculture alone contributed 34% of the GDP in the same year. In 2005 the share of agriculture was only 8.2%, whereas manufacturing (31.4%) and services (58.1%) contributed substantially to the GDP's growth. It is evident that Malaysia has made a major shift from an agrarian to an industrial economy.

The onset of globalization, combined with the technological revolution, especially in Information and Communication Technology (ICT), has given rise to the knowledge economy, which needs an educated, highly skilled workforce.

In 1991, Vision 2020 was announced by the former Prime Minister Tun Dr. Mahathir Mohamad which set the target for the country to be a developed nation by that year. The attainment of Vision 2020 will be accelerated by the strategies enshrined in the National Development Policy (NDP) 1991–2000 and the National Vision Policy (NVP) 2001–2010. The New Economic Policy (NEP) 1971–1990 laid the foundation for the launch of Vision 2020.

In 1996, the Multimedia Super Corridor was established with the purpose of making Malaysia one of the leading global ICT and multimedia hubs in the region. Information and communication technology was considered as the next engine of growth in the knowledge economy. This information superhighway project has involved both international and local companies which needed about 30,000 knowledge workers.

D. Johnson, R. Maclean (eds.), *Teaching: Professionalization, Development and Leadership,*
© Springer Science + Business Media B.V. 2008

Today MSC Malaysia ranks as the third most attractive country after India and China to conduct shared services and outsourcing. It is home to world class companies and local outfits which perform ICT services for multinationals and other global customers (*Straits Times*, Nov. 6, 2006).

In order to meet the skilled manpower needs of the knowledge economy, upper secondary education was universalized in 1991. Hitherto all pupils had only nine years of common schooling after which they had to take the Lower School Certificate Examination, which promoted only about 50% of the cohort. From now on all pupils can move automatically till the eleventh year, when they will take the School Certificate Examination.

This process of democratization further increased the demand for higher education. Normally, only about a third of all applicants to public universities were successful in securing a place. In 1992, the estimated shortfall was about 150,000 places (Marimuthu et al., 1999). In order to meet the demand for places in higher education, the government increasingly sought the involvement of the private sector in higher education.

Another factor that contributed towards the liberalisation of private higher education sector was the increasing cost of supporting Malaysian students overseas. In 1985, there were 68,000 Malaysian students studying overseas, mainly in the United Kingdom, Australia, United States of America, Canada and New Zealand. In the year 2000 this number has been reduced to 50,000 students, 30% of whom were sponsored students. The outflow of funds for the overseas education was about RM 2 billion (US$1 = RM3.80) (INPUMA, 2000: 18). The major reason for the higher cost of overseas education was the introduction of full-fee payment for overseas students by the Thatcher government in UK, followed by Australia and other Commonwealth countries, which have been the popular educational destinations for Malaysian students. In 2006, there were only 11,900 government-sponsored students thus reducing the financial burden of the government substantially.

The reduction in the number of overseas students added to the social demand for higher education in Malaysia.

The paradigm shift in the economic structure of the country, the external pressure brought about by globalisation and the technological revolution, the democratization of secondary education, the decrease of student numbers in overseas higher educational institutions, the increasing local demand for higher education, and the demand for an highly skilled workforce for the knowledge economy, all impacted on the need for the democratization of the private higher education sector.

Educational Acts

All these forces led to the introduction of legislation governing the educational sector. In 1996 a series of bills on tertiary education were tabled in Parliament. These bills were:

1. National Accreditation Board Act (Lembaga Akreditasi Negara) 1996. This Act established the National Accreditation Board (LAN) in 1997, which functions as the quality assurance and accreditation agency for private education.
2. National Council on Higher Education Act, 1996. This council formulates policy for both public and private education.
3. Private Higher Education Institutions Act (PHEI) 1996. This act permits the establishment of degree granting private universities and the establishment of branch campuses by foreign universities. It also permits private colleges to conduct their courses in English with the approval of the Minister of Education.
4. University and University Colleges Act 1971 (Amended 1996) This act was amended to enable to universities to be corporatised and to modernize the management of the universities to meet the needs of the society and the industry.
5. National Higher Education Funding Board Act, 1997. This act established the higher education funding board to provide loans for both public and private students in tertiary institutions.

The Education Act 1961 was amended in 1995 and reinforced the position of Malay as the national language and extended the use of Malay as the medium of instruction to the private sector.

These six acts which were passed by parliament between 1995–1997 enabled the liberalization of the private higher education sector and the corporatisation of public universities.

Private Education Sector

Private education in Malaysia has a long history. Private educational institutions have been in existence since the 1950s and have contributed to the growth and development of the nation. At the time of Independence in 1957, there were two parallel education systems, the public and the private schools. The private schools, which were mainly Christian mission schools, catered for those over-aged pupils who could not enter government schools. There were other private educational institutions such as the religious schools, correspondence schools and tutorial institutes. These tutorial institutes provided training in bookkeeping, type-writing, shorthand, and some elementary accounting preparing the students for the various local and foreign qualifications in the respective fields.

With the implementation of the selection examinations both at the primary and lower secondary levels, recommended by the Razak Committee Report on Education (1956) many youths were 'pushed' out of the public education system. In the 1960s these private educational institutions assumed greater importance for they provided an alternate educational route for these drop-outs. Many new private institutions sprung up throughout the country to cater for this educational need. These were the 'second chance' institutions providing tuition to prepare these young people for the various public national examinations such as the Lower Certificate Examination, the School Certificate Examination and the Higher School Certificate Examination.

The abolition of the primary selection examination in 1964 and the Lower Secondary Examination in 1991, democratized the whole education system, thus exerting pressure for educational opportunity both at the secondary and post secondary levels. The increasing demand for places was at the post-secondary and tertiary levels, with which the public institutions were unable to cope. This is the 'Diploma Disease' at work, where there is an increasing demand for more and more qualifications thus leading to a situation of educational inflation or devaluation of qualifications.

By the 1980s these private institutions were shedding their image as 'second chance' institutions for drop-outs and were beginning to offer courses leading to the award of degrees from foreign institutions. The private sector was encouraged to establish private colleges to respond to the increasing social demand for higher education, brought about by the imposition of full fees by the overseas universities and the structural change in the nations economy from an agricultural economy to an industrial one, which also resulted in the shortage of skilled labour.

These private colleges were not allowed to confer degrees on their own but they could award degrees in collaboration with foreign universities. This situation gave rise to the most innovative and creative arrangements such as twinning, credit transfer, external degrees, distance learning, joint programmes and e-learning.

The most popular method of delivery was the 1 + 2, 2 + 1 and 3 + 0 mode of twinning, whereby the students would spend one two years in the local institutions following the curriculum of the partner institution and complete the degree overseas. The 3 + 0 mode allowed the students to complete the entire programme in the local institution, with quality control mechanisms put in place by the overseas institutions. This 3 + 0 arrangement was only permitted in the mid 1990s after the Asian financial crisis. Only 19 private institutions were allowed to conduct the 3 + 0 degree programmes with 34 overseas universities comprising of 17 from United Kindgom, 14 from Australia, one each from France, Switzerland and the United States of America.

The courses conducted by the various arrangements included management, business, ICT, engineering, administration, social science, law, education, medicine, fine arts, science and maths, hospitality, tourism and hotel management, art and design and architecture.

Not all the existing private colleges conducted the degree programmes but they conducted certificate and diploma programmes in the disciplines outlined above. The majority of the colleges were multidisciplinary colleges and some were devoted to a single discipline, such as medicine, or art and design. Some of these colleges also offered MBA and DBA programmes mainly through part-time study. The awarding of licences to establish private colleges continued through 1980s and 1990s but accelerated after the enactment of the Private Higher Educational Institutions Act of 1996 and the Asian financial crisis in 1997.

In 1992, there were only 156 private institutions with an enrolment of 55,111 but by 2001 there were 706 private higher educational institutions including private universities and university colleges and foreign branch campuses. In 2002, there were 294,600 students enrolled in the private higher educational institutions compared with 15,000 in 1985. The majority of students were enrolled in non-university status private colleges, while about 14% of this total were enrolled in the private university sector.

In 2005, there were 18 public universities and university colleges compared with 22 private universities and university colleges. There were five foreign university branch campuses. They are Monash University, Curtin University and Swinburne University of Technology from Australia and University of Nottingham and FTMS-De Montford from the United Kingdom. There were also 532 private colleges of non-university status. The reduction in the number of private colleges from 706 in 2001 to 532 in 2005 is due to these colleges conducting programmes without the approval of the Ministry of Education, resulting in their closure. These private institutions of higher education had an enrollment of 342,310 students compared with the public institutions of higher education which had a total of 390,388 students. This enrollment figure for public institutions includes the enrollment for the 20 polytechnics, 27 teacher training colleges and 34 community colleges. This enrolment in the public sector constitutes 53.4% while the private sector contributed 46.6% of the total enrolment of 731,698 students. The public sector contribution is expected to increase to 64.4% in 2010.

The data in the Table (see Appendix) show that the majority of the students in the private higher educational sector were enrolled at the Certificate and Diploma levels while the public sector had more students at the undergraduate and post graduate levels.

The significant contribution made by the private higher educational institutions towards tertiary education has been acknowledged. The Ninth Malaysian Plan 2006–2010 (9MP) states that the total output from public and private educational institutions at all levels of study increased from 130,161 in 2000 to 252,730 in 2005, of which 58.5% was from the private tertiary educational institutions (Malaysia 2006 a: 244)

The important contribution made by the private sector towards the development of higher education in the last two decades is largely due to the entry of 'plurality of players' into the private educational sector market (Tan, 2002).

The entry of private individuals for profit, private companies, government corporations, not-for-profit philanthropic organisations and political parties have all entered the educational market, for different reasons.

Public listed companies and other private entrepreneurs have considered the private education sector as a business opportunity to make profits, taking over the smaller private colleges, which have been pioneered by educationalists. The non-profit organisations and political parties have set up colleges and universities to increase the educational opportunities for higher education. Two such efforts are the Asian Institute of Medicine, Science and Technology (AIMST) set up the Malaysian Indian Congress and the University Tunku Abdul Rahman (UTAR) set up by the Malaysian Chinese Association.

With the entry of the business corporations into the private education sector, private education has become a billion dollar business. In 1992 a report by the Indsutry Commission of Australia estimated that the global market for export of education is about RM32 billion a year. The privatization of education has led to the emergence of an education market thus commodifying education itself.

Appendix

Enrolment in tertiary education institutions by levels of study 2000 - 2010

Level of Study	Number of Students									Average Annual Growth Rate %			
	2000			2005			2010			2001 - 2005		2006 - 2010	
	Public	Private	Total	Public	Private	Total	Public	Private	Total	Public	Private	Public	Private
Certificate	23,816	81,754	105,570	37,931	94,949	132,880	141,290	143,480	284,770	9.8	3.0	30.1	8.6
Diploma	92,398	117,056	209,454	98,953	131,428	230,381	285,690	188,680	474,370	1.6	2.3	23.6	7.5
First Degree	170,794	59,932	230,726	212,326	110,591	322,917	293,650	134,550	428,200	4.4	13.0	6.7	4.0
Masters	24,007	2,174	26,181	34,436	4,202	38,638	111,550	5,770	117,320	7.5	14.1	26.5	6.5
PhD	3,359	131	3,490	6,742	140	6,882	21,410	270	21,680	15.0	1.4	26.0	14.0
Total	314,374	261,047	575,421	390,388	341,310	731,698	853,590	472,750	1,326,340	4.5	5.5	16.9	6.7

Source : Ministry of Higher Education, Malaysia

The commercialization of education is not confined to Malaysia alone but this process has been in place in US, UK and Australia since the 1980s. In these countries the reasons for finding off-shore education markets were the budget cuts for the universities, the rising cost of higher education and the global recession of the 1980s.

The commercialization and commodification of higher education has irked some educationists. They complain that the commodification of higher education have turned the universities into "knowledge factories" where academic ideas are compromised for the sake of money. (Bok, 2003: 16)

Corporatisation of Universities

The objectives of privatization and corporation of higher education were to reduce the financial burden of the state in the provision of higher education and to increase the access to higher education to fulfill the ever-increasing demand for tertiary education, to improve the efficiency of the organizations and to ensure the relevance of the courses to national labour requirements (Middlehurst and Woodfield, 2004: 17). It is to be noted that after the passing of the six education acts relating to private education, 11 private universities, 11 private university colleges and five branch campuses of foreign universities were established between 1997 and 2005 by public corporations. The 11 private universities were established by public corporations, private companies and political parties, whereas the private university colleges were upgraded to university college status from the existing private colleges. The enrolment of students in the private higher education sector increased from 15,000 in 1985 to 127,594 in 1995. This number increased almost three fold to 341,310 in 2005. This rapid increase in the number of private higher educational institutions and the student enrolment shows the important role played by the private sector in higher education in Malaysia.

The amendment to the 1971 Universities and Universities Colleges Act (UCCA) in 1996 facilitated the corporatisation of the public universities. In 1998, five of the older public universities were corporatised. By corporatisation, these universities were freed from the "shackles of government bureaucratic provision and would be run like business corporations. Corporatised universities are empowered to borrow money, enter into business ventures, raise endowments, set up companies acquire and hold investment shares" (Lee, 2002: 58). These corporate universities are expected to be managed like business corporations: to minimize costs, increase efficiency and to be more market oriented.

They should also increase their links with the industry and orientate their courses to meet the manpower needs of the economy.

The corporate culture of management is not confined to the corporatised universities alone but are being adopted by all the public and private tertiary education institutions in the country. The benefits resulting from the adoption of business management techniques in administering academic institutions in terms of efficiency, cost, quality of teaching and learning, research output and the morale of the staff are as yet unknown.

Quality

With the democratisation and liberalization of the tertiary education sector, the quality issue has been one of the main concerns of both the government and the public. To maintain the quality control of the increasing number of private higher educational institutions, the government set up the National Accreditation Board (NAB) after the Act was passed in Parliament in 1996. NAB overseas the quality of the courses delivered by making site visits, reviewing the curriculum materials, examination scripts, assignments, students' learning outcomes, student support, academic faculty and interviewing both the staff and students. Each of the courses delivered in the private higher education institutions should go through the process of obtaining the minimum standards status and then the accreditation of the course. Once the course is accredited it has satisfied the NAB's standards of quality and the institutions can market their courses as having been recognized by NAB.

The foreign partner universities, especially those from UK and Australia, have their own Quality Audit Agencies to audit the courses delivered in Malaysia. The personnel from these agencies make site visits and go through similar procedures adopted by NAB and send reports of their visits to the respective universities and colleges. The scope of NAB does not cover the public universities but they require the Ministry's approval to conduct new courses. Most of the public universities have their own Quality Audit Units, to assess their quality.

The Ministry of Education has set up a Quality Assurance Division (QAD) in 2001, similar to that of NAB to provide quality assurance to public universities by faculty and discipline. Recently the NAB and QAD have been merged to form the Malaysian Qualifications Agency (MQA) in order to implement the Malaysian Qualification Framework (MQF). The MQA will provide quality assurance for the public and private higher educational institutions as well as to the training and skill based providers (Malaysia, 2006b).

These various agencies monitoring the quality of tertiary educational institutions will no doubt increase the public confidence with regards to the quality of these institutions.

Professional Development

Another issue which is related to the quality of the institution is the overall quality of staff in the higher educational institutions. In the public universities the minimum academic qualification to be employed as an academic staff is a Masters degree in the respective disciplines. Whereas the minimum academic qualification in the private sector to be appointed as a lecturer is an undergraduate degree but these lecturers are only allowed to teach the Certificate and Diploma courses.

Only those with Masters qualifications can teach the undergraduate courses and those who possess a PhD can lecture the Masters students. In 1998, there were a total of 7,140 members of staff in the private higher educational institutions with

25.3% holding PhD degrees, 21.5% Masters, 32.6% first degree and 12.2% Diploma qualifications. Recent data on the staff qualifications are not available but it can certainly be stated that the post-graduate qualifications of the faculty in the private higher educational institutions would have increased.

According to the 9MP, the target for public universities is to achieve 60% of the total staff with PhD qualifications by 2010. In this regard 9MP has allocated RM 40.3 billion for the public educational sector out of which 39.8% is for higher education. This allocation is 4.5% more compared to the 8th Malaysia Plan. This 40% allocation for higher education demonstrates the commitment of the Government to promote the universities to world class status. The private higher educational institutions are encouraged to employ staff with post graduate qualifications.

Another important factor that will enhance the quality of the teaching and learning process in the institutions of higher education is the acquisition of pedagogical skills by the faculty. The majority of the members of the staff of both the public and private sectors do not possess any teaching credentials.

In the public universities the staff often resist the introduction of pedagogical training for the faculty. However, many of the public universities have established units or centres for pedagogical training, to be attended on a voluntary basis.

The private higher educational institutions organize their own in house training programmes for their staff, where they are exposed to theories of learning, teaching methods, and other pedagogical skills. This mode of training may vary according to the resources available in these institutions. Some conduct workshops and seminars on selected topics. Others have set up centres for provision of professional training. One such development has occurred at the Monash University Campus in Malaysia which has set up the Centre for Higher Education Quality (CHEQ), which organizes courses, workshops and conferences to upgrade the pedagogical skills of its staff.

The three professional associations representing the private education sector namely: the Malaysian Association of Private Universities and Universities Colleges (MAPCU), the National Association of Private and Independent Educational Institutions (NAPEI), the Association of Bumiputera Private Higher Educational Institutions (GIPTSB) also organize professional courses and seminars from time to time for their members. Though some efforts are being done in this direction, much more needs to be done to upgrade the pedagogical skills of the staff, both in the public and private higher education institutions.

The rapid growth and expansion of the private educational sector was in response to the demands of a knowledge economy brought about by globalization and to fulfill the increasing social demand for higher education in the country. The liberalization of the private higher educational sector was legitimized by the enactment of six educational acts in the mid 1990s. Another factor that contributed to rapid development of this sector was the failure of the public universities to respond to the changing needs of the globalised environment.

This process of democratization of the higher educational sector has given rise to a dual system of education with different distinguishing characteristics. These dual systems have grown separately, with little interaction between them.

The public higher educational system's policy has been guided by the social and political considerations of the nation. The admission policy to the universities has been guided by the ethnic quota of 55% for Bumiputera students and 45% for the non-Bumiputera students.

This "political arithmetic" tradition has been in place since the New Economic Policy (NEP) introduced in 1970. This ethnically based admissions policy was replaced by meritocracy in 2002 which continues to be a controversial issue amongst the Bumiputera community members.

However, the admissions of students under the meritocratic system seems to have normalized with about 62% Bumiputera, 32% Chinese, 5.5% Indians and the rest, others entering the universities between 2002 and 2006.

On the other hand the private higher educational sector's growth has been market driven. It pioneered the transnational model of higher education where degree courses from foreign universities were delivered locally. It introduced a variety of new innovative courses in keeping with the changing demand of a knowledge economy. Business corporations entered the private higher educational sector, developing it as an industry, and commodifying education. The big players also displaced the small colleges run by the educationists. These private institutions use English as the medium of instruction, while the main medium of instruction in public higher educational institutions is Bahasa Malaysia. The graduates from overseas universities and the private universities and colleges are more marketable compared to the graduates from the public universities. It is estimated that there are about 60,000 unemployed graduates largely from the public higher educational institutions and the majority of whom are Bumiputera graduates. The main reason is the 'mismatch' between the degrees obtained and the skills required by the job market. The Ministry of Human Resource organizes courses through the private colleges to provide graduate training between three to six months, in the English Language, ICT and management skills so as to fit them into the job-market.

The private higher educational sector has played an important role in the export of education. As of July 31, 2006, there are 31,159 foreign students studying in the private universities and colleges. Several private universities and private university colleges have established their branch campuses in China, India, Indonesia, Pakistan, Sri Lanka and Yemen, thus earning foreign exchange for the nation. The Government has also established promotion offices in Beijing, Ho Chih Minh City, Jakarta, Dubai and Yemen to attract foreign students to study in Malaysia. The target under the 9MP is to have 100,000 foreign students by 2010.

To achieve the Ministry of Higher Education's goal of making Malaysia as an international hub of educational excellence, the partnership between the public and private educational institutions should be strengthened.

The Minister of Higher Education, Hon'ble Dato Mustapa Mohamed addressing the Conference on Globalizing Malaysian Higher Education in August 2006 focussed on the issue of partnership between the public and private higher educational sectors and has suggested four areas for consideration. They are the issue of quality, capacity building, building the Malaysian Brand and the provision of relevant education, responsive to the needs of the industry and society at large.

The Hon'ble Minister has further suggested that the public and private higher institutions should share their physical and intellectual resources, offer a number of twinning and joint programmes between institutions, implement a mutual recognition of courses and credit transfers and conduct joint promotion overseas of Malaysian higher education.

One other important area suggested is the partnership in research and development. The public institutions of higher education are well endowed with funds and facilities and the conduct of collaborative research projects will certainly help the private higher education staff to obtain research experience. The private higher educational institutions are teaching institutions and conduct very little research or publish academic papers.

To attain the objective of world class status for the tertiary institutions, this partnership between the public and private institutions of education is an important one. This will increase efficiency in the use of scarce resources, upgrade the quality of teaching and learning and promote research and development. The Benchmark Report (2005) has also recommended the collaboration of public and private institutions of higher learning to achieve academic excellence in higher education.

The issue of quality of higher education has entered the arena of public debate and discussion when the University of Malaya, the premier public university in the country lost its position in the Times Higher Education Supplement's ranking from 89 in 2004, and 169 in 2005, to 192 in 2006. This down grading of the status of the University of Malaya has been taken seriously both by the government and the society at large. It has led to intense public debate in the media and in educational conferences and seminars. Action plans and strategies are being formulated to upgrade the quality of teaching and learning, research and publication, staff development and other areas of concern.

The funding for higher education has increased substantially. All these efforts augur well for higher education as a whole in the country.

The private higher educational sector has entered the consolidation phase. The Ministry of Higher Education has imposed a moratorium on the issuing of licences for the establishment of new medical and nursing colleges. Small colleges are being merged so as to be viable institutions in a very highly competitive market. Private universities and university colleges are moving into spacious purpose built campuses. They too are concerned that the quality of their product should be such that it attracts the discriminating student population.

The contribution made by the private higher educational sector in terms of access and equity in higher education is widely acknowledged. It is expected that the private higher educational sector in collaboration with the public higher educational institutions will achieve the social and economic agenda of higher education in Malaysia in the new millennium.

References

Bok, Derek (2003) Universities in the Market Place: The Commercialisation of Higher Education, Princeton, Princeton University Press

INPUMA (2000) Policy Issues in Higher Education in the New Millennium Proceedings of International Conference, Kuala Lumpur, University of Malaya

Lee, MNN (2002) Education Change in Malaysia, Penang, Universiti Sains Malaysia

Malaysia (1998) National Economic Recovery Plan: Agenda for Action, Kuala Lumpur, Govt. Printers

Malaysia (2005) The Benchmark Report on Higher Education: Towards Academic Excellence, Shah Alam: Pusat Penerbitan Universiti

Malaysia (2006a) The Ninth Malaysia Plan (2006–2010), Kuala Lumpur, Govt. Printers

Malaysia (2006b) Education Guide Malaysia (10th Edn), Kuala Lumpur, Challenger Concept

Marimuthu, T, Jasbir Singh, Chew Sing Buan, Norani Mohd Salleh, Chang Lee Hoon and Rajendran, NS (1999) Higher Education: Policies, Practices and Issues, Malaysia. The World Bank

Middlehurst, R and Woodfield, S (2004) The Role of Transnational, Private and For-Profit Provision in Meeting Global Demand for Tertiary Education: Mapping, Regulation and Impact (Case Study: Malaysia), Vancouver, UNESCO and Commonwealth of Learning

Readings, Bill (1996) The University in Ruins, Cambridge, Harvard University Press

Tan, AM (2002) Malaysian Private Higher Education: Globalisation, Privatisation, Transformation and Market Places, London, Asean Academic Press

Reflections

Chapter 19
Changing Conceptions of Teaching as a Profession: Personal Reflections

Eric Hoyle

This chapter provides me with an opportunity to reflect on the concept that has constituted the *leitmotif* of my academic writing: the concept of *profession*. This has been linked throughout with my two other main interests. One is the nature of the school as an organization, and particularly the relationship between teacher autonomy and bureaucratic control. The other is the leadership and management of schools, and particularly the role of school leaders in supporting teachers in their professional task.

In retrospect, my approach has entailed a constant engagement with a series of dilemmas, the fundamental dilemma being rooted in the tension between two modes of organizing work in public sector organizations: the *professional* and the *bureaucratic* (*managerial*). Although I had throughout my writing implicitly adopted a 'dilemmas' approach, I hadn't pondered on the nature of dilemmas until I encountered the following: "Dilemmas are neither problems to be solved nor issues to be faced. Problems are presumed solvable; issues can be negotiated and thus are resolvable. As we use the term in this chapter, we assert that dilemmas reveal deeper, more fundamental dichotomies. They present situation with equally valued alternatives. As a consequence, dilemmas cannot be solved or resolved" (Ogawa et al., 1999: 278).

An acceptance of the endemic nature of dilemmas does not preclude the making of choices or the expression of values. However, it does entail being sensitive to ambiguity, contingency and – clumsy word but important concept – 'satisficing' (March and Simon, 1958). I take the view that one of the defining characteristics of members of a profession is the ability to function effectively in uncertain and indeterminate situations. Some might argue that a sensitivity to ambiguity and contingency marks the beginning of the slippery path to relativism. However, I long ago made peace with myself over the foundationalism-relativism tension. I am unable to take a definitive position on whether or not 'truth' exists beyond consciousness, and from the massive and growing literature on this topic it would seem that many others are in the same boat. I nevertheless believe that it is worthwhile to maintain the Enlightenment position with regard to the search for truth without holding great hopes of a philosophical solution. Finality on this matter is elusive and we must live with ambiguities and dilemmas. Schumpeter (1942) wrote: "To realize the relative validity of one's convictions and evidence and argument and yet to stand for them unflinchingly, is what

D. Johnson, R. Maclean (eds.), *Teaching: Professionalization,*
Development and Leadership,
© Springer Science + Business Media B.V. 2008

distinguishes the civilized man [sic] from the barbarian". To which Berlin (1969: 170) adds: "To demand more than this is perhaps a deep and incurable metaphysical need, and more dangerous, moral and political immaturity".

Although this chapter, and my writings generally, engage with ultimately irresolvable dilemmas, there is no pretence that they are value-free. And, since values are expressed throughout this chapter, they might as well be made explicit at the outset. They can be summarized as follows: The quality of education is ultimately in the hands of teachers and hence the professionalization and professional development of teachers are central to the improvement of education; moreover the core function of leadership and management in schools is to support teachers in their professional task. Observation of changing conceptions of teaching as a profession over my career has led me to the conclusion that the educational reform movement consti- tuted a salutary corrective to the somewhat romantic – some would argue ideological – 'idea of a profession' which had previously prevailed, but that the response was an overcompensation that led to *managerialism* – management to excess, management as an ideology embodying the view that not only *can* everything be managed but that everything *should* be managed. This excess would appear to have had a deleterious effect on teaching. It has especially had a negative impact on the diffuse role of the teacher – a role that eludes the usual measures of accountability – as well as consid- erably reducing the work satisfaction of many teachers.

Teaching as a Profession: Key Dilemmas

This section begins with a defence of the viability of the concept of *profession*. Each of the subsequent sections focuses on the dilemmas embedded in the terms: *professionalization*, *professional and professionalism*.

Profession: In Defence of a Concept

It may seem odd to feel the need to defend a concept that has a lengthy history (see Freidson, 1986), remains in widespread use in English, and has its equivalents in other languages. Yet it has to be accepted that *profession* falls into the category of an 'essentially contested concept', thus the 'idea of a profession' as a universal phenomenon on which there is consensus ultimately has to yield to a more relativistic view. Yet this does not detract from its continuing value. There are three reasons for sustaining an academic interest in the word.

There is a strong *semantic* case for persevering with the concept of a profession.

As it remains a term in widespread use in public discourse, it is vital to explore just how the term is deployed. *Profession* represents an aspiration for many occupa- tions and for individual members because it offers psychic rewards and the more tangible rewards of remuneration and congenial work conditions. Thus the word has a symbolic function connoting the worth of one's occupation and hence one's self. It also has an ideological function since it is deployed as a counter by occupational elites in their quest for enhanced status – and, contrariwise, by those who would seek to thwart such aspirations There is also the issue of the ways in which *profession* can have a denotative meaning. For example, in some countries profession is a legal status with accompanying rights and responsibilities, and in many countries official statistics classify certain occupations as professions (though, of course, it could be argued that this is a social construct).

There is a *heuristic* case for persevering with the concept. It provides access to a particular configuration of educational issues relating to knowledge, skill, power, status, ethics, control, practice, development and leadership thereby enhancing our understanding of them. But, beyond enhancing understanding, the concept generates debates about the future and informs the formulation of policy. *Profession* is not the only way of framing these issues, but it is a powerful one.

Finally there remains a *normative* case for the concept of a profession. Given the essentially contested nature of the term, it may appear as quixotic – not to say philosophically dubious – to retain *profession* as connoting an ideal to which teaching and other public service occupations might aspire. The meanings of profession and professionalism are undoubtedly contingent but it does not follow that one need adopt the position that *profession* is inevitably so relativistic a concept that it retains little value. A universally accepted definition and an agreed set of criteria may be elusive but this would be to apply an impossibly demanding standard.

My own stance towards the concept of profession has been a mixture of the semantic, the heuristic and the normative. From my earliest writings I have taken the view that: "the term 'profession' is not a precise descriptive concept but more an evaluative concept" (Hoyle, 1969a: 80). Despite the fact that much that I have written has been concerned with the semantic and the heuristic it has also been suffused with values and despite my acceptance of many of the arguments of the critics of the idea of a profession, I have always held that, as T. H. Marshall put it: "Professionlism is an idea based on the real character of certain services. It is not a clever invention of selfish minds" (Marshall, 1963: 166).

Engaging with 'profession' entails confronting a number of endemic dilemmas. The following sections address such dilemmas from a heuristic, a semantic and a normative position.

Professionalization

The central dilemma of professionalization is that it has two components which may not always be as tightly linked as is often assumed. This has been of continuing interest since my initial exploration of this dilemma (Hoyle, 1974). I there drew a distinction between these two components. One I would now retrospectively term the *institutional* component of professionalization connoting the collective aspiration of an occupation to meet and sustain certain criteria: strong boundary, academic credentials, a university connection, a self-governing professional body, practitioner autonomy, a code of ethics and so forth. The other I would now refer to as the *service* component connoting the process whereby the knowledge, skill and commitment of practitioners is continuously enhanced in the interests of clients. Although these two processes are often presented as proceeding *pari passu*, this need not necessarily occur. Their divergence has long been the focus of critics of the teaching profession (e.g.: "It is time that teachers started to demand for themselves, not more money, but higher professional standards. One of the problems with their occupation is that they want the trappings of a profession but not its consequences" [*Spectator* leader: 22 April 1995]).

The paradigm professions of medicine and law established such institutions over a lengthy period of time. With 'the rise of professional society' (Perkin, 1989) from the late nineteenth century, many other occupations, including teaching, aspired to professional status not least because of the benefits that such recognition appeared to offer. The professionalization project of these aspirant occupations took the alleged criteria of a profession – theoretical knowledge, academic credentials, professional body, code of ethics, etc. – as the benchmarks of their aspirations. The implicit, and frequently explicit, claim was that meeting these criteria was to the benefit of clients as well as to the benefit of practitioners.

The rhetoric of bodies representing the professions was accorded academic legitimacy by the functionalist theory of the professions developed by sociologists in the United States. The basis of this theory was that the professions performed a distinctive social function in the exercise of which judgements concerning the interests of clients often had to be made in conditions of uncertainty. The autonomy necessary to make these judgements had the sanction of academic credentials and lengthy training and was guaranteed by a professional body consisting of members of the profession. There had long existed a more sceptical view of the professions – *vide* George Bernard Shaw's famous aphorism that a profession is "a conspiracy against the laity" – but it was only in the 1960s that there emerged a systematic critique of the professions. Briefly the argument was that professionalization was driven by an self-interested ideology which exaggerated the knowledge claims of the professions, promoted autonomy as a means of avoiding accountability, and proclaimed a code of ethics that was more concerned with the interests of practitioners rather than the interests of clients (see Larson, 1977; Abbott, 1988).

However, the subsequent 'reform' of the professions stemmed less from this academic critique than from a political critique centring on the growing costs of public services, the fact that the organized professions had become perceived as constituting a constraint on market forces, and that provider interests were prevailing over client (consumer) interests. This generated an accountability movement designed to reduce the power of the professions. In terms of the dilemma which is the focus of this section, the *institutional* dimension of professionalization was considered to have overwhelmed the *service* dimension. The accountability movement had the purpose of redressing this balance. What ensued has been differently interpreted as de-professionalization (Hoyle, 1980) or 'the new professionalism', an issue to be discussed further below.

The professionalization trajectory of the teaching profession in Britain followed the general pattern of seeking to meet the benchmarks derived from the established professions. However, the characteristics of these professions – self-employed, autonomous practitioners remunerated on a fee basis – could only function to a limited degree as a model for an occupation such as teaching whose members worked in organizations and whose salaries were largely out of public funds, Occupations in the second wave of professionalization confronted the choice between two major strategies: essentially the 'professional body' strategy and the 'trade union' strategy. Although during the later nineteenth and early twentieth centuries several attempts were made to establish a professional body for teachers these foundered and advancement depended largely on a 'union' strategy combined with a 'professional' rhetoric. Thus there was a tendency on the part of government and local education authorities to make an initial presumption of self-interest in teacher union proposals to enhance quality but they accepted the professional rhetoric of teacher unions when it was politically expedient to do so (see Gosden, 1972; Lawn,1987; Dale, 1989; Grace, 1987). For an account of recent relationships between teachers and the state see McCulloch et al. (2000).

Nevertheless, the organized teaching profession in England and Wales can be judged to have been reasonably successful in terms of advancing the *institutional* dimension of the professionalization project. By the late 1960s, which marked the apotheosis the professionalization project of many occupations, teaching had achieved a strong boundary around those with a licence to teach, four year programmes of education and training, an all-graduate profession, a growing body of research, a relatively high degree of teacher autonomy, and a powerful voice in the shaping of educational policy (Manzer, 1970) – but no self-regulating professional body – at least in England – until 2000. The apotheosis of the institutional dimension of teacher professionalization was reached in the late 1960s and early 1970s.

The accountability movement, later termed the educational reform movement, emerged in the late 1970s and proceeded apace under Conservative and New Labour Governments. From an *institutional* perspective, the changes brought about by the educational reform movement can be viewed as de-professionalization: reduced teacher autonomy, the marginalization of teacher associations, the weakening of the links with the academy in terms of initial training and continuous professional development and so forth. The reform movement represented a massive shift in the locus of accountability from self-regulating professional bodies to a mixture of managerial and market forms.

The reform movement was the outcome of a growing discontent with schooling. The basic problem was that the high level of school and teacher autonomy facilitated a shift in curriculum, pedagogy and assessment in a direction that confused and alienated many politicians, parents and some teachers, and generated a concern about standards. This shift can be summarized in the metaphor of 'open-ness'. Existing boundaries – between school subjects, between teacher and taught, between categories of pupil, between teacher roles, between components of the school day, between school and community and even, in the case of new 'open plan' schools, between the physical components of the school – were eroded or became more permeable. These changes denoted a radical shift in the nature of schooling towards what would later be termed constructionism. However, their implementation depended on new patterns of school leadership and new forms of professionalism amongst teachers. These meta-changes proved to be difficult to achieve in the short term and problems inevitably ensued. Moreover these changes in schooling were predicated upon quite fundamental changes in society as captured in the title of a prescient article by Bernstein (1967): 'Open schools, open society?' The interrogative was settled by the reform movement: radical change was indeed to occur but it took a different direction.

The effect of the reform movement has been to reinforce in terms of policy and practice the conceptual distinction between the *institutional* and the *service* dimensions of professionalization. It can be argued that deprofessionalization has occurred on the institutional dimension but one can be less categorical in relation to the service dimension. It is perhaps paradoxical that teachers have increasingly engaged in professional development activities that, though they may have enhanced their skills and thus been of benefit to pupils, have been at odds with traditional criteria of a profession, particularly those relating to academic knowledge (see Hoyle, 1982a; Hoyle and John (1995)). There can be little doubt that institutional professionalization has more or less run its course in Britain and there is little opportunity for the organized teaching profession to make further progress on this dimension, in fact, it is in retreat. The current emphasis on the service dimension of professionalization has entailed improving the skills and competence of teachers in the direction of ensuring that they become more 'professional'. This shift was perhaps timely but, of course, much turns on the changing connotations of *professional* and this will be discussed later in this chapter. This changing emphasis has been labelled, 'the new professionalism' which is used variously and by no means consistently (see Sykes, 1999 for a review) The main issue on which connotations vary is the degree to which the new professionalism interpenetrates with the new managerialism.

Professional

Protagonists of the reform movement argue that as a result of the reforms teachers have become more 'professional'. This apparent paradox arises because of the changing use of the term *professional* as both noun and adjective. There has in recent years occurred a semantic shift whereby the term has now acquired connotations of 'efficiency', 'competence', 'detachment' and even 'ruthlessness'. In the process of the reform movement 'professional' has become uncoupled from the concept of a 'profession' and has assumed a confluence of two modes of organizing work: the bureaucratic and the professional. In the process of this confluence management has become the more powerful stream and 'professionalism' has to a degree become assimilated into managerialism. I sought to capture this changed conception of *professional* as both as a noun and an adjective by noting a number of dimensions of change (Hoyle, 1995) I summarized these as follows:

...to be professional is to have acquired a set of skills through competency-based training which enables a practitioner to deliver, according to contract, a customer-led service in compliance with accountability procedures collaboratively implemented and managerially assured.

(Hoyle, 1995: 60 amended)

This is clearly something of a caricature and in the original paper I conceded that it was deliberately 'overstated'. Nevertheless there remains a tension which is caught in the conflicting connotations of *professional*: with politicians associating the term with efficiency and teachers associating the term with autonomy. This is not to suggest that teachers are unconcerned with efficiency. The likelihood is that teachers attach different meanings to what it is to be considered *professional*. At one level to be professional is to conform to the basic expectations of the teacher's role in relation to, for example, punctuality, marking work, completing reports, dealing with pupils and dealing with colleagues. Violation of such norms is dubbed 'unprofessional'. At another level to be professional is to exercise autonomy in making judgements in relation to clients. At a third level, *to be a professional* is to command the deference that is considered due to a member of a socially-important occupation. Professional workplace studies have suggested that teachers are not too preoccupied with 'being a professional' in terms of the traditional discourse of profession but are focussed more on 'acting professionally' (Helsby, 1999).

Professionalism

This section provides an opportunity for me to reflect upon a dilemma which I first explored more than thirty years ago and which still intrigues me. I hypothesized a distinction between *restricted* and *extended professionality* (Hoyle, 1974). A *restricted professional* was construed as a teacher for whom teaching was an intuitive activity, whose perspective was restricted to the classroom, who engaged little with wider professional reading or activities, relied on experience as a guide to success, and greatly valued classroom autonomy. An *extended professional* was construed as a teacher for whom teaching was a rational activity, who sought to improve practice through reading and through engaging in continuous professional development, who was happily collegial, and who located classroom practice within a larger social framework.

Many innovations in curriculum, pedagogy, grouping and assessment in the 1960s and early 1970s were predicated upon the enhancement of the professionality of teachers in the direction of *extended professionality* and this was my own value preference. However, some retrospective comments on the original formulation are appropriate.

There are clearly many problems associated with this formulation. The use of the term *professionality* was unfortunate. It was used in contradistinction to *professionalism* – a term used to connote the strategies used by teachers' organizations to enhance status. However, the only people who sustained this terminology were myself and some of my students! I have therefore now reverted to the single term *professionalism*.

The use of the term *restricted* was also unfortunate since it carried an negative connotation yet restricted professionals may well be classroom practitioners of the highest professional skill; it was only the *scope* of professionalism that was restricted. It was not made clear whether the two kinds of professionalism were to be treated as ends of a continuum or whether they constituted different 'factors'. This ambiguity has implications for the policy question of whether extended profession-alism can be achieved without undermining classroom skills. Nor was it made clear whether the terms referred to behaviour, perceptions, expectations, or prescriptions. Finally, at the time, the concepts were not empirically validated, though subsequent studies have attested to their validity.

In view of the above problems it is highly surprising that the distinction has remained in use for over thirty years, referred to in passing in many publications but also incorporated in empirical studies (see, e.g. Nias, 1989; Evans, 1998; Evans et al., 1994; Jogmans et al., 1998; Osborn et al., 2000; van Veen et al., 2001. This suggests that whatever weakness the formulation might have, it has retained a reso-nance for many subsequent students of the teaching profession.

The policy implication of the original formulation was the extension of teacher professionalism without detriment to classroom skills. Initially, the initiative for extending the professionalism of teachers lay with heads and teachers themselves supported by HMI and the local advisory service with the expectation that teachers would both enhance their skills and broaden their perspectives. However, as with so much else, this aspiration was overtaken by the changes ushered in by the reform movement. Ironically, the reform movement not only encouraged extended profes-sionalism, but *required* it. Equally ironical was the requirement of what might be termed *extended-but-constrained* professionalism. This ostensibly entailed teachers specifically relating classroom activity to the school charter or mission statement, conforming to appraisal procedures, reading a plethora of policy and curriculum documents, and participating in school-based professional development.

This brings out the paradox of the 'restricted' nature of the new 'extended pro-fessionalism'. One must again emphasize that it was probably too optimistic to assume that the great majority of teachers would choose to transform themselves into extended professionals. At least the reform movement has ensured that it has become difficult for a teacher to ignore the wider aspects of the role; as van Veen et al. (2001) demonstrate, it is now difficult to identify *any* restricted professionals in teaching as originally conceptualized. Ironically the changes in the provision of professional development as an element of the reform movement, particularly its problem-solving focus, is congruent with the proposals advanced for extending professionalism in the 1960s and 1970s but, as so often has been the case, the scope for teacher agency has been reduced resulting in an excessive swing towards one pole of the endemic dilemma whereby 'extended professionalism' is marked by the *expansion* of the teacher's role (the requirement that teachers will engage in many more activities related to accountability) and by the *intensification* of the role (the requirement that teachers will devote increased amounts of time and energy to prescribed tasks). There is thus a case for conceptualising a bifurcation *within* the category of extended professionalism, one branch of which might be termed *constrained professionalism* and the other *enabled professionalism* (see John in Chapter 1 of this volume).

Professionals in Organizations

In this section I outline the influences on my perspective on educational organizations and outline its implications for this core dilemma arising from the two major modes of organizing work

Loose and Tight Coupling

Organization theory is concerned with such social units as schools, universities, prisons, hospitals, factories and so forth. I have had an interest in the school as organization since the early 1960s (Hoyle, 1965). The term *organization* can be misleading since it can be taken to connote the ontological priority of structure. However, I have always assumed that organization theory does not preclude a perspective that embraces the *emergent* properties of organizations, particularly the view that structures can emerge from practice. I have also assumed that organization theory can embrace a number of frames, for example the structural, human relations, political and symbolic frames proposed by Bolman and Deal (1984).

An endemic dilemma characterizes organizations staffed by professionals. This stems from the interpenetration of professional and bureaucratic (managerial) ways of organizing work. Configurations resulting from the interaction between the these two principles varies according to organizational type, contextual factors and leadership style. The shifting nature of these configurations has been the focus of many studies of schools as organizations. In an influential review Bidwell (1965) noted the 'structural looseness' of the school and Lortie (1969) noted 'the balance between control and autonomy' in the school', but probably best-known is Weick's (1976) metaphor of *loosely coupled system*. Typically, the headteacher undertook the task of co-ordination, determined the general direction of the school and maintained relationships with the community. There was limited teacher involvement in these tasks. On the other hand, teachers enjoyed a relatively high degree of autonomy in matters of curriculum and method.

I was wholly committed neither to the system paradigm nor to the phenomenological paradigm – elaborated in relation to educational administration by Greenfield (1975). In organizational terms this meant a commitment to a bureaucratic component which was sufficiently robust to provide structure and support for teachers yet provided sufficient space for the exercise of agency in conditions of relative autonomy. I explored this largely through a micropolitical frame (Hoyle, 1982b, 1986, 1999), a frame that has generally remained underdeveloped both theoretically and empirically.

In relation to the structure-autonomy dilemma I perhaps hardly need repeat at this point my view that the constructionist trend in the 1960s and early 1970s led to excesses – which high profile events such as the case of William Tyndale primary school (Auld, 1976) came to symbolize. But that the excesses of rebalancing were based upon an over-rationalistic conception of the nature of schools and of what they might become.

Ambiguity

I could be very wrong but I believe that there are inherent limits to managerialism in schools and that the movement will recede, though it is likely leave a strong residue of management with an emphasis on effectiveness, efficiency and accountability. Relentless managerialism is based upon a misunderstanding of the nature of organizations in general and in the nature of the school in particular. My initial reading in the field of organizational theory in the early 1960s led to me to the work of James March which has remained an important influence. In *Organizations*, March and Simon (1958) explored the limits to rational decision-making in organizations without throwing rationality out the window. But I became very much taken by his notion of *ambiguity* (See March, 1999; March and Olsen, 1976).March writes:

> *ambiguity refers to a lack of clarity or consistency in reality, causality or intentionality. Ambiguous situations are situations that cannot be coded precisely into mutually exhaustive and exclusive categories. Ambiguous purposes are intentions that cannot be specified clearly. Ambiguous identities are identities whose rules or occasions for application are imprecise or contradictory. Ambiguous outcomes are outcomes whose characteristics or implications are fuzzy.*
>
> (March, 1994: 178)

In relation to educational organizations March has explored the ambiguities in the relationship between goals, structures, technology and outcomes. His explorations of how organizations actually work forces us, through the use of some telling metaphors, to question many deeply held assumptions. He writes of organizations as 'running backwards" in the sense that rationality is imposed *post factum* on features that have emerged from a complex set of interactions. Thus decisions often not 'made' but 'happen' and solutions often precede problems, His famous *garbage can* metaphor draws our attention to the fact that problems, solutions, participants, and choice opportunities are all in the mix together than being rationally sequenced and that universities are *organized hierarchies* in which order emerges from activities.

This approach is so counter to linear approaches to the management of organizations that it is initially difficult to accept and, despite its importance for *understanding* organizations, its contribution to the skills of *managing* organizations comes, if at all, only through deep reflection. Introducing these counter-intuitive ideas to students of management is initially confusing. However, in terms of understanding organizations it seriously questions managerialism. A latent function of the reform movement has been the reduction of ambiguity, particularly the ambiguities that stemmed from the constructionist approach to curriculum, pedagogy and organization that occurred in the 1960s and early 1970s, hence the emphasis on objectives, targets, measured outcomes, etc. But unless education is to be reduced to a narrow and specific set of outcomes, the diverse and diffuse goals of schools will continue to create ambiguity and hence, in my view, call to the fore the professional judgement of teachers.

Samizdat Professionalism

Mike Wallace and I have argued (Hoyle and Wallace, 2005, 2007. See also Chapter 19 by Wallace in this volume) that a fundamental irony of these educational times is that many national policies have been saved from unintended consequences through teachers exercising what we have termed '*samizdat* professionalism' in the interests of pupils in contingent contexts. There is no empirical evidence that directly supports the existence of this form of 'underground' professionalism. However, we have inferred its presence from a number of case studies (e.g. Helsby, 1999; Moore et al., 2002; Osborn et al., 2000; Pollard et al., 1994; Woods, 1995; Woods et al., 1997) conducted in the era of reform. These studies suggest that many heads and teachers develop strategies of adaptation whereby they 'work round' the requirements of policy and management and do their best by their pupils based on their professional judgement of contingent conditions – what we have termed *ironies of adaptation*. We have also inferred that many heads and teachers have succeeded in this through what we have termed *ironies of presentation*, strategies whereby they ostensibly appear to meet the demands of accountability but allow themselves space in which to make judgements in what they see as the best interest of pupils. Such heads and teachers thereby keep alive some of the traditional aspects of professionalism in unpropitious circumstances.

It would be unwise, however, to over-romanticise *samizdat* professionalism. There is no valid evidence of the incidence of such professionalism and there can be little doubt that there are many teachers who do not act in this way. Nor can it be assumed that the professionalism of teachers is all of the same kind, nor that the judgements made by teachers on what is best for pupils in contingent circumstances is sound. One is saying no more than it would appear that many teachers are striving to sustain a client-centred professionalism despite a shift towards a system-centred managerialism. If such is the case it gives hope for the future development of teacher professionalism.

Teaching: Careers, Status and Satisfaction

The confluence of the principles of professionalism and managerialism has had an impact on occupational identities. The tension between professional and managerial identities was felt long before the reform movement as promotion took practitioners into administrative roles and away from front-line professional practice. But this tension has been greatly exacerbated in recent years with the increasing pressure on individuals at almost every level of a profession to adopt a managerial identity. Coping with this tension is an individual matter but political trends are leading to an emphasis on the rewards of managerial identities. There are undoubtedly increased material rewards for managerialism but this may be at the heavy const of psychic rewards. This section briefly explores some of the implications of managerialism for career, status and satisfaction.

The Lure of Entrepreneurial Careers

As late as the mid-1950s there was a very limited career structure in teaching and little teacher turnover resulting from promotion. Teachers tended to remain in the same school for many years, often for a professional lifetime. This changed with the Burnham pay agreement of 1956 which introduced a range of salary differentials and thus an extended career hierarchy. I subsequently argued that the stratification of teaching was likely to increase work dissatisfaction (Hoyle, 1969b). At the time these changes generated discussion about the irony arising from the fact that a successful teaching career almost inevitably led a teacher out of teaching. I later made a distinction between two forms of career 'success': success in the task of teaching and success in terms of career advancement (Hoyle, 1981) and noted that the increasing salience of career advancement could re-shape the professionalism of the teacher.

With the reform movement a successful career in education has increasingly become signified by perceived success as a manager. This applies not only to managerial positions but also to professional roles which have become increasingly specialized. In some areas this has led to the phenomenon of 'a solution in search of a problem': if one is trained and credentialled to engage with a particular set of problems then one will be tempted to 'find' such problems. The reform movement has generated many new roles in the accountability and surveillance areas. The old adage: "If it ain't broke, don't fix it!" must now be replaced by the adage: "If it ain't broke, fix it anyway!"

There is doubt about the motivation provided by career enhancement. Very few professionals will be indifferent to career advancement but there is a need to be aware of the costs, and perhaps it is this awareness that is leading to an alleged reluctance of many teachers to seek promotion to a headship. Teachers need to be aware of the chimera of enhanced status.

Status

The professionalization project has been very much a matter of attaining, retaining and enhancing status. It has long suited governments to hold out the possibility of enhanced status in their negotiations with teachers. Sagging morale and the need to recruit and retain teachers has led to increased attention being paid to the status of teachers, at least in terms of rhetoric. Thus in 1999 the then Prime Minister spoke of the need 'to improve the status and morale of teachers' (Tony Blair the *Guardian* 19 January 1999). However, *status* is a complex term with different connotations and I have taken the view that an appreciation of the possibility of teachers enhancing their status requires distinctions to be made *within* the overall category of status. I have hypothesized a distinction between three dimensions of status: *occupational prestige, status* – used in a specific rather than a general sense, and *esteem* (see Hoyle, 2001 for a full discussion).

Occupational prestige is used to denote the relative rank accorded an occupation in a hierarchy if occupations. The most common method for determining this rank is to have members of the population rank a number of occupational titles according to some criterion of 'higher' or 'lower'. A large number of studies of prestige have been undertaken in countries with different political systems and at different levels of economic development. These studies, despite some individual variations, show a surprisingly high level of inter-correlation (typically +0.93) between prestige scales. Although there are intra-professional differences within teaching, the profession as such is typically at the lower end of the upper quartile of the range of occupations – therefore not 'low' in any general sense but lower than the occupations generally taken as a reference group of aspiration: medicine, law, architecture, etc. The relatively invariant character of prestige suggests that the possibility of teaching enhancing its relative prestige is remote.

Occupational status is the global term for social standing. However, it is here used in the limited sense of official recognition, in this context the formal recognition of the status of teaching as a profession. Status can be denoted in a number of ways. For example, in some systems *profession* is a legal status having certain rights and responsibilities and teaching has been accorded such a status Another indicator is the allocation of teaching to the various categories of 'profession' in official statistics. There is perhaps some – limited – scope for the enhancement of the status of teaching in this sense. What is perhaps of more significance to teachers is the semantic issue: whether their occupation is conventionally referred to as a profession by politicians, commentators and the general public. This is very difficult to determine since the term *profession* is used symbolically or ideologically to claim – or withhold – status.

Occupational esteem is here used to denote the regard in which on occupation is held by the public by virtue of the qualities that members bring to their task. In the case of teachers these could be grouped into the categories of dedication, care and competence. Esteem is complicated by the fact that it is determined not only by the direct experience of clients but also by the representation of the occupation in various media and as directly experienced by the public. This can often result in the esteem accorded to teachers on the basis of experience being more positive than media representations.

These three dimensions of 'status' in the global sense can vary independently. *Prestige* is the most intractable and teaching would always struggle to enhance its prestige because of factors endemic in the teacher's work. There is the long-term possibility of enhancing the *status* of teaching, perhaps more so in developing

than developed countries. The enhancement of the *esteem* of teachers is a possibility and very much depends on the enhancement of client-centred professionalism by teachers themselves. But enhanced esteem does not necessarily lead to
enhanced prestige: in some Asian and African countries high esteem is bestowed
on the teaching role but prestige rankings in those countries conform to the usual
hierarchy.

It is sometimes suggested that the status – in the general sense – of teachers would
be enhanced to the degree that they take on managerial roles. Perhaps some teachers
believe this to be the case and this would account for the apparent fondness for mana-
gerial-sounding titles. But it is highly unlikely that managerialism would constitute a
basis for improved prestige since the status of management as a profession is ambiguous. *Management* does not, perhaps, have the same aura as *profession* – and to invoke
the highly diffuse term *leadership* does not help. By re-badging themselves as managers, educators are unlikely to enhance their prestige, status or esteem. Parents are
much more likely to accord esteem to teachers as teachers and not as managers, and
even headteachers are much more likely to be accorded esteem on the basis of perceptions of professional commitment to pupils and their parents rather than on their display of managerial efficiency.

Satisfaction

This is not the place for a review of the extensive literature on the work motivation
and job satisfaction of teachers (see Evans, 1998, for a discussion). I want only to
claim the continuing relevance of Herzberg's two-factor theory of motivation
(Herzberg et al., 1959). This theory has generated a substantial literature, some it
critical. Nevertheless the basic notion that the factors that generate work satisfaction are relatively independent of the factors that generate work dissatisfaction is an
important one. The majority of studies of teachers make clear that by far their greatest source of satisfaction derives from *teaching*. The two major sources of teacher
dissatisfaction are pupil indiscipline and managerialism.

Professional Leadership

This phrase has two connotations which point to a key dilemma. Professional
leadership can refer to the professionalism of leaders; it can also refer to the process of leading other professionals. It might be assumed that the two processes are
so intertwined that there is little point in making this distinction. Not so. An irony
of policy is that just as teaching was being deprofessionalized, school management
was actually being professionalized. The process of professionalizing school
leaders and managers has followed the familiar trajectory: knowledge base, credentials, a technical language, and professional associations – which had in to a degree
preceded the reform movement. However, there were limits to this institutional

professionalization. Although the restraints which emanated from local education authorities were largely removed, and headteachers thereby enjoyed increased autonomy as leaders of 'self-managing schools', in practice this autonomy was limited by the accountability procedures emanating from central government reflecting the dominant strategy of change of central decision-making and local implementation. There was pressure on headteachers to demonstrate their 'professional managerialism' if the were to advance their careers.

The relationship between 'management' and 'leadership' has been the focus of interminable conceptual analysis that needn't be rehearsed here yet again. However it is worthwhile noting a shift in the metaphors of management (Hoyle and Wallace, 2006). The early years of the reform movement saw the incorporation into educational discourse of a range of managerialist metaphors such as *efficiency*, *objectives*, *resource allocation*, *performance monitoring*, *accountability* (metaphors taken from a single sentence in Coopers and Lybrand, 1988). However, from the mid-1980s the metaphors of management were 'gentled' by an overlay of the metaphors of 'leadership', 'culture' 'vision', 'mission' and so forth. School leadership was depicted as 'transformational' notwithstanding the fact that heads had very little scope for 'transforming' schools outside the parameters set by policy and constrained by accountability measures. There is little doubt that there has been inspirational leadership in schools in difficult circumstances but this has largely been concerned with doing the basic things better rather than transforming the goals of the school. It has also depended upon building on the professional leadership acts of teachers that emerge from practice. In short, it has entailed fostering the unobtrusive professionalism of teachers rather than seeking to convert them into manage-ment professionals.

The value of this approach to leadership has been captured by the protagonists of 'distributed leadership' (e.g. Gronn, 2000; Harris, 2004) Mike Wallace and myself (Hoyle and Wallace, 2005) have used the metaphor of *temperate leadership* to capture the pattern of leadership that is most likely to support teachers as professionals. This would be characterized by a reduction of managerial activity, supporting teachers by taking the strain and absorbing the stress, and by focussing on local, incremental improvements. This unheroic approach to leadership is less likely to stir the blood than an appeal to transformational leadership. There is a certain incongruity in unfurling a standard bearing the slogan: "Moderates of the world, unite!" But this approach to an improvement in the quality of education through increasing teacher professionalism is congruent with the nature of education as a social institution that has its basic, relatively unchanging 'grammar' and, as we have seen time and again, is not amenable to rapid large scale change.

Conclusion: Possibilities

This reflection on forty years engagement with the idea of teaching as a profession suggests that there is an endemic dilemma entailed in the relationship between two modes of organizing teachers' work: the bureaucratic (managerial) and the professional. At the heart of this is the balance between autonomy and control. Through institutional professionalization from the late nineteenth century until the early 1970s teaching had been moving towards the 'professional' pole of the dilemma, particularly in terms of autonomy. However, this came to be seen by politicians and others as inimical to the interests of clients (consumers) leading to the initiation of a movement towards greater accountability – the educational reform movement. However, my view is that this movement, by initiating managerialism – management to excess – has had deleterious consequences, not least for the creativity and work satisfaction of teachers. As the quality of education is ultimately a matter of quality teaching this is not insignificant. The current problem turns on whether there can be a return to a new professionalism that does not equate to the new managerialism.

It is unlikely that there will be a return to the days of high teacher autonomy. Nevertheless, although there are few solid indications of a deceleration in the reform movement, there are straws in the wind that might presage a shift in perspective that will provide scope for the further development of teacher professionalism. All the indicators show that there are high levels of teacher dissatisfaction with the continuing policy frenzy and the managerialism that accompanies this. This has not led thus far to any great a problem of recruitment and retention because, it would appear, teachers still derive satisfaction from teaching itself and, I would suggest, from the scope that is still offered for *samizdat* professionalism. Politicians are conscious of the level of teacher dissatisfaction but tend to treat this as resolvable by reducing teachers' workload – though the irony is that that solutions to the workload problem appear to have generated new kinds of workload.

A second possibility is that the economic cost of accountability and surveillance will become prohibitive. Despite the much greater levels of investment in education and other social services, polls indicate that members of the general public appear not to perceive any substantial improvement in the system, although they appear to be reasonably satisfied with the service they receive directly from professionals. It is most unlikely that there will be a complete *demarche* from the accountability measures that have been put in place, nor should there be a complete abandonment as they have enhanced important aspects of what it means to be *professional*. There are limits to accountability in teaching and the distinction between *accountability* and *responsibility* (Hoyle and John, 1995) remains valid: professional responsibility reaching the areas that are to diffuse to be accessible to measures of accountability. But responsibility is predicated on *trust*. Perhaps the most challenging issue for politicians and professionals at the present time is how to resuscitate *trust*, an issue that is currently generating an important literature (see, e.g. O'Neill, 2002; Bottery, 2003).

A third possibility is that there may be a slow movement in public opinion which brings back into favour an earlier conception of schooling. At the present time the dominant concerns of parents centre on the labyrinthine complexities of school choice and test and exam scores. But there is perhaps a recessive concern about the loss of the wider goals of schooling and the diffuse nature of the teacher role in the face of increasing instrumentalism There is at the moment the lack of any widely-accepted metaphors to capture this aspiration. Some have suggested *community* as a preferable metaphor to *organization* and certainly that is central to headteachers' talk about their schools. But, of course, *community* is itself is a hyper-referential concept.

Given that the institutions governing professional practice are now dominated by the state, the locus of professionalization is now the school. I have suggested that at the present time, to an unknown degree, this currently takes the form of *samizdat* professionalism. But teachers can go beyond this defensive stance. I am impressed by the approach that not only identifies the potential for advances in school-based professionalism, particularly the development of communities of professional practice (see Stoll and Louis, 2007) However, this school-based approach is not without its limitations. One is the ever-present tendency in these managerialist times to stifle emergent professionalism through the sequence: support leading to accountability leading to routinization. Another is the potential threat to teacher autonomy of 'collaboration', 'collegiality' or 'participation'. One of the enduring dilemmas of the teaching profession lies in the endemic tension between the two desirable principles of autonomy and collaboration. This was identified long ago by Lortie (1964) and has been explored by Little (1990) and Hargreaves (1994) amongst others. A third problem is that developments in professional practice may bloom and die in small communities of practice without making a contribution the professionalization of teachers more generally.

The current focus of work on teaching as a profession is, rightly, on the service aspects of professionalism. But there remains a need to engage with the future of the teaching profession as an institution. This is the focus of a number of chapters in this collection and others who are making distinctive contributions to this work include Sachs (2003), Bottery (1998), Eraut (1994), Whitty (1996), Darling-Hammond (1990), and Ginsburg (1997). In the light of the fact that there appears little scope for the teaching profession as an institution recovering its pre-accountability levels of power, influence and autonomy, perhaps the central question turns on the role of the profession in relation to the state on the one hand and in relation to families on the other hand. Of course, politicians would argue that the interests of the state and the interests of families are identical. This is dubious. Contrariwise there are those who argue for a coalition of the teaching profession and 'community' in opposition to the state. This, too, is dubious. The particularistic concerns of families with their own members may be at odds with the teaching profession's universalistic concern with all pupils. Notwithstanding the undoubted value of parent-teacher collaboration at the individual level, at the general level there remains a distinction between the lay and the professional.

Despite all the problems attaching to the concept, it is becoming even more vital to sustain the *idea of a profession*. The effect of the 'reform' project in politics is to replace professionalism by managerialism. Whether this is a conscious act of policy or a by-product of policy is a matter of current debate. Nevertheless, it is affecting all the professions. In my view, there remains the need for a principled defence of the idea of a profession. Elliott Freidson, the doyen of writers on the professions, has made a call for such in defence (Freidson, 2001):

> It is aggressive in joining the attack on the pathologies that stem from material self-interest
> in the market place, and from the reduction of work and its products to formal procedure

in bureaucracy. But it can no less aggressive in joining the attack on the practices or professionals that compromise the integrity of the model. Only by maintaining its own integrity can it leave no doubt of its superiority over the atomistic play of self-interest or the iron cage of formal rationality.

It is a call that resonates even more strongly today.

References

Abbott A (1988) *The System of Professions: An Essay on the Division of Expert Labour.* Chicago, IL: University of Chicago Press

Auld R (1976) *Report of the Public Enquiry into the William Tyndale Junior and Infant Schools.* London: Inner London Education Authority

Berlin I (1969) *Four Essays on Liberty.* Oxford: Oxford University Press

Bernstein B (1967) 'Open schools, open society?' *New Society* 10: 152–154

Bidwell C (1965) 'The school as a formal organization' in J G March (ed) *Handbook of Organizations.* New York: Rand McNally, 927–1002

Bolman L and Deal T (1984) *Modern Approaches to Understanding and Managing Organizations.* San Francisco, CA: Jossey-Bass

Bottery M (1998) *Professionals and Policy: Management Strategy in a Competitive World.* London: Cassell

Bottery M (2003) 'The management and mismanagement of trust'. *Educational Management and Administration* 31(3) 245–261

Coopers and Lybrand (1988) *Local Management of Schools.* London: Her Majesty's Stationery Office

Dale R (1989) *The State and Educational Policy.* Milton Keynes, UK: Open University Press

Darling-Hammond L (1990) 'Teacher professionalism: When and how?' in A Lieberman (ed) *Schools as Collaborative Cultures: Creating the Future Now.* London: Falmer

Eraut M (1994) *Developing Professional Knowledge and Competence.* London: Falmer

Evans L (1998) *Teacher Morale, Job Satisfaction and Motivation.* London: Paul Chapman Publishing

Evans L, Packwood A and Neill S (1994) *The Meaning of Infant Teachers' Work.* London: Routledge

Freidson E (1986) *Professional Powers.* Chicago, IL: University of Chicago Press

Freidson E (2001) *Professionalism: The Third Logic.* Chicago, IL: Chicago University Press

Gosden P H J H (1972) *The Evolution of a Profession: The Contribution of Teachers' Associations.* Oxford: Basil Blackwell

Grace G (1987) 'Teachers and the state in Britain: A changing relation' in M Lawn and G Grace (eds) *Teachers: The Culture and Politics of Work.* London: Falmer

Ginsburg M (1997) 'Professionalism or politics as a model for teachers work and lives?' *Educational Research Journal* 12, 1–15

Greenfield T B (1975) 'Theory about organizations' in M Hughes (ed) *Administration Education: International Challenge.* London: Athlone

Gronn P (2000) 'Distributed properties a new architecture for leadership'. *Educational Management and Administration* 28(3) 317–338

Hargreaves A (1994) *Changing Teachers, Changing Times.* London: Cassell

Harris A (2004) 'Distributed leadership and school improvement: Leading or Misleading? *Educational Management Administration and Leadership* 32 (1) 11–24

Helsby G (1999) *Changing Teachers' Work.* Buckingham: Open University Press

Herzberg F, Mausner B and Snyderman B (1959) *Motivation to Work.* New York: Wiley

Hoyle E (1965) 'Organizational analysis in the field of education'. *Research in Education* 7(2), 97–114

Hoyle E (1969a) *The Role of the Teacher*. London: Routledge/Kegan Paul

Hoyle E (1969b) 'Professional stratification and anomie in the teaching profession'. *Paedagogica Europaea 5 The Changing Role of the Teacher Education*. Amsterdam: Elsevier, 60–71

Hoyle E (1974) 'Professionality, professionalism and control in teaching' *London Educational Review* 3(2), 13–19

Hoyle E (1980) 'Professionalization and deprofessionalization in education' in E Hoyle and J Megarry (eds) *World Yearbook of Education, 1980: The Professional Development of Teachers*. London: Kogan Page, 42–54

Hoyle E (1981) 'The teacher's career' in *The Management of Staff*. Open University Unit E323 Block 6 33–44

Hoyle E (1982a) 'The professionalization of teachers: A paradox'. *British Journal of Educational Studies* 30(2) 161–171

Hoyle E (1982b) 'The micropolitics of educational organizations'. *Educational Management and Administration* 10(2)

Hoyle E (1986) *The Politics of School Management*. London: Hodder and Stoughton

Hoyle E (1995) 'Changing concepts of a profession' in H Busher and R Saran *Managing Teachers as professionals in Schools*. London: Kogan Page

Hoyle E (1999) 'The two faces of micropolitics'. *School Leadership and Administration* 19(2) 213–222

Hoyle E (2001) 'Teaching: Prestige, status and esteem'. *Educational Management and Administration* 29(1) 139–152

Hoyle E and John P (1995) *Professional Knowledge and Professional Practice*. London: Cassell

Hoyle E and Wallace M (2005) *Educational Leadership: Ambiguity, Professionals and Managerialism*. London: Sage

Hoyle E and Wallace M (2006) 'Beyond metaphors of management: the case for metaphoric redescription in education' *British Journal of Educational Studies* 55(4) 426–442

Hoyle E and Wallace M (2007) 'Educational reform: An ironic perspective'. *Educational Management, Administration and Leadership* 35(1) 9–25

Jogmans K, Biemans H and Beijaard D (1998) 'Teachers' professional orientation and their involvement in school policy-making: The results of a Dutch study'. *Educational Management and Administration* 26(3) 293–304

Larson M S (1977) *The Rise of Professional Society*. Berkeley, CA: University of California Press

Lawn M (1987) *Servants of the State: The Contested Control of Teaching 1910–1930*. London: Falmer

Little J W (1990) 'The persistence of privacy: Autonomy and initiative in teachers' professional relations'. *Teachers' College Record* 91(4) 509–536

Lortie D (1964) 'The teacher and team teaching' in J J Shaplin and H Olds (eds) *Team Teaching*. New York: Harper & Row

Lortie D (1969) 'The balance between control and autonomy in elementary school teaching' in A Etzioni (ed) *The Semi-Professions and their Organization*. New York: Free Press

Manzer R A (1970) *Teachers and Politics*. Manchester, UK: Manchester University Press

March J G (1994) *A Primer on Decision Making: How Decisions Happen*. New York: Free Press

March J G (1999) *The Pursuit of Organizational Intelligence*. Oxford: Blackwell

March J G and Olsen P (1976) *Ambiguity and Choice in Organizations*. Bergen, Norway: Universitetsforlaget

March J G and Simon H (1958) *Organizations*. New York: Wiley

Marshall T H (1963) 'The recent history of professionalism in relation to social structure and social policy' in T H Marshall (ed) *Sociology at the Crossroads*. London: Heinemann, 150–170

McCulloch G, Helsby G and Knight P (2000) *Politics and Professionalism: Teachers and the Curriculum*. London: Continuum

Moore A, George R and Halpin D (2002) 'The developing role of the headteacher in English schools: Management, leadership and pragmatism'. *Educational Management and Adminitration* 30(2) 175–198

Nias J (1989) *Primary Teachers Talking: A Study of Teaching as Work*. London: Routledge

Ogawa R, Crowson R and Goldring E (1999) 'Enduring dilemmas in school organization' in J Murphy and K Seashore Louis (eds) *Handbook of Research on Educational Administration*. San Francisco, CA: Jossey-Bass, 277–295

O'Neill O (2002) *A Question of Trust* Cambridge: Cambridge University Press

Osborn M, McNess E, Broadfoot P with Pollard A and Triggs P   (2000) *What Teachers Do. Changing Policy and Practice in Primary Education* London: Continuum

Perkin H (1989) *The Rise of Professional Society*. London: Routledge

Pollard A Broadfoot P Croll P Osborn M   and Abbott D (1994) *Changing English Primary Schools? The Impact of the Education Reform Act at Key Stage One* London: Cassell

Sachs J (2003) *The Activist Teaching Profession*. Milton Keynes, UK: Open University Press

Schumpeter J (1942) *Capitalism, Socialism and Democracy*. London: Allen & Unwin

Stoll L and Louis K S (eds) (2007) *Professional Learning Communities: Divergence, Depths and Difficulties*. Maidenhead, UK: Open University Press

Sykes G (1999) 'The 'new professionalism' in education: An appraisal' in J Murphy and K S Louis (eds) *Handbook of Research in Educational*. San Francisco, CA: Jossey-Bass, 227–249

van Veen K, Sleegers P, Bergen T and Klaasen C (2001) 'Professional orientations of secondary school teachers towards their work'. *Teaching and Teacher Education* 17(2) 213–226

Weick K (1976) 'Educational organizations as loosely-coupled systems'. *Administrative Science Quarterly* 21(1) 1–19

Whitty G (1996) 'Marketization, the state and the re-formation of the teaching profession' in A H Halsey et al. (eds) *Education, Culture, Economy and Society*. Oxford: Oxford University Press

Woods, P (1995) *Creative Teachers in Primary Schools*. Buckingham, UK: Open University Press

Woods P, Jeffrey B, Troman G and Boyle M (1997) *Restructuring Schools, Restructuring Teachers: Responding to Change in the Primary School*. Buckingham, UK: Open University Press

Author Index

Subject Index